The role of terrorism in twenty-first-century warfare

MANCHESTER
1824
Manchester University Press

NEW DIRECTIONS IN TERRORISM STUDIES

A series edited by

Max Taylor

Professor in International Relations (retired), University of St Andrews, Scotland where he was formerly Director of the Centre for the Study of Terrorism and Political Violence

P. M. Currie

Senior Visiting Fellow at the School of International Relations at the University of St Andrews, Scotland

John Horgan

Associate Professor of Science, Technology and Society and Director of the International Centre for the Study of Terrorism at Pennsylvania State University, USA

New Directions in Terrorism Studies aims to introduce new and innovative approaches to understanding terrorism and the terrorist. It does this by bringing forward innovative ideas and concepts to assist the practitioner, analyst and academic to better understand and respond to the threat of terrorism, challenging existing assumptions and moving the debate forward into new areas. The approach is characterized by an emphasis on intellectual quality and rigor, interdisciplinary perspectives, and a drawing together of theory and practice. The key qualities of the series are contemporary relevance, accessibility and innovation.

The role of terrorism in twenty-first-century warfare

SUSANNE MARTIN AND LEONARD WEINBERG

Manchester University Press

Published by Manchester University Press
Altrincham Street, Manchester M1 7JA

www.manchesteruniversitypress.co.uk

British Library Cataloguing-in-Publication Data
A catalogue record for this book is available from the British Library

Library of Congress Cataloging-in-Publication Data applied for

ISBN   978 1 7849 9408 2   hardback

ISBN   978 1 7849 9409 9   paperback

First published 2017

Typeset by
Servis Filmsetting Ltd, Stockport, Cheshire
Printed in Great Britain
by Bell & Bain Ltd, Glasgow

Contents

Figures

Tables

Acknowledgements

We owe a substantial debt of gratitude to many groups and individuals for helping us to prepare this volume. We would especially like to express our thanks to Sharon Martin, Elizabeth Francis, Ami Pedahzur, Kristen Kabrin, the staff at Mathewson-IGT Knowledge Center, the staff and physicians at Renown Medical Center in Reno, and the readers and editors at Manchester University Press. We also appreciate the constructive comments and suggestions offered by anonymous reviewers of this manuscript, whose thoughtful contributions have had a substantial impact on the final product.

Abbreviations

17N	Revolutionary Organization 17 November (Greece)
AK	Justice and Development Party (Turkey)
ALF	Animal Liberation Front
ANC	African National Congress (South Africa)
AQAP	al Qaeda in the Arabian Peninsula
AQI	al Qaeda in Iraq
AQIM	al Qaeda in the Islamic Maghreb
AS	al Shabaab (Somalia)
ASALA	Armenian Secret Army for the Liberation of Armenia
AUC	United Self-Defense Forces of Colombia
AZAPO	Azanian People's Organization (South Africa)
CIA	Central Intelligence Agency (United States)
COIN	counterinsurgency
COW	Correlates of War
ELA	Revolutionary Popular Struggle (Greece)
ELF	Earth Liberation Front
ELN	National Liberation Army (Colombia)
ETA	Basque Fatherland and Liberty (Spain)
EU	European Union
FARC	Revolutionary Armed Forces of Colombia
FMLN	Farabundo Marti National Liberation Front (El Salvador)

FTO	Foreign Terrorist Organization
GIA	Armed Islamic Group of Algeria
GTD	Global Terrorism Database
IDF	Israeli Defense Forces
IED	improvised explosive device
IRA	Irish Republican Army
ISI	Islamic State in Iraq
ISIL	Islamic State of Iraq and the Levant
ISIS	Islamic State of Iraq and Syria, Islamic State of Iraq and al-Sharm
JDP	Justice and Development Party (Turkey)
JVP	People's Liberation Front (Sri Lanka)
LAF	Lebanese Armed Forces
LeT	Lashkar-e Tayyiba (Pakistan, India)
LTTE	Liberation Tigers of Tamil Eelam, Tamil Tigers
M-19	19th April Movement (Colombia)
NATO	North Atlantic Treaty Organization
NGO	non-governmental organization
PAC	Pan Africanist Congress (South Africa)
PFLP	Popular Front for the Liberation of Palestine
PIJ	Palestinian Islamic Jihad
PIRA	Provisional Irish Republican Army, Provos
PKK	Kurdistan Workers' Party (Turkey)
PLO	Palestine Liberation Organization
PRIO	Peace Research Institute Oslo
RAF	Red Army Faction (Germany)
RAHOWA	racial holy war (United States)
RMA	revolution in military affairs

START   National Consortium for the Study of Terrorism and Responses
                to Terrorism (University of Maryland, United States)

TTP   Tehrik-e Taliban Pakistan

UCDP   Uppsala Conflict Data Program

UHRO   Ustasha – Croatian Revolutionary Organization

UN   United Nations

USSR   Union of Soviet Socialist Republics

WMD   weapon of mass destruction

Introduction

Most observers cannot help but notice that each of the major armed conflicts that occurred during the 1990s and the first decade of the present century – Bosnia, Kosovo, Chechnya, Afghanistan, Iraq, and Syria – has involved the use of terrorism by one or more of the contestants, at one time or another. Conflicts involving armed non-state actors challenging states and each other have become the main form of warfare thus far in the new millennium. The main participants are insurgents and counterinsurgents. Their conflicts are primarily internal, though they occasionally cross borders. They often involve outsiders, including states and other non-state actors, supporting one side or the other. The conflicts are carried out with a type of brutality that can be expected when the people of a country turn on each other and the institutions responsible for upholding law and order and protecting the population begin to fail. The types of weapons used by contestants in the armed conflicts of the twenty-first century are less sophisticated than those available to states. Whereas states may carry out wars from the sky or sea, or at least from a distance, with the aid of satellites, long-range missiles and other sophisticated technologies, the armed non-state actors fighting in the present century's armed conflicts do so primarily on the ground and at close range.

Another feature of warfare in the twenty-first century – the global battle being waged against perpetrators of terrorism – was not part of earlier warfare. The "global war on terrorism" began with the aim of eliminating the threat posed by transnational terrorists, al Qaeda in particular. As the "war" progressed, political vacuums were opened, insecurities were manifested, and new violent actors emerged. Localized violence pitted armed groups (some of them affiliated with al Qaeda) against states, local communities, and each other. Meanwhile, some of the same armed groups, which are identified at times as "terrorists" and at other times as "insurgents," have contributed to sectarian conflict in Iraq, civil war in Syria, and civil unrest in Afghanistan and elsewhere. Some of the "terrorist" groups that have received so much of the focus during the "war on terrorism" have become "insurgents," though they continue to use the types of violence typically identified as "terrorism."[1]

The discussion that follows concerns the role of terrorism in twenty-first century warfare.[2] This is a study of the ways in which militants use terrorism to trigger and sustain insurgency. It is also a study of the ways in which the resort to terrorism may signal an end to insurgency, or its failure. The text that follows introduces, describes, and analyzes patterns in the incidence of terrorism as a tactic used in wars past and present. Drawing insights from these patterns, this study addresses implications for efforts to counter the continuing threat.

An evolving threat

There are reasons to believe that terrorism's role in wider-scale warfare has changed since the beginning of the new millennium. The ways in which the use of terrorism has changed are apparent through observations of terrorists and their tactics, targets, and objectives. These changes are not occurring in a vacuum. They are not disconnected from the groups currently using terrorism or the ideologies that drive these groups. Nor are these changes occurring independently of other changes in the international environment.

The new millennium began a decade after the apparent end of communism as an ideological rival to Western ideas and influence in the world.[3] This period also marked the decline of a communist bloc capable of challenging Western hegemony and power. Communism and the superpower seemingly spearheading its spread ceased to be a common threat for its Western and non-Western opponents. The new era brought with it new ideas, which are shared via new technologies. This era has also seen the rise and fall of state and non-state actors, a new distribution of power and new perceptions of threats, as well as a continuation of an old competition among state and non-state actors seeking to maintain or increase their power. The relevance of non-state actors in this competition for power and influence represents a continuation of earlier efforts with two notable exceptions – the introduction of a religious ideology and objectives and the more global nature of some of these objectives. Among the armed non-state actors of the twenty-first century are some seeking not to change the government or political system within a single state but rather to establish a religious system of governance that bridges continents and incorporates (or subsumes) otherwise diverse national and religious communities.

In this context, non-state actors challenge states – including the strongest states – as they learned to do decades earlier in places like Vietnam, Iran, and Afghanistan. These are archetypal weak actors, whose targets include even weaker actors: civilians. Most of their attacks take place locally, close to the groups' primary areas of operations. The same groups attacking civilians also target states and their militaries, as well as each other. These groups are the main actors in the first wars of the twenty-first century.

There are precedents regarding the use of terrorism by weak actors in warfare and, in particular, in insurgency. There is also observable evidence that terrorism and warfare are changing. Terrorists and terrorist groups have "adapted."[4] The tactics they use have changed as have the tools available for their use. In some cases, the same groups have been labeled as "terrorist" and "insurgent." Similarly, references to "counterterrorism" and "counter-insurgency" have become practically interchangeable.[5] Given attention to specifying definitions and references to these terms – in particular to "terrorism" in the first decades of the twenty-first century – it is possible that these developments indicate the evolution of a modern threat more than a lack of conceptual clarity.

Changes in terrorism are not surprising; they are practically expected. David Rapoport, for instance, observes changes in the dominant ideologies of groups using terrorism at different periods in time, as well as the targets of attacks and types of attacks that are prevalent at a given time.[6] Despite these variations, one understanding that has not changed much over the years is that terrorism is a "weapon of the weak."[7] Those groups relying primarily or exclusively on terrorism tend to do so when they are too weak to engage their adversaries directly. They are weak actors in military terms, especially in comparison to the military strength of states. They are also weak in political terms. They often lack popular support and legitimacy, even among their presumed or desired constituency. Their primary targets – unarmed civilians – are even weaker.

If terrorism is the weapon of these weak actors, then one may expect that terrorists could be easily quashed by the superior power of states and their militaries. This is not always the case. Terrorists' strength lies in their clandestine nature, their ability to hide among a noncombatant population, and their capacity to survive, even when they cannot achieve their objectives. In reality, some terrorist groups are more capable challengers than others. Hence, some terrorist groups may pose a greater threat than others.

There is another point of reference for the question of whether or not states can defeat terrorists. This is the twenty-first century's "global war on terror." The goals expressed by those administering this "war" seem straightforward enough: reduce the threats posed by non-state actors willing to use terrorism, and especially those threatening national security and international peace.[8] With this goal in mind, it would seem like an oversight not to make note of the ways in which the armed groups on which the war on terrorism has focused – for instance, al Qaeda and its affiliates – use terrorism as one tactic within a more diversified arsenal. Moreover, it would also seem like an oversight to discount the violent conflicts that have followed the initiation of the war on terrorism. Many of these new wars are occurring in or near the places where the war on terrorism has been focused. Among the participants in these wars are some groups previously identified as terrorists. Some of the groups known to have used terrorism before and after September 11, 2001, are also engaging in forms of wider-scale warfare, including insurgency. This is not to suggest that the same groups have abandoned terrorism; instead, terrorism is a tactic they may continue to use in the context of insurgency.

The threat posed by insurgent groups in the twenty-first century is not limited to terrorism employed outside of war. These terrorists and now insurgents are engaging in wider-scale warfare. They seek to replace some prevailing order. In the process, insurgent groups can be expected to carry out the same types of attacks against military and civilian targets.[9] If their coercive capacity grows, they may find harder, better fortified state and military targets more accessible. As this happens, they are likely to expand their repertoire of tactics and targets. This does not mean that the terrorists-turned-insurgents will cease to attack civilians, nor does it mean that they will use different types of weapons when targeting state or military entities. Rather, they will likely continue using the same types of weapons (e.g., guns, bombs, suicide vests) with which they have become familiar and adept. They can apply the weapons and tactics rehearsed in attacks against softer (e.g., civilian) targets in their attacks on harder targets. To the extent that perpetuating fear is a goal of these groups, they may continue to pursue this goal and achieve it regardless of the targets of their attacks. There is an assumption that with sufficient resources, terrorist-insurgents may begin engaging in the types of activities more commonly associated with guerrilla warfare, including sabotage, hit-and-run attacks, and other tactics used by the weaker parties in militarized disputes. There is, however, no reason to assume that these activities must exclude terrorism, nor is there reason to believe that guerrilla warfare will be played out according to the styles set by earlier guerrillas. As Walter Laqueur has suggested, the conditions for guerrilla warfare as seen during the Cold War may no longer exist.[10]

Furthermore, the association between counterterrorism and counterinsurgency (COIN) is not surprising given the evolving threat posed by the armed actors of the twenty-first century. In the years since the invasions of Afghanistan and Iraq, attention has shifted somewhat from countering terrorism to countering insurgency. At the same time, COIN operations coincide with and may include counter-guerrilla operations and "unconventional warfare," as well as other operations aimed at addressing the threats posed by insurgent forces operating in weak states.[11] In the twenty-first century, these are among the duties of a conventional military's special operations forces.

Focus and objectives of this book

What is the role of terrorism in twenty-first century warfare? Answers to this question draw on assumptions regarding the strategies of armed groups as well as understandings of historical precedents and contemporary realities. Answers to this question also rely on assessments of the ways in which warfare and the actors responsible for waging it have changed and may continue to change in the twenty-first century.

"Terrorism" is a tactic, which may be used by a variety of groups to achieve a range of objectives. As a tactic, terrorism may be one part of a more comprehensive strategy that includes other tactics. References to terrorism do not refer only to particular acts of terrorism but rather to the purposeful attempt to perpetuate fear among a target audience for the purpose of achieving political goals.[12] As such, something is known about the use of terrorism as a tactic of armed resistance and within the context of wider-scale warfare.

As a tactic of armed resistance, terrorism is widely thought to be a weapon of the weaker actors.[13] Some armed groups turn to terrorism when they are unable or unwilling to engage in other forms of violent or nonviolent political action. A common assumption is that these groups use terrorism strategically. The "strategies of terrorism" serve some of these groups' shorter- or intermediate-term objectives.[14] Groups relying on terrorism may trigger a desired response from an adversary or create fear among a target audience; however, they are unlikely to achieve their ultimate objectives.

Though its use has been documented, terrorism is less frequently discussed as a tactic of wider-scale warfare. In some cases, terrorism is a tactic used by those who wish to incite insurgency, though they may be unsuccessful.[15] The types of attacks described as "terrorism" are also used by armed groups when their insurgency takes the form of wider-scale warfare.[16] It is unclear whether or not the identification of a conflict as "war" requires the relabeling of "terrorist" attacks as something else. This is apparent given the varying labels assigned to wider-scale armed conflicts ("civil war," "intra-state war," "insurgency") and the multiple, often interchangeable, labels given to the armed groups participating in them ("terrorists," "guerrillas," "insurgents").

The question of the uses of terrorism within wider-scale warfare takes on new significance if the ways of waging wars are changing. There are suggestions that the "great wars" of the past, involving states engaging each other on battlefields, are to be replaced by smaller-scale armed confrontations primarily involving non-state actors.[17] To the extent that this is the case, an understanding of the conduct of new wars requires giving attention to the tactics and strategies available to and employed by these non-state actors engaging in them.

It is from this point that interest turns to the uses of terrorism within wider-scale warfare and, in particular, to the timing of terrorism. Terrorism may be used prior to or early in a violent confrontation to incite further violence, gain attention, or for some other purpose. Terrorism used in these early stages is likely a sign of military weakness. Terrorism used later in the context of wider-scale warfare may indicate something different. It may indicate a weakening of an armed group. Terrorism may serve as a weapon of last resort, used when alternative forms of armed action are no longer available or seen as viable.[18] This situation may be due to losses incurred during an armed conflict or because the insurgents' adversary becomes more committed or organized in its fight. Terrorism may also be used throughout a conflict. Armed groups may remain relatively weak and their capabilities may vary over time and across geographic space. As a result, a group may rely on the kinds of attacks most identified as terrorism in places where, and at times when, it is a weak actor. Alternatively, the use of terrorism throughout the duration of insurgency or wider-scale warfare may indicate the adoption of a strategy combining terrorism with other tactics regardless of a group's relative strength or weakness. This outcome would suggest that armed groups include terrorism as one tactic within an armed struggle that is used concurrently with other tactics in attempts to achieve the group's objectives. As such, terrorism becomes one part of a group's strategy.

Some assumptions deserve further consideration. Terrorism is not, as many have suggested, necessarily the weapon of last resort.[19] Part of the debate regarding this point depends on how cases are interpreted and whether or not the interpreter accepts that there are no alternative courses of action. Second, while terrorism is a tactic used by groups that are weaker than their adversaries, the relative weakness or strength of these actors and their adversaries varies widely. Moreover, relative weakness is difficult to measure. Measurements based on military capabilities would differ from those based on popular support or ideological attractiveness. Assessments of relative weakness also fail to take into account the relative strength of clandestine armed actors when it comes to surviving and posing a continuing threat, even if not achieving their objectives.

Other aspects of terrorism's use in warfare are unknown. Apart from anecdotal evidence, it has not been clear whether there are variations in the use of terrorism as a tactic of war across place and time. It has also been unclear whether groups with different ideologies or different types of capabilities use terrorism differently over the duration of a violent confrontation. We have not known how the numbers of terrorist attacks look when mapped onto the timeline of a war. And, while we know that the success of insurgents varies on the basis of whether terrorism – especially attacks on civilians – is used sparingly or liberally, and discriminately or indiscriminately, we have not necessarily known whether or how variations in the numbers of terrorist attacks over the course of an insurgency may signal insurgent success or failure.

We also have not known whether the "new" terrorists of the twenty-first century will use terrorism differently than their predecessors did. The insurgent groups using terrorism in wars of the twenty-first century are distinct from their predecessors in ways that may be important. Their ideologies tend to be religious. Their objectives tend to be grander, more global, and less achievable. In most cases, their main fields of operation are areas with majority Muslim populations. Although their tools are both rudimentary (beheadings, burnings) and innovative (bombings, suicide attacks), few are militarily sophisticated. They may, however, gain access to more sophisticated technologies unavailable to their predecessors. They already have access to information and means of communication that were unavailable to most of their earlier counterparts.

Some of these questions are difficult to answer on a cross-national or cross-case basis with the types of data that is available. Despite such limitations, on which we elaborate further, many of the tools needed to acquire a better understanding of terrorism as a wartime tactic are available. This study builds on existing insights and adds descriptive analysis in order to begin to fill some of the gaps in our understanding of the role of terrorism in twenty-first warfare.

The study also bridges the largely separate literatures on terrorism and warfare, focusing on the ways in which these two literatures inform our understanding of the tactics and goals of armed non-state actors. The study of terrorism, a relatively young field that grew in the early 1970s and exploded in 2001, has developed independently of the literature on warfare. The literature on wars, in contrast, is much older, drawing on foundations established by ancient scholars and philosophers, such as Thucydides, and their modern counterparts, including Carl von Clausewitz.[20] The divide in the studies of terrorism and warfare – and especially wars involving insurgency – is hardly realistic. Terrorism is a tactic used by insurgents. It was a tactic used by armed anti-colonial and nationalist groups during the twentieth century; in the early twenty-first century, it is a tactic used mostly by groups with nationalist and religious ideologies. Terrorism may be used in various stages of insurgency, such as at the beginning or ending stages, or it may be used throughout insurgency alongside other tactics of warfare. More importantly, terrorism is a tactic used frequently in the first years of the twenty-first century. Meanwhile, the twenty-first century's terrorists have become insurgents engaging in wider-scale warfare. Recognizing this, the present study draws insights from both literatures.

Notes

1 Or, as Michael Boyle states, "many insurgent organizations also employ indiscriminate attacks that are not significantly different from terrorism." Michael J. Boyle, "Progress and Pitfalls in the Study of Political Violence," *Terrorism and Political Violence*, 24, no. 4 (2012): 536. See also James Khalil, "Know Your Enemy: On the Futility of Distinguishing between Terrorists and Insurgents," *Studies in Conflict & Terrorism*, 36, no. 5 (2013).

2 Few terms in the English language have been more disputed than "terrorism." After reviewing the history of terrorism Walter Laqueur threw up his hands and concluded a simple definition was virtually impossible. Bruce Hoffman, another widely respected analyst, defines terrorism as "the deliberate creation and exploitation of fear through violence or the threat of violence in the pursuit of political change." Bruce Hoffman, *Inside Terrorism* (New York, NY: Columbia University Press, 2006), 40. Nineteenth-century revolutionary anarchists referred to "propaganda by deed." One could do worse. These days most countries in the Western world have devised legal definitions. These tend to expand and contract with the severity of the threat.

3 Francis Fukuyama, "The End of History?" *The National Interest*, 16 (1989).

4 Bruce Hoffman, "The Changing Face of Al Qaeda and the Global War on Terrorism," *Studies in Conflict & Terrorism*, 27, no. 6 (2004).

5 For a discussion, Khalil, "Know Your Enemy: On the Futility of Distinguishing between Terrorists and Insurgents;" Michael J. Boyle, "Do Counterterrorism and Counterinsurgency Go Together?," *International Affairs*, 86, no. 2 (2010).

6 David C. Rapoport, "The Four Waves of Modern Terrorism," in *Terrorism Studies: A Reader*, ed. John Horgan, and Kurt Braddock (New York, NY: Routledge, 2012).

7 Martha Crenshaw, "The Causes of Terrorism," *Comparative Politics*, 13, no. 4 (1981).

8 See, for instance, "National Strategy for Combating Terrorism" (The White House, President George W. Bush, September 2006).

9 Ariel Merari, "Terrorism as a Strategy of Insurgency," *Terrorism and Political Violence*, 5, no. 4 (1993).

10 Walter Laqueur, "Postmodern Terrorism," *Foreign Affairs*, 75, no. 5 (1996).

11 United States Department of the Army, *Military Police Operations*, Field Manual No. 3-39 (August 26, 2013), for instance, xii–xiii.

12 See, for instance, Hoffman, *Inside Terrorism*, Chapter 1.

13 See, for instance, Martha Crenshaw Hutchinson, "The Concept of Revolutionary Terrorism," in *Terrorism: The Second or Anti-Colonial Wave*, ed. David C. Rapoport (New York, NY: Routledge, 2006), 74.

14 Andrew H. Kydd and Barbara F. Walter, "The Strategies of Terrorism," *International Security*, 31, no. 1 (2006).

15 See, for instance, Max Boot, *Invisible Armies: An Epic History of Guerrilla Warfare from Ancient Times to the Present* (New York, NY: Liveright Publishing Corporation, 2013).

16 For example, see Andrea J. Dew, "The Erosion of Constraints in Armed-Group Warfare: Bloody Tactics and Vulnerable Targets," in *Armed Groups: Studies in National Security, Counterterrorism, and Counterinsurgency*, ed. Jeffrey H. Norwitz (Newport, RI: U.S. Naval War College, 2008), 255–68; Andrew C. Janos, "Unconventional Warfare: Framework and Analysis," *World Politics*, 15, no. 4 (1963): 638–9.

17 See, for instance, Robert Jervis, "Theories of War in an Era of Leading-Power Peace, Presidential Address, American Political Science Association, 2001," *American Political Science Review*, 96, no. 1 (2002); Monty G. Marshall and Ted Robert Gurr, *Peace and Conflict 2005: A Global Survey of Armed Conflicts, Self-Determination Movements, and Democracy* (College Park, MD: Center for International Development and Conflict Management, 2005); John Mueller, "War Has Almost Ceased to Exist: An Assessment," *Political Science Quarterly*, 124, no. 2 (2009); John Mueller, *The Remnants of War* (Ithaca, NY: Cornell University Press, 2004); G. Easterbrook, "The End of War?" *New Republic*, 232, no. 20 (2005); Nils Petter Gleditsch et al., "The Forum: The Decline of War," *International Studies Review*, 15, no. 3 (2013); Joshua S. Goldstein, *Winning the War on War: The Decline of Armed Conflict Worldwide* (New York, NY: Dutton, 2011).

18 Whether or not terrorism is a tool of last resort is a topic of debate. See, for instance, Max Abrahms, "What Terrorists Really Want," *International Security*, 32, no. 4 (2008); E. Chenoweth et al., "Correspondence: What Makes Terrorists Tick," *International Security*, 33, no. 4 (2009).

19 Abrahms, "What Terrorists Really Want;" Chenoweth et al., "Correspondence: What Makes Terrorists Tick."

20 Thucydides, *Thucydides: History of the Peloponnesian War*, trans. C. Forster Smith (Cambridge, MA: Harvard University Press, 1951); Carl von Clausewitz, *On War* (Princeton, NJ: Princeton University Press, 1976).

1

The "new" terrorism in warfare

What role will terrorism play in twenty-first century warfare? While there is evidence that wars are changing, the reasons for and consequences of these changes remain largely unknown. This study represents an effort to better understand changes in the conduct of wars and implications of these changes. In the pages that follow, the first task involves specifying the meanings of terms such as "terrorism" and "insurgency." The chapter continues with a discussion of changes in the uses of terrorism over time, not only with regard to the actors responsible for using terrorist tactics but also the weapons they have at their disposal and the ideas that drive their violence. This discussion includes a description of the ways in which insurgent groups fought or attempted to initiate wars in the twentieth century as well as changes in the ways in which wars are being fought in the twenty-first century. A review of insurgent groups' uses of terrorism over the last several decades within and outside of war helps to ground this analysis in its contemporary context. In addition, an explanation of counterterrorism and counterinsurgency policies, and especially the evolution of these policies in the twenty-first century, helps to bring the discussion of terrorism and insurgency together. The present chapter concludes with an overview of the varying patterns and uses of terrorism in the context of war.

The analysis that follows serves several purposes. The primary objective is to offer insights into the conduct of current and future wars. Many of the wars of the present century involve armed non-state actors engaging in warfare against states and each other and using terrorist tactics in the process. A secondary objective involves bridging the largely separate literatures on terrorism and warfare. These are the literatures on which this study draws and to which it contributes. Although scholarship on terrorism has developed largely independently of scholarship on warfare, this separation makes little sense when referring to wars in the twenty-first century. Moreover, this separation makes little sense for a large number of wars (or "conflicts"), which took place during the twentieth century. As such, the need to bridge the literatures on terrorism and warfare is not entirely new.

Changing patterns of war

Terrorism is a type of violence being used by armed non-state actors in the context of wider-scale warfare. While the use has been seen in the past, it seems to be more prevalent – or at least evident – in the first decades of the twenty-first century. An outline of changing features of warfare is a useful starting point for this discussion.

There are indications that violent conflicts pitting non-state actors against states and each other may become the most common form of warfare in the years to come. This has something to do with a decline in the number of interstate wars,[1] though it likely has more to do with an anticipated decline in the "scale of wars."[2] The expectation of many students of warfare is that twenty-first century wars will be smaller and less deadly overall than wars in the previous century. Whereas wars involving direct confrontations between states may be less prevalent, non-state actors will continue to take part in armed conflicts and wars.

Modern wars and warriors share another new feature: the prevalence of religiously motivated militants seeking to achieve religious objectives. These are not the ethnic conflicts of the relatively recent past – including the 1990s – in which groups distinguishing themselves on the basis of religion sought political control over a territory they called "home," along with something approaching an ethnically pure society. Instead, the religious militants of the twenty-first century seek to create a new political system. This political system will impose a set of religious beliefs held by a minority group over a multi-ethnic and multi-national population. Although it is framed in religious terms, their battle is a political one. Appeals drawing on religious beliefs are often framed as existential battles between good and evil. These are the types of battles that are thought to be consecrated by a higher authority. In existential battles, death results from fighting or not fighting. As such, these battles may be fought to the death. In addition, groups with religious ideologies tend to have a built-in base of support, both active and passive. This includes believers and others who follow their lead or subscribe to their rhetoric. For these reasons, it is likely that the violent confrontations occurring today will continue for some time into the future.

There is another element to this story. Laurence Iannaccone and Eli Berman suggest that political-religious groups may be more likely to engage in violence – and are organized and incentivized to do so – when competing against other religious parties for political favor and when doing so within a weaker state.[3] Their take-away point, they say, is that violence associated with religiously motivated groups may be a function of "the religious-political environment rather than the religion itself."[4]

In addition, it is not far-fetched to think of some of the ongoing insurgencies – and especially those that have taken place in Iraq, Syria, and Afghanistan – as derivatives of the "global war on terrorism." Some evidence points to a connection between foreign troop deployment and transnational terrorism aimed at the state from which the troops are deployed.[5] Foreign intervention follows instability; it may also produce it. More importantly, it is the coincidence of locations and timing, especially in Iraq, that suggests a connection between the "war on terrorism" and the wars that have followed. Based on this coincidence, one may wonder whether efforts to end terrorism have had the opposite effect of increasing it.

This would not be an unexpected outcome. Efforts to counter terrorism may fuel even more terrorism. This is most pronounced when the means employed by those countering terrorists are brutal. When this happens, efforts to counter terrorism may produce a "backlash" that results in the vilification of the counterterrorism forces.[6] Gary LaFree and Gary Ackerman point out that efforts to "harden targets" may lead terrorists to use new tactics and attack new targets.[7] Softer (civilian) targets may replace harder (state, armed) targets as attacks on the latter become more difficult to carry out. In addition to an increasing frequency of terrorist incidents, there also appears to be an increase in the use of terrorism by insurgent groups engaging in various forms of armed conflict. Included among those that seem to illustrate this pattern are al Qaeda's various affiliates, ISIL (Islamic State of Iraq and the Levant), and the myriad nationalist and religious groups competing for power within some of the weakest states in Asia and Africa.

Defining key terms

Before the discussion proceeds, it is appropriate to offer definitions and outline the meanings of the terms used throughout this analysis. It will not be surprising to readers that the terms to which we refer remain highly contested. There is no true consensus definition for terms such as "terrorism." Nor, when it comes to applying a definition, is there agreement regarding the designation of events and the actors responsible for them. This is an issue affecting studies of terrorism and other forms of political violence and a point of departure for much criticism within the literature.

When it comes to specifying a definition, one matter worth considering is whether or not the definition being used is appropriately inclusive and exclusive so as to delineate a specific subject of study.[8] The conceptual problem follows from the necessity of distinguishing among the labels that may be given to groups and their actions. It may be necessary to distinguish between "terrorism" and other forms of political violence. In some cases more than one label aptly describes a group. Terrorists – and others – may employ a variety of tactics. Conceptual clarity is crucial.

Following this line of thought, it can be problematic to include a specific political objective – a long-term outcome rather than a short-term effect – as part of a definition for the actions of an armed non-state group. For instance, when asked to distinguish between freedom fighters and terrorists, it is useful to note that freedom is an objective while terrorism is a tactic, and one that may be used to achieve any number of objectives. Freedom fighters may use terrorism as a tactic in their fight for freedom.[9] Similarly, terrorists may fight for freedom (or freedoms).

Another issue is whether the definition can be applied to specific examples so as to establish which cases meet the definitional criteria and which do not. Problems may arise when the elements of a definition are not observable. This may be especially problematic when the unobservable features in question are the same ones used to distinguish one type of violence from another. If terrorism is distinguished from other forms of political violence by the intent to create fear or produce a psychological impact – as a short-term outcome to help bring about a longer-term objective – then knowing whether or not this was the terrorists' intent matters. In some cases, the presence or absence of such definitional features may be reasonably assumed. The issue then becomes applying the same criteria for making these assumptions to various cases.

A third issue, in no small part related to the first two, involves identifying differences between the phenomenon one seeks to study and the phenomena represented in available collections of data. This is especially important in situations in which large numbers of cases are analyzed together without in-depth (or even cursory) consideration of most of the cases. Much trust is placed in coders of data, their application of identifying criteria, and the reliability of "filters" used to include or exclude cases on the bases of specific features. Variations in definitions will have an effect on case selection. Case selection, in turn, may affect conclusions.

A final issue has much to do with the data that is available. Available data on terrorist incidents and the groups using terrorism and other types of political violence is incomplete. At least to some extent, it is also flawed. Events occurring in some regions and at some times receive more attention than those occurring in others. For this reason, information is more likely to be available for some cases than for others; consequently some events are more likely to be included in data collections than others. The effect is to create a bias in the available data. The same may be said of designations of larger-scale wars. Although there are quantifiable features of wars – such as, numbers of battle deaths within predetermined periods of time – these may seem insufficient or even arbitrary. As with terrorist attacks, less information is known about some armed confrontations than others.

Defining terrorism

Understanding these issues and limitations, we draw on an often-referenced definition of terrorism, which captures the main elements of the phenomena in which we are interested. Bruce Hoffman defines terrorism as involving "the calculated use of unlawful violence or threat of unlawful violence to inculcate fear; intended to coerce or to intimidate governments or societies in the pursuit of goals that are generally political, religious or ideological."[10]

We draw attention to four main elements of this definition. This definition of terrorism describes a type of act (violent), a non-specific long-term objective (political change), a target (likely noncombatants), and a short-term, strategic objective (fear).

Terrorism is inherently violent. Violent acts are easier to identify and count than are threats of violence. Data on violent attacks is more likely to include actual attacks. Information on failed attacks and those that were planned yet not carried out will be scarcer.

The second component of the definition of terrorism draws attention to the perpetrators' longer-term goal of bringing about some form of political change. Such objectives may be determined by reference to the aspirations of the groups responsible for carrying out attacks, to the extent that the perpetrators are known. The connection between an attack and a particular objective – especially a long-term one – is often assumed. The large number of unclaimed attacks, many of which are included in data on terrorist incidents, complicates the identification of attacks with particular objectives. Afghanistan offers an illustrative case for consideration. In 2014, unknown attackers were responsible for around 40 percent of "terrorist" attacks in this country. The proportion of events with unknown attackers was higher for attacks carried out against softer targets (e.g., civilians, businesses) than for those carried out against harder targets (e.g., state, military).[11] Noting this, it is possible that the targets of attacks will provide some insight into the objectives of attackers, even when actual perpetrators are unknown.

The third element draws further attention to targets. Although the excerpt from Hoffman's definition does not elaborate on specific types of targets, we may presume that terrorists direct their attacks against civilian and noncombatant targets more so than against a state's armed forces. Attacks on armed targets, such as militaries, may be more appropriately designated as an act of war or take place in the context of armed conflict. It is not uncommon for definitions of terrorism to specify that the targets of attacks are civilians or noncombatants.[12] While adding an assumption that terrorists tend to target noncombatants would be consistent with this subset of definitions, this would not necessarily serve the interests of this study. The same "terrorists" may engage in acts of war and terrorism, and they may alternate between attacking combatant and noncombatant targets. While it is true that attacks on noncombatants may send a message to a wider audience, so may attacks on combatant targets. Moreover, which groups are included in the category of "noncombatant" is a subject of debate. Attacks on the barracks of the U.S. Marines and the French paratroopers – peacekeepers operating in Lebanon during that country's sectarian civil war – are just one example. Some may consider peacekeepers to be noncombatants; others may see them as armed actors or foreign occupiers.

A fourth element is the "terror" or fear that results from a terrorist attack. While fear is not easily measured, it may be presumed to be a byproduct of violence perpetrated against noncombatant targets. The perpetuation of fear is a short-term objective. It is also strategic. For the terrorist, fear is a tool that can be utilized to influence a larger target audience.

It is also useful to point out what terrorism is not. Terrorism may be a tactic of war, but it is not a type of warfare, unconventional or otherwise.

For the purposes of this study, it is not helpful to refer exclusively to "terrorism" or "terrorist" groups. Terrorism is understood to be a tactic, and one among many tactics a political group may use.[13] It is a tactic used within and outside of war. The groups of interest in this study are armed non-state actors. All have used terrorism; many, if not most, have used other tactics in addition to terrorism. We may refer to those groups relying almost exclusively on terrorism as "stand-alone" groups. Stand-alone groups are generally small and clandestine. They tend to operate in urban settings. They tend not to have much in terms of popular support or resources.

Groups using terrorism may also be labeled as "armed groups," "violent groups," "militant groups," "non-state actors," or some related term. These labels help to capture the nature of the groups carrying arms and willing to use violence, including terrorism; however, even these terms leave us wanting for specificity. Groups may be armed and violent yet not use terrorism. Terrorism and political violence are not synonymous. Terrorism is a type of political violence, but not all political violence is terrorism. Armed groups may use terrorism or other types of violence, or they may not. In fact, armed groups may or may not threaten to use violence. The same holds for violent political groups, which may use violence (e.g., in riots, in warfare, in criminal activities) that would not qualify as terrorism. Their intent may be to destroy or murder rather than produce fear or a .psychological impact. For practical purposes, terms such as "armed groups" and "violent groups" may be considered synonymous. Attention is given to specifying whether or not these groups also engage in "terrorism."

Armed (or violent) groups use a variety of tactics. Some armed groups have political wings; others are the militant wings of political parties.[14] Some groups provide services to their presumed constituencies. The groups may participate in criminal activities, perhaps using these activities as a means of funding their operations. The groups of interest here have a variety of objectives. Some groups seek revolutionary change; others wish to preserve a status quo or return to an idealized (perhaps imagined) past. Some groups are guided by secular ideologies, others by religion. Armed groups may have plentiful resources, including popular support and varying types of assistance from states. Other armed groups may be relatively weak, a fringe group with little or nothing in the way of support or broader appeal. Armed groups carry out operations in a variety of settings. They operate in peaceful, democratic environments as well as in conflict-ridden, stateless surroundings. Armed groups may use terrorism during peacetime or wartime. They may use terrorism in the conduct of war, as part of a wartime strategy. Many armed groups combine tactics. They may engage in guerrilla warfare in addition to terrorism.

Defining guerrilla warfare

Guerrilla warfare has been distinguished from terrorism on the bases of targets, tactics, objectives, organization, resources, and location (rural versus urban). Guerrilla attacks occur in the context of warfare – specifically "small wars." Their attacks tend to be aimed at combatants, which is a term also requiring further consideration. Combatants may be understood to include military, police, and government entities. Other violent non-state groups or political parties may also be considered combatants. Each of these entities may be considered combatant even when they are not actively engaged in fighting in general or at the times in which they are targeted. These weaker non-state actors cannot attack armed adversaries through what are considered to be conventional means or on a battlefield. The category of noncombatants typically includes non-state, unarmed, and civilian targets. Civilians may or may not be armed and they may or may not be employed by a state. With the exception of targeted killings or assassinations, it is more likely the location of an attack that indicates whether the targets are combatant or noncombatant. An attack in a typically civilian setting (e.g., a marketplace, public transportation), appears to target noncombatants. If, on the other hand, an individual is targeted because he or she is a representative of the government or a member of the military, then the individual may be deemed combatant, and the label given to the attack may be affected accordingly. Unfortunately, these distinctions are difficult to make on a case-by-case basis given the large number of incidents, incomplete information, and a lack of access to the perpetrators' rationales for attacks.

Guerrilla warfare may involve attacks that resemble terrorist attacks, excepting that the targets of guerrilla attacks tend to be harder than those of terrorists and tend to occur in the context of armed conflict. The same types of attacks used against noncombatants may also be used against combatants. For instance, violent groups may aim suicide attacks at civilians as well as at military and government targets. Guerrillas are likely attacking the harder military and government targets. These are the types of targets that tend to be better fortified and protected than civilians. In order to carry out attacks on harder targets, guerrillas need to be better organized. They also require the types of resources that facilitate arming and training.

Guerrilla warfare is also distinguished as an "unconventional" manner of waging war. Guerrilla warfare involves at least two parties, including a non-state armed group and a state or its representatives. Guerrilla forces are far weaker than states. Unable to challenge their adversary on a battlefield, they rely on "unconventional" or "irregular" forms of warfare. Guerrillas may resort to sabotage or hit-and-run attacks on the military, law enforcement, and representatives of the state. Their short-term objectives include undermining the state's ability to respond to their threat. Guerrilla tactics are among the tactics used by insurgents in armed conflicts. Other references to "guerrilla tactics" refer specifically to the types of attacks guerrillas employ – sabotage and hit-and-run – even when the purpose is fraud or theft rather than military advantage.[15]

Other descriptions of guerrilla warfare draw attention to guerrilla forces and fighters. Some writers distinguish guerrillas (or guerrilla forces) from terrorists by their organization, resources, and objectives.[16] In terms of objectives, the most common distinction may be the desire to control territory. Distinctions based on group objectives can be problematic, however. One distinction between guerrilla warfare and terrorism draws attention to the intermediary objectives of the militant groups involved: guerrillas want to win territory while terrorists want to capture publicity, influence their target audiences, and gain supporters. However, this distinction ignores the fact that many terrorists – nationalist-separatists, in particular – seek territory. This distinction also supposes that guerrilla leaders do not also seek attention or support, resources that may help them in carrying out in guerrilla warfare.

Organization and organizational resources go hand-in-hand. In terms of organization, guerrilla forces may have a hierarchical organizational structure resembling that of a military. There is a presumption that the armed group has a leader. Guerrilla forces may don uniforms and operate more openly than their clandestine counterparts who carry out terrorist attacks. Guerrilla forces tend to have access to more resources than groups relying solely on terrorism. Their resources may include external support, a supply of weapons, large numbers of militants, and control over territory.[17] With territory, they are more likely to have "safe" areas from which they operate without a significant threat from the state. They are likely to operate in places where state authority is limited.

Of course, having any of these resources should make it easier for a guerrilla force to obtain other resources. Having territory may create opportunities to gain financial resources, perhaps through extortion or extraction or through business. Financial resources facilitate the purchase of weapons and the payment of monetary incentives to militants and potential supporters. Territory may also facilitate the creation and training of a force that can be organized along military lines. In turn, larger, better trained and equipped forces should find control over territory easier to maintain. In sum, guerrilla forces should be stronger and more sophisticated in military terms than terrorists. This is one of the reasons they should also be more capable of attacking harder targets. It is also why they may pose a more serious challenge to their adversaries.[18] Since guerrilla warfare involves attacks on a state and its representatives, the ability to challenge the state may also be part of the definition.

Making a distinction between terrorists, guerrillas, and insurgents is more difficult in large part because the same actors may engage in terrorism, guerrilla warfare, and insurgency and, they may do so for the same reasons and to achieve the same objectives.[19] The point is not to confuse guerrilla warfare with terrorism; rather, an armed group may use terrorism and engage in guerrilla warfare, and it may do both at the same time. Militant groups may alternate between attacking harder and softer targets for any number of reasons, for instance as a result of variations in group strength or strategic or tactical advantages. Moreover, militants may not distinguish between combatant and noncombatant targets. Alternatively, they may perceive distinct benefits from attacking both. Many of Central America's

Cold War-era "terrorists" were also "guerrillas" engaging in civil wars, with targets ranging from civilian to military to state. In their early years, the first modern suicide attackers of Lebanon and Sri Lanka used suicide attacks almost exclusively against embassies and militaries.[20] At times, the types of tactics often associated with terrorism seems to be more consistent with a form of guerrilla warfare.

Defining insurgency

The groups of interest in this study are those that use terrorism as a tactic within an "insurgency." These same groups are likely engaging in terrorism and guerrilla warfare. As with the cases of "terrorism" and "guerrilla warfare" there is no shortage of definitions of "insurgency," including those provided by states and those privately specified. Definitions of insurgency, unlike those used here for terrorism and guerrilla warfare, include references to objectives, adversaries, and tactics. Insurgencies can be a type of wider-scale war. The United States military uses the concept to mean "an organized, protracted politico-military struggle designed to weaken the control and legitimacy of an established government, occupying power, or other political authority while increasing insurgent control."[21] Others identify insurgency with "fourth gen-eration warfare," a post-World War II development involving a combination of guerrilla tactics, civil disobedience, disinformation campaigns and other political activity aimed at weakening the enemy's will to resist.[22] Insurgencies are typically protracted efforts, persistent struggles in which the challengers wear down or hope to wear down the authorities over a long period of time. Insurgencies tend to begin as asymmetrical conflicts in which the authorities enjoy a great advantage in human and material resources – hence the need to launch an insurgency and use tactics that allow the armed non-state group to avoid a direct and immediate confrontation with the state or powerful outside forces. David Galula describes this effort as "a competition between insurgent and government for the support of the civilian population, which provides the sea in which the insurgent swims."[23] Insurgents characteristically believe that they will prevail in the long-run. Moreover, if evidence on internal wars provided by Arreguín-Toft is accurate, insurgencies have become significantly more successful since World War II than they were previously.[24] Terrorist vio-lence, at least when it is directed at specific targets, appears to be a contribut-ing factor. Viewed in these terms, a modern insurgency is a way of waging war adopted by challengers who are relatively weak compared to those in power.

Not all insurgencies produce wars, and using methods to wage war does not necessarily mean that war results. Some insurgencies never reach the level of violence or scale often associated with war, which is often defined in terms of the numbers of battle-related deaths per year. Some insurgent groups fail altogether. Other insurgent groups may use terrorism as part of a strategy to incite government repression, which may lead to popular uprisings and divisions within the government or the security forces. In such cases, insurgents would not operate under conditions of wider-scale warfare. Our interest is primarily in those groups that do engage in insurgencies resulting in war.

Insurgent groups may participate in civil wars. Civil wars are wars involving a specific type of relationship between the adversaries; they are fought within a state. As Steven Metz puts it, "A civil war is simply a violent conflict within a nation – the antagonists share a citizenship. If there is a significant asymmetry between the antagonists, the weaker may resort to a strategy of insurgency."[25] James Fearon and David Laitin refer to insurgency, which they equate with rural forms of guerrilla warfare, as "a mode of military practice that can be harnessed to various political agendas."[26]

The more pressing question may be how we differentiate civil wars from other types of "civil violence" or armed confrontations.[27] Nicholas Sambanis points out a troubling reality: we have "no consensus" to which to turn when it comes to identifying what constitutes a civil war.[28] In comparisons across cases we expect to find variations in the numbers of battle-deaths, the types of participants and their levels of organization, and the types of threats the participants pose. Without giving attention to such details, we may be considering – and comparing – very different manifestations of armed conflict under the same label. This can be particularly problematic in cases in which data sources adjust the methods of measurement on which they rely over time.[29] In addition, there is not an established way in which to determine when civil wars begin and end.[30] The "intermittent" nature of violence in internal wars complicates the identification of these dates.[31]

It is clear that insurgency may take place in the context of civil war as well as in contexts where other types of armed confrontations are taking place. There is a certain irony in this.

We accept insurgencies as attempts by non-state actors aiming to replace a political system. These attempts may or may not result in wider-scale war. As weaker actors, the non-state groups engaging in insurgency carry out attacks on combatant and noncombatant targets. Often they are terrorists. When they have the capabilities to do so, these same insurgents may engage in guerrilla warfare. Forming an organized militia would be one step in the process of establishing a legitimate challenge to the state. Obtaining control over territory and the resources needed to organize a military represents another, possibly preceding, step in this process. Insurgents may also seek publicity and "freedom," along with other objectives.

Applying these terms

Some examples will help to illustrate these points. During 2012, al Qaeda in the Islamic Maghreb (AQIM), a foreign terrorist organization,[32] controlled a substantial part of the African state of Mali. Is AQIM now less (or more) of a terrorist group by virtue of its conquest?[33] As a member of the al-Qaeda franchise, AQIM seeks to abolish the political systems in place in parts of Africa that include Mali, Algeria, Libya, and Niger, and work with al Qaeda to establish a caliphate throughout these lands. Is AQIM thus also engaging in insurgency? The same questions may be asked about the ill-fated Tamil Tigers in Sri Lanka, who controlled the country's Jaffna Peninsula for years. Adding to the complexity of these designations, the Tamil Tigers, though labeled as a "terrorist organization," created a military. This military was more than an armed militia. It included a navy, "nascent" air force, and a suicide squad.[34] The Tigers attacked military, police, and government targets, and did so, by some estimates, around 60 percent of the time.[35]

Focusing instead on the insurgent groups' tactics and targets, we may wonder how best to apply these labels. The United States and its North Atlantic Treaty Organization (NATO) allies have certainly fallen victim to attacks by "unconventional" forces in their struggle against the Taliban in Afghanistan.[36] Suicide bombers have been deployed to maim and kill soldiers, as well as civilians. The U.S. Marines stationed at Beirut International Airport in October 1983 can also attest to the ambiguity in labels. The immediate effects – death, destruction, and fear – are much the same regardless of whether the attacks are called "terrorism" or "guerrilla strikes."

Patterns of terrorism

It makes sense to consider how terrorism is and has been used in the context of insurgency. Frequencies of terrorist attacks serve as an indicator of variations in the use of terrorism over time. If terrorism is the "weapon of the weak," we may expect would-be insurgents to use terrorism early on, before they gain the resources they will need to augment their struggle. Insurgents are likely to be weak when they begin their resistance, when they are organizing their efforts. We expect terrorism to be concentrated at the beginning or in the early stages of insurgency for insurgent groups that have not yet developed the capacity needed to pose a stronger resistance. We expect terrorism to occur throughout an insurgency in cases in which insurgent groups fail to gain such capacity. A depiction of terrorism concentrated during the early stages of war would show the number of terrorist attacks at its highest level at the initial stages of war. A depiction of terrorism occurring throughout wider-scale armed conflict could take any number of forms. The frequencies of terrorism employed throughout an insurgency may increase and decrease over time. A key distinction between earlier terrorism and terrorism used throughout an insurgency is the presence or absence of a spike or peak in frequencies of terrorism. Figures 1.1 and 1.2 illustrate hypothetical distinctions between these patterns.

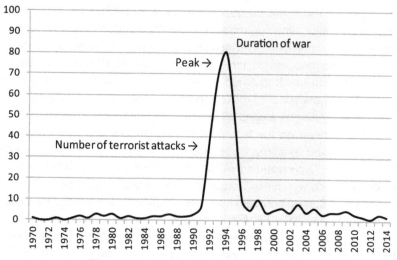

Figure 1.1   Terrorism early in insurgency

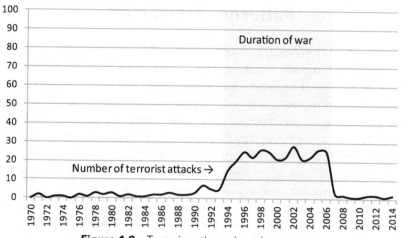

Figure 1.2   Terrorism throughout insurgency

There are several possible explanations for a reduction in terrorism after the initial phases of insurgency. We may expect a reduction in terrorism following a successful counterterrorism or counterinsurgency effort. We may also expect a reduction in terrorism following an increase in an insurgent group's capacity to direct attacks at harder targets associated with the state, police, or military. As such attacks may serve a tactical purpose – weakening the adversary – we may expect increases in attacks on these targets to coincide with fewer attacks on civilians. In addition, attacks on civilians may cost insurgents potential sources of support.

Our expectations are different in cases in which terrorism occurs primarily during the later stages of insurgency. Terrorism is the weapon of the weak, and it could also be a weapon of the weakening. Insurgents may turn to terrorism during the later phases of their resistance or during the later stages of insurgency when their positions have weakened vis-à-vis more powerful counterinsurgents. Perhaps ironically, an increase in terrorism may also follow successful counterterrorism or counterinsurgency efforts. Attempts to counter insurgents may weaken these groups, which may correspond with an increase in terrorism rather than a decrease. Figure 1.3 shows a hypothetical case with an increasing frequency of terrorism toward the end of wider-scale warfare.

There is another scenario to consider. What we think of as "terrorism" may be a tactic used throughout wars in the twenty-first century. The main competitors in twenty-first century wars thus far have been groups identified as "terrorists," some of these are "transnational" terrorist groups. Among these are groups engaging in insurgencies while continuing to carry out acts of terrorism. Although the threats of global terrorism remain, their activities,

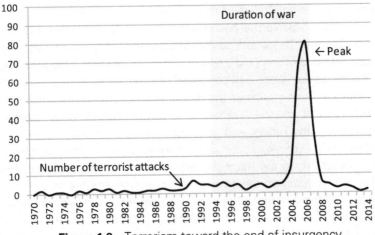

Figure 1.3   Terrorism toward the end of insurgency

including their terrorism, are more local than global. Terrorism may become a regular part of warfare as "terrorist" groups go to war.

Modern terrorism

It is useful to start a discussion of "modern" terrorism – usefully understood to include terrorism dating back to the nineteenth century[37] – by noting how terrorist activity caught the public's attention, especially during the middle to latter twentieth century. Walter Laqueur and other observers have characterized the era beginning in the late 1960s as the "Age of Terrorism."[38] This "Age" has yet to abate, much less come to an end. This discussion begins with a look at how it started.

The "Age of Terrorism" started with a long list of what one might label, for want of better terminology, as "armed struggle" groups. Various groups so engaged appeared in the Western world in the late 1960s. This was an era characterized by youth rebellion, opposition to the war in Vietnam, and the widespread expression of Maoist ideas about the possibilities of revolution and societal change. Israel's victory in the June 1967 Arab-Israeli War created challenges and opportunities, as well as new realities and questions among those claiming rights to govern and occupy this part of the Arab world. There were numerous movements pushing for equality and other liberties as well as some opposing such challenges to the status quo.

The "armed" groups of the era held a variety of ideologies, the most common being those associated with left-wing politics and nationalist or separatist objectives. Groups adhering to one of the various far-right movements were also present. In America, for instance, these include racist, religious-fundamentalist, and anti-federalist movements.[39] Many of the groups unique to this era asserted ideological agendas based vaguely on the views of Marx, Lenin, and Trotsky. These left-leaning groups were inspired in part by the ideological divisions of the Cold War era. Although they imported their ideas, many of the groups were self-contained, having localized objectives and local operations. Such groups as the Red Brigades, Red Army Faction (RAF), Revolutionary Road, and the Weather Underground formed in Italy, what was then West Germany, Turkey, and, to a lesser extent, in France, Greece, and the United States. These groups often formed among young people who had been caught up in the mass protests of the era, many of them young and educated. A common theme among the groups was the struggle for a form of revolutionary change. The armed groups active at the time began to stage well-publicized attacks, often targeting symbols of state power and the capitalist economic system. Bankers, businesspeople, elected officials, and judges were typically the targets of kidnappings, or worse. Contrary to the expectations of the groups' ideologues, these escapades mostly failed to raise the revolutionary consciousness of the masses or, for that matter, anyone else.

Groups with nationalist ideologies fared better during this time. Particularly in the Basque region of Spain and in Northern Ireland, Basque Fatherland and Liberty (ETA) and the Irish Republican Army (IRA) and Provisional IRA (PIRA) sought to separate their territories from their respective states, the newly democratic Spain and the United Kingdom. Diaspora populations of Armenians, Croats, South Moluccans, and others stimulated nationalist groups to launch terrorist attacks on Turkish, Yugoslav, Dutch, and other targets.[40] Oftentimes spokespersons for the populations championed by these "bands" expressed embarrassment at what was being done in their names. Nonetheless, nationalist-separatist groups achieved considerable resonance with their respective nationals, including those residing abroad. While there were times when Basque nationalists, Irish republicans, Palestinian nationalists, and others leaned to the political left, their main objectives remained primarily nationalist.

Nationalist Palestinian groups were also active during the initial phases of this era. Militants associated with the Palestinian national movement brought worldwide attention to their cause, largely through the use of terrorism. The background for the emergence of Palestinian terrorism was Israel's swift defeat of Arab armies during the Six-Day War of June 1967. Images of Arab strength, unity, and regional hegemony were among the casualties of the war. Bahraini scholar Mohammed Jabar al-Ansari described the Arab states' loss as "the mother of all defeats" and as a "defeat [that] was first and foremost existential."[41] Fawaz A. Gerges refers to the loss as having lasting "catastrophic civilizational and psychological repercussions on Arabs."[42] Another consequence of the loss was support from Arab states – self-interested as it may have been – for Palestinians' national aspirations. Palestinian leaders who had come together under the umbrella of the Palestine Liberation Organization (PLO) responded by acting more independently of their Arab-state backers.[43]

After initial experimentation with a "people's war" campaign in the Israeli-occupied West Bank, some of the PLO groups – most conspicuously the Marxist Popular Front for the Liberation of Palestine (PFLP) – turned their attention to Western Europe.[44] During this time PFLP fighters skyjacked and blew-up commercial airliners in European air space. On the ground there was a series of spectacular terrorist attacks carried out against Israeli and Jewish targets by the PFLP, its various Marxist-Leninist offshoots, and other militant Palestinian groups.

PFLP founder George Habash summarized the logic of the Palestinian groups' strategies in a well-publicized statement recorded in 1970: "When we hijack a plane, it has more effect than if we kill a hundred Israelis in battle ... For decades, world public opinion has been neither for nor against the Palestinians. It simply ignored us. At least the world is talking about us now."[45] Terrorism was a tool for gaining attention. There were limits, however, in terms of what could be gained through this form of violence. Nearly three decades later, in an interview published in 1998, Habash offered a point of distinction between the attacks perpetrated by his group and those carried out by others. According to Habash, the PFLP sought attention, though not necessarily by way of harming or killing.[46]

In fact, it was a Palestinian group that carried out the most widely publicized of terrorist attacks during this time. This was the internationally televised hostage-taking and killing of Israeli athletes at the 1972 Olympic Games in Munich. Members of Black September (the *nom de guerre* of a group with ties to Yassir Arafat's Fatah) gained immediate attention through the media, which was already in place to cover the Olympics. Images of masked gunmen at the Olympic dorms were distributed widely as negotiations and the tragedy unfolded.[47] Along with broad media coverage and attention came widespread disdain for the terrorists' tactics.

In another way, however, the terrorists' operations seemed to "work" up to a point.[48] If attention to the Palestinian cause was the primary objective of this terrorist attack, then we may presume that this one attack was successful.[49] From relative obscurity, the Palestinian cause became a central concern for the United Nations (UN), the Arab world, and Western democracies. If we seek to gauge the success of a single attack, we may focus on its immediate effect rather than any unforeseen future effect the attack may have by way of bringing a group closer to achieving its broader objectives. On the other hand, if success is measured in terms of achieving these broader objectives (e.g., a Palestinian state) or intermediate objectives (i.e., the release of Palestinian prisoners), the attack at Munich was unsuccessful, as was the sum of all other efforts (terrorist or otherwise). None of their terrorist operations led to the elimination of Israel or to significant territorial concessions by the latter. By the mid-1980s, the PLO headquarters were located in Tunis, more than a thousand miles removed from the object of Palestinian hatred.

The failure of Palestinian nationalists is not exceptional. Neither Basques nor Irish republicans achieved their long-term objectives. In contrast to the European nationalist-separatists, however, the Palestinians enjoyed a considerable measure of external support.[50] Syria, Iraq, Libya, and other Arab states, along with the Soviet Union (USSR), poured money and supplies into their favorite Palestinian factions.[51] Groups affiliated with the PLO enjoyed sanctuaries in Lebanon and what was then the People's Republic of South Yemen. By comparison, their European counterparts operated largely on their own.

The situation in Latin America was more complicated and quite distinct. Unlike the leftists in the West and the nationalist-separatists elsewhere, the Latin American groups were residing in what could be considered a significant front in the ideological battle between capitalism and communism. Much of the Cold War was fought in this arena. For those in the West, the Cold War was a battle between "good" and "evil." Latin America was clearly within the United States' "sphere of influence," as designated by the Monroe Doctrine of 1823. Communism in the Western hemisphere was seen as a real threat to U.S. national security.

In this context, the success of Fidel Castro's Cuban Revolution in 1959 inspired dreams of glory among young people throughout the region. It was around this time that the belief became widespread that the Cuban Revolution could serve as a model for toppling other authoritarian regimes in power throughout much of Latin America.

Ernesto "Che" Guevara, Castro's second in command, was the man who would try to export this model. Che was an Argentine by birth who traveled through much of Latin America during the early 1950s. He later became the equivalent of a rock star, with his poster displayed on dormitory room walls at universities throughout the continent. Che's celebrity, however, is not a product of his success in exporting the Cuban model.

There were problems with the expectation that the Cuban Revolution could be replicated elsewhere. Castro's revolution had been a largely rural endeavor. His guerrilla fighters had waged their war against the Batista dictatorship from the Sierra Maestra Mountains and then managed to parade triumphantly into Havana, as the dictator and his entourage fled into exile. According to Castro, cities were places where revolutions died.[52] Having experienced the revolution with Castro, Che Guevara agreed. Looking beyond Cuba, he saw Latin America's rural territories as fertile grounds for revolution.[53] This was Che Guevara's thinking when he sought to bring about revolutionary insurgency from the Andes. As it turned out, however, the South American countryside became a "graveyard for revolutions as well as revolutionaries."[54] It seems that the revolutionary plan did not account for the United States' interest in the politics of the region or the likelihood of foreign intervention, for which there was sufficient precedent. The revolutionaries also seem to have underestimated the likelihood that their adversaries might learn from previous events and adapt their counterrevolutionary responses accordingly.[55] With some assistance from the United States, including from the U.S. Central Intelligence Agency (CIA), the Bolivian military was able to track down and kill Guevara in 1967.[56]

This defeat of the famous rural guerrilla led various Latin American revolu-tionaries and revolutionary theorists, including Carlos Marighella and Abraham Guillen, to rethink their strategies. One result of their cogitations was the birth of the "urban guerrilla." Cities could support insurgencies by providing fighters with cover and access to targets. Marighella drafted guidelines for the urban guerrilla, which drew on insights taken from Maoist insurgency and lessons drawn from Guevara's experience.[57] For Marighella, the urban guerrilla was a terrorist, residing in cities and blending among the population. Terrorists would organize into small cells. They would engage in criminal activities in order to accumulate resources for carrying out attacks. Their form of warfare was unconventional. Their targets were to include the state and its representatives. They would attempt to disrupt the government, society, and economy, and demonstrate its weaknesses; they would also provide support for rural guerrilla forces.[58] Marighella centered his attention and efforts on Brazil.

Abraham Guillen, a Spaniard who left Argentina to settle in Uruguay, may have been more sensitive to the politics and the need to avoid unneces-sary violence, which could turn the civilian population – their presumed constituency – against the urban guerrillas.[59] Guillen's concern was that a guerrilla movement could fail if it lacked popular support, rendering its efforts futile.[60] When it comes to popular support, there is an intrinsic competition between insurgents and counterinsurgents. As Weinstein points out, vio-lence is a byproduct of this competition: "violence emerges as a strategy in different contexts and to different degrees as a consequence of the interac-tion between rebels and governments battling for control of the state on the one hand and civilians who choose to offer or withhold support from the com-peting parties on the other."[61] Yet, insurgents who rely on support from the public cannot simultaneously target this public.[62] The same is true of states and counterinsurgents. Protecting the public and gaining their support is a point of emphasis in counterinsurgency efforts.[63] Although Marighella and Guillen saw roles for urban and rural guerrilla operations, each seems to have focused attention on the importance of the urban arena.[64] Both also saw guer-rillas as potential state-builders.[65]

Urban terrorism was something of a scourge in Uruguay, Argentina, and Brazil as revolutionary groups launched their campaigns of urban terrorism in their major cities. Marighella became a practitioner of urban guerrilla warfare with his founding of the National Liberation Action (ALN) in Brazil.[66] Guillen served as an advisor and critic to Uruguay's Tupamaros, also known as the Movement of National Liberation. Argentina's leftist challengers included the Montoneros and the People's Revolutionary Army (ERP). Unlike their rural counterparts, none of these movements was successful.[67] Instead, they were defeated after the states' militaries turned to exceptionally brutal means (e.g., "death squads," abductions, torture) to repress them.

Other Latin American revolutionaries had better luck, especially those in Peru, Colombia, Nicaragua, and El Salvador. Through a combination of urban terrorism and rural guerrilla operations, insurgents in these countries posed serious challenges to the prevailing order for a number of years. Examples include the Shining Path in Peru, the Revolutionary Armed Forces of Colombia (FARC), the Sandinistas in Nicaragua, and the Farabundo Marti National Liberation Front (FMLN) in El Salvador.

This record hints at something of general significance. Groups such as the IRA or ETA were unable to pose a serious challenge to the prevailing political order even when they enjoyed a certain amount of support from their natural constituencies. Although their targets included the military (particularly in Northern Ireland) and the police (more so in Spain),[68] these groups did not use some of the tactics most closely associated with guerrilla warfare, such as attempts to sabotage the state's ability to respond to its challenge. When the IRA attacked harder targets, such as police headquarters, their attacks were more "demonstrative" and disruptive than they were effective at undermining the British state's response.[69] Their aim was to produce fear and gain attention. Bombings and shootings were within their repertoires; the types of military confrontations typically considered to be conventional or regular were not. For practical purposes, guerrilla forms of warfare, even when undertaken within the cover provided by urban or rural settings, remained largely outside of their repertoires.

On the other hand, the groups that employed some mixture of tactics – including terrorist and guerrilla tactics along with an effective use of the mass media – appear to have enjoyed greater success, at least in terms of gaining and maintaining attention, challenging a political status quo, achieving intermediary objectives, and even in some cases obtaining political power. The Shining Path did not defeat the government in Lima but it certainly posed a serious challenge for some years, taking control of rural territory and carrying out thousands of attacks. The same may be said about FARC in Colombia. In Central America's weak states, both Nicaragua's Sandinistas and El Salvador's FMLN were able to displace their respective states' incumbent regimes while transforming themselves from armed movements into more or less democratic political parties. While the threats posed by the Latin American groups have diminished, the surviving militant groups on the other side of the world are taking control of mass media. Palestinian groups, such as Hamas, have made use of martyr videos and posters to advertise the groups' accomplishments. Hezbollah has had its own television station. The radio has been a less expensive tool for the spread of propaganda, especially in more remote areas. Many groups – including armed groups, their political wings, or their representatives – publish their propaganda and arguments via newspapers and magazines. The Irish republican movement has a long history of publications, including the monthly *Saoirse – Irish Freedom*. The shift to transmitting information via the Internet has further eased the sharing of ideas. In the first decade of the twenty-first century, al Qaeda seemed to have provided a new model for using the Internet to facilitate the business of carrying out jihad. More recently, it appears that ISIL is establishing a new norm, using media to manage its own publicity and distribute its own message.

"New" terrorism

Toward the end of the Cold War many of the older terrorist groups either departed the scene, lost their relevance, or gave way to what many have called the "new" terrorism.[70] Notable events frame this period of history. Left-wing ideologies went out of style, a casualty of the end of the ideological arm-wrestling between capitalism and communism; victory belonged to the liberal West.[71] It was around this time that Afghan Arabs (with some assistance from the United States) pushed the Soviet Union out of Afghanistan.[72] It seemed that the weaker actors had defeated the superpower. This was viewed by some as a victory of the devout over the atheists. Around the same time, Iran's Islamic Republic survived the war against the secular Iraq, and Sudan experienced its own an Islamic revolution. Soon, the Third World would no longer be the territory over which the First and Second Worlds competed. The Third World would, however, remain an area of interest for the surviving superpower, whose influence among Arab regimes, military capacity and willingness to intervene in foreign affairs, and liberal culture would begin to be seen as a threat to the Muslim world. In particular, some among the newly empowered Afghan-Arab mujahideen, who succeeded in Afghanistan with Western aid, began to focus on the West and the United States as a new threat.

The end of the Cold War did not bring the hoped-for "new world order." Rather than "international peace and security,"[73] there were new civil wars, ethnic conflicts, and recurrences of genocide, something the states of the world had sworn to prevent. Pondering this changing climate of violent conflict, Samuel Huntington proposed that the new point of ideological contention would be cultural, a designation he assigned largely on the basis of religion. Huntington described this as a "clash of civilizations."[74] Ethnic conflicts broke out in places near some of the borders of Huntington's civilizations (e.g., Yugoslavia, Kashmir, Israel, Chechnya, Sudan). Former Yugoslavia began its violent breakup. In Israel-Palestine, the First Intifada was already underway. In contrast, Latin America was relatively quiet during this time.

Conflicts also broke out within the boundaries of Huntington's "civilizations." Rwanda's 1994 genocide stands out among these. The more recent case of Ukraine's war against pro-Russian separatists is another example. Violence within larger religious communities – for example, Sunni Muslims battling Shi'a Muslims in Iraq – suggests the relevance of differences within these communities in addition to differences between them. Conflicts have not arisen in all places where the borders of civilizations intersect. The arrival of the "new" terrorism has coincided with these developments.[75]

Observers saw this "new" terrorism as exhibiting certain distinctive features.[76] First, while the groups belonging to the earlier manifestation of terrorism "wanted a lot of people watching, not a lot of people dead," the new generation of terrorists seemed to want both.[77] Mass killing was the *sine qua non* of the new groups. Second, the new groups typically drew their inspiration from religious ideas. The obvious cases include Muslim groups claiming a Salafi-jihadist ideology, which have launched a holy war against the West and the Middle Eastern regimes with ties to the United States, including Egypt and Saudi Arabia. Despite the most obvious cases in the greater Middle East, these outgrowths of religious revivalism have not been restricted to Islam. Sikh groups in the Indian Punjab launched a terrorist campaign aimed at the Hindu-dominated government in Delhi. Ultra-orthodox Jewish groups in Israel waged a bitter campaign against the Oslo peace agreements between Israel and the PLO that culminated in the 1995 assassination of Prime Minister Yitzhak Rabin. While the bombing in Oklahoma City was perpetrated by individuals with peripheral ties to the militia movement in the United States, the ideology of this movement has "a significant religious dimension" drawing references to the Bible.[78] In Sri Lanka, the secular Liberation Tigers of Tamil Eelam (Tamil Tigers, LTTE) employed an extensive array of terrorist tactics in an effort to secede from the Buddhist-controlled state. Their members were predominantly Hindu.

Third, at least some of the new constellation of terrorist groups employed suicide as a tactic. Terrorist groups' use of suicide attacks began in Lebanon in the early 1980s before being adopted some years later by the Tamil Tigers of Sri Lanka and others. The LTTE's first suicide attack was a truck bombing at an army installation in 1987. Most conspicuously, suicide attacks were taken up by Hamas and Palestinian Islamic Jihad (PIJ) in the mid-1990s in their seemingly endless attempts to destroy the Jewish state. Other Palestinian groups, including the secular Fatah and PFLP, soon joined their religious counterparts in using suicide tactics. The increasing numbers of suicide attacks that resulted have been described as an exercise in "outbidding," during which competing political groups use violence in order to demonstrate their commitment to the Palestinian people.[79] Despite the attention given to the Palestinian groups, especially following their suicide attacks on civilians in busses, cafes, and shopping centers, it was Sri Lanka's LTTE who perpetrated the highest number of such attacks in the years prior to the introduction of the tactic in Iraq in 2003.[80] Al Qaeda and its affiliates were relative late-comers to the world of suicide terrorism. Like the LTTE and Palestinians before them, al Qaeda sought guidance from Hezbollah, the original innovators of modern suicide attacks.[81] The first al-Qaeda-linked suicide attacks were against American embassies in Kenya and Tanzania in 1998 and an American naval vessel in Yemeni waters in 2000. Since that time, the most deadly and destructive suicide attacks were carried out by al Qaeda and al-Qaeda-linked groups and individuals against an array of targets throughout the Middle East, South Asia, and against the U.S. and its allies. The September 11, 2001, attacks aimed at New York City and Washington, DC, and the July 7, 2005, bombings of mass transit, both underground and above-ground, in London stand out among these events.

There has been some debate over other features of the "new" terrorism. One point of contention is the extent to which the terrorist groups seek to acquire and use weapons of mass destruction (WMDs). This is not a new concern; the discussion of terrorists seeking access to and using such weapons preceded the advent of the "new" terrorism.[82] Fears regarding terrorists' (and others') interests in obtaining WMDs were augmented with the collapse of the USSR and concerns over which parties, if any, were securing the former republic's nuclear arsenal. Concerns have also followed al Qaeda's reported pursuit of radioactive material and even a nuclear bomb, an effort that began in the years shortly after the USSR's collapse.[83] Others believe these fears are vastly exaggerated.[84] Nuclear weapons are not the only concern. Aum Shinrikyo experimented with biological and chemical weapons prior to carrying out its sarin gas attack in Tokyo and reportedly researched alternative means of mass destruction.[85] While the Aum case may be isolated, the possibility remains that others could do the same. These considerations seem more relevant in an era in which terrorists seem to "want ... a lot of people dead."[86]

Another point of dispute is the way in which the "new" terrorist groups are organized. Some observers have stressed the evolving structure of terrorist organizations and the increasing prevalence of loosely connected cells organized as networks, which are more horizontal and more decentralized in terms of decision-making. Horizontal organizational structures are described as "flatter"; they are more likely to resemble a network in which members may be more or less connected to others within the network.[87] We should expect most organizations to be more or less hierarchical rather than approximating one of these ideal types.

These organizational features presumed to belong to "new" terrorist groups differ from the strictly hierarchical organizational structures thought to be characteristic of earlier and presumably easier-to-defeat terrorist groups.[88] In fact, horizontal organizational structures with networks of militants organized into separate, semi-independent cells are well-established among militant groups. The Ku Klux Klan (KKK) established an early version of "leaderless resistance," in part in response to successful efforts to counter the national organization in the 1940s.[89] Marighella's and Guillen's "urban guerrillas" were organized as cells operating within cities. The Viet Cong employed suicide cells.[90] Moreover, the horizontal structure is not the description immediately given to groups such as al Qaeda in Iraq (AQI), which now refers to itself as the Islamic State. Jacob Shapiro describes AQI and its successor organizations – Islamic State in Iraq (ISI), ISIL, which has also been referred to as Islamic State of Iraq and Syria (ISIS) – as having hierarchical characteristics with some local-level autonomy.[91]

Horizontal and hierarchical organizations may have centralized or decentralized decision-making. Decentralized decision-making is something different, referring to the level of concentration of decision-making in an organization's central leadership. The extent to which bin Laden was in charge of "calling the shots" for al Qaeda has been the subject of considerable debate, even while his organization has been recognized as a transnational, "franchise" system of terrorist groups and affiliates.[92] There is still much to learn about ISIL, including the extent to which control over the group is concentrated under its leader, Abu Bakr al-Baghdadi.

Studies of the "new" terrorism and its newest actors suffer from a recognizable problem: time. Much of the work done in the fields of terrorism and warfare, in general, is done after the fact, when the dust has died down, body counts are known, perpetrators have been identified, victims can be met, and access to each of these is easier. Even though interest lies with the most proximate threats, we cannot help but have incomplete information about many of the most important actors and events taking place today.

Terrorism in warfare

A discussion of terrorism in the twenty-first century would be incomplete without some discussion of the evolution of terrorism as a tool used by non-state actors in modern warfare. Max Boot reminds us that "conventional warfare is the relatively recent innovation" in the history of warfare. In contrast, "irregular" or "unconventional" forms of warfare have been more common in human history. These types of warfare are also common in modern history. Guerrillas and terrorists "simply assumed different forms."[93]

Few seem to recall that the Viet Minh and Viet Cong made extensive use of terrorism in their successful insurgencies against the French and, later, against American forces in Vietnam.[94] In the process, attacks against civilians were one tactic used to exert control over the local Vietnamese population.[95] In more recent times, terrorism has been employed by the Taliban groups in Pakistan and Afghanistan, al-Qaeda affiliates in Africa, the Arabian Peninsula, and Asia, AQI and ISIL, and as part of the anti-Assad insurgency in Syria. Western states and their citizens are not the primary targets of these terrorists or their terrorism. Rather, their targets are more local; their fights are primarily on the ground in the places these groups seek to control or claim to govern. Or, as Gary LaFree, Sue-Ming Yang, and Martha Crenshaw put it in their study of threats to United States security, "Most groups operated primarily at home against local targets."[96]

At this point it is worth considering why terrorism may be used in the context of war. Insurgent groups and others use terrorism strategically, as part of a strategy that combines various tactics in order to achieve the groups' goals.[97] These groups use terrorism to create fear and gain attention. Terrorism serves a coercive role.[98] Insurgent groups may use terrorist attacks to "punish" an opposition and "prevent" others from joining in opposition to the group.[99] Insurgent groups may use terrorism to signal their strength or a state's weakness. When there is competition between insurgent groups, these groups may use terrorism to demonstrate that their commitment to representing the interests of a target constituency is greater than that of others.[100] Terrorism may also serve as a tool for recruitment.[101] Insurgent groups often use terrorism as part of a strategy that includes other tactics.[102] Terrorism may be used to achieve proximate (immediate) objectives more so than longer-term (ultimate) objectives.

If we make the assumption of insurgent or terrorist rationality (i.e., they hope to win and choose tactics that will help them do so),[103] then we should expect insurgents to consider the ways in which their chosen means may affect their chances for achieving their desired ends. We need not, of course, assume that insurgents or terrorists have complete or correct information,[104] nor should we assume that they have the capacity to alter their tactics or strategies.[105] We may focus instead on the assumption that groups use terrorism because it "works," or at least because they think it will work. As such, the decision to commit terrorist attacks would be strategic, and there would be costs and benefits associated with this choice.[106]

This assumption deserves further discussion, especially in the context of the "new" terrorism. For one, we may wonder whether today's insurgents and terrorists are capable of acting strategically, given their size, span, and organizational structures. Are organizations such as al Qaeda "unitary" actors; must they be unitary in order to act strategically? Given a guiding ideology that is shared among members of the group or movement, are autonomous actors within a network able to make strategic decisions that are consistent with the interests of the larger collective? We may also wonder whether a guiding ideology has any effect on strategic choices. If the guiding ideology is based on religious beliefs, are decision-makers actively weighing costs and benefits? Might they be influenced by an assumption of greater popular support than they have, by an expectation of divine intervention, or by a compulsion to fight to an end, even if that end is their own destruction? Because so many of the "new" religiously motivated groups remain active at the beginning of the twenty-first century, it is not likely that these questions can be definitively answered.

If terrorism "works,"[107] then we might also expect to see clear indicators of success on the parts of terrorists or insurgents. Such evidence is not easy to find in terms of insurgent groups realizing their ultimate objectives. This lack of success poses a problem for the strategic explanation. Terrorism may be more effectively used for achieving short-term or intermediate objectives, such as publicity, coercion, or recruitment, than for achieving longer-term goals. The success or failure of terrorist attacks at achieving other short-term or more proximate objectives – such as influencing electoral outcomes – is also easier to assess. As elections resulting in the return of hard-line governments may suggest, however, such outcomes are not always consistent with the terrorists' interests or those of their constituency.

Another issue is how success is measured. As Robert Pape points out, "successes are more ambiguous than failures."[108] A group's long-term success is not necessarily determined by the number of people it kills or the number of attacks it carries out. These may be tactical successes, yet they may have no relationship to strategic success.[109] In terms of achieving their longer-term objectives, terrorists – namely those relying solely or almost entirely on terrorism – are overwhelmingly unsuccessful.

A further point – really a process – also deserves attention. An insurgent (or terrorist) group's objectives may change, even moderate, over time. This process may lead to new definitions of what it means to be successful. At some point, an insurgent group's survival may become its primary goal. Transitioning to legitimate participation in party politics may become more acceptable after a group's failure to achieve other objectives through violent means. In fact, insurgent groups may have more success when they do not rely primarily or exclusively on terrorism. Rather, they may find that terrorism is more effective when used in combination with other tactics.

If we presume that insurgent groups use terrorism strategically, then we may presume that these groups also recognize and take into account the consequences and costs associated with using terrorism. We may also expect that insurgent groups understand the types of messages their use of terrorism sends to various audiences.

One of the potential costs of using terrorism is a loss of popular support. This is not surprising, as attacking civilians goes against efforts to win their support. What is more surprising is the notion that insurgent groups do not need local support. If a population is unlikely to be supportive of an insurgent group, the most the group may hope to gain is the type of acquiescence that is achieved through coercion. Brutality against civilians may also be a sign that insurgents do not seek popular support.[110]

On this point, the Taliban and AQI provide useful examples. After experiencing "popular backlash," the Taliban "learned to discriminate in its use of terror."[111] AQI (now ISIL) took a different approach in its use of terrorism. AQI lost support among Iraq's Sunnis following the group's attacks on the country's Shi'a population.[112] The reasons for this type of backlash may be more obvious to outsiders. A group's ideology may contribute to its miscalculations regarding the effectiveness of a particular strategy. Armed groups (including insurgents, terrorists, and extremists) may be more likely to underestimate the people's preferences for peace and development over war and the resulting destruction, displacement, and death associated with it. Ideologies may lead groups to overestimate the appeal of their conservative beliefs, especially when these beliefs are imposed on a population. Alternatively, groups may ignore the differences between the beliefs they profess and those of a more moderate majority. Adding to this, the relationship between Sunni and Shi'a populations in Iraq is more complex than it is often portrayed. Members of these communities have lived side-by-side; they have intermarried. Not all members are politically motivated or religiously devout. Some do not actively practice their faith, and even among those who do, most do not practice the conservative forms represented by fundamentalist religious groups. Regardless of their beliefs or practices, the majority most certainly does not condone murder.

Attacking civilians may send another type of message: the insurgents are weak. A group shows weakness when it relies on violence against civilians, a community's softest targets. A stronger insurgent group – one with resources – should be better equipped to challenge harder targets. Strength in these terms is based on an assessment of a group's coercive capacity. From a political point of view, attacking civilians seems more likely to indicate that the group and its ideology are not sufficiently popular to appeal to the masses, or a sizeable segment within a population. In other words, the group's actions suggest that it has limited appeal or capacity to influence politics through nonviolent means.

Salafi-jihadists such as AQI would not view members of Shi'a and other non-Sunni communities as potential supporters. Iraq's Shi'a community makes up a majority of the population within Iraq and its neighboring areas. They are the stronger community in terms of numbers and representation in government. In addition to targeting Iraq's Shi'a, AQI's targets have included moderate Iraqi Sunnis. For AQI and other militant Sunni groups, attacks on Shi'a are a sign of their political weakness. Because Sunnis are a community presumably more likely to be sympathetic to AQI, attacks on Sunnis are an even greater sign of weakness. Another indication of AQI's (and ISIL's) weakness follows from the group's recruitment of non-Iraqi militants to carry out its insurgency in Iraq.[113] Weakness is also accentuated by the group's presumed reliance on foreign militants in suicide attacks on local Sunnis and Shi'a.[114]

In addition to signaling "weakness," targeting civilians may be a sign of "overconfidence."[115] Overconfidence may lead an insurgent group to assume that there will be support for the group's tactics, including its use of violence.

These points raise questions about the likelihood of insurgent groups' success in using terrorism. Two studies offer insights into the likelihood of terrorist and insurgent success. In one study, Max Abrahms assessed the efforts of twenty-eight foreign terrorist organizations (FTOs), designated as such by the United States Department of State for the years between 2001 and 2006.[116] Abrahms then identified forty-two terrorist campaigns carried out by the twenty-eight groups at some point during their history, including campaigns occurring prior to 2001. Terrorist campaigns include "clusters" of attacks carried out "by an organized group to achieve a specific political goal."[117] The groups in Abrahms' study had a variety of goals, and some groups waged more than one campaign in attempts to achieve these goals. Despite what amounted to repeated engagements with their adversaries, by Abrahms' calculations only two of the campaigns were fully successful. Both involved Hezbollah, which is often credited with driving the United States and France from Lebanon in 1984. By 2000 the same organization seems to have compelled the Israelis to withdraw their forces from the southern part of the same country. In five other cases terrorist groups appeared to have found "limited" or "partial" success. In two of these cases, though, the LTTE in Sri Lanka and FARC in Colombia, subsequent developments suggest rather negative outcomes for these somewhat successful groups. The LTTE was defeated in 2009 by the Sri Lankan military, which used exceptionally brutal means. FARC, after serious setbacks, formally entered negotiations with Bogota in 2012, with the aim of ending their operations. These negotiations were ongoing as of early 2015. Abrahms describes Hamas' and PIJ's campaigns to establish autonomy within the Palestinian territories and al Qaeda's campaign to rid the Arabian Peninsula of an American presence as partially successful. What followed these campaigns has been costly for the groups involved. The quality of life in the Gaza Strip, the Palestinian territory where Hamas and PIJ are strongest, has decreased substantially. While al Qaeda had some initial success with a reduction in America's military and civilian presence in Saudi Arabia, the repercussions for al Qaeda have been costly, including the group's loss of safe haven in Afghanistan.[118]

The record of failure described by Abrahms stands out against a RAND Corporation study carried out by Ben Connable and Martin Libicki.[119] The point of comparison is more complicated than one of success or failure, however. Connable and Libicki's interest is with the outcomes of insurgencies and the roles played by terrorism in these conflicts.[120] Drawing on a larger number of cases that includes eighty-nine insurgencies, Connable and Libicki find that some insurgencies succeed while others fail. They also find that the type of terrorism used by those engaging in armed conflicts against states – specifically, whether violence is used discriminately or indiscriminately – bears a meaningful relationship to the outcome of the conflict.

The apparent discrepancy between the Abrahms and the Connable and Libicki findings requires some explanation. Much can be explained by the cases they study and the different focuses of their studies. Abrahms limited his study to FTOs, as labeled during the first years of the twenty-first century. Terrorist groups are identified as FTOs when they are seen as posing a threat to the security of the United States.[121] The list is purposely exclusive. The groups are relatively weak in comparison to their adversaries. Hezbollah – the most successful group by Abrahms' calculations – aimed its attacks at foreigners on Lebanese soil.

Connable and Libicki study insurgencies, along with insurgents' conduct, the contexts within which they operate, and the outcomes of their efforts. Most of their insurgencies occur during the twentieth century; all are involved in wider-scale warfare. Drawing on insurgencies dating as far back as 1934, Connable and Libicki's study is more representative of the diversity of insurgent groups, their ideologies, and the contexts in which they fought. The study includes insurgencies and terrorism before and during the "Age of Terrorism." In short, their study offers a broader analysis.

Some groups were included in both studies (Hezbollah, Hamas, the Kurdistan Workers' Party (PKK), and AQI); many more were not. Insurgencies in Colombia (FARC), Algeria (Armed Islamic Group, GIA), and Afghanistan

(Taliban) are not included in Abrahms' study. Abrahms' study includes Tehrik-e Taliban Pakistan (TTP), which has been included on the U.S. State Department's FTO list, but excluded Afghanistan's Taliban, which was not.[122] Connable and Libicki's study covers insurgencies that began or took place prior to 1970 for which quantitative data on terrorist incidents is scant or non-existent.

There is more to this comparison. The ways in which insurgent groups use terrorism may have an effect on the outcomes of insurgencies. Some insurgents are more discriminating than others in attacks on civilians. Connable and Libicki provide evidence suggesting that insurgents using terrorism indiscriminately come out ahead in a smaller number of cases than those using terrorism more discriminately: "In other words, those insurgent groups that were able to restrict their use of terrorism by minimizing civilian – vice government – casualties were more likely to win than those that did not" (see Table 1.1).[123] There is also evidence that insurgents who launched indiscriminate attacks on civilian targets (post-Saddam Iraq might serve as an example) tend to lose, while insurgents who employ terrorism on a selective basis tend to succeed in their struggles.

Connable and Libicki describe insurgents who primarily attack civilians as engaging in "indiscriminate" terrorism and those primarily targeting non-civilians, including government officials, as engaging in "discrete" terrorism.[124] A more nuanced classification distinguishes between targets chosen on the

Table 1.1   Terrorism and outcome of insurgency*

	Descriptions of insurgents' use of terrorism				
Outcome	Indiscriminate use of terrorism	Discriminate use of terrorism	Insurgents and state use indiscriminate violence	Insurgents use little or no terrorism	Total
Insurgents win	20% ($n = 5$)	56% ($n = 14$)	8% ($n = 2$)	16% ($n = 4$)	30% ($n = 25$)
Neither side wins	28% ($n = 5$)	33% ($n = 6$)	17% ($n = 3$)	22% ($n = 4$)	21% ($n = 18$)
Government wins	42% ($n = 11$)	31% ($n = 8$)	12% ($n = 3$)	15% ($n = 4$)	31% ($n = 26$)
Ongoing	47% ($n = 7$)	20% ($n = 3$)	27% ($n = 4$)	7% ($n = 1$)	18% ($n = 15$)
Total	33% ($n = 28$)	37% ($n = 31$)	14% ($n = 12$)	15% ($n = 13$)	100% ($n = 84$)

* This table shows information collected and presented by Ben Connable and Martin Libicki in their study of the ends of insurgencies ($n = 84$).

Source: Connable and Libicki, *How Insurgencies End*, Table 4.3, p. 109.

basis of "selective" or "indiscriminate" criteria. "Selective" targets are those chosen on the basis of "personalized information about their actions." These targets pose or have posed a threat to the insurgent group. Other targets may be identified for their membership within a community (ethnic or otherwise) from which other threats have emerged. Attacks on such targets are described as "indiscriminate" because they are chosen on the basis of association rather than guilt. In other words, these targets are not known to have engaged in any specific form of opposition to the insurgent group.[125]

The effects of (and likely the motivations for) "indiscriminate" and "selective" terrorism differ, as do the outcomes. The indiscriminate use of terrorism by insurgents is more likely to turn a population against the insurgents and eliminate a potential base of support. Indiscriminate attacks may suggest weakness in terms of local appeal or overconfidence. Insurgent groups' use of discriminate attacks on civilians may suggest that the groups do not require local support. Indiscriminate attacks will also leave the impression that negotiations and compromise will be unlikely. A government may conclude that it is engaged in a fight to the death and react accordingly.

A more "selective" reliance on terrorism, on the other hand, may indicate that a group has resources on which to draw. This may signal military strength, with insurgent groups carrying out a greater number of attacks on harder targets, such as attacks on military, government, and police targets or against other violent groups. Selective violence may signal political strength in the form of an existing or potential base of support. Selective attacks on civilians may send the message that a group is more likely to be moderate and more willing to support nonviolent forms of conflict resolution. In sum, the conditions under which insurgents are likely to exercise "selective" or "indiscriminate" terrorism vary, as do the groups using these tactics.

The issue is more complicated than selecting a strategy that will succeed or fail. While Connable and Libicki find that insurgents tend to have better results when attacks on civilians are carried out selectively, they also point out that this relationship is not perfect.[126] Some insurgent groups with a more selective record of attacks on civilians fail in their efforts; while other groups succeed despite attacking civilians indiscriminately (see Table 1.1).[127]

One issue is that it is not hard to imagine conditions under which it would be difficult, if not practically impossible, to identify whether or not civilians are being targeted selectively. Counts of attacks against civilians and numbers of civilian deaths per attack offer approximations of selectivity, though they cannot be exact. In addition, such counts may not be comparable across cases.

Another issue is that insurgent groups differ in terms of their capacity to carry out attacks on various targets; their incentives also differ when it comes to choosing between selective and random violence. Jeremy Weinstein finds a connection between the resources available to an armed group and the group's use of violence against civilians. As such, a group's strategies – and its use of violence – are a function of the group's resources. Militants with access to natural resources or external sponsorship rely less on public support and, as it turns out, may be more likely to target the public. These militants may be less concerned about having a base of support among members of a potential constituency and more concerned about using local resources to fund their activities or enrich themselves. Militants lacking these types of resources are less likely to resort to random violence against civilians. Instead, they will "perpetrate far fewer abuses and employ violence selectively and strategically."[128]

Focusing on numbers of civilians attacked rather than types of attacks, Max Abrahms and Philip Potter find that an absence of leadership affects the likelihood of attacks on civilians. Such "leadership deficits" may coincide with conditions that place soldiers outside of their leaders' control, such as leadership decapitation (loss of leadership) or a decentralized command structure. Leaders are more likely to consider the implications for the organization while soldiers may be more willing to exercise violence.[129]

An interesting caveat to the focus on targets is the observation that the groups carrying out attacks may be less likely to claim those carried out against civilians than those against military targets. Even unclaimed attacks may be used strategically.[130] For instance, not claiming attacks on civilians allows the group to maintain whatever benefits may accrue from the use of violence without paying all of the costs that could also accrue. In addition, attacks on harder targets may have higher payoffs. This may be true strategically, in terms of weakening an adversary, as well as by way of demonstrating the weakness of this adversary. Abrahms posits that violent groups are more likely to influence a government through attacks on its military than through attacks on its civilians.[131]

Regardless of the level of violence perpetrated against civilians, it seems counterintuitive that weaker contestants would defeat stronger ones in any sort of military contest. The weakest contestants seldom manage to pose a significant challenge. Attacks on harder targets require greater skill and more training than many groups have.[132] Those groups that are better equipped from the beginning are more likely to challenge a state.[133] In an effort to explain how the weak win in asymmetric conflicts Ivan Arreguín-Toft selects data from the Correlates of War (COW) Project on 202 asymmetrical conflicts fought between 1816 and 2003.[134] In the process, Arreguín-Toft investigates a number of alternatives, including the unwillingness of publics in modern democracies to support an armed conflict over a protracted period. The evidence, however, leads him to another conclusion. In contrast to Weinstein's findings, Arreguin-Toft finds that the weaker side (measured in terms of resources and population) tends to win when it uses "unconventional" means, including what he labels "barbarism," terrorism in other words. This is a common feature of internal wars and insurgencies.[135] Despite military superiority, the United States could not defeat the "unconventional" tactics used by the North Vietnamese and Viet Cong during its decade-long struggle in Southeast Asia, neither could the Soviet Union rout the Afghan-Arab mujahideen. Consequently, these examples also demonstrate the relevance of a "home field advantage." Even strong states struggle against insurgents operating on the insurgents' home territory.

It is important to note that insurgencies are not just military contests; they are also political. Insurgents benefit from popular support, something over which they and counterinsurgents may find themselves competing.[136] Moreover, insurgents may be more likely to obtain popular support within their local community than are counterinsurgents coming from outside this community.

Furthermore, it is possible that insurgents and terrorists will learn over time and adapt their strategies and tactics according to their needs and capabilities,[137] which are also likely to change. Some groups have shown their capacity for change by adopting suicide tactics, which are thought to be more effective tools of coercion.[138]

The record suggests that groups using terrorism, and especially those using terrorism almost exclusively, have enjoyed little success beyond winning publicity for their various causes. Most of the groups using terrorism outside of wider-scale warfare are, almost by their very nature, unable to mount a serious challenge to the prevailing order. Their lack of coercive capabilities is a symptom of their weakness. Moreover, whatever successes groups using terrorism have achieved have been made when terrorism was used in conjunction with other tactics, such as guerrilla warfare in the countryside and urban warfare (or terrorism) in the cities; when the terrorists have some level of support, either popular support or passive acceptance; and, at least in recent years, when the terrorists make adroit use of social media. It also appears that the odds of a weaker side's victory have improved as we move into the twenty-first century,[139] aided at least in part by a selective use of terrorism. Given these developments, it makes sense to expect more of the same over the course of the twenty-first century.

New warfare: new contestants, new means

The nature of warfare has been going through some serious changes in recent times. The smaller-scale of warfare and the prevalence of non-state actors are not the real changes; these characteristics are common through-out history.[140] Instead, changes in twenty-first century warfare involve its conduct and the weapons used to wage it. We summarize these changes by discussing the ways wars are being fought and the means available to fight them.

Twenty-first century wars have become what David Kilcullen labels "hybrid" conflicts involving the use of a wide repertoire of means and devices, along with a diverse set of new actors.[141] Some of what makes these newcomers and their tactics so interesting has to do with the ways in which they challenge states. They take advantage of the weaknesses of weak or failing states.[142] This is not surprising given expectations – and evidence – that non-state actors tend to challenge the states less capable of answering their challenges.[143] This is part of an economic understanding of the incidence of civil war, which is also associated with explanations for insurgency.[144] Insurgent groups are usually weak in comparison to states; however, their local adversaries also tend to be relatively weak. Their distant adversaries (in the case of al Qaeda, this would include Western states) are stronger in military terms, though they are less so when engaging in warfare on the insurgents' home territories. Some insurgent groups are carrying out a form of "transnational guerrilla warfare"[145] and producing their own media in the process. Others are advocating for an identity group which they claim to represent. In contrast, the causes may be more political than economic in cases of internal wars waged for the protection or promotion of the interests of one identity group residing within a multi-ethnic society.[146] There is also an expectation, supported by empirical evidence, that strong democracies are less likely to see the emergence of "new" terrorist groups, especially when they avoid intervention in foreign conflicts.[147] Regimes transitioning to democracy are not as fortunate.[148] The "new actors"[149] participating in the wars of the twenty-first century – pirates, private militaries, and independent and networked affiliates of transnational terrorist networks, among them – have become equipped to carry out a type of warfare that is unconventional by today's standards and to which states' conventional armed forces have been less equipped to respond.[150]

In another influential commentary Mary Kaldor outlines the attributes of what she calls "new wars."[151] Kaldor asserts that the new type of warfare should be distinguished from its predecessors by three characteristics: its goals, methods, and finances.[152] Kaldor's new wars take place within rather than between the types of communities Huntington identified as civiliza-tions.[153] Kaldor links the aims of those conducting new wars to the pursuit and reassertion of identities based on clan, tribe, nation, and religion. By contrast to earlier types of war staged around identity, the new form occurs in the context of globalization. She writes, "the upsurge in the politics of particularistic identities cannot be understood in traditional terms. It has to be explained in the context of a growing cultural dissonance between those who participate in transnational networks ... [a]nd those who are excluded from global processes and are tied to localities, even though their lives may be profoundly shaped by these same processes."[154]

Kaldor's observation is hardly self-explanatory. She cites the fighting over Bosnia-Herzegovina and Kosovo as examples during the collapse of Yugoslavia. We might also mention that the fighting over Afghanistan's fate involves a struggle over identity with the Ghilzai tribal grouping giving rise initially to the Taliban among the Pashtun communities and then waging war against the Durrani tribe and its leaders in Kabul – President Karzai and his NATO-backed government.[155] The Ghilzai and Durrani tribes make up a majority of the community identifying itself as Pashtun in Afghanistan.[156]

Other than the fundamental matter of identity, Kaldor goes on to note the growing presence of a new cast of players. An observed decline in interstate wars is expected to continue.[157] Wars between states have been replaced not by peace, but by wars within states. There are new warriors. Kaldor also mentions the "privatization" of warfare.[158] Private armies, rebel bands, local warlords, shadowy arms dealers, criminal drug gangs, and non-governmental organizations (NGOs) with a variety of agendas now play important roles in twenty-first century warfare. These are roles previously played by the armed forces of states and the governments that deployed them. More specifically, the forces found in twenty-first century warfare constitute a heterogeneous collection of armed groups. These include regular armed forces, paramilitary groups, self-defense units, foreign mercenaries, and foreign troops usually present under the auspices of the UN, NATO or the Organization of African Unity (OAU).[159] Among the non-state actors opposing a given status quo, it is likely that the insurgents (often labeled as "terrorists") will be among the most prolific rebels in current and future warfare.[160] They are, however, not alone. Thomas X. Hammes describes the new security threats as originating in "the increasing power of smaller and smaller entities" that are part of networks, sharing information and resources in order to wreak large-scale havoc. These non-state actors represent "causes" not states or nations.[161] The threat these entities may pose is a new type of warfare requiring a new type of preparation.[162]

At the individual level, children make up a growing proportion of these units. Among these are young people who have been abducted by paramilitary groups, for example, the Lord's Resistance Army in Uganda, and then trained to kill.[163] Sometimes the children are sold by their impoverished families to help meet ends – one less mouth to feed – or perhaps because of a promise of education or a better life for their child. In Afghanistan and Pakistan, TTP, Lashkar-e Tayyiba (LeT) and the groups linked to al Qaeda have made extensive use of children, boys aged twelve to fourteen years, to serve as suicide bombers in Islamabad, Kabul, Kandahar, and other sites of armed conflict. Instead of candy, the boys are offered immediate entry into Paradise, a strong temptation if ever there was one. There is evidence that some youths seek membership in ISIL, al Qaeda, and other groups. Whether or not the children are motivated by religious beliefs, a particular ideology, honor, or some other motivation remains unclear.

Twenty-first century wars also differ from their predecessors in the means that are used to wage them. Defense analysts at the Pentagon and elsewhere refer to a "revolution in military affairs" (RMA).[164] This RMA is composed of several elements. First and foremost among these are the vast changes brought about by transformations in communication technologies. In regard to the Arab Spring of 2010, young people in Egypt were able to share images and stories of their discontented peers' successful toppling of Tunisia's long-time dictator Ben Ali and then focus their animosity toward Egypt's own dictator Hosni Mubarak. Acts of government repression in one country may be displayed on a worldwide basis within seconds of the brutality, as the Assad regime in Syria has discovered. These days most insurgent groups have their own websites, which describe their goals and objectives and the villainy of their opponents. On the other side of the ledger, it was possible for U.S. President Obama and his national security advisers to follow in real-time the movements of Seal Team Six as it carried out its attack on Osama bin Laden's compound in Abbottabad, Pakistan, halfway around the world from the White House.

At the same time, these revolutions have given the new insurgents of the twenty-first century access to new technologies, which they may adapt to suit their political and military needs. Thanks to the Internet and the satellite transmission of messages and images, insurgents and potential insurgents, along with terrorists and potential terrorists, now are able to communicate with one another almost instantaneously via various means, including Facebook and Twitter. Access to the Internet and other new technologies has revolutionized the ways in which organizations of all types – including armed groups – operate, communicate, plan, and train. It has also revolutionized the ways in which insurgents share propaganda and seek publicity. With their own production capabilities, insurgents can provide clips of executions, allowing them to validate their barbarism to large audiences.

Another aspect of this RMA involves the abilities of computer-savvy individuals, groups, and states to seriously disrupt the military operations and key infrastructures of their targets. Cyber-warfare has now become a serious concern for defense planners. For instance, the August 2008 five-day war between Russia and Georgia over the contested region of South Ossetia began with the former's armed forces taking down Georgia's command and control systems via the Internet. Stuxnet, a computer virus that infected Tehran's centrifuges causing them to spin out of control, evidently delayed the development of Iran's nuclear weapons capabilities. As recent hacks seem to suggest (including the copying and publicizing of private customer information from the AshleyMadison dating site), we can assume that the skills needed to carry out cyber attacks already lie in the hands of at least some non-state actors.

The RMA has also meant major changes in the weapons used by insurgents and counterinsurgents. For challengers, many of the weapons they now employ have become miniaturized and made easier to use (e.g., hand-held rocket launchers). These weapons were employed, for example, to great effect in Somalia by General Aidid's militias in 1994 to coerce the U.S. humanitarian mission into withdrawing from the country – as depicted in the 2001 film *Black Hawk Down*. Such technologies have become relatively cheap. On the other hand, counter-RMA weapons have also been used to great effect. Drones are another new tool, as well as a toy – easily accessible for children, hobbyists, and militants. These "toys" have been an intruder into privates spaces and an occasional nuisance to guests at sporting events. More importantly, drones have been a real menace to air traffic safety, and they could be used for more nefarious activities. More sophisticated weapons – including biological and chemical weapons – may also be within reach of non-state actors, even small groups or individuals. Hammes describes how advances in biotechnology may be used to turn synthesized viruses into weapons with the help of a moderate level of scientific knowledge and what essentially amounts to over-the-counter ingredients.[165]

Despite these RMAs, other, quite unsophisticated, weapons have also been used to great effect and insurgent groups have demonstrated their ability to use some of the most rudimentary (and easily accessible) of weapons. These are not the nano-technologies or new, more lethal types of weapons, to which Kilcullen refers. The single most lethal weapon used by the Taliban in Afghanistan has been the improvised explosive device (IED) whose basic ingredient is common fertilizer. The 9/11 skyjackers seized control of American airliners through the use of box-cutters, tools easily purchased at most hardware stores. Using these most basic of weapons – such as the daggers used by ancient "terrorists"[166] – requires close contact with the targets of attacks. ISIL has publicized its use of swords and fire to execute its captives.

Other characteristics of twenty-first century wars are the propagation of "terror," which may be distinct from "terrorism," and the realization that noncombatants are treated like combatants.[167] "Terror" in the context of warfare may take many forms. In his seminal book *The Logic of Violence in Civil War*, Kalyvas draws our attention to the particularly barbaric nature of internal wars, in general, and civil wars, in particular.[168] While not a new tactic, rape has become an increasingly discussed aspect of war. Sexual violence such as that reported in the Balkans, Rwanda, and the Kivu provinces of the Congo falls within the category of what Arreguín-Toft labels a strategy of barbarism: "the deliberate or systematic harm of noncombatants (e.g., rape, murder, and torture) in pursuit of a military or political objective."[169] Dara Kay Cohen offers another explanation for the use of wartime rape. After finding little support for existing explanations, Cohen proposes that militant groups use rape to facilitate something akin to team-building used in an attempt to create "social cohesion" among combatants. This is a condition that may be most common, she suggests, when militant groups are made up of fighters who were kidnapped or coerced into participating. Within these groups, child fighters would be the most easily influenced.[170]

Brutality – or barbarism – against civilians knows few boundaries, and it is not reserved for "regulars" or "irregular" fighters in local armed conflicts. After an extensive discussion of the Greek Civil War following World War II, Kalyvas concludes that such wars "provide powerful incentives for the production of 'indirect' violence by 'ordinary' civilians. For the many people who are not naturally blood-thirsty and abhor direct involvement in violence, civil war offers irresistible opportunities to harm everyday enemies."[171]

These insights help to resolve what Lee Ann Fujii describes as the "puzzle of extra-lethal violence."[172] The "puzzle" for Fujii is why militants would spend time torturing and brutalizing their victims. It is an "inefficient" practice in terms of the "extra time and effort" required to torture individuals whom the militants plan to kill or have already killed.[173] For example, in many internal conflicts, the public execution of suspected opponents and the subsequent mutilation of their bodies appear to be a common practice. The purpose behind all this mayhem is usually some version of ethnic cleansing, removing some identity-based group, or subordinating one ethnic group to the group that is better able to prosecute the war. The systematic murder of those with "other" identities, as with the Tutsis killed by Hutus in Rwanda in 1994 and the efforts of the Janjaweed to eliminate various groups from the Darfur region of Western Sudan, provide further illustrations.

Also, as Kaldor notes, areas may be rendered uninhabitable by the planting of landmines, poisoning of crops, and other related chemical measures. Access to and control over the drug trade along with such resources as oil and diamonds are often subsidiary objectives.[174] Such objectives may take precedence over other interests.

Support for the groups using these tactics comes from a variety of sources. Philanthropically minded individuals may be the most conspicuous of supporters. Wealthy individuals from the oil-rich Persian Gulf sheikdoms have provided large amounts of money in support of various militant groups in the Middle East and elsewhere. Foreign governments also provide support. The Syrian insurgency receives assistance from Saudi Arabia and Qatar.[175] At the same time, the Assad government in Damascus has been the beneficiary of help from Iran and Russia to wage its counterinsurgency aimed at repressing the country's Sunni population.[176] Damascus has also benefited from its decades of support for Hezbollah, which now aids its former state sponsor.[177] Ironically, Hezbollah, the "founding father" of suicide tactics has itself become a target of suicide attacks by anti-Assad Syrian rebels.[178]

Diaspora communities, often residing in adjacent countries or the West, also render important assistance to their fellow ethnics and co-religionists living on their home territory. The LTTE's armed struggle to separate the Tamils from Sri Lanka received enormous help from other Tamils living across the narrow strait separating the Jaffna Peninsula from the Indian state of Tamil-Nadu. Palestinians living in North and South America have raised money over many years on behalf of the groups, principally Hamas, seeking to defeat Israel.

Today's insurgents also support themselves. Insurgents (and terrorists) from Colombia to Afghanistan have used the drug trade to fund their operations. In some cases, these groups are more criminal than political.[179] Groups today also engage in "legitimate" business.[180] ISIL controls a healthy share of the oil business in Syria and Iraq.[181] The oil business is a big business with a larger market than cocaine, even when it must be smuggled and traded at a discount. Moreover, ISIL reportedly earned an estimated $1,000,000 per day in 2014 through its underground oil trade at a time when al Qaeda's resources are "squeezed."[182] Through "corruption and crime," even ISIL's "enemies" become wealthy.[183]

ISIL does not rely solely on revenues from oil; rather, its activities and investments are diversified, providing multiple sources of income.[184] For most terrorists and insurgents, diversification implies engaging in a variety of criminal activities, which would tend to involve some combination of kidnappings for ransom, smuggling of goods and people, theft, fraud, and extortion, including the extortion of others engaging in theft or smuggling.[185] One may wonder, are these activities illegal in the absence of law, as may be the case in Somalia and parts of Libya, Syria, Iraq, and elsewhere.

Insurgents (and terrorists) also engage in non-criminal activities. Hezbollah's business ventures include ownership of shops and farms; the group also collects fees for some of the services it provides, such as schooling.[186]

ISIL's activities include establishing a state bureaucracy, encouraging and monitoring local businesses, and providing education, including programs for professional and religious education.[187] ISIL also collects "taxes" from local businesses and traders using its territory for transport.[188] It is not uncommon for non-state actors with control over land to collect "taxes;" in reality, this may be a form of extortion.[189] Extortion was a main source of revenue for FARC, accounting for more than 40 percent of the group's income.[190] Under ISIL, collecting taxes is referred to as a "Zakat," which under Sharia law requires financially capable Muslims to give money to the state.[191]

The sum of changes in warfare since 2001 has been described as the onset of a "fifth generation of war."[192] New non-state actors with new means and lacking old constraints pose the types of threats that challenge states, including those with the strongest militaries.[193]

Countering the new insurgents

What role does terrorism play in the new "fifth generation" warfare? Forecasting future developments is a notoriously hazardous undertaking. However, some possible outcomes seem clear when we apply what is already known about the effects of terrorism in the recent past.

Terrorism seems to be a more effective tactic when those challenging a state's power use it in conjunction with a number of different means of waging unconventional warfare. Terrorism tends to be a less effective tool for those using terrorist violence on an indiscriminate basis. Indiscriminate violence is more likely to lead to an insurgent group's failure than its success.[194] Terrorist violence employed on a selective basis, as used by the Viet Minh and Viet Cong against locals during their wars against the French and Americans, may be more effective. The Viet Minh and Viet Cong's use of terrorism included assassinations of local leaders and key figures at the center of public life, especially those linked to an incumbent government. It also helps if the insurgents represent more than a few dozen individuals. The former Symbionese Liberation Army in the United States, Direct Action in France, and the Communist Combatant Cells in Belgium are three examples of would-be insurgents, all active for a few years during the 1970s, whose efforts gathered little momentum, much less support. With twenty fatalities, the Black Liberation Army was the deadliest terrorist group in the United States in the 1970s. The group was somewhat more successful in gaining attention than it was in raising a significant following.[195]

Many of the groups posing the greatest challenge in the twenty-first century are quite a bit more capable of initiating wider-scale armed conflict than their predecessors. It is among these more powerful terrorists that we find insurgents. If we were to assume that terrorists and insurgents belong to distinct categories of violent actors, then we may also assume that counter-ing one would require a different strategy than countering the other. It is pos-sible that any distinction between counterterrorism and counterinsurgency would only apply when the authorities confront the smaller stand-alone terror-ist groups, referring to those groups that rely almost exclusively on terrorism. This distinction does not seem to apply when authorities must respond to the larger groups of insurgents employing some mixture of tactics.

The insurgent groups engaging in warfare in the twenty-first century will likely be more destructive and deadly than their predecessors.[196] It is also possible that the majority of casualties of this warfare will be civilian. Civilian casualties are not a feature that is unique to twenty-first century warfare. In his study of episodes of violence during the twentieth century, Benjamin Valentino estimates between 60 and 150 million deaths (a significant spread) occurred outside of interstate and civil wars. These include deaths in the process of carrying out genocide. These counts do not include non-lethal atrocities perpe-trated against civilians. Valentino compares this estimate to around 34 million battle deaths in wars during the same century.[197] We should not expect the same numbers of deaths in twenty-first century wars that were seen in the wars of the twentieth century, which included two "great" wars.[198] In addi-tion, we may need to redefine what we understand as "battle deaths."

Civilian casualties of war are not necessarily a direct result of fighting.[199] Fatalities may be indirectly related to conditions associated with living in or fleeing a state of war. Alternatively, civilian deaths may be directly related to attacks aimed at civilians for the purpose of perpetuating fear, punishing a pop-ulation, or exerting authority. There are also variations in civilian deaths across countries and wars. For instance, there is evidence suggesting that civilian deaths outnumber combatant deaths in Iraq, though not in Afghanistan.[200] It is unclear how many Syrians and Iraqis will become casualties of the civil war and sectarian conflicts being fought within the boundaries of these states. When deaths resulting solely from terrorism are counted, it should be true, practically by definition, that civilian deaths outnumber those of combatants.

These developments in warfare call our attention to a change in think-ing regarding how to fight twenty-first century wars.[201] Here we enter the realm of counterinsurgency warfare or COIN. Just as there is more than one type of insurgent threat, there is more than one approach to counter-ing these threats. Defense analysts, journalists, and other observers initially attached the label "terrorist group" to the clandestine bands that plagued Western Europe, North America, and the Middle East in the 1960s and 1970s. Accordingly, the states confronted by these relatively inconsequential threats developed their own counterterrorism strategies aimed at defeating the small groups they faced. Some stressed a law-enforcement model while others advocated what was labeled a warfare model.[202] The groups posing challenges to states differ in terms of their operational capacities, popularity, objectives. They also differ in terms of their threat. While a law-enforcement model may have been appropriate for dealing with relatively weak and isolated terrorist groups, it would not likely be the best approach in contexts characterized by stronger insurgent groups or wider-scale warfare. Thanks to the Vietnam experience and the various "wars of national liberation" that characterized the period from the 1950s through the 1970s, military planners in the United States, Great Britain, and elsewhere devised a framework for waging counterinsurgencies against the challenges posed by these typically self-defined national liberators, who were, consequently, often Soviet-backed.[203]

In the years following America's defeat in Vietnam, U.S. military officers, frequently ones teaching social science courses at West Point, sought to change the country's approach to the types of armed conflicts in which American forces were likely to become engaged.[204] The result of this rethinking was a new COIN doctrine.

We should bear in mind the effects of counterinsurgency operations. Political leaders may be reluctant to see their forces suffer more casualties for fear, if nothing else, of losing popular support at home. Elements in the armed forces of an incumbent regime may go through a process of demoralization and quit, physically and psychologically.[205] And not uncommonly, soldiers targeted by suicide bombers or IEDs or fired upon at night by unseen enemies may lose self-control and carry out indiscriminate attacks on civilian targets, precisely what insurgents may hope to see. Attacks by armed forces against civilians may transform otherwise indifferent villagers and city-dwellers against the counterinsurgents. The civilians could become what David Kilcullen calls "accidental guerrillas."[206] The new approach to countering insurgencies aims to avoid this.

Based in part on the successful British counterinsurgency campaign in Malaya during the 1950s, the new approach to fighting insurgents requires keeping the violent elements of a state's response to a minimum. Rather than a military victory, the real war involves winning the struggle for the support of the affected population. Accordingly, economic and social development projects (e.g., school construction, road-building) were assigned a high priority, as were the reform of local governmental institutions and the elimination of corruption, or at least its significant reduction. In theory, when these changes were accompanied by copious amount of propaganda, the local population would come to trust the incumbent government and the American forces, which would be on hand to offer physical protection from insurgents. Over time, as this thinking goes, the insurgents would become isolated from the population, the metaphorical fish (the insurgents) would no longer find a sea in which to swim (hiding among civilians), and they would consequently dwindle to insignificance.

The new counterinsurgents carry out their less violent approach with the aid of a new toolkit. The weapons and means of surveillance available to governments, and especially the American government, have clearly undergone major changes. Weapons have become more precise. Cruise missiles as employed by the U.S. Navy during the 2003 war against Saddam Hussein's Iraq were able to strike at targets in downtown Baghdad without inflicting much "collateral" damage on the surrounding civilian population. Pilotless and remote-controlled aircraft such as the American Predator are able to maintain surveillance over potential targets while hovering above them for long periods of time. And, if the situation appears to warrant, these drones are able to launch Hellfire missiles at these targets.

Technological advances also serve insurgents' purposes. New drone technologies are hardly a monopoly enjoyed by the American military, or any other state's military. From time to time both the Israelis and the Iranians use these unmanned aircrafts to maintain surveillance over each other's military deployments. Hezbollah, the Iranian-backed militia in southern Lebanon, has its own drones to monitor the Israelis.

Given the focus of counterinsurgency efforts on groups previously identified as "terrorists," we may wonder what insights from counterterrorism may be applicable to countering insurgents. One practice, "leadership decapitation," seems worth mentioning. Leadership decapitation refers to removing the leader of a terrorist group. The idea is that removing a leader will hinder a group's operations. This strategy seems to have worked in at least a few instances. The Shining Path and the LTTE insurgencies effectively ended with the removal of their leaders by capture and killing, respectively. Aum Shinrikyo suffered similarly from the arrest of its leader. The capture or killing of leaders who are thought to be "above the law" and described in almost god-like terms not only deprives a group of their leadership; it may also lead members of groups to question their beliefs and affiliation. This process may be further prompted by images of former leaders in prison attire and behind bars. Images of an incarcerated Abimael Guzman, the founder and leader of the Shining Path, and Aum Shinrikyo's Shoko Asahara seem to have had this effect on large numbers of their followers.

One difference between these groups and some of their modern counterparts may affect the applicability of this strategy today. The former groups were thought to have hierarchical organizational structures with centralized decision-making. In a sense, the loss of leadership caused the organizations to "die." In contrast, some of the twenty-first century groups may be more horizontally organized than their predecessors, with greater local autonomy. Leadership decapitation may remove key figures, even charismatic leaders, from their networks, but it will not necessarily cause the groups to lose their purpose. Moreover, these newer networks may lack the central figures associated with groups such as Shining Path and Aum Shinrikyo. They may have many local leaders or "hubs" of influential individuals, who are more difficult to identify and whose loss would be less detrimental to the functioning of the organization.[207]

Leadership decapitation may not produce the anticipated or desired outcomes. The removal of bin Laden from his position as al Qaeda's leader followed a long period in which he was secluded from the larger organization and largely out of the public's eye. The al-Qaeda network continued to operate despite his seclusion. Local leaders made decisions for al-Qaeda operations in their areas. After his death, some of these leaders competed to fill his vacant leadership position. This led, within a short while, to a division within the al-Qaeda network. This was followed, first, by the eviction of the former AQI leader, Abu Bakr al-Baghdadi, and his ISIL group in Iraq and Syria and, shortly thereafter, by the changing affiliations of other groups seeking to shift alliances from al-Qaeda Central to al-Baghdadi's ISIL. ISIL's approach has been described as (and demonstrated to be) more brutal and forceful than al Qaeda's, and further removed in practice from Salafi-jihadist ideology. It also seems to be the more popular and powerful, at least in terms of growing prestige and influence, of the two groups. Moreover, the newly divided Salafi-jihadist organization may pose an even greater challenge to its adversaries, especially if the two networks enter into an "outbidding" competition that entails increasing violence against the West.[208]

We may wonder what further impact insurgent groups' use of terrorism may have on COIN doctrine and the effectiveness of COIN efforts. If the insurgents carry out terrorist attacks in the course of their operations, does it become more or less difficult for the counterinsurgents to achieve their aims?[209] It makes sense now to give attention to the time at which those challenging the authorities apply this tactic.

Time for terrorism

At what point in an armed conflict do insurgents use terrorism? And, does the timing make a difference in terms of the success or failure of insurgents' efforts? The following alternatives come to mind.

Terrorism may be employed during the early "agitation-propaganda" phase of an insurgency. If we use the language of Mao, this is the phase in which insurgents are engaged in "strategic defense," because they are weak and must seek support.[210] We might think of this phase as involving terrorism prior to the initiation of guerrilla warfare: "Subversive activities are frequently executed in an organized pattern, but major combat is avoided. The primary military activity is terrorist strikes. These are executed to gain popular support, influence recalcitrant individuals, and sap enemy strength."[211]

Another possibility is that insurgents will use terrorism along with other tactics throughout the violent stages of a conflict. This is a departure from Mao's description of the stages of insurgent operations. As with the Viet Cong and North Vietnamese fight against the United States during the late 1960s and early 1970s, terrorism was a tool employed concurrently with other means of waging war after the insurgency was well-underway. Consider the January 1968 TET Offensive by the Viet Cong or the recent operations of the Taliban in Jalalabad, Kandahar, Kabul, and other Afghan cities.

A third possibility is that terrorism may be a trailing indicator occurring as part of what Mao called the "strategic counter-offensive,"[212] when the insurgents organize themselves into larger-scale units and confront their enemy's armed forces directly.[213] At this stage, terrorism may by symptomatic of either success or failure. If the insurgent group is on the verge of winning its struggle, the fighters may stage purges aimed at killing key figures within the failing regime and intimidating their followers into quiescence. This may amount to an increase in terrorism. The murders carried out by the Khmer Rouge in Cambodia shortly after they marched into Phon Penh in 1976 are illustrative. Terrorism may also be an indicator of failure. Insurgents who have fought and lost may decide to continue their fight at a lower level of violence until such time as they are able to re-launch a serious bid for power. In this case terrorist activity is a means of letting the government and the population know they are still active and have not yet abandoned what they intend to be a protracted struggle.

There are also cases in which terrorism signals nothing. Some writers have stressed that terrorist groups often emerge as mass movements of social and political protest subside. These groups include members belonging to a category of fighters Charles Tilly labels as "specialists in violence," which continue the fight after most movement activists have returned to normal life.[214] These are the most extremist members of the movement. If these terrorists fail to raise the level of violence to something resembling wider-scale warfare, it is likely because they remained too weak. As such, terrorism is also a tactic of those would-be insurgents who will not be able to pose a more substantial challenge.

Looking ahead

In the pages that follow we look to past and present insurgencies in order to analyze the timing of terrorist attacks in the context of war. To speculate about terrorism's role in more recent conflicts, we rely on evidence drawn from the recent past. Is terrorist violence usually a leading indicator of broader conflicts to come? How commonly is terrorism used alongside other tactics? How often is terrorism a trailing indicator, a tactic symptomatic on occasion of both success and failure? Last on our agenda is the intent to discover whether the application of terrorism is more successful at one phase or another of insurgent campaigns.

This investigation draws on a combination of descriptive statistics and case analyses. In the following chapter we review the sources from which we derive information regarding terrorist attacks, insurgent groups, and wider-scale wars. We also discuss the techniques we use to analyze this data. In Chapters 3, 4, and 5, we consider the role of terrorism as a leading, concurrent, or trailing indicator of armed conflict. Our focus is on the ways in which terrorist attacks coincide with or occur independently of wider-scale warfare. We identify trends across cases by mapping the frequencies of terrorist attacks within a state's borders along a timeline that also shows when armed conflicts are being fought in that territory. We categorize these trends according to whether terrorism is occurring at the onset of wider-scale armed conflict, taking place throughout these conflicts, or increasing toward the end of an armed conflict. Each of these represents a pattern in the use of terrorism within insurgency. We also identify cases in which terrorism occurs without wider-scale warfare. We illustrate our general findings through comparisons among cases. Through case analyses, we expound upon selected insurgent groups, the conflicts in which they are engaged, and their stated or presumed motivations for using terrorism. We also consider the benefits, if any, that may accrue to the insurgents who choose terrorism as one of their tactics. In our concluding chapter, Chapter 6, we discuss observations regarding the timing of terrorism within wider-scale warfare.

Notes

1   See, for instance, Mueller, *The Remnants of War;* Goldstein, *Winning the War on War;* Marshall and Gurr, *Peace and Conflict 2005;* Martin van Creveld, *The Transformation of War: The Most Radical Reinterpretation of Armed Conflict since Clausewitz* (New York, NY: The Free Press, 1991); Benjamin

A. Valentino, *Final Solutions: Mass Killing and Genocide in the 20th Century*, ed. Robert J. Art, Robert Jervis, and Stephen M. Walt, Cornell Studies in Security Affairs (New York, NY: Cornell University Press, 2004); Easterbrook, "The End of War?"; Mueller, "War Has Almost Ceased to Exist."

2 Goldstein, *Winning the War on War*; van Creveld, *The Transformation of War*; Mueller, "War Has Almost Ceased to Exist."

3 Laurence R. Iannaccone and Eli Berman, "Religious Extremism: The Good, the Bad, and the Deadly," *Public Choice*, 128, no. 1–2 (2006): see, for instance, 121.

4 Ibid., 125–6.

5 Alex Braithwaite, "Transnational Terrorism as an Unintended Consequence of a Military Footprint," *Security Studies*, 24, no. 2 (2015).

6 Gary LaFree, "Editorial Introduction: Loner Attacks and Domestic Extremism, Lone-Offender Terrorists," *Criminology and Public Policy*, 12, no. 1 (2009); Gary LaFree and Gary Ackerman, "The Empirical Study of Terrorism: Social and Legal Research," *Annual Review of Law and Social Science*, 5 (2009); Richard K. Betts, "The Soft Underbelly of American Primacy: Tactical Advantages of Terror," *Political Science Quarterly*, 117, no. 1 (2002).

7 LaFree and Ackerman, "The Empirical Study of Terrorism: Social and Legal Research," 365.

8 David Collier and James E. Mahon, "Conceptual Stretching Revisited – Adapting Categories in Comparative-Analysis," *American Political Science Review*, 87, no. 4 (1993).

9 Leonard Weinberg, *Global Terrorism* (New York, NY: The Rosen Publishing Group, Inc., 2009), 9.

10 Hoffman, *Inside Terrorism*, 31; Leonard Weinberg and William Eubank, "An End to the Fourth Wave of Terrorism?," *Studies in Conflict & Terrorism*, 33, no. 7 (2010); Jeffrey Kaplan, "The Fifth Wave: The New Tribalism?," *Terrorism and Political Violence*, 19, no. 4 (2007).

11 It should be added that a large number of attacks were carried out against harder and softer targets. This calculation includes attacks meeting the Global Terrorism Database's (GTD's) three terrorism criteria and excluding attacks perpetrated solely against government, police, military, and violent non-state actors, based on data accessed September 12, 2015. "Global Terrorism Database [Data File]," National Consortium for the Study of Terrorism and Responses to Terrorism (START), 2015, www.start.umd.edu/gtd (last accessed April 4, 2016).

12 See, for instance, Hoffman, *Inside Terrorism*, 31.

13 Susanne Martin and Arie Perliger, "Turning to and from Terror: Deciphering the Conditions under Which Political Groups Choose Violent and Nonviolent Tactics," *Perspectives on Terrorism*, 6, no. 4–5 (2012).

14 Leonard Weinberg, "Turning to Terror: The Conditions under Which Political Parties Turn to Terrorist Activities," *Comparative Politics*, 23, no. 4 (1991).

15 See, for instance, John Coulter, "Guerrilla Tactics," *China Business Review*, May 1, 2007.

16 For a discussion of the problems confronting guerrillas in Third World settings see Jeremy Weinstein, *Inside Rebellion: The Politics of Insurgent Violence* (New York, NY: Cambridge University Press, 2007), 27–60.

17 See, for instance, Hoffman, *Inside Terrorism*, 35.

18 Ignacio Sanchez-Cuenca, "The Dynamics of Nationalist Terrorism: ETA and the IRA," *Terrorism and Political Violence*, 19, no. 3 (2007).

19 Hoffman, *Inside Terrorism*, 35–6.

20 Ami Pedahzur, *Suicide Terrorism* (Malden, MA: Polity Press, 2005), 52.

21 United States Department of the Army, *Counterinsurgency*, Field Manual No. 3-24, Marine Corps Warfighting Publication No. 3-33.5 (Washington DC: Department of the Army, December 15, 2006), 1-1. http://usacac.army.mil/cac2/Repository/Materials/COIN-FM3-24.pdf (last accessed 20 April 2016).

22 David Betz, "Cyberspace and Insurgency," in *The Routledge Handbook of Insurgency and Counterinsurgency*, ed. Paul Rich and Isabelle Duyvesteyn (New York, NY: Routledge, 2014), 54–66.

23 David Galula, *Counterinsurgency Warfare: Theory and Practice* (Westport, CT: Praeger Security International, 2006), xiii.

24 Ivan Arreguín-Toft, "Contemporary Asymmetric Conflict Theory in Historical Perspective," *Terrorism and Political Violence*, 24, no. 4 (2012); Ivan Arreguín-Toft, *How the Weak Win Wars: A Theory of Asymmetric Conflict* (New York, NY: Cambridge University Press, 2005). See also Ben Connable and Martin Libicki, *How Insurgencies End* (Santa Monica, CA: RAND, 2010).

25 Steven Metz, "Rethinking Insurgency," in *The Routledge Handbook of Insurgency and Counterinsurgency*, ed. Paul Rich and Isabelle Duyvesteyn (New York, NY: Routledge, 2014), 38.

26 James D. Fearon and David D. Laitin, "Ethnicity, Insurgency, and Civil War," *American Political Science Review*, 97, no. 1 (2003): 88.

27 Ibid.

28 N. Sambanis, "What Is Civil War? Conceptual and Empirical Complexities of an Operational Definition," *Journal of Conflict Resolution*, 48, no. 6 (2004).

29 Ibid.

30 Ibid.

31 Ibid., 816.

32 Bureau of Counterterrorism, "Chapter 6. Foreign Terrorist Organizations," in *Country Reports on Terrorism 2014* (Washington, DC: United States Department of State, 2014).

33 See for example, Oliver August, "Al-Qaeda's Land Grab," *The Economist: The World in 2013* (2013): 80.

34 Office of the Coordinator for Counterterrorism, *Country Reports on Terrorism 2009* (Washinton, DC: United States Department of State, 2010).

35 "Global Terrorism Database [Data File]," 2015.

36 For discussions see Peter Bergen, *The Longest War* (New York, NY: The Free Press, 2011), 309–49.

37 Laqueur, "Postmodern Terrorism," 24–36. David C. Rapoport, "The Fourth Wave: September 11 in the History of Terrorism," *Current History*, 100, no. 650 (2001): 419–24.

38 Walter Laqueur, *The Age of Terrorism* (Boston, MA: Little, Brown and Company, 1987), 1–9.

39 Arie Perliger, *Challengers from the Sidelines: Understanding America's Violent Far-Right* (West Point, NY: The Combating Terrorism Center at West Point, 2012).

40 For a discussion of Croatian terrorism during this era, see Stephen M.

Sobieck, "Democratic Responses to International Terrorism in Germany," in *The Deadly Sin of Terrorism: Its Effect on Democracy and Civil Liberty in Six Countries*, ed. David A. Charters (Westport, CT: Greenwood Press, 1994), 48–50.

41   Mohammed Jabar al-Ansari, as quoted in Fawaz A. Gerges, "The Transformation of Arab Politics: Disentangling Myth from Reality," in *The 1967 Arab-Israeli War: Origins and Consequences*, ed. Avi Shlaim and William Roger Louis (New York, NY: Cambridge University Press, 2012), 295.

42   Ibid.

43   For further description, see Kirsten E. Schulze, *The Arab-Israeli Conflict*, 2nd edn (New York, NY: Routledge, 2013), for instance, p. 33. See also Schulze, *The Arab-Israeli Conflict*.

44   See, for instance, Hoffman, *Inside Terrorism*, 65–71, 234.

45   The quote is restated, among other places, in a 2008 *New York Times* obituary for George Habash, see Edmund L. Andrews and John Kifner, "George Habash, 82, Founder of Popular Front for the Liberation of Palestine," *New York Times*, January 27, 2008.

46   George Habash and Mahmoud Soueid, "Taking Stock: An Interview with George Habash," *Journal of Palestine Studies*, 28, no. 1 (1998).

47   See, for instance, Mark Ensalaco, *Middle Eastern Terrorism: From Black September to September 11* (Philadelphia, PA: University of Pennsylvania Press, 2008), 29–32, see also 50–9.

48   See the argument of Alan Dershowitz, *Why Terrorism Works: Understanding the Threat, Responding to the Challenge* (New Haven, CT: Yale University Press, 2002), 36–88.

49   See also ibid.

50   Daniel Byman, *Deadly Connections: States That Sponsor Terrorism* (New York, NY: Cambridge University Press, 2005).

51   For an in-depth discussion, see ibid.

52   This reference is to an oft-quoted and paraphrased statement attributed to Fidel Castro that a city would be the "graveyard of revolution." See, for instance, William Rosenau, "Counterinsurgency: Lessons from Iraq and Afghanistan," *Harvard International Review*, 31, no. 1 (2009): 56. See also Regis Debray, *Revolution in the Revolution?* (New York, NY: Grove Press, Inc., 1967).

53   Che Guevara, *Guerrilla Warfare* (New York, NY: Monthly Review Press, 1961).

54   Debray, *Revolution in the Revolution?*, 67.

55   This type of learning has been relevant in explanations for dictators' responses to the "Color Revolutions" taking place within their borders. Wolchik refers to this as "authoritarian learning." See, for instance, Sharon L. Wolchik, "Can There Be a Color Revolution?" *Journal of Democracy*, 23, no. 3 (2012); Valerie Bunce and Sharon Wolchik, "A Regional Transition: The Diffusion of Democratic Change under Communism and Postcommunism," in *Democracy and Authoritarianism in the Poscommunist World*, ed. Valerie Bunce, Michael McFaul, and Kathryn Stoner-Weiss (New York, NY: Cambridge University Press, 2010); Vitali Silitski, "Contagion Deferred: Preemptive Authoritarianism in the Soviet Union (the Case of Belarus)," in *Democracy and Authoritarianism in the Postcommunist World*, ed.

Valerie Bunce, Michael McFaul, and Kathryn Stoner-Weiss (New York, NY: Cambridge University Press, 2010); Regine A. Spector, "The Anti-Revolutionary Toolkit," *CACI Analyst* (2006).

56 For further discussion, see Henry Butterfield Ryan, *The Fall of Che Guevara: A Story of Soldiers, Spies, and Diplomats* (New York, NY: Oxford University Press, 1998).

57 Connable and Libicki, *How Insurgencies End*, 8.

58 Carlos Marighella. *Manual of the Urban Guerrilla*, The Terrorist Classic. Chapel Hill, NC: Documentary Publications, 1985.. See also, Anthony Joes, *Urban Guerrilla Warfare* (Lexington, KY: The University of Kentucky Press, 2007), 76–9.

59 Walter Laqueur, *A History of Terrorism* (New Brunswick, NJ: Transaction Publishers, 2012), 184–5.

60 Abraham Guillen, "Urban Guerrilla Strategy," in *Guerrilla Strategies: An Historical Anthology from the Long March to Afghanistan*, ed. Gerard Chaliand (Berkeley, CA: University of California Press, Ltd., 1982), 317–23.

61 Weinstein, *Inside Rebellion*, 27.

62 See, for instance, ibid.

63 See, for instance, the United States Counterinsurgency (COIN) Manual. United States Department of the Army, *Counterinsurgency*.

64 See, for instance, Thomas C. Wright, *Latin America in the Era of the Cuban Revolution* (Westport, CT: Praeger Publishers, 2001), 93–6. See also Connable and Libicki, *How Insurgencies End*.

65 Marighella, *Manual of the Urban Guerrilla*; Guillen, "Urban Guerrilla Strategy," 317–23. See also Connable and Libicki, *How Insurgencies End*, 7–8.

66 Joes, *Urban Guerrilla Warfare*, 76–9.

67 Wright, *Latin America in the Era of the Cuban Revolution*, 93–6.

68 Sanchez-Cuenca, "The Dynamics of Nationalist Terrorism: ETA and the IRA."

69 Pape differentiates between types of terrorism. Demonstrative terrorism is the type least likely to alienate a terrorist group from its target population. It is also the least destructive. R. A. Pape, "The Strategic Logic of Suicide Terrorism," *American Political Science Review*, 97, no. 3 (2003).

70 See, for example, Pedahzur, *Suicide Terrorism*; Walter Laqueur, *The New Terrorism: Fanaticism and the Arms of Mass Destruction* (New York, NY: Oxford University Press, 1999); David C. Rapoport, "The Four Modern Waves of Terrorism," in *Attacking Terrorism*, ed. Audrey Kurth Cronin and James Ludes (Washington, DC: Georgetown University Press, 2004), 46–73.

71 Fukuyama, "The End of History?"

72 For instance, James M. Scott, *Deciding to Intervene: The Reagan Doctrine and American Foreign Policy* (Durham, NC: Duke University Press, 1996); Artemy M. Kalinovsky, *A Long Goodbye: The Soviet Withdrawal from Afghanistan* (Cambridge, MA: Harvard University Press, 2011).

73 Anne-Marie Slaughter, *A New World Order* (Princeton, NJ: Princeton University Press, 2004); Anne-Marie Slaughter, "The Real New World Order," *Foreign Affairs*, 76, no. 5 (1997).

74 Samuel P. Huntington, *The Clash of Civilizations and the Remaking of World Order* (New York, NY: Simon and Schuster, 1996).

75 See, for instance, Mark Juergensmeyer, "Understanding the New

Terrorism," *Current History*, 99, no. 636 (2000): 158–63; Ersun N. Kurtulus, "The 'New Terrorism' and Its Critics," *Studies in Conflict & Terrorism*, 34, no. 6 (2011): 476–500; Walter Laqueur, "The New Face of Terrorism," *Washington Quarterly*, 21, no. 4 (1998): 169–78; Laqueur, *The New Terrorism: Fanaticism and the Arms of Mass Destruction*.

76 See, for instance, Laqueur, *The New Terrorism*; Juergensmeyer, "Understanding the New Terrorism;" Hoffman, *Inside Terrorism*. For examples of critiques, see Isabelle Duyvesteyn, "How New Is the New Terrorism?" *Studies in Conflict & Terrorism*, 27, no. 5 (2004); David Tucker, "What Is New About the New Terrorism and How Dangerous Is It?" *Terrorism and Political Violence*, 13, no. 3 (2001).

77 Brian M. Jenkins, "Will Terrorists Go Nuclear?" (November 1975), www.rand.org/content/dam/rand/pubs/papers/2006/P5541.pdf (last accessed March 15, 2016); Brian M. Jenkins, "The New Age of Terrorism," in *Mcgraw-Hill Homeland Security Handbook* (McGraw-Hill Companies, Inc., 2006), 118–19, www.rand.org/content/dam/rand/pubs/reprints/2006/RAND_RP1215.pdf (last accessed April 20, 2016).

78 Michael Barkun, *Religion and the Racist Right: The Origins of the Christian Identity Movement* (Chapel Hill, NC: The University of North Carolina Press, 1997), 273–5.

79 Mia M. Bloom, *Dying to Kill: The Allure of Suicide Terror* (New York: Columbia University Press, 2005); Kydd and Walter, "The Strategies of Terrorism."

80 See, for instance, Mohammed M. Hafez, "Suicide Terrorism in Iraq: A Preliminary Assessment of the Quantitative Data and Documentary Evidence," *Studies in Conflict & Terrorism*, 29, no. 6 (2006): 591–619; Assaf Moghadam, "Motives for Martyrdom: Al-Qaida, Salafi Jihad, and the Spread of Suicide Attacks," *International Security*, 33, no. 3 (2009): 46–78.

81 Michael C. Horowitz, "Nonstate Actors and the Diffusion of Innovations: The Case of Suicide Terrorism," *International Organization*, 64, no. 1 (2010): 33.

82 See, for instance, Jenkins, "Will Terrorists Go Nuclear?"

83 Hoffman, *Inside Terrorism*, 273.

84 A. O'Neil, "Terrorist Use of Weapons of Mass Destruction: How Serious Is the Threat?," *Australian Journal of International Affairs*, 57, no. 1 (2003); K. A. Lieber and D. G. Press, "Why States Won't Give Nuclear Weapons to Terrorists," *International Security*, 38, no. 1 (2013).

85 Laqueur, *The New Terrorism*, 263–5.

86 Jenkins, "The New Age of Terrorism."

87 Arie Perliger and Ami Pedahzur, "Social Network Analysis in the Study of Terrorism and Political Violence," *Ps-Political Science & Politics*, 44, no. 1 (2011).

88 See, for example, Marc Sageman, *Leaderless Jihad: Terror Networks in the Twenty-First Century* (Philadelphia, PA: University of Pennsylvania Press, 2008); Marc Sageman and Bruce Hoffman, "The Reality of Grass Roots Terrorism [with Reply]," *Foreign Affairs*, 87, no. 4 (2008): 163–6; Bruce Hoffman, "Leaderless Jihad: Terror Networks in the Twenty-First Century," *Foreign Affairs*, 87, no. 3 (2008): 133–8; M. Sageman, "Does Osama Still Call the Shots? Debating the Containment of Al Qaeda's Leadership,"

Foreign Affairs, 87, no. 4 (2008). See also Ami Pedahzur and Arie Perliger, "The Changing Nature of Suicide Attacks: A Social Network Perspective," *Social Forces*, 84, no. 4 (2006): 1987–2008.

89   Perliger, *Challengers from the Sidelines*, 40–50.

90   Stephen Hosmer, *Viet Cong Repression and Its Implications for the Future* (Lexington, MA: Heath Lexington Books, 1970).

91   Jacob N. Shapiro, *The Terrorist's Dilemma: Managing Violent Covert Organizations* (Princeton, NJ: Princeton University Press, 2013), 94–7.

92   Sageman and Hoffman, "The Reality of Grass Roots Terrorism [with Reply]."

93   Max Boot, "The Evolution of Irregular War: Insurgents and Guerrillas from Akkadia to Afghanistan," *Foreign Affairs*, 92, no. 2 (2013).

94   See, for example, Walter Laqueur, *Guerrilla* (Boston, MA: Little, Brown and Company, 1976), 262–77.

95   See, for instance, Stathis N. Kalyvas and Matthew Adam Kocher, "The Dynamics of Violence in Vietnam: An Analysis of the Hamlet Evaluation System (HES)," *Journal of Peace Research*, 46, no. 3 (2009).

96   For an additional discussion of similar patterns in attacks on United States and foreign interests, Gary LaFree, Sue-Ming Yang, and Martha Crenshaw, "Trajectories of Terrorism: Attack Patterns of Foreign Groups that Have Targeted the United States, 1970–2004," *Criminology and Public Policy*, 8, no. 3 (2009): 468.

97   Martha Crenshaw, "Theories of Terrorism – Instrumental and Organizational Approaches," *Journal of Strategic Studies*, 10, no. 4 (1987); Crenshaw, "The Causes of Terrorism;" Kydd and Walter, "The Strategies of Terrorism."

98   Max Abrahms, "Why Terrorism Does Not Work," *International Security*, 31, no. 2 (2006); Pape, "The Strategic Logic of Suicide Terrorism."

99   Weinstein, *Inside Rebellion*, for instance, 6.

100   See, for instance, Bloom, *Dying to Kill*; Mia M. Bloom, "Palestinian Suicide Bombing: Public Support, Market Share, and Outbidding," *Political Science Quarterly*, 119, no. 1 (2004); Kydd and Walter, "The Strategies of Terrorism."

101   Nick Ayers, "Ghost Martyrs in Iraq: An Assessment of the Applicability of Rationalist Models to Explain Suicide Attacks in Iraq," *Studies in Conflict & Terrorism*, 31, no. 9 (2008).

102   Henar Criado suggests that violence may be used and abandoned strategically in an effort to gain popular support as well as a better bargaining position. Henar Criado, "Bullets and Votes: Public Opinion and Terrorist Strategies," *Journal of Peace Research*, 48, no. 4 (2011). There is also a sizeable literature on 'dual strategies.' See, for instance, Susanne Martin, "Dilemmas of 'Going Legit': Why Should Violent Groups Engage in or Avoid Electoral Politics?," *Behavioral Sciences of Terrorism and Political Aggression*, 6, no. 2 (2014).

103   For instance, Crenshaw, "The Causes of Terrorism."

104   B. D. Jones, "Bounded Rationality," *Annual Review of Political Science*, 2 (1999).

105   Stathis N. Kalyvas, "The Paradox of Terrorism in Civil War," *Journal of Ethics*, 8 (2004).

106   See, for instance, M. I. Midlarsky, Martha Crenshaw, and F. Yoshida, "Why

Violence Spreads – the Contagion of International Terrorism," *International Studies Quarterly*, 24, no. 2 (1980); Crenshaw, "The Causes of Terrorism;" Kalyvas, "The Paradox of Terrorism in Civil War."

107 Max Abrahms, "Why Terrorism Does Not Work," *International Security*, 31, no. 2 (2006): 42–78.

108 Pape, "The Strategic Logic of Suicide Terrorism," 351.

109 See, for instance, Aaron Edwards, "Abandoning Armed Resistance? The Ulster Volunteer Force as a Case Study of Strategic Terrorism in Northern Ireland," *Studies in Conflict & Terrorism*, 32, no. 2 (2009).

110 See, for instance, Weinstein, *Inside Rebellion*.

111 Connable and Libicki, *How Insurgencies End*, 48.

112 Ibid., 103–4.

113 Hafez, "Suicide Terrorism in Iraq."

114 Ibid.

115 Connable and Libicki, *How Insurgencies End*, xvii.

116 Abrahms, "Why Terrorism Does Not Work." For a description of the cases, see especially 43, 49–50.

117 Pape, "The Strategic Logic of Suicide Terrorism," 344.

118 See, for instance, Hoffman, "The Changing Face of Al Qaeda and the Global War on Terrorism."

119 Connable and Libicki, *How Insurgencies End*.

120 The U.S. Military defines an insurgency as follows: "an organized movement aimed at the overthrow of a constituted government through the use of subversion and armed conflict." United States Department of the Army, *Counterinsurgency*, 1-1.

121 Bureau of Counterterrorism, "Chapter 6. Foreign Terrorist Organizations," in *Country Reports on Terrorism 2014*.

122 Ibid.

123 Connable and Libicki, *How Insurgencies End*, xvii.

124 The ways in which insurgencies were assigned classifications as indiscriminate or discrete seems somewhat subjective, with ratios of civilian to non-civilian deaths remaining something of a mystery. Ibid., 205.

125 Kalyvas, "The Paradox of Terrorism in Civil War," 101. See also Weinstein, *Inside Rebellion*.

126 Connable and Libicki, *How Insurgencies End*.

127 Ibid.

128 Weinstein, *Inside Rebellion*, 7.

129 Max Abrahms and Philip B. K. Potter, "Explaining Terrorism: Leadership Deficits and Militant Group Tactics," *International Organization*, 69, no. 2 (2015).

130 Erin M. Kearns, Brendan Conlon, and Joseph K. Young, "Lying About Terrorism," *Studies in Conflict & Terrorism*, 37, no. 5 (2014).

131 Max Abrahms, "The Political Effectiveness of Terrorism Revisited," *Comparative Political Studies*, 45, no. 3 (2012).

132 Horowitz, "Nonstate Actors and the Diffusion of Innovations."

133 See, for instance, Weinstein, *Inside Rebellion*.

134 Arreguín-Toft, *How the Weak Win Wars*, 23–47.

135 Stathis N. Kalyvas, *The Logic of Violence in Civil War* (New York, NY: Cambridge University Press, 2006).

136 For instance, Stathis N. Kalyvas, "Review Symposium: Counterinsurgency

Manual," *Perspectives on Politics*, 6, no. 2 (2008); Boot, "The Evolution of Irregular War."

137 For instance, Midlarsky, Crenshaw, and Yoshida, "Why Violence Spreads – the Contagion of International Terrorism;" Lawrence C. Hamilton and James D. Hamilton, "Dynamics of Terrorism," *International Studies Quarterly*, 27, no. 1 (1983); Horowitz, "Nonstate Actors and the Diffusion of Innovations."

138 See, for instance, Pape, "The Strategic Logic of Suicide Terrorism."

139 Arreguín-Toft, *How the Weak Win Wars*.

140 Boot, *Invisible Armies*.

141 David Kilcullen, *The Accidental Guerrilla* (New York, NY: Oxford University Press, 2009), Chapter 1.

142 LaFree and Ackerman, "The Empirical Study of Terrorism: Social and Legal Research."

143 Refer, for instance, to the contributions found in Philip Keefer and Norman Loayza, eds, *Terrorism, Economic Development, and Political Openness* (New York, NY: Cambridge University Press, 2008); see also Erica Chenoweth, "Terrorism and Democracy," *Annual Review of Political Science*, 16 (2013).

144 Fearon and Laitin, "Ethnicity, Insurgency, and Civil War." See also N. Sambanis, "Do Ethnic and Nonethnic Civil Wars Have the Same Causes? A Theoretical and Empirical Inquiry (Part 1)," *Journal of Conflict Resolution*, 45, no. 3 (2001).

145 Kilcullen, *The Accidental Guerrilla*, 6.

146 Sambanis, "Do Ethnic and Nonethnic Civil Wars Have the Same Causes?"

147 Chenoweth, "Terrorism and Democracy."

148 LaFree and Ackerman, "The Empirical Study of Terrorism: Social and Legal Research."

149 Kilcullen, *The Accidental Guerrilla*, 5, 79.

150 Ibid., 5–6.

151 Mary Kaldor, *New and Old Wars*, 2nd edn (Stanford, CA: Stanford University Press, 2006), 7–14. For an account of recent insurgencies in sub-Saharan Africa see Weinstein, *Inside Rebellion*, 61–95. For another overview see Bruce Berkowitz, *The New Face of War: How Wars Will Be Fought in the 21st Century* (New York, NY: The Free Press, 2003), see especially Chapter Four, 'The Asymmetric Warrior'.

152 Mary Kaldor, *New and Old Wars: Organized Violence in a Global Arena* (Stanford, CA: Stanford University Press, 2001), for instance, 6–9.

153 Huntington, *The Clash of Civilizations*.

154 Kaldor, *New and Old Wars: Organized Violence in a Global Arena*, 69–70. See also Sidney Tarrow, *The New Transnational Activism* (New York, NY: Cambridge University Press, 2005).

155 Thomas Johnson and M. Chris Mason, "Terrorism, Insurgency and Afghanistan," in *Countering Terrorism and Insurgency in the 21st Century*, ed. James Forrest (Westport, CT: Praeger International, 2007), 453–78.

156 Hayder Mili and Jacob Townsend, "Tribal Dynamics of the Afghanistan and Pakistan Insurgencies," *CTC Sentinel*, 2, no. 8 (2009), www.ctc.usma.edu/v2/wp-content/uploads/2010/06/Vol2Iss8-Art3.pdf (last accessed April 29, 2016).

157 On this point, see Jervis, "Theories of War in an Era of Leading-Power Peace, Presidential Address, American Political Science Association, 2001;"

Marshall and Gurr, *Peace and Conflict 2005*; Mueller, "War Has Almost Ceased to Exist;" Mueller, *The Remnants of War*; Easterbrook, "The End of War?"; Gleditsch et al., "The Decline of War;" Goldstein, *Winning the War on War*.

158 See also Colonel Thomas X. Hammes, "Fourth Generation Warfare Evolves, Fifth Emerges," *Military Review*, 87, no. 3 (2007).

159 Kaldor, *New and Old Wars*, 2nd edn.

160 Susanne Martin and Leonard B. Weinberg, "Terrorism in an Era of Unconventional Warfare," *Terrorism and Political Violence* (forthcoming).

161 Hammes, "Fourth Generation Warfare Evolves, Fifth Emerges," 23.

162 Ibid.

163 Kaldor states, "In Charles Taylor's National Patriotic Front of Liberia, for example, which invaded Sierra Leone ... some 30 per cent of the soldiers were said to be under the age of seventeen." Kaldor, *New and Old Wars*, 2nd edn, 99.

164 See, for example, Keith Shimko, *The Iraq Wars and America's Military Revolution* (New York, NY: Cambridge University Press, 2010), 213–37. See also Berkowitz, *The New Face of War*.

165 Hammes, "Fourth Generation Warfare Evolves, Fifth Emerges."

166 David C. Rapoport, "Fear and Trembling – Terrorism in 3 Religious Traditions," *American Political Science Review*, 78, no. 3 (1984).

167 Martin and Weinberg, "Terrorism in an Era of Unconventional Warfare;" Quintan Wiktorowicz and John Kaltner, "Killing in the Name of Islam: Al-Qaeda's Justification for September 11," *Middle East Policy*, 10, no. 2 (2003).

168 Kalyvas, *The Logic of Violence in Civil War*, 52–86.

169 Arreguín-Toft, *How the Weak Win Wars*, 31.

170 D. K. Cohen, "Explaining Rape During Civil War: Cross-National Evidence (1980–2009)," *American Political Science Review*, 107, no. 3 (2013).

171 Kalyvas, *The Logic of Violence in Civil War*, 389.

172 Lee Ann Fujii, "The Puzzle of Extra-Lethal Violence," *Perspectives on Politics*, 11, no. 2 (2013): 410–26.

173 Ibid., 410, 15.

174 Kaldor, *New and Old Wars*, 2nd edn.

175 See, for instance, Derek Henry Flood, "An Overview of Syria's Armed Revolution," *CTC Sentinel*, 5, no. 4 (2012).

176 Ibid.

177 Mona Yacoubian, "Hezbollah's Gamble in Syria: The Dangerous Calculation Behind the Group's Decision to Back Assad," *Foreign Affairs*, June 2, 2013.

178 Pedahzur, *Suicide Terrorism*, 52.

179 Audrey Kurth Cronin, *How Terrorism Ends: Understanding the Decline and Demise of Terrorist Campaigns* (Princeton, NJ: Princeton University Press, 2009).

180 For further discussion of the "legitimate" and quasi-legitimate business activities of terrorists, see Louise I. Shelley, *Dirty Entanglements: Corruption, Crime, and Terrorism* (New York, NY: Cambridge University Press, 2014).

181 Audrey Kurth Cronin, "ISIS Is Not a Terrorist Group: Why Counterterrorism Won't Stop the Latest Jihadist Threat," *Foreign Affairs*, 94, no. 2 (2015);

Louise Shelley, "Blood Money: How ISIS Makes Bank," *Foreign Affairs*, November 30, 2014.

182 Cronin, "ISIS Is Not a Terrorist Group;" Shelley, "Blood Money."

183 Shelley, "Blood Money."

184 Ibid.

185 For a more in-depth discussion, see Shelley, *Dirty Entanglements*, for instance, 1–5, 173–218. See also Brian Michael Jenkins, "Brothers Killing Brothers: The Current Infighting Will Test Al Qaeda's Brand" (Santa Monica, CA: RAND Corporation, 2014), www.rand.org/pubs/perspectives/PE123. html (last accessed April 20, 2016); Matthew Levitt, "Al-Qa'ida's Finances: Evidence of Organizational Decline?," *CTC Sentinel*, 1, no. 5 (2008); Jacob Zenn, "A Biography of Boko Haram and the Bay'a to Al-Baghdadi," *CTC Sentinel*, 8, no. 3 (2015).

186 Shelley, *Dirty Entanglements*, 178.

187 Laith Alkhouri and Alex Kassirer, "Governing the Caliphate: The Islamic State Picture," *CTC Sentinel*, 8, no. 8 (2015).

188 Cronin, "ISIS Is Not a Terrorist Group."

189 Shelley, *Dirty Entanglements*.

190 Ibid., 188.

191 Alkhouri and Kassirer, "Governing the Caliphate."

192 Hammes, "Fourth Generation Warfare Evolves, Fifth Emerges."

193 See, for instance, Donald J. Reed, "Beyond the War on Terror: Into the Fifth Generation of War and Conflict," *Studies in Conflict & Terrorism*, 31, no. 8 (2008).

194 Weinstein, *Inside Rebellion*; Connable and Libicki, *How Insurgencies End*.

195 W. Rosenau, "'Our Backs Are against the Wall': The Black Liberation Army and Domestic Terrorism in 1970s America," *Studies in Conflict & Terrorism*, 36, no. 2 (2013).

196 For instance, Juergensmeyer, "Understanding the New Terrorism."

197 Valentino, *Final Solutions: Mass Killing and Genocide in the 20th Century*, 1, 255.

198 For a broader discussion of the decline in violence and deaths over time, see Steven Pinker, *The Better Angels of Our Nature: Why Violence Has Declined* (New York, NY: Viking Penguin, 2011).

199 See, for instance, Neta C. Crawford, "Costs of War: War-Related Death, Injury, and Displacement in Afghanistan and Pakistan 2001–2014" (Watson Institute for International Studies, Brown University, 2015), http://watson. brown.edu/costsofwar/files/cow/imce/papers/2015/War%20Related%20 Casualties%20Afghanistan%20and%20Pakistan%202001-2014%20FIN% 20%288%29.pdf (last accessed April 20, 2016). See also Human Security Report Project, *Human Security Report 2013: The Decline in Global Violence: Evidence, Explanation, and Contestation* (Vancouver, Canada: Human Security Press, 2014), 105–13.

200 Neta C. Crawford, "Assessing the Human Toll of the Post-9/11 Wars: The Dead and Wounded in Afghanistan, Iraq, and Pakistan, 2001–2011" (2011), http://watson.brown.edu/costsofwar/files/cow/imce/papers/2011/ Assessing%20the%20Human%20Toll%20of%20the%20Post911%20 Wars.pdf (last accessed April 20, 2016).

201 See especially John A. Nagl, *Learning to Eat Soup with a Knife: Counterinsurgency Lessons from Malaya and Vietnam* (Chicago, IL: University of Chicago Press, 2005). See also, David Kilcullen, *Counterinsurgency* (New York, NY: Oxford University Press, 2010). For some of the ideas on which COIN was based, see Galula, *Counterinsurgency Warfare*.

202 See for example, Cronin, *How Terrorism Ends*, 207–22; Paul Wilkinson, *Terrorism Versus Democracy: The Liberal State Response*, 2nd edn (New York, NY: Routledge, 2006).

203 For the origins and development of these ideas see Fred Kaplan, *The Insurgents* (New York, NY: Simon and Schuster, 2013), 11–34.

204 For a detailed discussion see ibid., 126–52.

205 See for example, Bruce Watson, *When Soldiers Quit* (Westport, CT: Praeger, 1997), 156–73.

206 Kilcullen, *The Accidental Guerrilla*.

207 Pedahzur and Perliger, "The Changing Nature of Suicide Attacks: A Social Network Perspective."

208 See, for instance, Justin Conrad and Kevin Greene, "Competition, Differentiation, and the Severity of Terrorist Attacks," *Journal of Politics*, 77, no. 2 (2015). See also Jeff Burdette, "Why the ISIS-Al-Qaeda Conflict Isn't All Good News," *Georgetown Security Studies Review*, March 26, 2014.

209 For the confusion caused by the use of both COIN and counterterrorism, see Boyle, "Do Counterterrorism and Counterinsurgency Go Together?"

210 See, for instance, Mao Tse-Tung, *On Guerrilla Warfare*, trans. Samuel B. Griffith (New York, NY: BN Publishing, 2007); Mao Tse-Tung, *Selected Works of Mao Tse-Tung*, Vol. 1 (Elmsford, NY: Pergamon Press, Inc., 1965).

211 United States Department of the Army, *Counterinsurgency*, 1-6. Early observations about the role of terrorism in internal wars identified it as an early stage tactic. See Brian Crozier, *The Rebels* (Boston, MA: Beacon Press, 1960), 151–95; Thomas Thornton, "Terror as a Weapon of Political Agitation," in *Internal War*, ed. Harry Eckstein (New York, NY: The Free Press, 1964), 92–5.

212 In Tse-Tung, *Selected Works*: see, for instance, 223–5.

213 See, for instance, Tse-Tung, *On Guerrilla Warfare*; Tse-Tung, *Selected Works of Mao Tse-Tung*.

214 Charles Tilly, *The Politics of Collective Violence* (New York, NY: Cambridge University Press, 2003), 35–6.

2

The logic of our approach: data and measurement

Our interest is in the study of terrorism as it is used in the context of warfare. Our main concerns lie in understanding the role terrorism has played in warfare and whether the role of terrorism in twenty-first century warfare has changed from previous eras to today and, if it has, in what ways? We investigate terrorism's role in warfare through an analysis of the timing of terrorist attacks during wider-scale warfare and the outcomes of these wars as regards the groups using terrorism. In the process, we seek answers to three more specific questions. In what ways does terrorism correspond with wider-scale armed conflict? Is terrorism a predictor of violent conflict to come or a tactic of last resort employed after wider-spread conflict has dissipated? Is terrorism used concurrently with other types of tactics in the context of wider-scale warfare?

In answering these questions, our first task is to identify patterns in the use of terrorism over time and across geographic space. Our second, and principal, task lies in identifying whether and how these patterns vary across contexts in which there is wider-scale warfare. Our third task involves analyzing whether and how these patterns relate to the outcomes of conflict. Our focus here is on whether groups tend to succeed or fail when terrorist tactics are employed at different stages in a wider conflict. We answer these questions through a combination of descriptive statistics and qualitative analysis.

Terrorism as an insurgent tactic

Clearly terrorism can be incorporated into the repertoire of tactics used by insurgents as part of their long-term struggles. In fact, it is hard to think of a contemporary insurgency in the Middle East, North Africa, South Asia, or elsewhere where terrorism has not played an important role at one point or another. If the prominent counterinsurgency analyst David Kilcullen is right in thinking that armed conflicts of this type are becoming increasingly urban in character, terrorism is likely to become an even more significant factor in these sorts of conflicts in the future.

It seems helpful at this point to restate our terminology. By "terrorism" we have in mind a politically motivated tactic involving the threat or use of violence in which the pursuit of publicity plays a prominent role. These attacks are not executed as part of an overt military campaign. The targets of these threats and acts of violence are typically noncombatants or civilians.[1] Terrorism is a tactic used by violent groups to garner particular types of attention from a stronger opponent or opponents (typically a state) and from target populations, including those in which the groups seek to instill fear as well as those whose support they hope to gain or maintain. Attacks on military forces on a battlefield are not acts of terrorism. In addition, the hit-and-run attacks and acts of sabotage used by non-state armed groups against other armed forces, including those of a state, would not typically be categorized as terrorism.

Terrorism as a revolutionary tactic

Modern terrorism became a significant tactic in revolutionary politics in the last decades of the nineteenth century. Those revolutionary anarchists and ultra-nationalists who believed "propaganda by deed" to be a crucial means of bringing the masses from passivity to action thought they had discovered a way of taking a shortcut on the path to revolution.[2] In their view, campaigns of assassinations and bombings would prove sufficient for terrifying rulers and igniting the revolutionary spark for workers and peasants.

Despite these expectations, the waves of assassinations and bombings that occurred throughout czarist Russia, Europe, and the Americas in the decades preceding the outbreak of World War I did little apart from inviting harsh repression by the authorities. This was the era of what may be thought of as the first international effort to combat terrorism, or the first "war on terrorism."[3] Left-wing critics (e.g., Marx, Lenin, Trotsky) of "propaganda by deed" regarded anarchist or social revolutionary terrorism as a juvenile and futile exercise more likely to put the masses to sleep than to lead them to revolution.

In practice, Bolshevik revolutionaries in Russia and their admirers elsewhere had little objection to the use of terrorism, including assassinations, kidnapping, and "proletarian expropriations," when it was used in conjunction with other means of mass mobilization. Terrorism was simply one tool among many.

The benefits of terrorist violence were also recognized by groups on the far-right as well as those drawn to the cause of national independence. Accordingly, during the interwar period, fascist bands in France (e.g., Street Followers of the King), Romania (e.g., Iron Guard), and Hungary (e.g., Arrow Cross), as well as those in Italy and Germany, carried out assassinations of prominent anti-fascist politicians and journalists. In Yugoslavia, the Ustasha combined rabid Croat nationalism with fascist ideas in its effort to establish an independent Croatia. Ustasha's most spectacular terrorist attack was the assassination of the Yugoslav King Alexander during the latter's visit to France in 1934.

World War II (1939–45) left the major European imperial powers in severely weakened circumstances. National independence movements emerged in the Middle East, North and sub-Saharan Africa, and South and East Asia. Their goal was to compel the British, French, Dutch, and Belgians to abandon their colonial enterprises and grant them freedom. After more than a decade of a revolutionary struggle, the Chinese Revolution culminated in 1949 with the victory of communist forces.

The principal means by which these Third World countries achieved their independence was through insurgency. With a few exceptions (e.g., Algeria, Palestine, and Vietnam), terrorism was a relatively minor ingredient in these insurgencies.[4] In some places, insurgents were worried that terrorist tactics would backfire, making more enemies than friends for their cause.

The role of terrorism during these insurgencies became an important consideration for Western observers somewhat later, largely after the fact. French and British writers placed their reflections under the broad heading of counterinsurgency. Their concern was how the authorities should go about defeating insurgent groups.[5]

Some American writers began to pay attention to the role of terrorism during insurgencies in the early 1960s, just as the Kennedy and Johnson administrations in the United States were becoming directly involved in the fights for control over Southeast Asia, and in South Vietnam especially. Counterinsurgency doctrines also caught the attention of Washington decision-makers at this time. Scholars interested in countering the Viet Cong, Pathet Lao, Khmer Rouge, and other insurgents paid particular attention to the works of Mao Tse-Tung. Mao, after all, had led a revolutionary insurgency that succeeded in toppling the nationalists and creating the Chinese People's Republic, ruling the most populous country on Earth. Given this enormous achievement – and perhaps, not coincidentally, the geographic proximity of this achievement to other leftist insurgents in Asia – Mao's ideas were taken with the utmost seriousness by Western strategists committed to thwarting revolutionaries' attempts to replicate this success elsewhere.

Mao thought that peasant-based revolutions went through a series of three stages. The first stage involved steps revolutionaries should take in order to draw attention to their cause and win the sympathy of the local population, what the Bolsheviks had earlier labeled "agitation-propaganda." Although Mao was himself leery of terrorism, because of its counter-productive potential, Western analysts saw things somewhat differently: terrorism was part of the revolutionary process. In other words, terrorism was a tool used by insurgents; it was one way in which insurgents could bring attention to their cause. Thomas Thornton and Brian Crozier, for example, also linked terrorism to the initial stages of an insurgency.[6] Once insurgents had attracted sufficient publicity and won a certain level of popular support, terrorism had achieved its purpose. This was essentially a short-term objective. The insurgents could then go on to conduct more extensive military operations.

It was the fighting over Southeast Asia that stimulated the formation of a long list of terrorist groups in the Western world. The 1960s was a time marked by revolutionary thinking and action. In Western Europe and Latin America, the various communist parties (e.g., Euro-Communism) were increasingly perceived as no longer possessing serious revolutionary credentials. They had become reformists bureaucratic organizations whose leaders seemed indistinguishable from their bourgeois counterparts, replete with double-breasted suits and homburg hats.

Against this background, the Viet Cong's highly romanticized achievements became a source of inspiration for young would-be revolutionaries throughout Western Europe and North America. The situations in the Middle East and Latin America were somewhat different than in the West. In the former case the outcome of the June 1967 Six-Day War led the various Palestinian groups to pursue new means for destroying their hated Zionist enemy. Some Palestinian figures stressed the benefits of a "people's war" or a "war of long duration." The successes of the Viet Cong in fighting the United States and its South Vietnamese ally to a standstill provided inspiration for this approach, as did the victory of the National Liberation Front in Algeria.

Unlike Western Europe, which was experiencing a period of unprecedented prosperity during the late 1960s, Latin America was a region, with its millions of desperately poor, where young revolutionaries could hope to win significant popular support. Initial attempts to follow Fidel Castro's route to revolution failed as illustrated by the 1967 defeat of Che Guevara's guerrilla band in Bolivia.[7] As a consequence of this and the failures of other rural-based insurgent groups, Latin America's revolutionaries turned their attention to the region's vast cities with their millions of slum-dwellers. From the late 1960s, governments throughout the region were confronted by bands of "urban guerrillas" who intended to take advantage of the urban setting to carry out their insurgent efforts.

With some exceptions, especially Latin American ones (e.g., Peru and Colombia), what emerged from this concatenation of radicalizing forces was a series of what should be labeled stand-alone groups. We may think of these stand-alone groups as simply terrorist groups; although, this grouping would include would-be insurgents. They used and continued to use terrorism in large part because they were unable to incite insurgency, much less to be successful in carrying out any such endeavor. A long list of revolutionary groups surfaced in Italy, Turkey, and what was then West Germany. These groups began to launch terrorist campaigns directed against their own governments, the United States, and the ubiquitous system of capitalism.

Several of the groups, including the Red Brigades in Italy, the RAF in West Germany's Federal Republic, Revolutionary Organization 17 November (17N) in Greece, and Revolutionary Road in Turkey, became sources of serious concern as they killed and kidnapped prominent politicians, bankers, businesspeople, and government officials. Their efforts, however, hardly constituted insurgencies. They were not like the Viet Cong. Virtually none of these groups possessed or could seriously hope to win a mass constituency of (largely non-existent) peasants and workers. Their appeal and coercive potential were limited. What they could hope to do was identify their cause with that of Third World national independence movements and an international proletariat.

The Palestinians, Latin America's urban guerrillas, and the Viet Cong offered practical substitutes for what the European terrorist groups lacked, namely a serious cause with a mass constituency. By identifying themselves with these Third World causes, the European terrorist organizations could claim to be acting on behalf of the "wretched of the Earth"[8] and so assert their legitimacy. In some cases the links were more than ideological affinity. The PFLP, for example, developed operational ties with German terrorist bands to the point of carrying out joint operations, including the July 1976 skyjacking of an Air France flight.

Despite the sense of identification with Third World causes, the European and North American terrorists were essentially small clandestine groups with little popular support beyond university campuses and counter-culture enclaves. It was the presence of such groups that grew to be the center of attention for scholars like Brian Jenkins, David Rapoport, Martha Crenshaw, Yonah Alexander, Bruce Hoffman, and a long list of others who became the founders of a new academic field of terrorism studies.

The focus of these founders of terrorism studies was largely on the stand-alone terrorist groups operating in the industrialized democracies. Given their small size and clandestine operating techniques, the founders sought to understand these terrorist bands in terms of small group dynamics and the individual personality traits of key figures.[9]

In addition to the focus on small clandestine groups operating within or targeting from without the industrial democracies, analysts drawn to the new field of terrorism studies tended in large part to limit their work to the revolutionary left. It was the terrorist groups that attacked American and NATO targets that drew the most attention. Other groups, including the far-right, neo-fascist, or neo-Nazi groups active in Italy, Turkey, and the United States and the "death squads" in Latin America, drew little attention despite their high levels of violence. And, with the exception of Northern Ireland, terrorism analysts wrote little about the relationship between religion and violence. For the Irish republicans and nationalists, religion is part of their identity. Unlike those of their successors in the "fourth wave" of terrorism,[10] the objectives of the Irish republicans were not religious.

Obviously much has changed since the founders of terrorism studies made their initial observations. These changes began with the Soviet invasion of Afghanistan in 1979 and the invasion of the Holy Mosque in Mecca by followers of a man claiming to be the Mahdi, or Redeemer. Since this time, religious doctrines – Salafi-jihadi doctrines especially – have become the organizing principles of the "new" terrorist and insurgents. This includes al Qaeda and an impressive list of groups committed to waging a holy war against the West and those governments in the Muslim world thought to be infected by Western ideas and unable or unwilling to adopt Sharia law as the basis of their legal and political systems.

Since the events of 9/11, there has been an enormous increase in scholarly work focusing on the terrorist phenomenon, especially its religious roots in the Middle East and South Asia. The same may be said about the subjects of insurgency and counterinsurgency. The fighting over Iraq, Afghanistan, Somalia, Sudan, and Yemen, along with other armed struggles, has stimulated a substantial volume of work devoted to the nature of insurgencies and the techniques the United States and its allies might use in countering these insurgents, at least those hostile to Western interests.

The problem, as we see it and as Michael Boyle points out, is that the study of terrorism proceeded largely independently of the study of insurgency and counterinsurgency.[11] One reason for this essentially two-track approach to what is really a common problem concerns the origins of these areas of study, academic and otherwise. Modern terrorism studies began with an investigation of the stand-alone groups operating primarily in the

West during the 1960s and 1970s. These were the relatively weak groups actively attempting to bring about revolution within otherwise peaceful Western democracies. In contrast, studies in insurgency and counterinsurgency grew out of efforts by British and French writers interested in understanding how their countries lost their empires to the seemingly weaker forces of insurgents. These views, including the lessons they taught, were then digested by American analysts and applied to the fighting over Vietnam.

In the twenty-first century it seems clear that studies of terrorism and insurgency belong together. Insurgents currently active in the Middle East, Africa, and Asia employ terrorism in conjunction with other tactics to advance their operations. These groups are also the participants in wars of the twenty-first century, and it is these groups that seem to pose the greatest challenge to national and international security, not only within the weak or failed states in which they operate but also in other contexts in which they may gain followers.

Overview

We expect that insurgent groups use terrorism strategically. A group's objectives and operational capabilities factor into strategic decision-making. We also expect that patterns in insurgent groups' use of terrorism in the context of wider-scale armed conflicts will reflect these strategies and constraints. We anticipate that some groups will use terrorism primarily during the early "agitation" phase of their insurgent efforts, while others will rely more heavily on terrorist attacks later in their insurgency. Still others may use terrorism throughout an armed confrontation. Patterns in these groups' resort to terrorism may be indicative of changes in strategies, along with changes in objectives and operational capabilities.

If we are correct in these views, we should be able to demonstrate these linkages by examining what the available data suggests. Accordingly, we derive information from a variety of sources, including datasets on terrorism, insurgencies, and various categories of wider-scale warfare. We use this data to identify patterns in insurgent groups' use of terrorism in the context of wider-scale armed conflicts. We follow this with analyses of illustrative cases, those corresponding to the patterns we identify. We draw conclusions from our analyses of these armed groups and the contexts within which each of these patterns emerge.

In conducting this analysis, we use a combination of qualitative and statistical methods. The unit of analysis is the insurgent group. The tactic of interest is terrorism. The insurgents of interest in this study use terrorism under one of two conditions: the absence or presence of wider-scale warfare. Wider-scale warfare includes armed conflicts, civil wars, and other types of internal wars. Insurgent groups can and do participate in each of these types of wars. The phenomena of most interest in this study are the frequencies of terrorist attacks throughout an armed group's engagement in insurgency and war.

Description of the data

Answering the questions of interest to this study requires information not only on terrorist attacks, but also on the attackers, particularly when these are insurgent groups, and the wider-scale wars in which they participate. As such, we use data on terrorist attacks, including the perpetrators, places, and times of attacks. We also require information on insurgents, understanding these to include a variety of types of groups using a combination of tactics in order to achieve some type of domestic political change. We also require information on wars, along with the start and end dates of wars, their locations, and the participants.

We gathered information from several sources. These include the Global Terrorism Database (GTD), the COW Project, and Max Boot's data on insurgencies.[12] We supplemented these with three additional sources of information on armed conflicts: the Uppsala Conflict Data Program/Peace Research Institute of Oslo (UCDP/PRIO) Armed Conflict Dataset, James Fearon and David Laitin's list of civil wars and Ben Connable and Martin Libicki's list of insurgencies.[13]

Terrorism

Our interest in terrorism follows a noticeable trend. If we glance at the frequency of terrorist events, we observe an increasing number of terrorist attacks over time, especially by groups engaging in modern-day warfare. If we plotted these frequencies on a graph there would be hills and valleys, to be sure, but the overall pattern is upward. The closer in time we come to 2015, the more terrorism we find.

The GTD, managed by the National Consortium for the Study of Terrorism and Responses to Terrorism (START) at the University of Maryland, provides data on terrorist incidents for the period of time including 1970 through 2014.[14] Overall we are dealing with almost 142,000 events that took place in more than 200 distinct locations over a forty-five-year period.[15] From this data, we make note of the perpetrators of attacks and the timing, location, and frequency of attacks.

Before we count terrorist attacks, we must identify which events we will include in our count. We check whether or not incidents match our definition of terrorism in order to confirm that we are studying what we say we are studying. The GTD includes events that may be designated as "not terrorism" on the basis of one or more definitional criteria. A small proportion of the attacks included in the dataset may be more appropriately labeled as examples of guerrilla warfare or criminal behavior. The GTD provides several criteria by which we may discern the match between an incident and predetermined definitional criteria. We use these criteria to sort and filter the data so as to identify, where possible, which attacks most closely match the definition of terrorism on which we rely.

We use several of the GTD's filters to eliminate cases that may not match our definition. The GTD provides three criteria by which to designate an attack as a "terrorist" attack. In order, these three "terrorism criteria" require that an attack (1) be used to achieve a specific goal, (2) represent an attempt to influence a "larger audience," and (3) not qualify as "legitimate warfare."[16] Around a quarter of the attacks included in the GTD dataset do not meet all three of the definitional elements used for distinguishing terrorism from other types of attacks.

In some cases there are also "doubts" regarding whether an attack should be deemed "terrorism proper."[17] The GTD also allows us to eliminate cases in which there is further "doubt" that an event is an example of terrorism beyond the three criteria. Having "doubt" suggests that an event may not be an example of terrorism. We treat this as a fourth criterion.

There are also differences in the coding of earlier and later incidents in the GTD data. The "terrorism proper" label, for instance, is available more consistently for attacks taking place since 1997.[18] An incident may meet the three criteria outlined above (specific goals, influence, and nature of attack), yet doubts may remain regarding the appropriateness of giving the attack the terrorism label. There are more than a few cases in which this occurs ($n > 2800$, or around 2 percent of "terrorist" incidents).

These four criteria say nothing specific about the nature of the groups, themselves. They do not, for instance, include information regarding whether or not insurgent groups hold or are attempting to hold territory. It would not be far-fetched to assume that guerrilla forces engaging in insurgency and warfare could carry out attacks meeting each of the three criteria. The data does not include information regarding the sizes of the groups, whether their memberships number in the dozens or in the hundreds or thousands. The data is silent on how much support the armed groups receive from their presumed constituency or outside supporters. The data does not provide information on the objectives of the groups, such as whether their goals

Table 2.1 Frequency of terrorist events by country (1970–2013)*

	Middle East, North Africa, Near East	Asia and the Pacific	Eastern Europe and former Soviet Asia	West	Latin America	Sub-Saharan Africa
More than 2,500 terrorist incidents	Iraq Pakistan Afghanistan Turkey Algeria	India Philippines		Northern Ireland Spain	Colombia Peru El Salvador	
Between 1,000 and 2,500 terrorist incidents	Israel Lebanon	Thailand Sri Lanka	Russia	United States Italy Corsica	Chile	Nigeria Somalia South Africa
Between 250 and 1,000 terrorist incidents	West Bank and Gaza Strip Yemen Egypt Syria Iran Libya	Nepal Bangladesh Indonesia		France Greece Great Britain West Germany	Guatemala Nicaragua Argentina Mexico	Angola Sudan Uganda Kenya Burundi
Between 100 and 250 terrorist incidents		Myanmar Japan Cambodia China	Georgia Kosovo Yugoslavia	Germany Ireland Belgium Portugal	Bolivia Puerto Rico Honduras Ecuador Venezuela Brazil	Mozambique Congo (Kinshasa) Rwanda Ethiopia

* The states and territories in each cell are listed from highest to lowest frequency of terrorist attacks.

Source: "Global Terrorism Database [Data File]," 2015.

include gaining attention, influencing electoral outcomes, inciting revolution, engaging in a war of attrition, or some combination of these.[19] Moreover, insurgent groups can (and do) attempt to achieve some of their objectives by using terrorism while also engaging in other unconventional tactics, including those associated with guerrilla warfare.

It is useful to keep in mind that terrorism is a tactic and a terrorist is an actor who uses this tactic. Accordingly, the insurgents using terrorism are also terrorists.[20] For most parts of our analysis, we limit our study to the attacks that meet all four criteria. We apply all three definitional features and exclude "ambiguous" cases (those that GTD coders label as "doubt terrorism proper").[21] We use these criteria to identify the events most closely matching our definition of terrorism. Once these have been identified, we examine where and to what magnitude terrorism has occurred, giving particular attention to the places where insurgents operate and where there is evidence of wider-scale warfare.

The overall pattern in the frequencies of attacks recorded by GTD does not change when incidents are included or excluded on the basis the three terrorism criteria and the "doubt terrorism" criterion. In fact, there is little difference in the frequencies of (1) all attacks, (2) attacks meeting the three terrorism criteria, and (3) attacks meeting the three terrorism criteria, which are not labeled as "doubt terrorism" (see Figure 2.1).

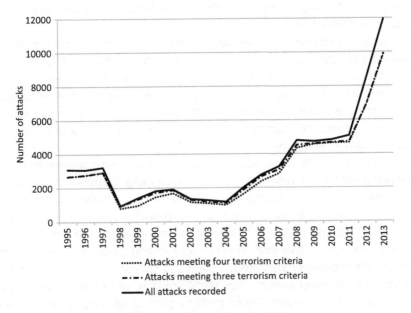

Figure 2.1 Categories of attacks

Source: "Global Terrorism Database [Data File]," 2014.

The frequencies of recorded terrorist attacks may not be comparable across cases. This is due in part to incomplete information. In addition, the count of terrorist attacks does not provide a direct measure of violence, especially in the context of warfare, where violence takes other conventional and unconventional forms. Unsurprisingly, the locations with the highest frequencies of terrorist attacks are also known to have experienced episodes of wider-scale armed conflict. These include terrorism "hot spots," places where large numbers of terrorist attacks have occurred, among them Iraq, Pakistan, and Afghanistan.[22] Other locations stand out for their relative lack of terrorism, including the Palestinian territories (perhaps because many attacks took place within Israel proper) and the Central American countries where guerrillas were also called terrorists.

The numbers of terrorist attacks are difficult to count in cases where warfare coincides with terrorism and terrorist incidents may be difficult to record due to a lack of information regarding attacks. Syria is an interesting, ongoing case for preliminary analysis. After more than three years of civil war involving insurgent groups, it is likely that Syria will see a considerable increase in the number of recorded terrorist attacks taking place within the state's borders. This is an important theater in which insurgent groups are using terrorism and other unconventional tactics of warfare and in which the more successful insurgent groups, as they gain strength, may make a transition to "regular" forms of warfare. It is too soon to know whether this will happen and what will be the outcome of this civil war.

In order to further disaggregate the data, we consider a fifth criterion, beyond the four mentioned above: the targets of attacks. This criterion allows us additional insight into the perpetrators of attacks. Attacks on harder targets provide some evidence that a group may be engaging in or capable of engaging the state more directly. Attacks on softer targets also tell us something about the objectives of a group, a group's levels and sources of support, and its strength.

Giving attention to harder and softer targets serves two purposes. First, our interest is not limited to groups using terrorist attacks. Terrorism is just one of a number of tactics insurgents may use. Our primary interest is in the timing of terrorist attacks in the context of insurgency and wider-scale warfare. Moreover, because we are investigating insurgency as well as terrorism, it is appropriate to give consideration to attacks meeting the GTD's four terrorism criteria that are perpetrated against state and non-state entities and against armed and unarmed entities. We recognize that attacks on harder state, police, and military targets may be part of a guerrilla campaign or an evolving threat from an insurgent group. While we may define attacks on state, police, and military targets as something distinct from terrorism, those attacks that otherwise meet the terrorism criteria provided by the GTD may be viewed as part of a campaign that includes terrorism.

Second, identifying patterns in targets is one way to distinguish between attackers who are simply terrorists and those who are also guerrilla fighters or insurgents. This distinction may offer insight into the strength, sophistication, and level of domestic or foreign support enjoyed by an insurgent group. Our interest is in distinguishing between attacks on harder targets, such as a state, military, police, or other armed groups, and those on softer targets, including civilians and private entities. Attacks on harder targets require the types of capabilities often associated with guerrilla groups, whereas attacks on softer targets do not. Softer targets are generally easier to access – they are everywhere – and less capable of protecting or defending themselves. It follows that the groups that are able to attack harder targets tend to be stronger, more sophisticated, better supported, and more likely to raise the level of conflict than those that are only capable of attacking softer ones.

Despite our interest in observing patterns of terrorist attacks, we expect that insurgents will carry out attacks on harder and softer targets at one time or another. Smaller, clandestine bands of insurgents (or would-be insurgents) should be less capable of attacking harder targets and would presumably concentrate attacks on softer ones. This may change as the insurgent groups gain strength and capacity.

We also recognize that contexts matter. The presence of wider-scale armed conflict affects the types of entities armed groups can and will target. Government policies and responses to insurgent groups may also affect the types of targets insurgent groups attack. The nationalist efforts of republicans in Northern Ireland and Basques in Spain help to illustrate this point. The republican campaign in Northern Ireland took the lives of a higher number of soldiers than police. Nationalist terrorists in Spain, on the other hand, aimed their deadly attacks at Spain's police forces, claiming a higher number of lives of law enforcement officials than of soldiers. Attacks carried out by both groups claimed civilian lives at approximately the same rate (as a percentage of total deaths attributed to the groups). Ignacio Sanchez-Cuenca explains the difference in patterns of military and law enforcement deaths in the United Kingdom and Spain as a function of these states' different approaches to countering the threats posed by these groups. The British answered terrorism originating in Northern Ireland with a military response, while the Spanish employed their police forces for the job.[23] This difference, however, is not as pronounced in the numbers of attacks perpetrated by terrorists, in general, or republican terrorists in Northern Ireland, in particular. Instead, the frequency of attacks on police has increased over time while the frequency of attacks on the military has decreased. The number of people killed in IRA attacks on military targets is approximately twice the number of people killed in attacks on police.[24]

A group's objectives will also influence target choice. Targeting civilians may create fear and discourage challenges aimed at the terrorists; targeting the state, military, or police may be part of a war of attrition or provocation.[25] In short, even though patterns in target choice may be informative, these patterns may not be a sufficient indicator of group strength, sophistication, and support.

Identifying whether or not terrorist attacks take place in a given place or at a given time is also not sufficient for answering our questions regarding the timing of terrorism within wider-scale warfare. The presence of a terrorist group and the timing, location, and frequency of attacks do not tell us enough when considered independently of each other and of the broader context. In order to tie the use of terrorism to a stage of insurgency, we must show that the insurgents or would-be insurgents are likely to be the ones responsible for the terrorism we observe. To accomplish this, we must identify, to the extent possible, who the likely perpetrators were. The GTD dataset allows us to do this in some instances but not in all.

This is an issue to which we must devote some attention in order to answer our question of the timing of terrorism in the context of wider-scale warfare. Many of the incidents included in the GTD dataset lack information regarding the attackers and, as a consequence, also of their intent. The missing information of most interest to us is the "unknown" attacker. On average, almost half of attacks included in the dataset were carried out by "unknown" actors or "others." The share is only slightly smaller for those carrying out attacks meeting the terrorism criteria. It is not surprising that there is considerable variation across contexts. The proportions of "unknown" attackers are smaller in some places than others (e.g., 13 percent of attackers in Northern Ireland versus 49 percent in India).

Our interest is in identifying the numbers of attacks perpetrated by particular insurgent groups. It is not quite as simple as ascertaining whether or not there is terrorism in a particular place or at a particular time. Oftentimes there is more than one group using terrorism within a given context. Sometimes armed groups use terrorism while competing against each other. An argument has been made that the Palestinian groups have done this in an attempt to outbid each other.[26] Loyalist paramilitaries traded attacks with Irish republicans in Northern Ireland in response to republican attacks as well as in support of the status quo in Northern Ireland. Other times the groups operating within the same context are unrelated (e.g., anti-abortion terrorists, animal rights terrorists, and left-wing revolutionary terrorists in the United States).

Again, the case of terrorism originating out of Northern Ireland provides a useful example. The IRA was the most active of the republican groups in

Northern Ireland for a period of time between 1969 and 1999. Others, includ-ing various loyalist paramilitaries and competing republican groups, also used terrorism during this time. Their attacks occurred during the same period of time and in roughly the same places – in some cases only blocks apart in the divided neighborhoods of West Belfast. When looking at patterns of terror-ism in Northern Ireland, however, we must pay attention to the numbers of incidents attributed to the various groups credited with carrying them out. In other words, we should not take descriptions of terrorism across the whole of Northern Ireland as a reflection of patterns of republican (or loyalist) terrorism.

In addition, when disaggregating the data, we should not focus solely on the terrorists' countries of origin. Some of the armed groups of interest in this study have operated in and outside of their home countries, though the attacks perpetrated outside of an insurgent group's home country tend to account for a smaller proportion of the total number of attacks carried out by these groups. Examples of attacks carried out close to home, but outside of the group's home base, include those carried out by Palestinians in Israel, by Tamil insurgents in India, and by Kashmiri separatists across the India–Pakistan border. Attacks by Lebanon's Hezbollah in Argentina, Egypt's al Gama'a al-Islamiyya's in Croatia, and by al Qaeda and its affiliates in the United States, Europe, and elsewhere are just a few examples of terrorist groups traveling distances to carry out attacks. These still account for a small number and proportion of these groups' total number of attacks.

Identifying attackers is a simpler task when terrorists take credit for their actions and when the attacks occur in places where information is available regarding the details of an attack. It may also be easier when there are two clear sides in a conflict, though this is not necessarily the case. We can expect it to be more difficult to identify the perpetrators and, hence, have an idea of their intent, when there are many insurgents operating in roughly the same area at the same time. This has been the case in India, where several insurgencies are ongoing and coinciding. India's Sikh, Naxalite, and Kashmiri insurgents are among those whose attacks overlap in terms of time, if not also in terms of place. At this point, a more detailed description of the data should be useful.

A majority of the nearly 142,000 attacks included in the GTD database (including attacks through the end of 2014) meet the definitional require-ments to be labeled "terrorism," as specified in this analysis. We apply the GTD's filters in order to limit the cases we consider when referring to terrorist attacks. Close to 85 percent of incidents, or over 120,000, meet the stricter "terrorism" criteria regarding group objectives and intentions, the nature of the attack, and the absence of "doubt," as recorded by the GTD.[27] Because our interest is in an evolution in the tactics used by insurgent groups in the context of wider-scale warfare, we find it useful in some parts of our analysis to report the total numbers of terrorist attacks regardless of the type of target. This includes those attacks that are perpetrated against the state – governments, military, and police – as well as those carried out against other armed targets, such as violent political parties and other armed groups. We find it useful to point out patterns in terms of attacks against these harder targets and those aimed at softer, civilian targets.

In order to illustrate some of the patterns, we report the numbers of all attacks and terrorist incidents recorded by the GTD. We also report the total numbers of terrorist attacks in three illustrative cases: India, Northern Ireland, and the United States. These three cases show some of the cross-national variation in terms of the recording of data. One of the most notable points of difference is the discrepancy in terms of "unknown" perpetrators and unattributed attacks in India as compared to the United States and Northern Ireland. The number of "unknown" perpetrators in India is 48 percent, which is slightly above average in comparison to the database as a whole (46 percent). The proportions of attacks carried out by "unknown" perpetrators in the United States and Northern Ireland is much lower (12 percent) (see Table 2.2).

In addition, a number of the incidents meeting the terrorism criteria are attacks on governments, militaries, police, and other violent armed groups. By some definitions and in some contexts, these types of targets could be considered combatant. A government represents the state, also playing a role in counterterrorism and COIN policy-making and implementation. Military and police tend to be armed and may be employed in the implementation of

Table 2.2 Patterns in the GTD data

	All attacks	Terrorist incidents*	Terrorism in India	Terrorism in Northern Ireland	Terrorism in the United States
Total	125,087	92,996	6,472	3,029	1,914
Unknown	56,905 (45%)	39,380 (42%)	3,045 (47%)	373 (12%)	226 (12%)
Other Target*	464 (4%)	346 (4%)	76 (1%)	10 (0%)	0 (0%)
Government	20,114 (16%)	18,152 (20%)	1,265 (20%)	211 (7%)	360 (19%)
Police	17,168 (14%)	14,826 (16%)	1,268 (20%)	701 (23%)	131 (7%)
Military	16,867 (13%)	3,078 (3%)	176 (3%)	61 (2%)	80 (4%)
Other violent groups	3,070 (2%)	2,183 (2%)	191 (3%)	129 (4%)	12 (1%)

* These counts include only cases designated in the GTD as terrorism.

Source: "Global Terrorism Database [Data File]," 2014.

counterterrorism and COIN activities. Violent armed groups, including violent political parties, are defined as such because they engage in various forms of violence or armed confrontation.

Our interest is in the pattern of insurgent groups' attacks, including patterns of attacks on harder and softer targets, focusing on incidents that are identified as terrorism. For this reason, we include attacks on these harder and softer targets (or combatant and noncombatant targets), though we report distinctions between the two. We do not expect the GTD database to include attacks that would be categorized as guerrilla attacks or insurgent warfare, when these do not otherwise match the description of terrorism or the stricter terrorism criteria used to identify "ambiguous" cases, or cases in which there is "doubt" regarding applying the terrorism label. In addition, we expect incidents classified as terrorist attacks to make up a smaller proportion of total attacks taking place in the context of wider-scale warfare than they would outside of wider-scale warfare. In short, terrorism is likely the main tactic of insurgents outside of warfare; other unconventional tactics will coincide with the use of terrorism within the context of wider-scale warfare.

Within the subset of incidents meeting the stricter GTD criteria for terrorism, nearly 20 percent target government entities (including domestic and diplomatic). More than 15 percent target police. While these descriptions are similar for all attacks and terrorist attacks, one difference is worth noting: attacks on military targets make up a much smaller proportion of attacks that meet the terrorism criteria than those included in the total incident count. Whereas military targets make up 13 percent of all attacks, they make up only 3 percent of attacks meeting the terrorism criteria (see Table 2.2). An explanation for this difference is relatively straightforward. Militaries are more likely than other types of targets to be viewed as combatant targets. Attacks on military targets are more likely to take place within a context of wider-scale warfare and are more likely to be labeled as something other than terrorism. Attacks on military targets may also correspond with an escalation to civil war or another type of armed conflict, which is more likely be considered as a type of legitimate warfare, as designated by the GTD terrorism criteria. In addition, attacks on military bases and infrastructure tend to require a relatively organized and sophisticated armed force. The forces capable of carrying out such attacks are less likely to be small bands of terrorists operating in isolation of a broader base of support. Of course, there is some variation in the capabilities required to attack military targets. Attacks on individual members of the military require less sophistication; they also have a far more limited impact on an adversary's military capabilities. Moreover, attacks carried out against members of the armed forces or police forces who are off-duty are more likely to resemble terrorist attacks.

We expect insurgents to attack various targets – including harder and softer targets – and we expect such attacks to be carried out for many of the same reasons. Insurgents can and do attack harder and softer targets during a single campaign, sometimes in a single attack. An attack can create fear or terror regardless of the type of target. Moreover, considering the adage that we will "know terrorism when we see it," it should not be surprising that what one person sees as terrorism is not necessarily what others see. Insurgents may not distinguish among targets on a combatant-noncombatant basis as defined by outside observers, further trivializing such a distinction. From the perspectives of insurgent groups, attacks on governments, militaries, and civilians may serve as part of a single campaign and may be used as part of a strategy to achieve the same ends.

Debates have raged in the United States in recent years over the classifications of events as terrorism or as acts of terror. We may wonder whether these are one classification or multiple ones. Perhaps a relevant distinction lies in the targets of attacks, the nature of the attackers, or something else. Alternatively, there may be no real distinction. The September 11, 2012, attack on the American embassy in Benghazi, Libya has been called many things, including "terrorism," an "act of terror," and an "act of terrorism."[28] These designations are interesting for the implications that these labels hold. For this study, the dilemmas of such classifications are interesting to the extent that they describe attacks that are part of a pattern of attacks used by insurgent groups to achieve particular objectives. Consequently, the GTD includes an attack on the American consulate in Benghazi on September 11, 2012, stating that this attack meets all three terrorism criteria and that there is no "doubt" of terrorism in this case. The GTD lists two (rather than four) fatalities in the attack.[29]

Issues such as these get to the heart of one of the most important considerations in dealing with terrorism data: its limitations. For our purposes, we accept the limitations of the available data. We recognize that the many "unknowns" will likely never be known. Assumptions can be made about the likely perpetrators of attacks on the basis of which groups are active at a given time, in a given place, and with a given set of grievances. Such assumptions, however, will do little to close the gap created by the large proportion of cases that will remain unattributed. We also recognize that the sheer number of attacks and attackers prohibits our in-depth study of the majority of these incidents.

We also expect that attacks taking place in some places and at some times will be underrepresented in the overall count of terrorist incidents. The GTD records 361 incidents meeting the four terrorism criteria in the United States in 1970 and 516 terrorist attacks meeting the same criteria in the world during the same year. If the numbers are correct, terrorism in the United States accounted for nearly 70 percent of the total number of terrorist attacks recorded in that year – worldwide.[30]

In fact, Vietnam comes to mind as one place where we might expect to find more recorded incidents of terrorism than are included in the GTD data. The Viet Cong was known to use terrorism against local Vietnamese as a means of instilling fear and controlling the population while engaging in its war for control of the territory.[31] In 1962, Raymond L. Garthoff described the Viet Cong's use of terror as "selective" and aimed at "local representatives of the incumbent regime in order to destroy its control."[32] Carol Winkler describes this "Communist terrorism" as a public rationale for America's involvement in Vietnam.[33] Even though most of the terrorist attacks likely occurred before the GTD's records began in 1970, the terrorism presumably continued at least through 1972, prior to the January 1973 ceasefire agreement and the subsequent withdrawal of America's combat forces.

In contrast to expectations, only one terrorist attack is recorded in South Vietnam during the early 1970s. This attack, however, had no relation to the insurgency or the Vietnamese. The GTD describes this attack as a plane bombing, which took place in the air above Vietnam during the summer of 1972 while war was ongoing on the ground. The flight did not originate in or intend to land in Vietnam; however, the plane's wreckage fell within Vietnamese territory. It has been suggested that the reason for the bombing was criminal (murder and insurance fraud) rather than political, raising questions regarding whether or not the event would meet a stricter definition of terrorism.[34] Beyond this event, there are no recorded incidents of terrorism or other attacks perpetrated by the Viet Cong against local Vietnamese populations within the GTD data collection.

Insurgent attacks on civilians are not all that uncommon. Intimidation of local populations is one of the strategies of terrorism.[35] This is a strategy that has been used in places such as Vietnam, Peru, Algeria, and Afghanistan and by groups as diverse as the Viet Cong, the Shining Path, the National Liberation Front, and the Taliban, in pursuit of their communist, nationalist, or religious ideologies.[36] Although the issue of what appears to be missing data on terrorism in Vietnam may be an extreme example, it is likely that records of other similarly situated attacks, occurring largely out of sight and during wider-scale armed conflicts, are also missing. The inclusion or exclusion of incidents may have been influenced by the timing and location of the acts, including whether or not the acts were observed or reported; the presence or absence of wider-scale warfare; and the designations of the groups responsible for the attacks.

Insurgents

The focus of this study is on insurgents' use of terrorism in attempts to initiate or continue an insurgency. It has not been uncommon to refer to insurgents as those fighting insurgencies without giving much additional consideration to the meaning of the term or how insurgents may differ from other actors using similar tactics. While it is far easier to find a definition of insurgency in the literature on the topic, it is not quite as easy to find a definition for insurgent. Various terms are sometimes used interchangeably in references to insurgents. Discussions of the individuals, groups, and movements involved in insurgencies may refer to these actors as guerrilla forces, irregulars, terrorists, militants, paramilitaries, or bandits. This mixture of terminology may lead one to question how (if at all) insurgent groups differ from other violent armed groups.

Max Boot describes insurgency, including conflicts involving guerrillas, as a form of "low-intensity conflict."[37] Stathis Kalyvas and Matthew Kocher describe insurgency, "guerrilla war," and "irregular war" as synonyms.[38] Insurgencies are a form of unconventional warfare to the extent that conventional warfare is thought to involve militaries facing each other on battlefields.[39] Insurgent groups are non-state actors employing irregular forces and small-war tactics against conventional armed forces, or the armed forces of a state. Insurgents are the armed actors who engage in the low-intensity conflict or irregular warfare associated with insurgencies.

The tactics of insurgent groups include terrorism and guerrilla tactics, or some combination of both. Insurgent groups rely on terrorism and guerrilla tactics because they are weaker actors facing stronger opponents. These tactics are not reserved for a particular type of armed group or a particular type of warfare. The ideologies of insurgent groups vary widely.[40] Many insurgent groups seek political change; others may be better understood as "preservationists,"[41] which are dedicated to "keeping things the way they are" (or were, also implying a need for change).[42] The U.S. Army's COIN Manual describes insurgents as a diverse and changing collection of actors, who nevertheless share one important characteristic: "In all cases, insurgents aim to force political change; any military action is secondary and subordinate, a means to an end."[43]

It appears that groups engaging in this type of warfare increasingly seek attention and legitimacy, use the media strategically, and organize politically. It also appears that insurgent groups are increasingly successful, often benefiting from external support for their insurgent activities.[44]

To clarify, we are not interested in all users of terrorist tactics; rather, we are interested in those who play a role – or seek to play a role – in bringing about the types of outcomes that often coincide with wider-scale warfare.

We include insurgent groups that succeed in bringing about the wider-scale warfare often associated with insurgency, as well as those would-be insurgents that have failed to do so.[45] In order to identify insurgent groups, we turned to Max Boot's work on insurgencies and, especially, the list of insurgents he includes in the appendix to *Invisible Armies*.[46]

The list to which we refer includes what Boot describes as "all significant insurgent movements since 1775." He explains his definition of "significant" insurgents as those who "caused some deaths and drew some attention from contemporaries and historians."[47] We find Max Boot's list of insurgents particularly useful for its inclusion of those would-be insurgent groups that did not bring about insurgency, much less achieve their objectives, or cause many deaths, but nevertheless managed to pose a challenge to authorities within their states and receive some attention in the process.[48]

A number of these insurgent groups have not engaged or have yet to engage in what most would define as wider-scale warfare. Boot includes in his list of insurgencies many that would be excluded from other databases due to their limited lethality, size, or impact. He compares these insurgents to "start-up companies" that "never get very far."[49] We also note that Boot's list of insurgent groups includes some whose activities are ongoing. These, as he points out, are an important part of the story of contemporary insurgency.[50] In some cases, insurgent groups may be considered successful for having survived for a period of time. On the other hand, their longevity is not necessarily an indicator of their success; it may be the opposite. An insurgent group may continue its operations but be unable to achieve its objectives. These groups may be among those enjoying sufficient support or resources so as to continue their efforts.

Because we are working with data on terrorist events that is confined to the post-1970 time period, our interest is with many of the insurgent groups that are still active in the second decade of the twenty-first century. These current operators – among them the Islamic State and al Qaeda, as well as Syria's al-Nusra Front, Nigeria's Boko Haram, Somalia's al Shabaab, China's Uighur minority, Colombia's FARC, Afghanistan and Pakistan's Talibans, and India and Pakistan's Kashmiri separatists, to name just a few – are also of broader contemporary interest in the study of terrorism, political violence, and warfare in the twenty-first century.[51]

Boot's data goes as far back as 1775, to the time when America's colonists engaged in insurgency against Britain's regular military force in the context of the colonists' fight for independence. We look ahead to 1970 and include in our count those insurgents whose operations took place after this time. While our primary interest is in those groups whose operations began after 1970, we analyze patterns in the use of terrorism for insurgents whose operations began prior to 1970 but continued into the 1970s. We also include in our analysis groups that continue to engage in insurgency, looking in particular at patterns in terrorist attacks before and during wider-scale warfare. We include these cases for comparative and informational purposes. While we can examine these groups' use of terrorism in the context of insurgency, we cannot comment specifically on the frequency of any groups' pre-1970 use of terrorism and, as a result, on the early stages of some insurgent campaigns. We also cannot comment on whether there is more or less terrorism during the latter stages of insurgencies that began prior to 1970. The same holds for those insurgencies continuing today.

Using Boot's list, we gather information on 167 insurgent groups operating during the period between 1970 and 2012 (see Appendix 1). The insurgent groups are diverse, having varying ideologies, objectives, and operating contexts. The list includes insurgents engaging in civil wars in Iraq and Syria during the first and second decades of the twenty-first century and would-be insurgents carrying out attacks in the 1970s in the United States. Some insurgents have persisted in their efforts for decades, while others disappeared within a decade of their formation. The higher median lifespan of the insurgent groups discussed here suggests that organizational and operational capabilities were above average for this subset of terrorist groups. Some insurgents have participated in wider-scale warfare, others have not.

While relying on Boot's list, we should clarify that our count does not include 167 distinct or unitary insurgent groups. It is not uncommon for the number of insurgent groups to change over the duration of an insurgency. Insurgent groups may cooperate and form alliances; they may establish umbrella organizations; they may split into competing factions. We began with Boot's list of insurgents.

Locations of insurgencies

This analysis requires identifying the main locations of insurgent groups' operations. It also requires matching terrorist attacks to these groups and the time period of wider-scale warfare in which insurgent groups are involved. In essence, the patterns in the use of terrorism that are of interest here are, at least to some extent, place-based and group-based. Insurgent groups' operations tend to be geographically bound. Insurgent groups are, by definition, weaker forces operating within a state (or states). A number of factors will affect their resort to terrorism. In addition to their organizational capabilities, other features of their operational context should have an effect on whether and how an insurgent group uses terrorism. These features may include the number of other insurgent groups operating in the same context, the frequency of other groups' use of terrorism, local and external support, and the presence or absence of wider-scale warfare.

We take locations into account when placing insurgent groups and insurgencies into the broader contexts within which they operate. Insurgents may reside in one state, yet carry out attacks in another state. Historically, at least, this would be a nearby state. Alternatively, their presumed constituencies may reside in more than one state and – as in the cases of some Islamist groups – they may reside within a larger cultural region. While earlier anarchist and communist terrorism had international aspects, it seems that the objectives of insurgent groups today have become more global than local.[52] The most obvious examples of this are the transnational terrorist networks affiliated with al Qaeda and its competitor, ISIL. Other examples include affiliates of these groups, which draw on the ideologies and resources of al Qaeda or ISIL, while having interests that may, in fact, be primarily local. Among these are Pakistan's Tehrik-e Taliban, Somalia's al Shabaab, and the Islamic Movement of Uzbekistan, to name just a few. In these and other cases, insurgent groups' interests cross borders. They may collaborate with like-minded groups, recruiting militants, finding safe haven, or spreading fear across porous borders. This type of action was demonstrated in a 2015 attack at Kenya's Garissa University College, which was credited to al Shabaab. During the incident, the attackers killed scores of Kenyans, most of them students.[53]

While there are similarities among groups within the Salafi-jihadist movement, there are also differences. The approach to achieving group objectives is among these differences. The group's dealings with its adversaries have been brutal. ISIL has attacked civilians, including Muslims and non-Muslims. ISIL has also engaged in confrontations against its former allies, the al-Nusra Front and al Qaeda.[54] In addition, ISIL has done something that al Qaeda has not. The group declared a caliphate, using force to secure its claim. ISIL has also declared a caliph, the group's leader Abu Bakr al-Baghdadi.

While the declaration of a caliphate may seem like a victory for the moment, the use of force to achieve and maintain this gives the impression that the movement is not sufficiently appealing to find support within the community in which it operates. This may not bode well for the group sustaining itself in the long run. Claims that the group appeals to its recruits through its use of violence and conquest, including conquest in sexual terms, suggest that the group has departed in important ways from the religious foundations of the larger Salafi-jihadist movement.[55] Moreover, al-Baghdadi's assertions, which include the creation of a caliphate with himself as caliph in parts of Syria and Iraq, have reinforced divisions within the larger movement.

There are many other examples of insurgents operating across borders.

These include the Lord's Resistance Army, which has had operations in Uganda, Sudan, and the Democratic Republic of Congo, and may have extended beyond these three states. The PLO and Lebanese Hezbollah have operated in and around Israel. Many groups operate on either side of the Afghanistan–Pakistan and Pakistan–India borders. In each of these cases, their objectives and presumed constituencies cross the same borders.

Rwanda's ethnic conflicts provide another example of insurgents crossing borders. Rwanda's various militant groups have at various times crossed borders into neighboring countries, hiding among refugees, where they could recruit and regroup.[56] It was just over twenty years ago when ethnic conflict in Rwanda turned to genocide. Warring Hutus and Tutsis resided not only in Rwanda but also in large numbers in neighboring Burundi. The two sides focused their fight on each other, politicizing ethnic divisions between Hutus and Tutsis, which were arguably created, or at least exacerbated, by the regions' previous colonial powers.[57] Their fight spread into neighboring Uganda. The result in Rwanda was an attempt on the part of one group, the Hutus, to eliminate (in some of the most barbaric ways) their Tutsi neighbors.

These cases differ from those in which insurgents seek independence from distant colonial powers. Independence-seeking insurgents under the control of faraway colonial powers are more likely to operate on the territory they claim as their own, as the Mozambicans, Angolans, Bissau-Guineans, and others have done. Recognizing these types of variations in the locations of insurgent activity, we focus mostly on the main areas in which any given insurgent group operates.

We should also note that we are not dealing with 167 distinct contexts or conflicts. We are dealing with insurgents whose main operations take place in no fewer than eighty-seven states, or approximately half as many locations as the number of groups. This, of course, means that some states have had more than one insurgency and more than one active insurgent group. Unsurprisingly, some states appear to be more prone to insurgency than others. Of those states with insurgent groups, some also seem to be more prone to having violent and long-lasting experiences with armed conflicts. We count twenty-three states in which two or more insurgent groups have operated simultaneously for a period of time. The issue we face in these cases is identifying whether the patterns in terrorism in these states reflect the activities of one insurgent group or another. This is complicated by the higher number of unattributed attacks in some of the territories with the largest numbers of simultaneous insurgencies (e.g., India) (refer to Appendix 2 and Table 2.2).

Warfare

The presence of an insurgent group does not mean that there is also wider-scale warfare. Many insurgent groups (or would-be insurgent groups) do not manage to incite the types of armed confrontations often associated with insurgencies taking place in the context of civil war or other types of internal armed conflict. We draw on six sources of data to identify cases in which the operations of insurgent groups correspond with wider-scale warfare. The first two of these, already discussed, include the GTD database and Max Boot's list of insurgents. The other four sources include the COW Project, Connable and Libicki's list of insurgencies, the UCDP/PRIO Armed Conflict Dataset, and James Fearon and David Laitin's list of civil wars.

Our goal is to identify the cases in which insurgent groups operate in the context of wider-scale warfare. We first turned to the Correlates COW Project in order to identify the "intra-state wars"[58] that occurred in places where insurgents on our list were also operating.

The COW Project provides data on armed conflicts taking place between 1816 and 2007. The dataset includes information on the types of armed conflicts, the beginning and ending dates of each conflict, the parties involved in these conflicts, and which party initiated the conflict. The COW dataset also provides information regarding the locations in which conflicts occurred. Combining this information with that already collected regarding insurgent groups and terrorist attacks, we are able to chart the times in which insurgent groups use terrorism during armed conflict. We can then identify cases in which terrorism is used, whether during the initial phases, throughout, or at the ending stage of wider-scale armed conflict. We can also point to terrorist campaigns that led nowhere in locations where a measurable volume of terrorism occurred but where there was no wider-scale warfare.

We began by coding COW designations of wars alongside countries on a year-by-year basis. We distinguished internal wars from other wars. We then matched these designations with the presence of insurgent groups and the numbers of terrorist events (overall) for each year.

In the process, we found several instances in which Boot's list of insurgencies does not match the wars listed in the COW data. Although we note that the label "insurgency" is not specifically coded in the COW database, there are examples of intra-state and non-state wars, which may have been described as insurgencies. Moreover, many of the insurgent groups included in Boot's list participated in more than one type of war. Boot's list also includes insurgents operating at times and in places where there was not war – inter-communal, civil, or otherwise – according to the data provided by the COW Project.

This is not surprising. Insurgencies do not necessarily escalate into wars. Also, as we mentioned, Boot's designation of "insurgencies" differs from the COW's definition of "war." Moreover, there has always been some disagreement regarding the classifications of armed events, drawing in large part on variations in definitions, applications of these definitions, and, to some extent, the availability of information followed by qualitative assessments of events. These are not debates we wish to participate in at this time, nor are they debates that will help us in answering our questions.

We do not specify numbers of battle deaths as is common in the COW and other data collections. Instead, we focus on the actors. Our interest is exclusive to identifying patterns in the use of terrorism by insurgent groups engaging in what would most likely be defined as insurgency in the context of wider-scale warfare. As such, we find ourselves approaching our question from a perspective closer to Boot's approach in assembling his list of insurgents.

We also found it useful to look to additional sources of data on armed conflicts, which more closely match our understanding of wider-scale warfare. We consulted four additional data collections on armed conflicts and wars in order to gain a more complete picture of the various designations of wider-scale warfare. The four sources differ in their definitions and, as a result, in their listings of armed conflicts and wars.

The UCDP/PRIO Armed Conflict Dataset provided us with a list of armed conflicts involving a government and at least one other group, in which at least twenty-five people died in battle during a given year.[59] To be included in this list, a conflict must involve issues of governance or territory and any non-state actors must be deemed to be sufficiently organized in their armed activities.[60] The UCDP/PRIO data includes information on conflicts taking place between 1970 and 2013, involving seventy-three countries and including 1,332 country-years of armed conflict. Referring to the Armed Conflict Dataset, we added thirty-two countries to our list of places experiencing armed conflict, defined to include armed confrontations between a state and another armed group with a minimum of twenty-five deaths in battle.[61] The insurgents identified by Boot figure prominently among the non-state actors involved in these armed conflicts.

We also referred to an earlier work by James Fearon and David Laitin on civil wars.[62] In their "Additional Tables," Fearon and Laitin include a list of civil wars occurring at some point between 1945 and 1999.[63] Similar to the armed conflicts included in the UCDP/PRIO dataset, Fearon and Laitin designate civil wars as conflicts between state and non-state actors over territory or governance. In addition, Fearon and Laitin apply criteria for the numbers of deaths in battle that fall in the middle of those used in the COW dataset and by UCDP/PRIO. Their designation fits nicely as a check on these other resources.[64]

Following a comparison of the Fearon and Laitin and the COW lists, we added an additional civil war as designated by Fearon and Laitin, which was not included in the COW dataset or in the UCDP/PRIO dataset. This was the case of the Irish Republican Army in Northern Ireland (1969–99).[65] Although it was a bloody, restless time in Northern Ireland's and Great Britain's history, this conflict, in particular, falls short of what many would consider a war. Nevertheless, the conflict met the criteria to be added to Fearon and Laitin's list. We also give consideration to this conflict.

The third source to which we turned was Ben Connable and Martin Libicki's listing of insurgencies in *How Insurgencies End*.[66] Connable and Libicki's list of insurgencies is, in part, a re-examination and updating of Fearon and Laitin's list.[67] As such, their list offers an additional resource for the identification of wider-scale armed conflicts. Connable and Libicki add to the records of civil wars for the few years between 1999 (the cut-off year for the Fearon and Laitin data) and the time of their writing.[68] Comparing the Connable and Libicki list against the others shows the effects of varying definitions and criteria; however, on the whole, the comparison leads to the addition of only one case (Brazil) (see Appendix 3 for a list of internal wars).

It is useful to note that the periods of insurgencies noted by Boot do not coincide with the periods of wider-scale warfare identified through other sources. As mentioned earlier, this is a result of Boot's inclusion of insurgent groups that were unsuccessful in creating insurgent conditions. These groups may have sought to carry out an insurgency but for any number of reasons, they did not. This also has quite a bit to do with the understanding that insurgency is not the same thing as war. The insurgent groups that are able to engage their adversaries may perpetrate violent acts and provoke a violent response; however, this exchange may fall well short of a designation as war. Moreover, in many of the cases analyzed, insurgent activities began well before the initiation of wider-scale warfare. This may be the equivalent of a warm up period in which insurgent groups worked toward increasing their capacity to prompt and engage in wider-scale armed conflict. This may also be a result of changing circumstances which made wider-scale warfare more likely to occur.

Analysis

The data described above offers a starting point for our analysis. We begin by counting the numbers of terrorist attacks on an annual basis. The actual numbers of attacks are less important than are changes in these numbers over time. We focus on patterns, not overall frequencies. We then map the numbers of terrorist attacks onto the timelines of armed conflicts taking place within the states in which insurgents primarily operate for the durations of the conflicts. We also map insurgents' use of terrorism for the duration of the insurgent groups' lifespans, which often precedes and follows episodes of wider-scale warfare. With this information we are able to visualize the coincidence between the timing of terrorist attacks with respect to the timing of wider-scale warfare. We identify patterns in the timing of terrorism in countries experiencing wider-scale warfare, particularly insurgency. This allows us to ascertain whether terrorist attacks tended to precede, coincide with, or follow these periods of wider-scale warfare. Our analysis includes insurgents with varying objectives and operational capacities, operating in diverse settings and within a variety of wider-scale armed confrontations. Because of this, we are able to examine which types of conflicts coincide with terrorist attacks and in what ways these incidents coincide. In other words, we have the information needed to disaggregate and match patterns in the uses of terrorism with specific actors and within specific contexts.

Although the coincidence of war and terrorism gives us some of the information we seek, we recognize the need to tie attacks to particular insurgent groups. Again, this is a challenge that follows from the large number and proportion of cases that are unattributed, as well as the expectation that some cases are missing. We deal with these challenges as follows. We focus on attacks credited to the insurgents included in our list. We also compare patterns of the total numbers of terrorist attacks within a context to patterns in the frequencies of attacks perpetrated by these groups. We use the data to identify patterns that, we hope, would exist even in cases in which some large portion of incidents are not counted or remain unattributed. We gain confidence in our identification of patterns when we find similar patterns in terms of the shape, peak(s), and distribution of attacks through analyses that include and exclude the large numbers of "unknown" perpetrators.

Using the available data, our goal is to identify patterns and offer a discussion of these patterns. We do not aim to offer prescriptions. Instead, we focus on learning what the patterns might tell us about the ways in which terrorist tactics are used by insurgent groups and the outcomes associated with them. Along these lines, we take an additional and necessary step. We identify insurgent groups for further study on the basis of patterns in their uses of terrorism. We supplement our analysis with discussions of these key cases.

As such, data analysis is only our first step in the process of examining the role of terrorism in warfare. Our research design draws more heavily on qualitative analyses and case descriptions in order to identify general patterns in the timing of terrorist attacks, categorize these cases, and offer explanations for trends in the varying contexts in which insurgent groups operate. This combination of descriptive statistics and case analyses is conducive to typological theorizing, by which we can distinguish among types of insurgent groups, conflicts, and contexts, and the relationships between each of these and the timing of terrorism.

The qualitative part of our study follows from the findings of our descriptive statistical analysis. We grouped cases according to the patterns in the use of terrorism they most closely matched. In some cases, as anticipated, terrorism preceded or coincided with the beginning of wider-scale warfare. In other cases, terrorist attacks coincided with the ending period of warfare. In still others, terrorism occurred throughout the period of wider-scale warfare.

Grouping cases required more than country-level analysis. In addition to focusing exclusively on the terrorist attacks taking place within each of the countries experiencing wider-scale warfare, we looked at the groups engaging in the conflicts and at patterns in these groups' uses of terrorism. The purpose of this step was, to the extent possible, to identify trends in the timing of each group's use of terrorism. Matching groups with their frequencies of terrorist attacks allowed us to determine whether terrorist attacks occurred along with or independently of a particular insurgent group's participation in the wider-scale warfare taking place within the state's borders.

We identify terrorist attacks occurring within each of our four categories we have identified: preceding, coinciding, trailing, or having no relation to wider-scale armed conflict. After classifying terrorist groups on the basis of the timing of terrorist attacks, we investigate whether or not general trends are present within each category. We focus on similarities and differences within each classification with regard to the objectives of the groups, the contexts within which the groups operate, their use of terrorist tactics, and descriptions of larger-scale conflicts that have taken place in their midst.

We supplement our investigation by drawing on in-depth analyses of the insurgent groups. We identify features of these groups and their contexts. Analyses of insurgent groups include descriptions of the groups' histories as well as discussions of their objectives and the contexts within which they operate. These analyses add background information that is useful for understanding the patterns we observe.

Investigating insurgent groups in this way informs our second question: in other words, is there a logic associated with the patterns we observe? We began by asking whether there is a relationship between the use of terrorist tactics and wider-scale armed conflict. We also seek to understand the nature of this relationship, if there is one.

Notes

1 Boaz Ganor, *The Counter-Terrorism Puzzle* (New Brunswick, NJ: Transaction, 2005), 17–18; Hoffman, *Inside Terrorism*, 37–9.

2 Laqueur, *The Age of Terrorism*, 24–71; Richard Jensen, *The Battle against Anarchist Terrorism* (New York, NY: Cambridge University Press, 2014), 6–36.

3 For further discussion, see, for instance, the work of Richard Bach Jensen, "The United States, International Policing and the War against Anarchist Terrorism, 1900–1914," *Terrorism and Political Violence*, 13, no. 1 (2001); Jensen, *The Battle against Anarchist Terrorism*; Jensen, "The Pre-1914 Anarchist 'Lone Wolf' Terrorist and Governmental Responses," *Terrorism and Political Violence*, 26, no. 1 (2014); Jensen, "The International Campaign against Anarchist Terrorism, 1880–1930s," *Terrorism and Political Violence*, 21, no. 1 (2009).

4 Laqueur, *Guerrilla*, 278–325. See also Metz, "Rethinking Insurgency," 32–44.

5 See for example, John Nagl, *Learning to Eat Soup with a Knife* (Westport CT: Praeger, 2002), ad passim.

6 Thornton, "Terror as a Weapon of Political Agitation," 92–5; Crozier, *The Rebels*, 159–61.

7 See for example, Richard Gillespie, *Soldiers of Peron* (Oxford: Clarendon Press, 1982); David Scott Palmer, "The Revolutionary Terrorism of Peru's Shining Path," in *Terrorism in Context*, ed. Martha Crenshaw (University Park, PA: Pennsylvania University Press, 1995), 266.

8 Frantz Fanon discusses the Third World populations to which this term refers in his book by the same name, *The Wretched of the Earth* (New York, NY: Grove Press, 1963).

9 See for example, Jerrold Post, "Terrorist Psycho-Logic: Terrorist Behavior as a Product of Psychological Forces," in *Origins of Terrorism: Psychologies, Ideologies, Theologies, States of Mind*, ed. Walter Reich (New York, NY: Cambridge University Press, 1990), 25–40; Albert Bandura, "Mechanisms of Moral Disengagement," in *Origins of Terrorism: Psychologies, Ideologies, Theologies, States of Mind*, ed. Walter Reich (New York, NY: Cambridge University Press, 1990), 161–91.

10 Rapoport, "The Four Waves of Modern Terrorism."

11 Boyle, "Do Counterterrorism and Counterinsurgency Go Together?" 38. See also Khalil, "Know Your Enemy: On the Futility of Distinguishing between Terrorists and Insurgents," 419–30.

12 "Global Terrorism Database [Data File]," National Consortium for the Study of Terrorism and Responses to Terrorism (START), 2013, www.start.umd.edu/gtd (last accessed April 4, 2016); Meredith Reid Sarkees and Frank Wayman, *Resort to War: 1816–2007* (Washington, DC: CQ Press, 2010); Boot, *Invisible Armies*, 569–89.

13 UCDP/PRIO, "Armed Conflict Dataset V.4–2014a, 1946–2013" (2014); James D. Fearon and David D. Laitin, "Additional Tables For 'Ethnicity, Insurgency, and Civil War'" (Stanford University, Department of Political Science, February 6, 2003); Connable and Libicki, *How Insurgencies End*, Table A.1, 159–62.

14 Despite any limitations in the available data that are known (and not known) to exist, the data offers a starting point for a more in-depth and differentiated study of terrorism than was available to the foundational scholars in the field. For a discussion of developments in this area, see LaFree, "Editorial Introduction: Loner Attacks and Domestic Extremism, Lone-Offender Terrorists," 61.

15 This is an updated count based on new data for 2014. For the previous data, the count was 125,000 "attacks." "Global Terrorism Database [Data File]," 2015.

16 Refer to "Global Terrorism Database (GTD) Codebook: Inclusion Criteria and Variables" (START, October 2012), 8.

17 Ibid.

18 Refer to ibid.

19 This is part of the description and distinction Max Boot draws. Boot, *Invisible Armies*, xx–xiv. Regarding terrorists engaging in a 'war of attrition', see Kydd and Walter, "The Strategies of Terrorism."

20 Weinberg, "Turning to Terror: The Conditions under Which Political Parties Turn to Terrorist Activities;" Susanne Martin, "From Parliamentarianism to Terrorism and Back Again," (Austin, TX: University of Texas at Austin, 2011); Leonard Weinberg, Ami Pedahzur, and Arie Perliger, *Political Parties and Terrorist Groups* (New York, NY: Routledge, 2008).

21 "GTD Codebook;" "Global Terrorism Database [Data File]," 2015.

22 For discussions of "hot spots," see Alex Braithwaite and Quan Li, "Transnational Terrorism Hot Spots: Identification and Impact Evaluation," *Conflict Management and Peace Science*, 24, no. 4 (2007); Gary LaFree and Bianca E. Bersani, "County-Level Correlates of Terrorist Attacks in the United States," *Criminology and Public Policy*, 13, no. 3 (2014); Lawrence W. Sherman, Patrick Gartin, and Michael Buerger, "Hot Spots of Predatory Crime: Routine Activities and the Criminology of Place," *Criminology and Public Policy*, 27, no. 1 (1989).

23 Sanchez-Cuenca, "The Dynamics of Nationalist Terrorism: ETA and the IRA."

24 "Global Terrorism Database [Data File]," 2015.

25 See, for instance, Kydd and Walter, "The Strategies of Terrorism."

26 Bloom, "Palestinian Suicide Bombing;" Bloom, *Dying to Kill*. For a critique, see R. J. Brym and Bader Araj, "Palestinian Suicide Bombing Revisited: A Critique of the Outbidding Thesis," *Political Science Quarterly*, 123, no. 3 (2008).

27 This is an updated count and it shows a higher percentage of events meeting the first four terrorism criteria (including the three GTD requirements and excluding cases with "doubt" or "ambiguous" cases. The previous count was that close to three-quarters of the 125,000 total attacks (or around 90,000) met these stricter terrorism criteria. "Global Terrorism Database [Data File]," 2015.

28 See, for instance, The White House, Office of the Press Secretary, "Remarks by the President on the Deaths of U.S. Embassy Staff in Libya" (September 12, 2012); "Obama's Claim He Called Benghazi an 'Act of Terrorism'," *Washington Post*, May 14, 2014.

29 The attack took the lives of four members of the United States Foreign Service. This included the American ambassador to Libya, a State Department officer (also a former member of the Air Force), and two security officers, who had been Navy Seals. The information given in the GTD lists only two fatalities. "Global Terrorism Database [Data File]," confirmed October 18, 2015.

30　Ibid.

31　See, for instance, Hosmer, *Viet Cong Repression and Its Implications for the Future.*

32　Raymond L. Garthoff, "Unconventional Warfare in Communist Strategy," *Foreign Affairs*, 40, no. 4 (1962): 573. See also Bernard B. Fall, "The Theory and Practice of Insurgency and Counterinsurgency," *Military Review*, 95, no. 5 (2015): 46; Kalyvas and Kocher, "The Dynamics of Violence in Vietnam."

33　Carol K. Winkler, *In the Name of Terrorism: Presidents on Political Violence in the Post-World War II Era* (Albany, NY: State University of New York Press, 2006), 17–36.

34　This record was made prior to events being coded as "ambiguous" or "doubt terrorism proper." For some additional discussion of the 1972 event, see John McBeth, "Technology May Hold Key to Answers About Malaysia Airlines Flight Mh370," *China Post (The Straits Times/Asia News Network)*, March 12, 2014.

35　Kydd and Walter, "The Strategies of Terrorism."

36　For a description of the National Liberation Front (FLN) terrorism in Algeria, see Alistair Horne, *A Savage War of Peace: Algeria, 1954–1962* (New York, NY: New York Review of Books, 2006), for instance, 133–5.

37　Boot, "The Evolution of Irregular War;" Boot, *Invisible Armies.*

38　Kalyvas and Kocher, "The Dynamics of Violence in Vietnam," for instance, p. 337.

39　In fact, unconventional warfare, at least as it is understood in modern terminology, is more likely the historical norm. See, for instance, Boot, "The Evolution of Irregular War;" Boot, *Invisible Armies.*

40　See, for instance, Bard E. O'Neill, *Insurgency and Terrorism: From Revolution to Apocalypse*, 2nd edn (Washington, DC: Potomac Books, Inc., 2005), 19–28.

41　Ibid., 27–8.

42　Bard E. O'Neill, "Forward," in Robert Taber, *War of the Flea: The Classic Study of Guerrilla Warfare* (Washington, DC: Potomac Books, Inc., 2002), p. viii.

43　United States Department of the Army, *Counterinsurgency*, 1-5.

44　See, for instance, Boot, *Invisible Armies*, xx–xxiii, xxvi–xxvii.

45　One question we may raise here is whether or not a group that fails to bring about insurgency is, nevertheless, an insurgent or, alternatively, whether insurgents are designated on the basis of their intent (as are terrorists) rather than the outcomes they produce.

46　Boot, *Invisible Armies*, Appendix, 569–89.

47　Ibid., 569–70.

48　Ibid.

49　Ibid.

50　See for instance, ibid.

51　Martin and Weinberg, "Terrorism in an Era of Unconventional Warfare."

52　For a discussion of "globalized" versus "localized" objectives, see Moghadam, "Motives for Martyrdom: Al-Qaida, Salafi Jihad, and the Spread of Suicide Attacks."

53　This attack, which occurred on April 2, 2015, follows less than two years after the attack at the Westgate Mall in Nairobi, also credited to al Shabaab militants, during which close to seventy people were killed. For one description of the group and its attacks, see BBC News Africa, "Who Are Somalia's Al-Shabab?" April 3, 2015, www.bbc.com/news/world-africa-15336689 (last accessed 4 April 2016).

54 Jenkins, "Brothers Killing Brothers."

55 See, for instance, Anita Peresin, "Fatal Attraction: Western Muslimas and ISIS," *Perspectives on Terrorism*, 9, no. 3 (2015); Cronin, "ISIS Is Not a Terrorist Group;" Boaz Ganor, "Four Questions on ISIS: A 'Trend' Analysis of the Islamic State," *Perspectives on Terrorism*, 9, no. 3 (2015).

56 For one discussion, see Philip Gourevitch, *We Wish to Inform You That Tomorrow We Will Be Killed with Our Families: Stories from Rwanda* (New York, NY: Farrar, Straus and Giroux, 1998).

57 See, for instance, James D. Fearon and David D. Laitin, "Review: Violence and the Construction of Ethnic Identity," *International Organization*, 54, no. 4 (2000); S. J. Kaufman, "Symbolic Politics or Rational Choice? Testing Theories of Extreme Ethnic Violence," *International Security*, 30, no. 4 (2006).

58 Meredith Reid Sarkees, "Codebook for the Intra-State Wars v.4.0. Definitions and Variables," COW Project, www.correlatesofwar.org/data-sets/COW-war (last accessed April 28, 2016); *Sarkees and Wayman, Resort to War.*

59 UCDP/PRIO, *UCDP/PRIO Armed Conflict Dataset Codebook, Version 4–2014a* (Uppsala Conflict Data Program (UCDP). Centre for the Study of Civil Wars, International Peace Research Institute, Oslo (PRIO), 2015).

60 UCDP/PRIO, "Armed Conflict Dataset V.4–2014a, 1946–2013," 1–3.

61 UCDP/PRIO, *UCDP/PRIO Armed Conflict Dataset Codebook, Version 4–2014a*, 1–2.

62 Fearon and Laitin, "Ethnicity, Insurgency, and Civil War."

63 Fearon and Laitin, "Additional Tables For 'Ethnicity, Insurgency, and Civil War'."

64 Fearon and Laitin require 1,000 or more deaths overall, not necessarily in battle, with at least 100 losses on the part of each party to the conflict and an average of 100 deaths per year, when all years of conflict are taken into account. Fearon and Laitin, "Ethnicity, Insurgency, and Civil War," 76.

65 Three other civil wars were identified in Fearon and Laitin, which were not included in the COW data, but were included in UCDP/PRIO data.

66 Connable and Libicki, *How Insurgencies End*, 157–62, 99–201.

67 Ibid., Appendix A, 157–62.

68 Ibid.

3

Terrorism as a leading indicator: insurgents' use of terrorism at the initial stages of conflict

Our initial concern is with terrorist activity carried out during the early stages of an armed conflict. We hope to measure the extent to which this activity is a precursor or leading indicator of a widening insurgency.

We begin this effort by discussing the reasons terrorists may fail to produce insurgency. In these cases, the terrorists (or would-be insurgents) used terrorism as an initial tactic in what would equate to the early stages of their insurgent campaign. This would typically involve the use of terrorism in the absence of wider-scale armed conflict.

These groups differ from the others in which we are interested. These are the cases in which terrorism leads to nothing, where further escalation in terms of the scale of conflict and warfare did not occur. In a sense, the early stages were the only stages for these would-be insurgents. Even when they lasted nearly three decades – as was the case with the leftist 17N in Greece – these insurgents failed to produce anything more than terrorism. There was no wider-scale armed fighting, or insurgency in the sense often associated with the term. We begin by identifying and offering a discussion of the terrorist campaigns that represented a "dead end."

Terrorism as a "dead end"

Terrorism is not always an indicator of wider-scale warfare to come. We explore two categories of cases in which terrorism does not lead to insurgency. The first category includes those cases in which terrorists are just terrorists. They are not seeking the type of political change or the level of violence often associated with insurgency. The second category includes cases in which would-be insurgents wish to produce an insurgency but fail in their efforts to do so. These are cases in which there is no wider-scale violence, much less warfare. We deal with each in turn.

Although insurgents are likely to be terrorists, not all terrorists are insurgents. One explanation for a terrorist group's failure to produce or engage in wider-scale warfare is their lack of desire to do so. Some of the armed groups that use terrorism are not insurgents, nor do they wish to be. They may not seek to overthrow or replace an existing system. Rather, they may seek something far less revolutionary, such as bringing attention to an issue and encouraging (perhaps attempting to coerce) a change in practice, policy, or law. Wider-scale warfare is not part of their agenda.

The types of groups that fit this profile are not among the most deadly or destructive of terrorists. They often have narrow objectives. They are more likely to seek change within an existing system than to seek that system's overthrow. We count militant animal rights groups and environmental groups among these, in the cases in which these groups use terrorism. We may think of these as special interest groups or activists, to the extent that they are bringing attention to particular issues and advocating for those that cannot speak. Changing the ways in which laboratories perform tests on animals or businesses dispose of waste products is more readily achieved by changing laws than by changing an entire legal system. When these groups turn to violent tactics, the acts are meant to draw attention to the groups' areas of concern. They may destroy infrastructure, but they do not typically aim to produce casualties. Their attacks tend to be less deadly than those carried out by other types of terrorist groups.

Two of the most well-known of these groups are the Animal Liberation Front (ALF) and the Earth Liberation Front (ELF). Out of a count of 188 incidents of terrorism associated with these and other like-minded groups, there were no fatalities; this count includes eighteen attacks on targets labeled as government, police, or military.[1] This track-record is not an accident. These groups purposely avoid fatalities, protecting human lives in a manner that may seem to be consistent with their desire to protect the environment or animals. Another incentive for avoiding casualties is the negative attention these would draw. Moreover, casualties would take attention away from the issues and make it more difficult for these groups to appeal to potential bases of support. They would become more like criminals than activists.

Anti-abortion terrorists are another type of terrorist seeking change within an existing system. As with other activist groups, the goal is to change practices, not a political system. The majority of recorded abortion-related terrorist events have been carried out in the United States, with ten incidents recorded elsewhere, including Canada, Western Europe, and Argentina. Anti-abortion terrorism has claimed eight lives (all in the United States) and caused nearly four times as many injuries.[2]

As with animal rights and environmental groups, anti-abortion groups have specific interests and targets. Their activities are sporadic and may be declining despite overall increases in the numbers of terrorist attacks.[3] Finally, many of those responsible for anti-abortion, animal rights, and environmentalist causes are part of what are best understood as loose networks of independent actors. Though they may share objectives, they are not necessarily coordinated in their activities.

Other terrorists seek insurgency. They tend to have a different type of ideology, which is more conducive to insurgency. This is due in large part to the nature of their objectives. Achieving the objectives associated with some ideologies requires changing a prevailing system rather than working within it. Attempting such an outcome would likely call for insurgency, both in terms of the goal of replacing a system as well as the types of activities and violence typically associated with attempts to do so.

For groups falling within this second category, terrorism may be a "dead end" for reasons other than intent or design. Insurgents are not always successful at initiating a wider-scale armed conflict, much less realizing the changes they seek. This seems to be the case for many of the insurgencies identified in this study.

Of course, an ideology and political objectives are not enough to produce insurgency. It may be that some would-be insurgents, regardless of their ideological positions or goals, are unable to pose a serious challenge to the systems they wish to change. They may be incapable of carrying out the types of attacks that give the appearance that they can threaten a system. They may fail to attract sufficient support among those whose interests they presume to represent or promote. Perhaps these are groups that would be insurgents if they could; they simply cannot. In the end, they are just terrorists.

Context is an important factor in insurgent success. It seems, for instance, that Western states are an unlikely location for wider-scale warfare on their home soil. In the United States, for example, "strong democratic traditions," constitutional protections for rights and liberties, respect for the rule of law and judicial processes combine with a relatively prosperous society.[4] Violence is stigmatized and prosecuted and there are nonviolent routes for recourse when the system seems to fail. In addition, U.S. counterterrorism and policing efforts have been relatively effective at preventing and deterring terrorism on American soil.[5] Terrorists, whether homegrown or not, tend to be captured and prosecuted. The same can be said for much of the West.

Democracy is not a necessary condition for stifling terrorism or insurgency.[6] Strong authoritarian regimes are also able to carry out effective counterterrorism and policing activities. Authoritarian regimes can limit the freedoms enjoyed by a population, which may inhibit the organization of an opposition and the acquisition of means to pose a challenge to the regime. In the absence of respect for the rule of law and human rights, authoritarian regimes may impose harsh forms of retribution against would-be insurgents and their associates, presumed or proven. Reverting to authoritarianism may appear to provide a short-term solution to what is perceived as a national security problem. Argentina's military regime carried out its own version of terrorism (state terrorism) between 1976 and 1983 against the perceived threats posed by Argentina's leftist revolutionaries.[7]

Groups operating within democratic contexts are less likely to present a challenge than those operating in authoritarian contexts. Democratic and authoritarian regimes may face insurgent groups that are homegrown and posing a challenge to a regime's authority within its own borders. Meanwhile, as Jason Lyall points out, democracies are more likely than autocracies to counter insurgent groups operating on foreign soils. They are more likely to engage in such operations because they elect to do so. According to Lyall, part of the issue here is the different capacities of democratic and nondemocratic regimes to respond to insurgent threats; another issue is the role of counterinsurgents as "occupiers" rather than their status as democracies or nondemocracies.[8]

This is not to say that the United States and other parts of the West are immune from terrorism or insurgency, either of a homegrown variety or imported. The United States has had more than a few terrorist groups and would-be insurgents operating on its soil.[9] Most of these groups appeared and disappeared with little notice; few received more than a modicum of attention. The GTD records more than 2,200 terrorist events in the United States between 1970 and 2014.[10] The highest yearly sum of attacks was in 1970, the first year covered by the GTD. This was the year in which terrorism in the United States accounted for almost 70 percent of terrorism worldwide. Putting 1970 into perspective, just over 516 terrorist attacks claimed 156 lives around the world. The deadliest attacks of 1970 were in Switzerland and the Philippines, claiming forty-seven and thirty-six lives, respectively. These attacks involved aircraft explosions. In the United States, twenty-seven lives were taken in twenty-one terrorist attacks. Out of 361 attacks in the United States that year, at least 338 (or greater than 93 percent) claimed no lives.[11]

While the number of recorded terrorist events declined in the United States, they increased elsewhere. Though there are wide variations across countries, terrorism rose sharply in Western Europe through the 1970s. Italy's peak in 1977 may be among the most dramatic.[12] Despite their high numbers of attacks, revolutionaries in Europe were not able to capture or maintain the attention or affection of the masses, nor were they able to upset the systems against which they fought. Location seems to be an important matter.

Insurgents without insurgency

The second category of cases discussed above includes those in which insurgents (or would-be insurgents) are present and using terrorism, but failing to produce insurgency. Max Boot lists several groups of would-be insurgents operating in the United States during and just prior to the period of time in which we are interested. His list includes white segregationists (1955–68), the Weathermen (1969–77), the Symbionese Liberation Army (SLA) (1973–77), and the Patriot Movement (1992–2001), as well as groups acting primarily outside of the United States, such as al Qaeda.[13] The ideologies of these domestic groups range from far-left to far-right; included among these are racists and black nationalists. None of the groups' efforts resulted in wider-scale warfare, much less full-blown insurgency.

Comparing the information presented in the various sources to which we turned to match armed conflicts and other types of internal wars with the activities of insurgent groups, we find twenty-five examples of insurgents operating in the absence of wider-scale warfare.[14] Of these, fourteen operated either in Western Europe, Japan, Canada, or the United States. In all such instances, it requires a strong and willful suspension of disbelief to regard these national experiences to be anything other than straightforward terrorist campaigns with little in the way of guerrilla activity at the beginning, middle or end of their proceedings. In most of these cases, insurgents failed to bring about the type of wider-scale warfare typically brought to mind when the term "insurgency" is used. A few cases are illustrative.

The late Italian publisher and multi-millionaire Giangiacomo Feltrinelli became a revolutionary and admirer of Fidel Castro during the second half of the 1960s. After a Third World conference in Havana in 1966, Feltrinelli returned to Italy where he attempted to establish a guerrilla force in the mountains of central Sardinia. He quickly discovered that some among the rural Sardinians at the time earned their livelihoods by grazing sheep and kidnapping tourists (to ransom them). These "primitive rebels"[15] had little interest in the publisher's revolutionary aspirations. As his efforts caught the attention of the press, Feltrinelli became a figure of fun among Italian newspaper readers.

Feltrinelli, though, refused to abandon his revolutionary dreams. Accordingly he created and lavishly funded the New Partisans. This group was particularly active in Northeast Italy. At one point in 1971 his followers were able to super-impose their revolutionary images on a Genoa television station, sending their revolutionary messages to the city's viewers. Later, in 1972, Feltrinelli managed to kill himself when a bomb he was planting on an electric power pylon in Milan exploded prematurely.[16]

Greece offers another instance in which the term "insurgency" really belongs in quotation marks. To be sure, Greece did experience an exception-ally brutal civil war following the end of World War II. During this conflict, com-munist insurgents employed techniques of guerrilla warfare and terrorism in order to prevent the restoration of the conservative monarchy in Athens. The conflict left thousands dead before the insurgents were defeated.[17] The revo-lutionary challenge whose beginnings followed democratization in Greece seems minor by comparison.

Greece's military dictatorship ended in 1973 and was followed by the restoration of democratic rule. At this time, two revolutionary terrorist groups emerged from the country's radical student protest movement: the Revolutionary Popular Struggle (ELA) and the 17N.[18] The ELA carried out hundreds of bomb attacks on places of business and government, often the Athens offices of multi-national corporations and NATO-related targets. The 17N group (named after November 17, 1973, during which the police used excessive force in repressing student protests) specialized in assassinations of the domestic and foreign officials that the group associated with American imperialism. Although these terrorist bands were active for two and three decades, respectively, neither group managed to transform its operations into a serious challenge to the country's newly restored democracy.[19]

At approximately the same time, the 1970s, during which the ELA and 17N were waging their Don-Quixote-like attacks in Greece, similarly imagina-tive groups appeared in the United States and the German Federal Republic (then West Germany). The Weathermen, SLA, and the Black Liberation Army appeared, claiming to fight on behalf of the world's oppressed masses. A handful of far-right organizations also appeared, seeking to unleash a racial holy war (RAHOWA) in the United States. For some, their cause was white supremacy, and they carried out a number of largely symbolic attacks on human targets. For others, the goal was something quite opposed to white supremacy – in fact enacted in response to it; this was "black national-ism."[20] The Weathermen combined a left-leaning ideology and opposition to the war in Vietnam, a position held by other groups, including the Black Liberation Army.[21] Some of these groups were insurgents in the sense of their revolutionary ideas and aspirations to change the American system. Despite their grandiose rhetoric, however, none of the groups amounted to very much.[22]

The situation in the German Federal Republic resembled that in America, although on a substantially wider scale.[23] Unlike America's insurgent groups, the German ones were able to develop links to various Palestinian groups, most notably the Marxist PFLP. In addition to providing training facilities in what was then the People's Republic of South Yemen, the Germans and Palestinians carried out a series of joint operations. The most famous of these was the Entebbe incident (June 27–July 4, 1976) in which a combined German and Palestinian commando team skyjacked an Air France jet bound for Tel Aviv and diverted it to the Ugandan airport outside Kampala, the state's capital. The incident is remembered today because it ended when Israeli special operations forces stormed the airport lounge, killed the terrorists and liberated the hostages.

The major German groups enjoyed somewhat greater success on the domestic front. For more than a decade, the RAF and the June 2 Movement kidnapped and often killed prominent public officials, bankers and businesspeople. The end of the Cold War and the collapse of the communist project, more generally, led those terrorists not yet in prison to abandon what had clearly become a hopeless cause. In West Germany, as in the other cases, none of the groups managed to attract anything approaching a mass constituency. They also failed to achieve the political changes they sought.

Japan stands out for the challenges the country averted as well as the one it faced. Even though Japan, like its counterparts in the West, experienced an episode of left-wing and student-based terrorism during the 1970s under the auspices of the United Japanese Red Army, these groups amounted to very little. The Japanese group that managed to capture the world's attention was a religious group known as Aum Shinrikyo. The group is perhaps best known for the March 20, 1995, dispersal of a chemical agent (sarin gas) in the Tokyo subway system during the morning rush hour. The attack left many commuters seriously ill and a dozen dead.[24]

As it turned out, Aum was an end-of-the-world religious cult led by a charismatic figure, Shoko Asahara. A partially blind man who declared himself a prophet and seer, Asahara aimed to ignite a worldwide conflagration so that a new world would emerge free of human corruption.[25] This would require, as Robert Jay Lifton describes, "destroying a world in order to save it."[26] Toward this end, Asahara's organization managed to recruit a large following, including a number of natural scientists. In Aum laboratories, his adherents experimented with various ways of simultaneously killing large numbers of people. The group reportedly had access to or attempted to use a variety of biological and chemical weapons, including Anthrax, botulinum toxins, Ebola, and other infectious diseases, along with sarin.[27] The thinking was that killing large numbers of people would act as a catalyst for repairing the world.

Terrorism analysts around the world believed that a threshold had been crossed and thereafter terrorists around the globe would seek access to WMDs. Although this development has not proven true, at least in terms of the size and magnitude expected by earlier analysts, once the Japanese authorities became aware of the threat posed by Aum, they wasted little time in dissolving the organization and bringing Asahara and other key figures to justice.[28]

Aum had the support of thousands, if not tens of thousands, in Japan, Russia, and elsewhere.[29] This is a substantial following by comparison with the various Western groups we have discussed. However, as was true in the West, Aum was never able to achieve a mass base of support within these societies. Their few thousand followers would not differ much from the presumed thousands of members belonging to right-wing militias or white-supremacist groups in the United States, though these may be organized in a "leaderless" form of resistance.[30] Like other would-be insurgent groups operating in the Western world, these terrorists may have had the desire to produce insurgency, but they lacked the means and support to do so in the places they operated. Moreover, they lacked the means and support despite having a relatively large following and significant resources.

In contrast to these, other groups operating in the West have had more success in raising the scale of armed confrontations, even when they still fall short of wider-scale war. Some terrorists with predominantly nationalist-separatist objectives have had a more natural base of support and a more sizeable impact. The protracted terrorist campaigns in Northern Ireland and the Basque country of Spain were more serious undertakings than those posed by leftist revolutionaries. Both campaigns involved secessionist drives. In Spain, members of ETA sought independence for the country's five northern Basque Provinces and the formation of a new state that would include the southern two Basque-dominated provinces of France. In the case of Northern Ireland, the IRA and, later, the PIRA (or Provos) sought to separate the region's six counties from the United Kingdom and have them reunited with the Republic of Ireland to the south.

Unlike the other cases we have discussed thus far, there was significant public support for these causes among the respective populations. Their terrorist campaigns continued for decades, with periodic breaks for temporary truces and negotiations, only ending when compromise agreements were reached at the end of the twentieth century for the Provos and at the beginning of second decade of the twenty-first century for ETA. It took several more years for the Provos to officially disarm. This was officially accomplished in 2005. The Provos foreswore armed violence just one month after the jihadist-inspired July 7 terrorist attacks on London's transit system.

Despite their longevity, neither terrorist campaign warrants the designation "insurgency" during the full duration of its activities. The IRA engaged in what has been labeled by some as a civil war, with the early period of the Troubles likely coming closest in appearance to such; the same designation has been withheld from ETA.[31] While both groups received some respite in the Irish Republic and southern France, respectively, for the most part, neither was able to capture territory, either on a daytime or nighttime basis, or carry out guerrilla-style attacks from remote redoubts beyond the easy reach of the British or Spanish authorities.[32] Nevertheless, insurgencies can and do occur in the absence of what scholars of various types of warfare would deem to be "war" in its moderate forms or otherwise.

The remaining cases of insurgencies stirring in the absence of wider-scale warfare are found in places where one might expect the conditions to be quite different from those in the West, including locations in Sub-Saharan Africa, the Middle East, and South Asia. The picture seems to have changed considerably since 2010. More recently, there is evidence of new conflicts and increasing violence in at least some of these places (e.g., Bangladesh, Libya, Saudi Arabia, and Yemen) where insurgents surfaced years prior to the beginning of this new era of warfare. Islamic extremism seems to be increasing in Bangladesh following an al-Qaeda expansion into the region. This move was announced in 2014 shortly after the group expelled ISIL, its former Iraqi branch.[33] In a December 2014 report, Rohan Gunaratna describes al Qaeda's return to South Asia in the form of al Qaeda in the Indian Subcontinent (AQIS) as bringing with it local participation and a more local, less "Arab" face. He notes that the leadership of the new AQIS is made up primarily of Pakistanis along with Indians, Bangladeshis, and other South Asians.[34] Other locations of failed attempts to create wider-scale warfare have been places in or near where insurgents are increasingly using violence in their operations (e.g., Kenya, Mali, Tanzania, and Yemen). Many of these places outside of the West are now the sights of wider-scale warfare. Although there are several examples, Syria's ongoing civil war stands out among these (refer to Table 3.1).

There has been turmoil in much of the Middle East and North Africa since the late twentieth century. Even where there has not been war, there have been coups and other examples of general unrest, as demonstrated by the Arab Spring and the regime changes and regime-administered crackdowns that followed. Newly weakened and failing states are among those where insurgents did not produce wars. These include Libya and Syria, two of the "hottest spots" of 2015. Israel, also on the list, is a state that has hardly known peace, despite the absence of full-scale war during most of the state's recent history. In Sub-Saharan Africa, Mali's Tuareg insurgents may not have engaged in what would be identified as a war prior to 2012, but there has been

Table 3.1 Insurgencies without war (1970–2010)

State	Insurgents
Bangladesh	Harakat-ul-Jihad-I-Islami (1992–ongoing)
Canada	Quebec Liberation Front (1963–71)
Chile	Movement of the Revolutionary Left (1965–ongoing)
France	Action Directe (1979–87)
Germany	Red Army Faction (1970–98)
Greece	Revolutionary Organization 17 November (1975–2002)
	Revolutionary Struggle (2003–ongoing)
Iran	People's Resistance Movement of Iran (Jundallah) (2003–ongoing)
Japan	Japanese Red Army (1969–2000)
	Aum Shinrikyo (1984–ongoing)
Israel/Jordan	Abu Nidal Organization (1974–ongoing)
Italy	Red Brigades (1970–88)
Kenya/Tanzania	Al Qaeda in East Africa (1998–ongoing)
Lebanon	Asbat al-Ansar (1991–ongoing)
Libya	Libyan Islamic Fighting Group (1995–ongoing)
	Transitional National Council (2011)*
Mali	Tuareg insurgents (2007–9)
	Tuareg insurgents, Ansar-al-Dine (2012–ongoing)
Morocco	Moroccan Islamic Combatant Group (1990–ongoing)
Northern Ireland	Continuity Irish Republican Army/Real Irish Republican Army (1999–ongoing)
Portugal	Popular Forces of April 25 (1983–84)
Saudi Arabia and Yemen	Al Qaeda in Saudi Arabia and Islamic Jihad of Yemen/al Qaeda in the Arabian Peninsula (2000–ongoing)*
Spain	Basque Fatherland and Liberty (1959–2011)
Syria	Muslim Brotherhood (1976–82)
Tanzania	Al Qaeda in East Africa (1998–ongoing)
United States	Weather Underground (Weathermen) (1969–77)
	Symbionese Liberation Army (1973–75)
	Patriot Movement (1992–2001)

* We expect the designations of some cases will change over time.

Sources: Boot, *Invisible Armies*, 569–89; Sarkees and Wayman, *Resort to War*; Fearon and Laitin, "Additional Tables;" UCDP/PRIO, "Armed Conflict Dataset V.4-2014a, 1946–2013;" Connable and Libicki, *How Insurgencies End*, Table A.1, 159–62.

much unrest in the region since that time. This unrest has pitted the separatist Tuareg insurgents against the state and other groups seeking to impose Islamic law over the population. Examples such as these illustrate the possibility that insurgents may spend years operating without producing or participating in wider-scale warfare, or even armed conflict. Yet, this may change along with changes in their environments, capabilities, support, or competition.

There are a few cases in which insurgent groups operate amidst minor armed conflicts falling short of war (refer to Table 3.2). Of the six insurgent groups

Table 3.2   Insurgencies with minor armed conflicts (1970–2010)

State	Insurgent	Conflict period*
Egypt	Gama'a al-Islamiyya (1973–ongoing)	1993–98
Mexico	Zapatista Army of National Liberation (1994–ongoing)	1994, 1996
Panama	Panama (versus United States) (1989)	1989
Spain	Basque Fatherland and Liberty (1959–2011)	1980–81, 1987
Uzbekistan	Islamic Movement of Uzbekistan (1991–ongoing)	2000
	Islamic Jihad Union/Jihad Islamic Group (2004–ongoing)	2004

* Conflict periods are based on UCDP/PRIO data on minor armed conflicts.

Sources: Boot, *Invisible Armies*, 569–89; Sarkees and Wayman, *Resort to War*; Fearon and Laitin, "Additional Tables;" UCDP/PRIO, "Armed Conflict Dataset V.4-2014a, 1946–2013;" Connable and Libicki, *How Insurgencies End*, Table A.1, 159–62.

included in this list, two are nationalist (Spain's ETA and Mexico's Zapatistas) and three are Islamist (Egypt's Gama'a al-Islamiyya and Uzbekistan's Islamist Movement and Islamic Jihad Union/Group). The remaining case of insurgency occurred in Panama during "Operation Just Cause," the December 1989 invasion of the country which coincided with the ousting and subsequent arrest of Panama's leader, General Manuel Noriega. The episode lasted just over three weeks.

Terrorism without insurgency

In addition to the cases outlined above, there are also many cases in which insurgent groups are not present, yet terrorist groups are present and active in times of peace. What can be said about those instances where there is terrorism without insurgency?

Perhaps what is most surprising about these cases is how few there are. Few states have experienced terrorism in the absence of insurgency, attempted insurgency, or wider-scale warfare.[35] The count of states that fits these criteria comes to thirteen. This count excludes states with almost no history of terrorism, as well as micro-states and island nations. Incidentally, micro-states and island nations have almost no history of terrorism. Their locations range almost as widely as their number is small. Europe figures more prominently than any other region in this list, with the persistence of terrorism without insurgency in five Eastern and Western European countries. Other locations range from Latin America to Sub-Saharan Africa. There is one case each in the Middle East, East Asia, and Southeast Asia. The political systems in these states vary; they include democratic and non-democratic regimes.

Their economies vary from among the wealthiest (Ireland and Switzerland) to among the poorest (Togo and Zambia) in the world. For the period between 1970 and 2013, these states range from fewer than twenty terrorist incidents in Slovakia (which is a relatively young state, the Slovak Republic having "divorced" the Czech Republic in 1993) to more than 200 terrorist incidents in Venezuela and Puerto Rico. There is also variation in terms of the types of targets to which terrorists are attracted in each state (see Figure 3.1).

One country – Ukraine – was excluded from the list because of its recent experience with a violent pro-Russia separatist movement. Ukraine's internal conflict advanced from protest in 2013 to war in 2014. At the same time, terrorism in Ukraine spiked, increasing from four attacks in 2013 to 405 in 2014.[36] There were only a fraction as many terrorist attacks in Ukraine during the preceding years, between 1991 and 2013 (n = 48), and almost all were carried out by "unknown" perpetrators. Two groups are responsible for

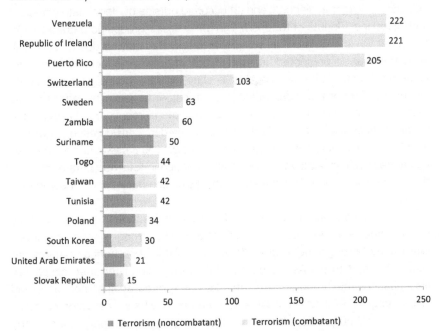

Figure 3.1 Terrorism without insurgency (1970–2014)*

*The information presented in Figure 3.1 includes attacks coded in the GTD as terrorism. For each country, terrorist attacks against government, military, police, and other armed targets are shown alongside terrorist attacks against other, typically softer, civilian, private, and non-state targets. In the cases in the GTD codes a single terrorist incident as having more than one type of target (for example, when the target is both civilian and military), the event is included in the noncombatant category. As such, each event is counted one time. This list excludes micro-states and island nations lacking a history of terrorism.

Source: "Global Terrorism Database [Data file]," 2013.

nearly half of the attacks in 2014. These two groups – the Donetsk People's Republic and the Luhansk People's Republic – take their names from two of Ukraine's easternmost provinces along the country's border with Russia. Another point worth noting has to do with the targets of terrorism in Ukraine. Despite 2014 being marked by wider-scale warfare in parts of the country, the proportion of terrorist attacks against civilian (non-state, unarmed) entities in this year is slightly higher than it was over the previous twenty-three years. Ukraine's insurgents are also terrorists.[37] In the context of this violence, pro-Russia separatists have claimed parts of the country for Russia. In 2014, Russia annexed Ukraine's Crimean peninsula, where a majority of residents speak Russian. The area is strategically valuable not for its Russian-speaking population but for its access to the Black Sea.

The terrorist incidents included in this analysis meet the four criteria outlined earlier: (1) being used to achieve a specific goal, (2) representing an attempt to influence a "larger audience," and (3) occuring outside of "legitimate warfare," and (4) lacking "doubt" of terrorism.[38] In many cases, groups perpetrate attacks that meet these criteria but do so against targets that may be deemed combatants. The analysis presented here differentiates between attacks on non-state, unarmed targets and attacks against a state, military, police, or other armed actors. The former are more clearly noncombatant targets. The latter may be better understood as combatant in the context of insurgency. Furthermore, the former entities are softer while the latter are harder. Consideration is given to attacks aimed at state and non-state entities as well as those aimed at unarmed and armed entities. Attacks are not counted twice in total numbers of attacks, though they are counted separately as attacks on combatant and noncombatant targets.

Attacks on combatant targets are of considerable interest to us as they may be classified as harder targets typically attacked by stronger insurgent forces, which may be engaging in guerrilla warfare. Attacks on noncombatants are also of interest to us. As we note an increasing use of terrorist tactics, we also observe the proportions of attacks perpetrated against non-state and civilian targets. Attacks on these softer targets may be indicative of a group's weakness. Alternatively, attacks on softer targets may be part of a strategy that involves the use of fear in order to achieve a group's objectives. This may be more prevalent in the absence of a higher authority (i.e., a state) capable of challenging the group and, hence, in cases where there is an absence of state, police, or military targets.

Distinguishing between terrorist attacks aimed at harder and softer targets allows us to investigate an additional dimension in the pattern of terrorism. Ireland and South Korea stand out in a comparison of groups on the basis of the targets of their attacks. Ireland sits at one extreme, with more than

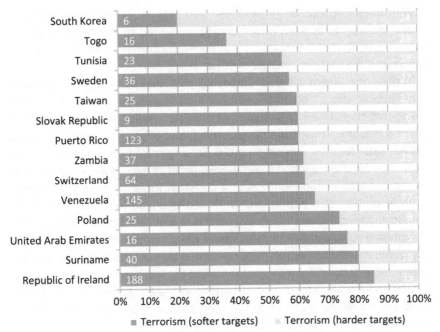

Figure 3.2   Targets of terrorism where there is not wider-scale warfare*

* The counts given in the table are the number of terrorist incidents coded in GTD. As in Figure 3.1, terrorist attacks against combatant targets (including the government) are shown alongside terrorist attacks against other, typically softer targets. Attacks perpetrated simultaneously against harder and softer targets are counted one time within the softer category.

Source: "Global Terrorism Database [Data file]," 2013.

80 percent of terrorist attacks targeting private or non-state entities. South Korea sits at the other extreme, with 80 percent of terrorist incidents, or twenty-four out of thirty attacks, aimed at combatant targets, despite the absence of an insurgency. In Togo, as in South Korea, terrorists have tended to attack harder targets (more than 60 percent). In the remaining states, terrorists aim their attacks at non-state, unarmed targets on average 63.5 percent of the time,[39] with softer civilian and non-state targets making up an even higher proportion of attacks in most of these cases (see Figure 3.2).

Terrorism and failed insurgency

Whereas the above states have had terrorism without insurgency or even attempted insurgency, there are many instances where insurgencies were attempted, terrorism was used, but the result fell short of wider-scale warfare.

With the exceptions of those in Northern Ireland (and by some estimates Spain), insurgents in the Western world amounted to little more than nuisances, managed and defeated, so to speak, by domestic law enforcement. This is also the case for insurgents in Japan.

It does not seem all that surprising that the advanced industrialized democracies should be largely immune from serious armed challenges. Insurgents have failed to produce wider-scale warfare in these places for obvious reasons. The insurgents lacked a broad base of support. Conditions did not exist for their support to grow. They appealed on largely ideological grounds – most were leftists, some were racist or exclusionary – rather than on the basis of shared identities or a common threat of the sorts felt by a sizeable portion of a population. They also operated in states with liberal democratic tendencies and respect for the rule of law. States such as these do not tend to target their populations in ways that turn the masses against the government. In other words, these states do not tend to act in ways that create more support for insurgents. Adding to this, insurgents who failed to induce wider-scale armed conflict resided in places where the populations were and are relatively secure and comfortable – economically and otherwise. The incentives for mass rebellion were largely absent.

Ted Gurr and other analysts observed this pattern in the mid-1960s.[40] Given the extent to which an insurgency requires a large number of "available" segments in the population, countries such as Sweden or Switzerland are unlikely to offer much of an opportunity to initiate insurgency. On occasion some would-be revolutionaries operating in such contexts are subject to self-delusion and a vastly exaggerated sense of self-importance, but this is unlikely to take them very far.

White supremacist groups in the United States provide a useful example. In the early 1980s, residents of an Aryan Nations compound in the American state of Idaho aspired to ignite a RAHOWA in the United States. They hoped the result of this so-called war would be the restoration of white racial dominance throughout the country. In 1983, a small group identifying itself as the Silent Brotherhood broke away from the parent organization and launched a series of terrorist attacks, murders, kidnappings, and bank robberies in the belief that the Brotherhood's operations would yield a genuine racist insurgency. Within less than two years, most members of the group were arrested, with the exception of its leader who was killed during a shootout with the Federal Bureau of Investigation (FBI). The Aryan Nations survives, along with the Ku Klux Klan, neo-Nazis, and other white supremacist groups, whose local clubs likely number in the hundreds.[41]

At the beginning of the twenty-first century, Germany was the site of a terrorist campaign waged by the National Socialist Underground. Between 2001 and 2010 young admirers of Hitler carried out a series of assassinations of Turkish immigrants and one Greek immigrant to the Federal Republic. Initially the authorities believed the killings were part of a struggle among immigrants associated with the drug trade; however, much to the embarrassment of the Federal Criminal Police, it took the authorities in Berlin to discover the organized and racist nature of the killings.

In neither case did these far-right terrorist operations cause much more than a mix of curiosity and revulsion on the part of the public witnessing these events.[42] Similar stories might be told about various "lone wolf" terrorists, including racist, anti-Muslim, anti-Sikh, and anti-Semitic terrorists, who have carried out killings and bombings in the other Western democracies. These "lone wolves" may have hoped the time was right to ignite a race war or a new anti-Muslim Crusade to repel followers of the Prophet from invading Christendom. Their efforts have clearly failed.

The exceptional case of republican terrorists and loyalist paramilitaries stands out for different reasons. Northern Ireland experienced terrorism as well as insurgency, if not full-scale war. The conditions that stifled insurgents in other advanced, industrialized states, however, were not present in Northern Ireland. The republican and loyalist sides drew support from distinct communities whose memberships were determined by religious affiliations. The loyalists tended to be Protestant; the republicans were Catholic. The two communities were unequal in many ways, perhaps most obviously in terms of economic opportunity. In their own ways, members of both groups lacked what one might identify as a sense of security. Local governance and democracy were suspended for a time and freedom of movement was limited. There were fences, gates and curfews. Many of the people in Northern Ireland were not satisfied with the status quo, with their governments, or with their situations. In short, they were easier to mobilize behind whichever extremist movement championed their preferred version of change. Despite this level of support, however, the conflict has largely subsided without the republicans having achieved their stated aims.

Two ongoing insurgencies are likely to meet similar ends. By most accounts, the end seems already to have come for the religious cult known as Aum Shinrikyo, later named Aleph. No longer engaging in terrorism, the group persists in its new form, under new leadership, and drawing much of its support from outside Japan, including from Russians.[43] Support for Aleph declined further as a result of disagreements regarding the group's ideology and leadership. These disagreements led to a formal split in 2007 and the introduction of a new, competing organization Hikari no Wa ("The Circle of Rainbow Light").[44]

It is too soon to know whether Greece's newest insurgents will pose a long-term challenge similar to the one posed by their predecessors. According

Table 3.3 Insurgencies that fizzled (1970–2012)

Territory	Timeline	Insurgents	Ideology
Canada	1963–71	Quebec Liberation Front	nationalist-separatist
France	1979–87	Action Direct	leftist
Germany	1970–98	Red Army Faction	leftist
Greece	1975–2002	Revolutionary Organization 17 November	leftist
Italy	1970–88	Red Brigades	leftist
Japan	1969–2000	Japanese Red Army	leftist
Portugal	1983–84	Popular Forces 25 April	leftist
Spain	1959–2011	Basque Fatherland and Liberty	nationalist-separatist, leftist
United States	1969–77	Weather Underground (Weathermen)	leftist
	1973–75	Symbionese Liberation Army	leftist, nationalist
	1992–2001	Patriot Movement	right-wing exclusionary
Ongoing insurgencies			
Greece	2003–ongoing	Revolutionary Struggle	leftist
Japan	1984–ongoing	Aum Shinrikyo	religious

Source: Boot, *Invisible Armies*, Appendix, 569–89.

to George Kassimeris, the Revolutionary Struggle and Conspiracy of Cells of Fire – successors to Greece's 17N and ELA – use violence more symbolically than as a tactic of war used to annoy or defeat an adversary.[45] Regardless of the new insurgents' longevity, it is safe to say that precedent in Greece and elsewhere suggests that the product will be something less than wider-scale war.

We should note here that all of the groups in the West and Japan that employed terrorism as a stand-alone tactic in the course of their respective campaigns lost.[46] The same is true of the insurgent groups whose efforts have ended without graduating from terrorism. The same may be expected for the remaining cases where insurgency continues in the absence of warfare (refer to Table 3.3).

The situation in Latin America is more perplexing. Certainly in some parts of the region we would think it likely that a sustained terrorist movement would spark an insurgency with wider-scale armed conflict. This happened in some places, such as Argentina, El Salvador, Guatemala, Panama, Peru, and Colombia; yet, in the other places it did not.

According to our review of the data, Brazil, Costa Rica, Honduras, Mexico, Bolivia, Paraguay, and Uruguay all served as locales for terrorist attacks during the 1970–2013 period but in none of these places was wider-scale warfare the result. Mexico came closest to having a war in its southern Chiapas region. Why was wider-scale warfare not the result in these cases? This is, after all, a diverse group of states. Costa Rica and Uruguay both have traditions of democratic participation and relatively wealthy economies. These political and economic characteristics presumably reduced the likelihood that these states would fall victim to manifestations of terrorism or civil war.[47] Paraguay and Bolivia, with their long-time right-wing dictatorships, did not have democracy throughout the entirety of this period; although, both underwent transitions to democratic rule during it. About the same may be said for Mexico.[48] Paraguay and Bolivia are among the poorer states in Latin America. Mexico's economy is comparatively wealthy, though the population is relatively poor.

Repression by the authorities seems to have been a key factor in the states lacking wider-scale warfare. State repression became more obvious after terrorism reached a high level of intensity. It appears as if the security police and the army in these Latin American countries limited themselves to modest levels of repression until the leaders of the terrorist groups sought to transform their fight into a full-scale insurgency, posing a more realistic threat to the status quo. Once the terrorist groups began to behave as potentially serious (or semi-serious) challengers for power, the police and military removed the proverbial "kid gloves" and used the resources available to them to destroy the insurgents. These responses were often carried out without regard for the rule of law and related forms of self-restraint.[49] The histories of state terrorism in Brazil and Uruguay during the 1970s illustrate the point.[50]

There is likely much more to the story, however. The harshness of responses within Latin American can only provide part of the answer. Argentina's response to the leftist terrorists produced what has been called that country's "Dirty War." Abandoning rule of law, Argentina's right-wing military regime carried out a systematic elimination of the leftist terrorists and their associates from the mid-1970s through the early 1980s. By some estimates, around 30,000 people are thought to have been "disappeared" during this time. The demise of leftist terrorism in Argentina can be attributed in part to the comprehensive and brutal nature of the state's response. Peru's response to its own guerrilla threat was a combination of counterterrorism and counternarcotics, at some points offering aid to Peru's mountain residents and at other times engaging in indiscriminate violence against the people, increasing their overall suffering.[51]

There seems to have been support for the government's harsh response to the terrorists' threat, at least among those whom the government did not target.[52] In Peru, the Shining Path eventually turned on the people whose interests the group had claimed to represent. In Argentina, the military intervention was seen by some as creating a welcome sense of order.[53] In both cases, the insurgents were leftists and their primary opponents were right-wing authoritarian regimes. This was also the height of the Cold War.

The Central American countries that experienced wars – El Salvador, Guatemala, and Panama – were also at the frontlines of the Cold-War-era competition between the West and those thought to be leaning too far to the left. The alignment of these states' governments with the West was viewed as an issue of national security. Democracies were especially challenged in these states with their dictators, leftist guerrilla fighters, ongoing civil wars, and comparatively poor economies.

In contrast to their counterparts in the relatively compact Central American states and Argentina's urban terrorists, Peru's and Colombia's guerrillas benefited from large land areas, terrains that were diverse and difficult to access, and limited infrastructure connecting the center to the periphery. The Peruvian and Colombian states were sufficiently weak in the peripheral areas to leave an opening for insurgent activities. For their part, Colombia's guerrillas provided "basic order" in parts of the country where they operated, largely in isolation.[54] The Shining Path, which began its operations in the remote mountainous Ayacucho region of Peru, also sought to create "an institutional alternative to the state." The population of this region was isolated and poor. According to estimates of the Shining Path's power in 1992, the year of its leader's arrest, the group had achieved a level of influence in somewhere between a quarter and 40 percent of the country.[55]

Over time, what remained of the leftist groups became less focused on revolutionary ideas and more on survival and economic gain. Several of these groups turned to narco-terrorism, becoming criminals as much as or more than anything else. Authorities addressing the terrorist threat in Peru, Colombia, and elsewhere have found themselves engaging in "counter-narcotics efforts" as well as counterterrorism.[56]

As the sole tactic used by insurgents, terrorism characteristically fails to produce the objectives its practitioners believe or hope it will. This is not necessarily true for a strategy that combines terrorism and other tactics.

Terrorism and wider-scale armed conflict

One of the most recent cases of a terrorist group turning to wider-scale warfare is that of ISIL (the Islamic State). While there remains much to learn, detailed analyses of the group and its tactics are now forthcoming at a rapid pace, and there is a growing monographic literature on this subject.[57]

Despite this growing literature, we would be shooting at a moving target if we attempted to offer a detailed accounting of ISIL or its activities. In 2015, the group's challenges to the governments in Baghdad and Damascus are still unfolding; efforts to uncover the nature of the group's expansion into Libya are underway. Suffice it to say, ISIL has managed to surmount the terrorism-to-insurgency hurdle within a short period of time. In fact, the group is more than a terrorist or militant group. A statement by Brett McGurk, U.S. State Department Deputy Assistant Secretary for Iraq and Iran, describes ISIL as a "full-blown army seeking to establish a self-governing state" in the part of the world we now know (or once knew) as Iraq and Syria.[58]

Noting these limitations in our knowledge, ISIL is one of the most widely discussed insurgent groups operating in the twenty-first century. The group's increasing use of terrorism and expanding operations also lend interest to the group as a case for consideration. Thus far, it seems that ISIL joins insurgencies that are already underway – as an adversary to the state and any group or individual that chooses not to align with it. Perhaps ISIL is opportunistic in this sense, seeking to fill voids where states have little or no control.

ISIL is not an insurgent group that must create conditions conducive to insurgency; it simply operates in places where insurgencies were already underway. The militant group al-Tawhid wal-Jihad (also known as Tawhid and Jihad) formed in the 1990s in response to Western support for Israel and military intervention "in the Islamic world."[59] The group became part of al Qaeda under the leadership of Abu Musab al-Zarqawi (a Jordanian). This was after the West's invasion of Iraq. The new group took the name al Qaeda in Iraq.[60] After Zarqawi's death in 2006, the group took another name, the Islamic State of Iraq (ISI). ISI's strategy and identity began to change again between 2012 and 2013, during which time ISI became the main player in the Islamic State in Iraq and the Levant, an umbrella organization of militant groups operating on both sides of the border between Iraq and Syria.[61] ISIL's affiliation with al Qaeda lasted until the group was expelled from the movement in early 2014. ISIL declared the creation of an Islamic Caliphate the same year.

At this point, it is also worth calling attention to differences between al Qaeda and ISIL. In following Osama bin Laden's original scheme, al Qaeda's goal is to strike first at the "far enemy," namely the United States and its European allies. In so doing, bin Laden's followers have sought to coerce their withdrawal from the Middle East. This was a shared objective for Zarqawi and bin Laden. The thinking behind al Qaeda's position was that once this goal was reached, the corrupt and heretical Arab regimes would likely collapse from their own weight. Al Qaeda has been sensitive to the killing of Muslims in this campaign. ISIL's focus, on the other hand, is on the "near enemy." It seeks to use some combination of social media, terrorism, guerrilla techniques and the deployment of conventional military forces to topple and replace the already weakened regimes in Damascus, Baghdad, and

Tripoli. The group's activities suggest its indifference regarding the killing of fellow Muslims. These killings seem to be part of its strategy.

Although ISIL's origins date to the 1990s, its first insurgency was in Iraq. In Syria, ISIL's early activities included staging attacks on military and civilian targets, which were loyal to Bashar al-Assad's Alawite regime in Damascus. The group presumably carried out these attacks on behalf of the country's majority Sunni population. The group was not known as ISIL at the time; it was, officially at least, al Qaeda in Iraq (AQI). This group also took the name Islamic State in Iraq (ISI). AQI/ISI worked alongside its al-Qaeda partner in Syria, the al-Nusra Front. There was talk in 2013 of the creation of ISIS (Islamic State of Iraq and al-Sharm) through an AQI–al-Nusra merger, but this did not go over quite as well as the ISIL leaders might have expected. Following some defections of al-Nusra militants to AQI/ISI/ISIL, it appears that the groups are now adversaries. The result has been fighting between the two former allies, which presumably has been combined, at least on occasion, with cooperation between them.[62] While it lost the al-Nusra Front, ISIL has managed to bring other militant groups into its fold through what Michael Knights has described as a "mergers and acquisitions approach."[63]

The Islamist beliefs ISIL claims to champion – Salafi-jihadist – stress the vital role of holy war in promoting a truly Islamic state. Creating an Islamic state also calls for the imposition of Sharia law. ISIL's brutality in pursuing this goal has drawn the support of many young jihadists from the Middle East, North Africa, and beyond. At the same time, this is a war with many sides, with some rebels fighting the Syrian state, others fighting on the side of the Syrian state, and many fighting each other. In its war, ISIL has managed to alienate some of the other groups fighting against Assad's repressive dictatorship (e.g., the Free Syrian Army).

In addition to drawing recruits, ISIL's actions have also galvanized militants wishing to fight against the group and its objectives. Among these opponents are Shiite militias in Iraq and Revolutionary Guardsmen from Iran. ISIL has also found opponents among Westerners and others outside the war zone. Some of these militants seek to join any group opposing ISIL. These militants wish to bring about the group's demise.

A more updated distribution of GTD data covers terrorist attacks through 2014. The previous distribution included attacks through 2013, just after ISIL's formation and before the group's declaration of an Islamic State in parts of Iraq and Syria. The GTD data records also include terrorism perpetrated by ISIL's predecessors.

As of 2015, the GTD includes information on attacks attributed to Tawhid and Jihad (2002–4), AQI (2004–13), ISI (2007–11), and ISIL (2013–14). The GTD credits the group, still listed as ISIL, with 1,443 terrorist attacks in 2014.

This equates to more attacks in one year than in all previous years combined.[64] The data paints a picture of quickly escalating violence.

This data can tell only part of ISIL's story, however. It is too soon to say whether ISIL's use of terrorism will be a leading indicator of the group's current insurgent activities, whether it will be a tactic used throughout its insurgent efforts, and whether and in what ways the group's terrorist operations may change in the future. Moreover, we cannot know how long the wars in which ISIL is engaged will continue. Given the ongoing nature of the group's insurgency in Syria and Iraq, its operations in Libya, and its potential to expand elsewhere, this much remains unknown.

Terrorism as a leading indicator

There are many examples where a terrorist campaign acted as a leading indicator of a growing insurgent threat and subsequent outbreak of wider-scale warfare. These are countries in which a "wave" of terrorism was followed by the initiation of an armed insurgency. Among these cases, the events may not have unfolded precisely in the manner of Mao's followers, but rather in a way that bears a close enough resemblance. In some instances the terrorism persisted for the entire duration of the conflict, while in other cases terrorism was largely replaced or superseded by other types of violence. The former cases are those in which terrorism coincided with insurgency. In this chapter we pay particular attention to the latter cases, or those cases in which terrorism coincided more closely with the beginning stages of wider-scale warfare (see Table 3.4). Terrorism in these cases was later abandoned in favor of other types of warfare. We examine several of these episodes and the contexts within which they occur in some detail. The descriptions that follow include accounts of terrorism used by insurgent groups in Turkey, India, and the Former Yugoslavia.

Turkey's Armenian insurgents

For more than one hundred years, Turkey has suffered through various episodes of terrorism, guerrilla warfare, and other less-organized forms of political violence. We should briefly review some of these.

First is the matter of the Armenian genocide. The mass murder of Ottoman Turkey's Armenian population during World War I (1915) has left an indelible impression on generations of Armenians living in the West, the Middle East, and now in their own post-Soviet state. During the 1970s, a new generation of young Armenians, most living in diaspora communities, created a handful

Table 3.4 Terrorism during the first stages of war

Country	Insurgents*	Peak (in terrorism)
Argentina	Argentina's "Dirty War" (1976–82)	1974
Bangladesh	Harakat ul-Jihad-i-Islami (1992–ongoing)	1992
China	Uighur separatists (1996–ongoing)	1996
Croatia	Republic of Serbian Krajina (1990–95)	1991
India	Kashmiri separatists and Islamists (1989–ongoing)	1990
India	Sikh separatists (1984–ongoing)	1983
Iran	Kurdish Democratic Party – Iran (1979–ongoing)	1981
Israel	Hezbollah (1982–2000)	1982**
Israel	Second Palestinian Intifada (2000–5)	2001
Israel	Hezbollah (2006)	2006
Lebanon	Hezbollah (1982–2000)	1983
Mexico	Zapatista Army of National Liberation (1994–ongoing)	1994
Rwanda	Interahamwe (1994–ongoing)	1994***
South Africa	African National Congress, Pan Africanist Congress, Azanian People's Organization (1961–90) (Note: Intra-state Inkatha–ANC war, 1987–94)	1988
Turkey	Revolutionary People's Liberation Party (1978–ongoing)	1977, 1991***
Turkey	Kurdistan Workers' Party (1983–ongoing)	1992****
Uganda	National Resistance Army (1981–86)	1981
Yemen	South Yemen	1992

* The period given in parentheses is the time of the group's insurgency. Insurgency in this case may not equate to wider-scale warfare. It also is not necessarily indicative of the duration of the group's lifespan.

** The number of terrorist attacks peaked in 1983 in Lebanon and in 1982 in Israel. Attacks attributed specifically to Hezbollah, which was formed around 1982, peaked in 1985 and again in 1994.

*** There was a second spike in the number of terrorist incidents in Rwanda in 1997 and by leftists in Turkey in 1991.

**** Turkey's Kurdistan Workers Party peaked early in their campaign, though not at the beginning of it. The highest number of attacks credited to the PKK occurred several years after the initiation of the group's wider-scale insurgent warfare against the state.

Sources: Boot, *Invisible Armies*, 569–89; Connable and Libicki, *How Insurgencies End*, 157–62, 99–201; Sarkees and Wayman, *Resort to War*; Fearon and Laitin, "Additional Tables;" UCDP/PRIO, "Armed Conflict Dataset V.4-2014a, 1946–2013;" "Global Terrorism Database [Data File]," 2013.

of terrorist groups. Nominally, the stated goal of the Armenian terrorist groups was to achieve an autonomous region for Armenians within Turkey or an independent state for the Armenian nation. This latter objective was eventually realized in 1991, following the collapse of the Soviet Union. The psychologically more meaningful objectives of these groups, however, involved drawing attention to the Armenian genocide, revenge for the atrocities perpetrated against Armenians, and coercing the Turkish authorities into admitting the state's guilt and responsibility for the killings.[65] The Armenian groups' targets were Turkish, but their terrorism was carried out largely against Turkish interests outside of the country.

Among the Armenian nationalist groups, the Armenian Revolutionary Army (ARA), the Justice Commandos of the Armenian Genocide (JCAG), and the Armenian Secret Army for the Liberation of Armenia (ASALA) carried out some hundreds of attacks on Turkish targets both inside and outside the country (around 95 percent of their attacks occurred on foreign soil). Turkish diplomats were attacked in the United States and Western Europe. The Armenian groups claimed responsibility for bombings of the offices of Turkish Airlines and other airlines in locations throughout Europe and in Lebanon, Iran, and Turkey. A 1983 attack by ASALA at Orly Airport in Paris may be one of the best known attacks due not to its success but rather to the backlash that followed from the group's presumed supporters.

This was the wrong kind of attention. The attack at Orly is an example of what Laura Dugan, Julie Huang, Gary LaFree, and Clark McCauley have called "overreaching." The incident caused Armenians, including those within the diaspora community, to question ASALA's and the other Armenian groups' use of terrorism on their behalf.[66] Among these presumed or potential supporters, the effect was revulsion.

In the end, the use of terrorism proved to be a dead end for the various Armenian groups, which never managed to mount a full-scale insurgency. The thousands of Armenians living in the United States, Western Europe, Lebanon, and elsewhere in the Middle East found the Justice Commandos, the Secret Army and other such groups more embarrassing than anything else.[67]

Turkey's leftist revolutionaries

The groups that took to the streets of Istanbul and Ankara posed a more significant challenge than the Armenian bands. These included groups of the revolutionary left and their far right-wing opponents. Leftist revolutionary terrorism in Turkey was an outgrowth of the university student protest movement of the late 1960s and early 1970s. Turkey's membership in NATO and, consequently, the country's link to the American adventure in Vietnam, were sufficient to spark a wave of student radicalism. Such groups as Revolutionary Path (Dev Yol) and Revolutionary Left (Dev Sol) emerged and sought to transform Turkey from an ally of the West into some version of a people's republic. Shooting and killing unarmed civilians, robbing banks, and bombing public buildings were the methods these groups chose. Whether or not, or the extent to which, these groups received covert support from the Soviet Union remains a matter of controversy.[68]

Terrorism during the earlier era of leftist insurgency in Turkey has been credited to two groups: the Turkish People's Liberation Army and the Turkish People's Liberation Front (TPLF). Before other leftists entered the scene (at least in name), these two groups were responsible for a spike in the incidence of terrorism in 1980, early in the leftist insurgency. The Turkish People's Liberation Army was also responsible for terrorist attacks prior to the onset of insurgency, with smaller spikes in terrorism in 1971 and 1976. Although these "insurgents" are still present in Turkey, their activities and the threats they pose have diminished significantly. In fact, the activities of these two groups largely came to an end prior to the beginning of the 1990s and prior to the later peak in terrorist attacks in Turkey in 1991 (see Figure 3.3).[69]

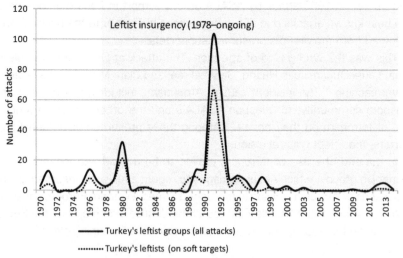

Figure 3.3   All attacks and attacks on soft targets by leftists in Turkey*

* The count of terrorist attacks includes attacks credited to five groups with organizational ties to the Revolutionary People's Liberation Party, including Dev Sol, Dev Genc, Devrimci Halk Kurtulus Cephesi, Turkish People's Liberation Army, and Turkish People's Liberation Front.

Sources: Boot, *Invisible Armies*, 569–89; Connable and Libicki, *How Insurgencies End*, 157–62, 99–201; Sarkees and Wayman, *Resort to War*; Fearon and Laitin, "Additional Tables;" UCDP/PRIO, "Armed Conflict Dataset V.4-2014a, 1946–2013;" "Global Terrorism Database [Data File]," 2015.

Dev Sol, which formed in 1978 out of the Revolutionary Youth (Dev Genc), appears to be the most active of the leftist groups in terms of its use of terrorism. In his list of insurgencies, Max Boot gives 1978 as the beginning of a leftist insurgency by the Revolutionary People's Liberation Party/Front (DHKP/C).[70] This is the name the group known as Dev Sol assumed in 1994, a few years before making the U.S. State Department's list of FTOs.[71]

The attacks in 1991 and later were almost entirely credited to Dev Sol. Although Dev Sol carried out its first documented terrorist attack in 1979, it was more than a decade later that the group was most active. The GTD credits Dev Sol with carrying out more than 100 attacks in 1991 alone.[72]

It appears that Turkey's original leftists demonstrate the pattern of terrorism as a leading indicator, while Turkey's later leftists used terrorism in what may have been an effort to keep the insurgency going. Another possibility is that the spike in terrorism in 1991 may have been an effort by the "new" leftists to start or re-start the insurgency (see Figure 3.4).[73]

Turkey's left-wing groups did not have a monopoly on the use of terrorism within the state. Right-wing groups were fighting nocturnal battles against the

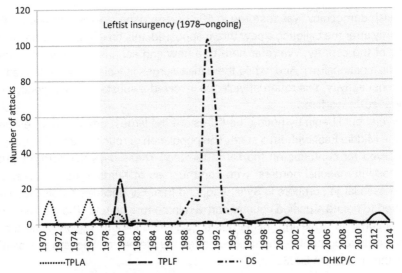

Figure 3.4 Attacks by Turkey's leftist groups*

* The count of terrorist attacks includes attacks credited to five groups with organizational ties to the Revolutionary People's Liberation Party, including Dev Sol (DS), Devrimci Halk Kurtulus Cephesi (DHKP/C), Turkish People's Liberation Army (TPLA), and Turkish People's Liberation Front (TPLF).

Sources: Boot, *Invisible Armies*, 569–89; Connable and Libicki, *How Insurgencies End*, 157–62, 99–201; Sarkees and Wayman, *Resort to War*; Fearon and Laitin, "Additional Tables;" UCDP/PRIO, "Armed Conflict Dataset V.4-2014a, 1946–2013;" "Global Terrorism Database [Data File]," 2015.

leftists. The neo-fascist and ultra-nationalist Grey Wolves may be the most well-known of the right-wing groups. Claire Sterling captures the atmosphere of the time: "Armed bank robberies ran to about twenty a day ... Journalists, professors, tradesmen, high school kids, might be found with their throats cut or bound tightly with wire, strangled, stabbed, mutilated, tortured, shot to death and laid on railroad tracks. The victims seemed to be chosen at random."[74]

The Turkish military intervened in 1971 after declaring a state of emergency. The youthful university students and others were detained without much difficulty. Peace and civilian rule were restored. By 1974, the government felt sufficiently comfortable to release Revolutionary Path and Revolutionary Left militants. The result was a return to violence at a level higher than occurred during the initial wave of terrorism. By 1978 and 1979, thousands of Turks drawn from virtually all walks of life were being murdered in the country's struggles between the extremists on the left and right. The military once again intervened; on this occasion through a bloodless coup.[75]

Kurdish nationalists

Turkish democracy was restored in 1983 when general elections were held. Shortly after the balloting a new threat appeared, this time in the southeastern part of the country. We refer here to a new and serious outbreak of violent Kurdish nationalism. And, while the earlier surges in violence were limited to terrorist activity, this round of violence involved a substantial insurgency and wider-scale warfare.

We should begin by noting the Kurds are the largest ethnic group residing in the Middle East without a state. The population of roughly 18 million people has lived for centuries on the same territory. These days this territory cuts across international borders, with communities of Kurds living in Turkey as well as in large numbers in Syria, Iraq, and Iran. For decades Kurdish leaders hoped to create a unified country and eliminate foreign rule. The closest they have come to achieving this aim is a quasi-autonomous region of northern Iraq, a development brought about after the defeat of Saddam Hussein's Baathist regime in 2003.

Over the decades, the country's leaders in Ankara showed little sympathy for the Kurds. They denied the existence of a Kurdish ethnicity. The Kurdish language was neither taught in the schools nor permitted to be used in public. Kurds were subject to various forms of discrimination. It was in this context during the late 1960s and early 1970s that radical student activism was ignited among the young Kurds attending Turkish universities. As with other nationalist-separatist movements, such as those in Croatia and the Basque country of Spain, for example, the Kurds expressed their support for

Marxist-Leninist ideas. This support, though, was simply a fad. Not too far below the surface was a commitment to Kurdish national independence, one which would supplant the existing international borders.

The Kurdistan Workers' Party formed in the mid-1970s and launched its insurgency the following decade under the leadership of Abdullah Ocalan, a former student of political science at the University of Ankara. The PKK announced its presence by launching an assassination campaign directed against the leaders of other Kurdish organizations in the heavily Kurdish southeastern part of Turkey. Its aim was to dominate the cause of Kurdish nationalism, at least in Turkey. Its strategy, as with other insurgent groups in Sri Lanka and Algeria, was to eliminate its competition. To quote Henry Barkey, "Following classic insurgency tactics, the PKK first tried to establish its domination over other Kurdish groups ... and then proceeded to terrorize the very population it wanted to free. Its use of violence was designed to spread fear among the rural Kurdish population and establish its bona fides as a serious organization."[76]

What then happened over the ensuing years were a large number of attacks on landlords and public officials, including, for example, attacks on school teachers, police officers, and administrators sent to Kurdish areas by Ankara. In other words, as the PKK consolidated its position, it shifted its tactics from terrorism to guerrilla warfare with occasional acts of terrorism.

Despite this history, the GTD does not record a single PKK terrorist attack before 1987. Reports that the PKK was actively engaging in terrorism prior to this time, including attacks on Turkey's government and fellow Kurds during the early and mid-1980s,[77] cannot be substantiated through a count of events, or at least not through GTD data. A search for terrorist attacks carried out by the PKK's various aliases yields no new information. In fact, the GTD lists almost no terrorist attacks in Turkey between 1981 and 1986, during what would be the first years of the PKK's insurgency. The PKK altered its approach later, focusing its attacks on Turkish targets.[78] This trend in attacks is more evident during the height of the PKK's terrorist activity between 1992 and 2011, when the proportions of PKK attacks aimed at harder targets (i.e., the government, military, police, and other armed groups) increased. This shift in targets is illustrated by an increasing gap between total terrorist attacks and those carried out against softer civilian and non-state targets (see Figure 3.5). These timing of these latter attacks corresponds with the first cases of PKK terrorism recorded in the GTD.

Armed exchanges between Turkey and the PKK were not uncommon in 1992. PKK terrorism increased dramatically around this time, peaking in March 1992. It was later in the same year that Turkey's military entered Iraq

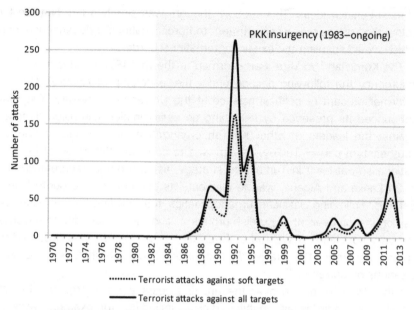

Figure 3.5   Terrorism by the Kurdistan Workers' Party

Sources: Boot, *Invisible Armies*, 569–89; Connable and Libicki, *How Insurgencies End*, 157–62, 99–201; Sarkees and Wayman, *Resort to War*; Fearon and Laitin, "Additional Tables;" UCDP/PRIO, "Armed Conflict Dataset V.4-2014a, 1946–2013;" "Global Terrorism Database [Data File]," 2014.

in search of Kurdish terrorists, an effort they would repeat in years to come. Turkey's military response to the PKK and the group's supporters was harsh. Towns were destroyed and residents were displaced.[79] The violent response may have begotten more violence.

The PKK's struggle and the Turkish government's response to it were influenced by the state's objectives and the international climate of the time. First, in responding to the PKK insurgency the Turkish government was restricted by its desire to join the European Union (EU). One of the EU's requirements for admission was a commitment to the protection of human rights (the EU's Helsinki Resolution of 2001). Repeated efforts at brutal repression of the Kurds by the government in Ankara would not help the state gain admission to the EU.[80]

Kurds were also the targets of serious abuse by Saddam Hussein in Iraq. Among other things, the abuse took the form of poison gas attacks on Kurdish communities in northern Iraq following the conclusions of the war with Iran in 1988 and the U.S.-led Operation Desert Storm in 1991. The Kurdish community in the northern part of the country achieved regional autonomy in the wake of Operation Enduring Freedom, the American-dominated invasion of Iraq in 2003. As a result, PKK fighters were able to use this territory as a refuge from the Turkish authorities.

The situation of Turkey's Kurds changed radically at the turn of the twenty-first century. After hiding for years in Syria, Ocalan was arrested in Kenya in 1999 and extradited to Turkey. Damascus had been willing to offer the PKK chieftain sanctuary at a time when it had an interest in reducing Turkish influence in the region. When this interest was supplanted by other considerations, Syria no longer had any use for the PKK or in protecting Ocalan. Accordingly, Ocalan was prosecuted for a number of capital crimes and sentenced to death. Faced with execution, he recanted and proclaimed an end to the PKK's armed struggle. Many of the organization's fighters followed his advice as the insurgency lost its momentum during the first years of the new century.

Having been approved as a candidate years earlier, Turkey entered negotiations to join the EU in 2005. The EU admitted Turkey to accession status with the understanding that the country's laws would be harmonized with the organization's regulations concerning human rights and civil liberties. The Kurdish community's situation improved somewhat with support from the Turkish business community and a shift in power in 2002 to the mildly Islamist Justice and Development Party (JDP or AK), headed by Recep Erdogan.[81] Among other benefits, the Kurdish language and Kurdish cultural practices were no longer subject to prohibition or discrimination. The Kurd's language could now be used in schools and universities, and the heavy-handed military and police presence in Turkey's Kurdish areas was lifted.

The PKK's original demands for complete independence have not been met. However, the JDP under Erdogan, first as prime minister and then as Turkey's directly elected president, have brought Kurdish citizens under the umbrella of democratic law.

Although neither Turkey's leftists nor its Kurdish nationalists have ended their campaigns, it has become evident that one resulted in wider-scale warfare while the other did not. Turkey's changing list of leftist revolutionaries used terrorism near the beginning of their insurgent efforts and again somewhere near what we may presume to be the mid-point of their ongoing campaign. Credit for the latter spike in terrorism went to a differently named (though ideologically similar) organization.

The violent Kurdish nationalist-separatist movement began its campaign at around the same time. The peak in Kurdish terrorism followed shortly after that of the leftists. One may wonder about the coincidence in the use of terrorism by these two groups. Another consideration would be the timing of Turkey's response to the Kurdish rebels. Turkey's efforts at undermining the Kurdish militants in 1992 coincided with the spike in Kurdish terrorism. This gives the appearance that the spike in terrorism corresponds to an early stage of what we may think of as wider-scale warfare between Turkey and the PKK. More than twenty years later, 1992 seems early in the ongoing campaign.

Indian democracy and its challengers

It would certainly be surprising if India, the world's largest democracy and a country consisting of more than a billion ethnically and religiously diverse peoples, lacked examples of violent conflict. In this case there are no surprises except, perhaps, the fact that the country has managed to sustain its democratic institutions in the face of so much bloodshed over the years.

The major challengers to democracy in India since the 1970s have come from a Sikh secessionist movement in the Punjab; a Pakistani-backed effort to detach the state of Jammu Kashmir from India in order for it to become part of Pakistan (along with some indigenous sentiment for an independent state); and the Naxalite movement, a Maoist group seeking to foment revolution in impoverished parts of central and eastern India.[82] All three groups have enjoyed significant popular support and carried out exceptionally brutal attacks on their perceived enemies but not one of them has been able to conquer and hold territory (the Naxalites come closest). This would be a key component, from our point of view, of what constitutes a serious insurgency.

These three cases make India an interesting country for this study. India's diversity is evident in the insurgent threats faced by the state over time. Several of the insurgent groups have been simultaneously active, meaning the threats they pose have overlapped. They operate independently of each other, in some cases within separate Indian states. The groups represent a diversity of interests, ranging from communist to nationalist-separatist to Islamist. The insurgent groups have been relatively durable; in some cases the organizations have survived even after their insurgencies have been suppressed by India's military. By one count, the sum of terrorist incidents in India between 1970 and 2014 exceeds 8,200 attacks. The annual frequency of terrorist attacks has been on the rise.[83]

A survey of the incidence of terrorism alongside insurgency in India suggests that in at least two periods – 1984 and 1988 – terrorism may have spiked at the first stages of insurgency (see Figure 3.6). These peaks marked

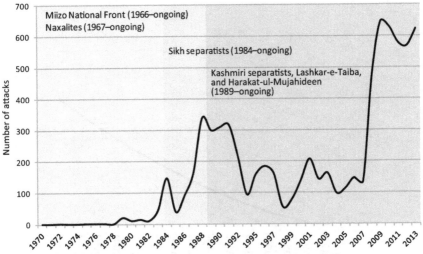

Figure 3.6 Terrorism and insurgency in India*

* The shaded areas indicate when insurgencies are taking place. The earliest insurgencies shown above are the Miizo National Front (1966–ongoing) and the Naxalites (1967–ongoing). The second shaded area shows the timing of Sikh separatist activities. The most recent insurgencies began in 1989 and include Kashmiri separatists, Lashkar-e-Taiba, and Harakat-ul-Mujahideen. These are ongoing.

Sources: Boot, *Invisible Armies*, 569–89; Connable and Libicki, *How Insurgencies End*, 157–62, 99–201; Sarkees and Wayman, *Resort to War*; Fearon and Laitin, "Additional Tables;" UCDP/PRIO, "Armed Conflict Dataset V.4-2014a, 1946–2013;" "Global Terrorism Database [Data File]," 2014.

the beginning of the Sikh insurgency (1984) and the initiation of activities by the separatist and also religiously motivated insurgent groups operating primarily in the northeast part of India (1988).

There was also a sharp increase in the recorded incidence of terrorism in India beginning in 2008. The presence of several ongoing insurgencies, the geographic size and population of the Indian state, and the introduction of transnational terrorism, primarily of a religious nature, add complexity to the story. The process of matching patterns of terrorist attacks to specific insurgencies is further complicated by the large number of attacks carried out by "unknown" perpetrators. These add up to some 2,300 of the 8,200 terrorist attacks carried out in the country between 1970 and 2014.[84] The number of "unknown" attackers has risen over time; however, the proportion of unattributed attacks has varied rather dramatically on a year-by-year basis (see Figure 3.7). In response to these observations, we look more closely at the perpetrators of terrorism within each context.

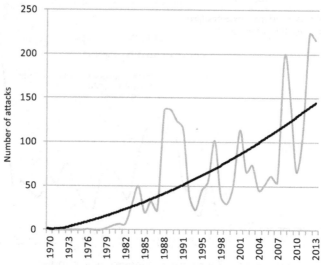

Figure 3.7 Terrorist attacks by "unknown" actors

Source: "Global Terrorism Database [Data file]," 2013.

Punjab and the Sikhs

In the case of the Sikhs, we are dealing with a cause that combined religion and nationalism. The Sikhs are a religious group whose faith combines elements of both Islam and Hinduism. Most of India's Sikhs live in Punjab, in the northeastern corner of India. A sizeable Sikh diaspora also resides in North America and Great Britain.

The Sikh effort to establish an independent state to be known as Khalistan began in the early 1980s, though some sources note an earlier appearance of Sikh violence.[85] The insurgency slowed down considerably by the early 1990s, and even though most efforts on the part of the Sikhs ended by the latter 1990s,[86] Max Boot lists the effort as ongoing.[87] During this period an estimated 20,000 people were killed as a result of the fighting.[88] The context for all this bloodshed was a powerful religious revival, one undertaken by a charismatic leader, Sant Jarnail Singh Bhindranwale.

Although Bhindranwale may be viewed as something of a "hero" by some, he and his group were also known widely as terrorists.[89] Their first target was local, within their own community. Bhindranwale and his growing band of followers sought to purify the Sikh community. In this process, they killed hundreds of fellow Sikhs, especially moderates, and Hindus as well as others who happened to be in the wrong place at the wrong time. It was these moderates who would support the Indian state against the Sikh separatists.[90]

Within a short time the Sikh militants launched an assassination and bombing campaign directed against Indian public officials in the Punjab region and beyond. In 1982, Bhindranwale and his group shifted their headquarters to the Golden Temple complex in the city of Amritsar, the holiest site for Sikh worshippers.[91] Understandably, the Indian authorities were reluctant to use force against this holy site to subdue the Bhindranwale group.

Despite this, the violence mounted. Finally, in 1984, the Indian government in New Delhi under the leadership of Prime Minister Indira Gandhi concluded that action was required. The government launched "Operation Blue Star." The military invaded the Golden Temple and engaged in a bloody fire fight with Bhindranwale's group. Some 1,000 people were killed during this episode, including Bhindranwale and his chief lieutenants. This was more the beginning than the end for the movement.

A few months after the Golden Temple killings, Indira Gandhi was assassinated by two of her Sikh bodyguards. In response, elements within her ruling Congress Party engaged in a series of indiscriminate attacks on Sikhs living in Delhi and elsewhere. Some 2,000 Sikhs were killed in the process.

There was a proliferation of Sikh terrorist groups in the aftermath of these killings. The Khalistan Commando Force, the Babbar Khalsa, and the Khalistan Liberation Force were the most prominent. Until the Indian government became more sophisticated in its use of force and steps were taken to restart the political process in 1990–91, these largely student-led groups killed some thousands of Hindus in the Punjab and beyond. The most spectacular attack attributed to the movement was carried out in 1985, presumably by a group of Canadian Sikhs who planted a bomb aboard an Air India 747 scheduled to fly from Toronto to London, killing 329 people when the bomb exploded over the Atlantic. Until 9/11, this event was the single most lethal terrorist attack in history.

Looking at domestic attacks, Sikh extremists and Sikh separatist groups used terrorism throughout the early and more active part of their insurgent efforts, beginning in 1983 and lasting until 1993. Sikh terrorism dropped considerably after 1993 when the terrorists were weakened by India's successful counterinsurgency strategy (see Figure 3.8).[92] About one third of the terrorist attacks in India that were attributed to Sikh terrorists were against harder targets, such as the government, police, military, and other violent groups in the region (see Figure 3.9).[93]

When we look at terrorism in the major cities of India's Punjab Province (Ludhiana, Amritsar, Chandigarh, Jalandhar Haryana, Chandigarh), as well as at attacks in nearby Punjabi areas within India (Haryana and Chandigarh), we have a much different picture. Terrorism in Punjab clearly spiked in 1982, the first year of the Sikh separatist insurgency (see Figure 3.10). In addition, terrorism

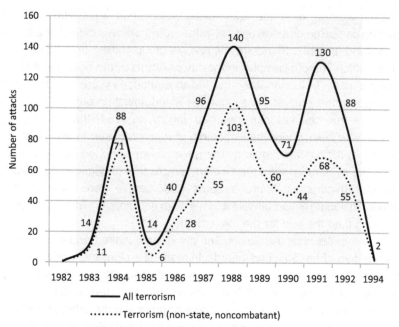

Figure 3.8 Terrorist attacks by Sikh extremists

Sources: Boot, *Invisible Armies*, 569–89; Connable and Libicki, *How Insurgencies End*, 157–62, 99–201; Sarkees and Wayman, *Resort to War*; Fearon and Laitin, "Additional Tables;" UCDP/PRIO, "Armed Conflict Dataset V.4-2014a, 1946–2013;" "Global Terrorism Database [Data File]," 2013.

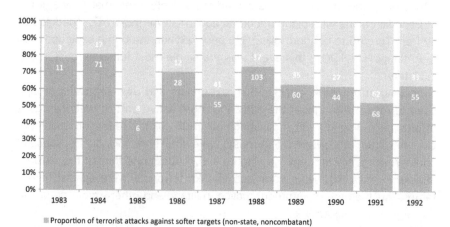

■ Proportion of terrorist attacks against softer targets (non-state, noncombatant)

Proportion of terrorist attacks against harder targets (state and combatant attacks)

Figure 3.9 All terrorist attacks by Sikh extremists

Source: "Global Terrorism Database [Data file]," 2013.

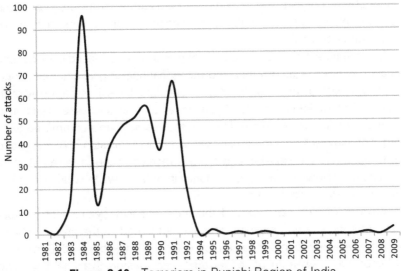

Figure 3.10   Terrorism in Punjabi Region of India

Source: "Global Terrorism Database [Data file]," 2013.

clearly ends around 1992 and is absent in the area in 1994 (recall that we do not have data for 1993). As we have found elsewhere in India, 144 of the attacks are labeled as having "unknown" perpetrators. Of 454 attacks in the major cities of this region, nearly 63 percent were attributed to Sikh groups. The remaining attacks were unattributed or "unknown."[94] None of the attacks within this subset were attributed to non-Sikh groups. Although this evidence suggests that Sikh terrorism spiked in 1982, terrorism was used until at least the early 1990s, when the movement was, for the most part, quashed by the Indian government. As such, Sikh terrorism continued during, and peaked again toward the end of, the active period of their separatist insurgency.

Jammu Kashmir

On three occasions (1947, 1965, 1971) the status of the Indian state of Jammu Kashmir has triggered wars between Pakistan and India. The origins of the conflict should be traced to the partition of the two states in 1947 at the time of their independence from Britain. The majority of the population of Jammu Kashmir was and is Muslim; however, the maharajah ruling the state in 1947 was a Hindu who opted for the state to remain a part of India.

Stress and tension over the anomalous situation has persisted over the decades. Terrorism has been a significant factor in the conflict since the 1970s when the Jammu Kashmir Liberation Front (JKLF), an indigenous organization, began attacking civilian and Indian military targets, the most notable of which was the kidnapping of the daughter of India's interior minister. The JKLF's aim was national independence for Jammu Kashmir, not merger with Pakistan.

Since that time, however, a number of groups have surfaced seeking amalgamation with Pakistan. Further, the purely nationalist goal has been superseded by a religious one. Hizb-ul-Mujahideen, Lashkar-e Tayyiba (Army of the Pure), Jaish-e-Mohammed, Harakat-ul-Ansar and its successor Harakat ul-Mujahidin (HUM), and others define themselves as jihadis committed to the merger of Jammu Kashmir with an Islamic state of Pakistan.[95] All the groups are headquartered in Pakistan and all have received support from Pakistan's military's Inter-Service Intelligence agency in order to wage what amounts to surrogate warfare with India.[96]

Lashkar-e Tayyiba has received the most publicity because of its spectacular attention-getting exploits. The acts attributed to the group include a terrorist attack on the Indian parliament in New Delhi and the 2008 massacre in Mumbai when a handful of LeT terrorists came ashore in a small boat, originating in Karachi, and proceeded to massacre passers-by at the city's railway station and at two of Mumbai's most prominent hotels, including the Taj, a popular outdoor café, and the local Jewish community center.[97] Moreover, LeT has a formal affiliation with al Qaeda and its aims are not restricted to Jammu Kashmir.[98] According to its literature, LeT doctrine expresses hatred for Hindus, Jews, Americans, apostates and infidels, more generally. Its long-range, and certainly far-fetched, goal includes bringing India into a caliphate.[99]

This analysis of the data suggests that Kashmiri separatists have carried out terrorist attacks continuously – though in varying frequencies – throughout their ongoing struggle (see Figure 3.11). The data of attributed attacks does not tell us anything about the attacks that are unknown or unclaimed, which add up to more than 25 percent of attacks in India. A separate analysis can provide insight regarding this question.

For this, we look at the terrorist attacks that were carried out in the province of Jammu Kashmir and, in particular, in the province's three main cities – Srinagar, Jammu, and Anantnag (see Figure 3.12). This allows us to study the distribution of terrorist attacks occurring within the same province most affected by the three insurgent groups: Lashkar-e Tayyiba, Jaish-e-Mohammed, Harakat ul-Mujahidin and Harakat-ul-Ansar. This analysis shows that the volume of terrorism did, in fact, peak in 1990 at the beginning stages of the insurgency, with 120 acts of terrorist (or almost 20 percent of all terrorist attacks between 1988 and 2013) occurring in this year. This number has not been matched, even by half, since that time. Moreover, the majority of known attackers fall into one or more of three categories: pro-Kashmiri, pro-Pakistani, and Islamist.

This analysis comes with some limitations. We cannot attribute the

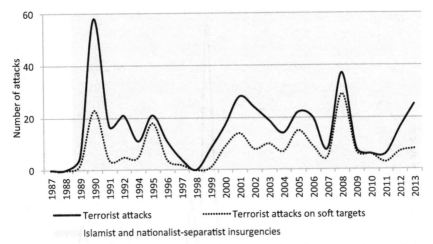

Figure 3.11   Terrorist attacks by Kashmiri nationalist-separatists and Lashkar-e Tayyiba*

* This data includes terrorist attacks perpetrated by the major Kashmiri nationalist-separatist groups, as well as several less prolific groups, all of which were identified and confirmed through a variety of sources, including START's "Terrorist Organization Profiles" and the Global Terrorism Database, as well as reliable news sources such as BBC News Africa. "Who Are Somalia's Al-Shabab?" April 3, 2015, www.bbc.com/news/world-africa-15336689 (last accessed April 4, 2016).

Sources: Boot, *Invisible Armies*, 569–89; Connable and Libicki, *How Insurgencies End*, 157–62, 99–201; Sarkees and Wayman, *Resort to War*; Fearon and Laitin, "Additional Tables;" UCDP/PRIO, "Armed Conflict Dataset V.4-2014a, 1946–2013," "Global Terrorism Database [Data File]," 2014.

"unknown" attacks to specific groups carrying out insurgency in Jammu Kashmir. We know that some of these insurgent groups have carried out attacks in other provinces, so we may assume that terrorists with other objectives and operating primarily outside of Jammu and Kashmir could carry out attacks within the province. At the same time, we note that most of the attacks attributed to the pro-Kashmiri and pro-Pakistani insurgents, including those with Islamist ideologies, do, in fact, occur within Jammu Kashmir. Less than 15 percent of Lashkar-e-Tayyiba's known terrorist attacks occurred outside of Jammu Kashmir. Around 20 percent of the terrorist attacks attributed to Jaish-e-Mohammed, Harakat ul-Mujahidin, and Harakat-ul-Ansar occur outside of Jammu Kashmir. The proportion of terrorist attacks carried out by the various other groups of Kashmiri militants outside Jammu Kashmir (as opposed to within Jammu Kashmir) is smaller.[100] Further support comes from the observation that approximately 2 percent of the more than 600 terrorist attacks in Jammu Kashmir are attributed to Sikh extremists. In fact, these observations provide additional support for the conjecture that some, if not

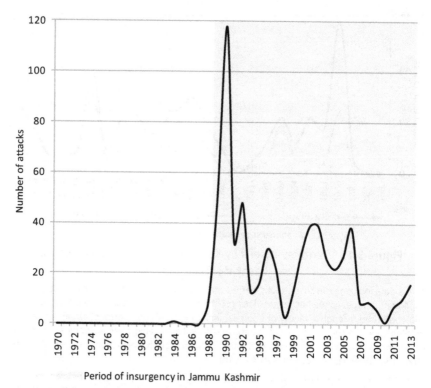

Period of insurgency in Jammu Kashmir

Figure 3.12   Terrorist attacks in the three major cities of Jammu Kashmir*

* This data includes terrorist attacks perpetrated in the three major cities of Jammu Kashmir: Srinagar, Jammu, and Anantnag.

Sources: Boot, *Invisible Armies*, 569–89, Connable and Libicki, *How Insurgencies End*, 157–62, 99–201; Sarkees and Wayman, *Resort to War*; Fearon and Laitin, "Additional Tables;" UCDP/PRIO, "Armed Conflict Dataset V.4-2014a, 1946–2013;" "Global Terrorism Database [Data File]," 2014.

most, of the "unknown" attacks were the work of these same Kashmiri and Islamist separatist groups. In other words, while there is no reason to believe that all of the "unknown" terrorists in the province were aligned with Kashmiri separatists, there is evidence to suggest that most of them were (see Figure 3.13).

Although we note the highest frequency of terrorism in the earliest stages of these groups' insurgencies, both overall and in their area of primary interest, there are limitations to the conclusions we can draw. As with the other insurgents in India, the Kashmiri separatist insurgents remain active. Terrorism has remained an important part of these groups' activities over the years. We cannot know the future patterns of attacks or the perpetrators of terrorism in the region. We cannot know how the expansion of Salafist-jihadist networks

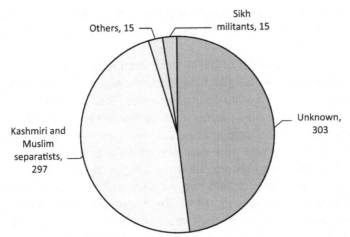

Figure 3.13   Perpetrators of terrorist attacks in the three major cities of Jammu Kashmir*

* This data includes terrorist attacks perpetrated in the three major cities of Jammu Kashmir: Srinagar, Jammu, and Anantnag.

Source: "Global Terrorism Database [Data file]," 2013.

may influence the competitions between the groups and the Indian state or among the groups, or the tactics they will use.

Croatia, the Ustasha and Former Yugoslavia

Croatia is a country with a population of some 6,500,000 predominantly Catholic Slavs, which became part of the new state of Yugoslavia as the result of the World War I Treaty of Versailles. Prior to this time, parts of the territory now within Croatia's borders had been under Romanian and Austro-Hungarian rule. The Ottoman Empire reached Croatia's borders before receding and dying at the end of World War I.[101] In the interwar period, this new state was dominated for most of its relatively brief history by the predominantly Eastern Orthodox Serb population, with its Serb monarchs ruling from Belgrade, Serbia to the East. At this time, Croatian nationalists seeking independence for Croatia led a resistance to Serb authority. Their nationalist resistance went by the name Ustasha.

Terrorism was one means by which Croat nationalists expressed their opposition to the highly authoritarian rule from Belgrade. The most substantial manifestation of this opposition was the Ustasha – Hrvatska revolucionarna organizacija (UHRO), or the Croatian Revolutionary Organization. Between 1929 and 1941, UHRO was responsible for several small-scale terrorist attacks inside Yugoslavia. Belgrade responded to these attacks by seeking to murder UHRO activists abroad. Ustasha terrorism included assassinations and bombings.[102]

The most spectacular act of UHRO terror occurred in 1934 when its operatives assassinated the Yugoslav King Alexander and the French foreign minister during the former's state visit to Marseilles. The killers had been trained in Fascist Italy and received support from Admiral Horthy's right-wing government in Hungary. Both Rome and Budapest had a shared interest in weakening Yugoslavia so as to promote their own territorial ambitions.

The 1934 assassinations prompted the League of Nations in Geneva to take action. The League drafted two treaties, one creating an international crime of killing or attempting to kill heads of state and other "internationally protected persons." The other draft treaty proposed an enforcement mechanism: an international court to try such cases. Neither agreement achieved enough signatures to come into force.[103]

The status of the Ustasha and its leader Ante Pavelic changed radically during World War II. Hitler seized control of Yugoslavia in April 1941. The Ustasha leadership allied with Nazi Germany, gaining independence for Croatia as a "Nazi puppet state." Pavelic was its leader. During the years of Pavelic's rule, Croatia modeled itself after Germany in a number of ways. Territorial expansion into Bosnia and parts of Serbia followed, along with genocide. Pavelic and his lieutenants organized concentration camps and carried out mass executions of Croatia's Serb, Jewish, and Roma populations, along with Croats who opposed the fascist regime.

Ustasha rule was brought to an end with the arrival of the Red Army in 1944 and with the assistance of Josef Broz "Tito" and his predominantly Serb Partisans. Pavelic fled to Argentina along with other key figures where they lived under the auspices of what came to be viewed as a pro-Axis regime under Juan Peron.[104]

Then, following World War II, the state became part of the Socialist Federal Republic of Yugoslavia under a communist regime headed by Tito. Postwar Croatia was re-formed as a republic. A Croatian by birth, Tito was a Partisan leader with a following made up primarily of Serbs. He established a federal system of rule under the overall direction of the League of Yugoslav Communists, headquartered in Belgrade, Serbia. As a shrewd political leader, he extended a certain measure of self-rule to the republics into which the country was divided. Tito experimented with local self-management of business enterprises, broke with the Soviet Union, and developed economic and political links to the West, including NATO. Yugoslavia officially became a non-aligned state during the Cold War.[105]

Under communist auspices no open political opposition was tolerated.

Croatian nationalism, though, was openly expressed among the Croatian diaspora. By the early 1970s this sentiment gave rise to a wave of terrorism. Accordingly, in 1971 two Croats forced their way into the Yugoslav embassy in Stockholm and assassinated the ambassador. The following year, other Croats planted a bomb aboard a Yugoslav airliner. The in-flight explosion killed all but one of its passengers. This incident was followed by a long series of terrorist attacks on Yugoslav targets located in the United States, Germany, France, and Australia. In 1972, Croatian nationalists even sent a guerrilla band into Yugoslavia proper, all nineteen of whose members were killed in a gun battle with the authorities.

The most spectacular terrorist episode occurred in September 1976 when a small group calling itself the Fighters for a Free Croatia skyjacked a TWA flight from Chicago bound for New York and diverted it to Paris. In exchange for the passengers' freedom the Croatian group coerced the *New York Times* into publishing its manifesto and dropped pamphlets with the same message from the jetliner while it was in flight. As may be imagined, this event achieved worldwide publicity for the Croats' cause.[106]

Tito did not remain passive in the face of this challenge. Rather, clandestine Yugoslav "hit teams" were sent abroad. A number of Croatian leaders in exile were assassinated. At the same time Belgrade demanded action on the part of those Western governments with sizable Croatian populations in exile so as to restrict the operations of the various violent nationalist groups that surfaced in these years.[107]

Yugoslavia changed with Tito's death in 1980. His successors, recognizing the problem of national integration, produced a new constitution, which among other things provided for a collective presidency in Belgrade, representing each of the country's six republics.[108] Although this arrangement lasted for a decade, the centrifugal forces pulling the country apart were too strong.[109]

A complete description of Yugoslavia's disintegration is beyond the scope of our analysis. It will have to suffice to say that for reasons having to do with internal economic problems, foreign indebtedness, the failure of economic experimentation at the local level and the revival of strong nationalist sentiments, the system began to fall apart in the period between 1989 and 1991. Matters were not helped by the fact that the president of the federal executive as well as Serbia was Slobodan Milosevic, a figure who was first and foremost a Serb nationalist.

What followed was the outbreak of a multi-sided civil war in 1991. Slovenia and Croatia were the first to secede in 1991. Their independence was recognized first by Germany. Serbia refused to accept this result and fighting ensued between its armed forces and Croatia's hastily assembled military. Slovenia, located on the opposite side of Croatia and sharing no borders, had an easier "divorce." Croats were the victims of Serb atrocities after Croatia's declaration of independence. This was particularly true in the early fighting. Examples of brutality and murder in the war between Slavs were shocking. Displays of murdered, mutilated corpses were part of the warfare and part of the message: those who stayed could expect the same treatment.[110]

Citizens of Bosnia and Herzegovina, the third largest of the republics and the one situated between Croatia and Serbia, also experienced atrocities during the Balkan Wars of the 1990s. Bosnia and Herzegovina was home to a mixed population of Croats, Serbs, and Muslims, none of these groups represented a majority of the population of the republic. At the same time, parts of the republic were ethnic enclaves in which one ethnic group made up a majority. The eastern region was predominantly populated by Bosnians identifying as Serbs. These Bosnian Serbs would distinguish themselves from other Bosnians primarily on the basis of their religion, with their Orthodox faith, or at least their self-identification as being culturally Orthodox, as the defining trait of their community.[111]

Milosevic was committed to the idea of a "greater Serbia," which would include territories in which Serbs lived outside of Serbia-proper. The eastern areas of Bosnia and Croatia, including the Krajina, were among the sought-after territories. At first glance, the formation of a Bosnian Serb republic and its military campaign of ethnic cleansing seem to be consistent with promoting this outcome.[112] The campaign included Serb militants seeking to rid the area of its Muslim population, often by carrying out atrocities against unarmed civilians. Despite this, there is evidence that the Serbs of Bosnia, and perhaps even Croatia, would not have sought unification with Serbia.[113] The idea that all Serbs would belong to a single Serbian state may have been accepted by the Serbian state and those desiring a "Greater Serbia." This idea was not necessarily shared within the broader ethnic Serb community.

The fighting resulted in some of the worst atrocities recorded in the post-Cold War era. Among these atrocities, the 1995 massacre of an estimated 8,000 Bosnian Muslim men and boys in Srebrenica and the killing of no fewer than 500 of Sarajevo's children during the city's nearly four-year siege, between April 1992 and December 1995, stand out.[114] The atrocities were not perpetrated solely by Serbs against Croats and Muslims. Croatian forces participated in mass murders and the destruction of buildings; accusations have also been made against Bosnia's Muslims.[115] Claims of attacks by members of one ethnic group against another, whether alleged or actual, were submitted in arguments supporting the need for violent responses against enemy combatants.

Given that violent conflicts were taking place throughout the former Yugoslav territories, we might ask what role terrorism played in the fighting for Croatia's national independence. The new country was both on the giving and receiving ends of terrorism and wider-scale violence. There was strong reliance on militias, which were presumably sponsored by the warring states. Here we enter the realm of "proxy warriors." As Ariel Ahram writes, "Studies of civil wars tend to depict internal conflict as dyadic engagements between the state and rebel groups, two-player games of incumbent versus challenger. Yet closer inspection belies such simplification."[116] He goes on to cite the civil war analyst Stathis Kalyvas's study of this type of war in Greece, pointing out that these conflicts often produce small, local, and semi-independent groups built around family and community ties that carry out attacks, perhaps with calculations of personal benefit taking precedence over any other cause. (Similar arguments have been made in other contexts, such as in the Palestinian territories.)[117] State and rebel groups employ these fighters, though the same fighters may work for the state and rebel groups at different times; their targets include hapless civilians living in close-by communities.[118] This is, in other words, terrorism (see Figure 3.14).

In summary, the period immediately after Croatia's declaration of independence in June 1991 and the international recognition of this status some seventeen months later was one of warfare between Serbia and the newly independent Croatian state. In addition to conventional armed forces, proxy warriors surfaced on both sides. In those areas of Croatia with a significant Serb minority, such as in Krajina and Slavonia where Serbs made up roughly 12 percent of the total population, such militia groups as the White Eagles,

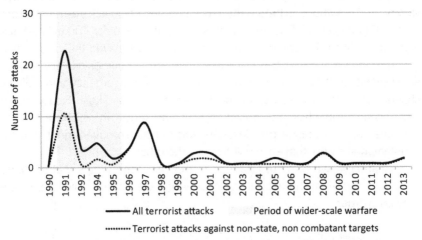

Figure 3.14   Attacks and terrorist attacks in Croatia (1991–2013)

Sources: Boot, *Invisible Armies*, 569–89;Connable and Libicki, *How Insurgencies End*, 157–62, 99–201; Sarkees and Wayman, *Resort to War*, Fearon and Laitin, "Additional Tables;" UCDP/PRIO, "Armed Conflict Dataset V.4-2014a, 1946–2013," "Global Terrorism Database [Data File]," 2014.

Chetniks, Tigers and Kninjas formed and proceeded to stage terrorist attacks and various atrocities. Their acts were carried out on behalf of the Serb minority's presumed intent to separate itself from the newly independent Croatian state. Croat paramilitary groups also played a significant role, particularly early in the fighting. Until a new Croatian national army could be organized, the militia of the neo-Ustasha, Croatian Defense Force and mercenary elements within the new National Guard directed terrorist attacks against Serbs and Bosnian Muslims.[119]

Conclusions

The cases we have sought to describe above are ones in which groups claiming to represent the grievances of sizeable ethnic, religious, and social populations, sometimes amorphous and at other times close-knit, made strategic decisions to use terrorism in order to achieve a separatist or revolutionary objective. However, terrorism could only carry them so far in pursuing their goals. At some point in their violent operations, leaders reached the conclusion that the conditions were ripe for a wider-scale confrontation with the authorities. What followed was insurgency within wider-scale warfare that led, as in the case of Croatia, to national independence – a goal pursued over many years. On other occasions, cooler heads prevailed and compromise solutions between the contestants were achieved. The third outcome was a decisive victory by the authorities before the terrorist group could achieve much more than self-gratification. This seems most likely the case for Turkey's leftists and India's Sikhs. Though elements of both groups survived their respective government's responses and still exist, their terrorist campaigns are far less significant than they once were and their hopes for insurgency and political change, at least through violent means, seem far less likely. Finally, there were instances in which the conflict remains unresolved, in which each of the contestants, for instance the Naxalites and the Indian government, remain constant in the view that each will destroy the other.

In Chapter 4, we turn our attention to the insurgent groups that continue to employ terrorism throughout the course of their armed challenges to the prevailing order.

Notes

1 In addition to ALF and ELF, this count includes acts by groups such as the Animal Defense League, Animal Rights Militia, Revolutionary Cells – Animal

Liberation Brigade, Earth Night Action, and Earth First! This count is based on data available in the Global Terrorism Database. See "Global Terrorism Database [Data File]," 2015.

2   These numbers are based on attacks recorded in the GTD dataset. "Global Terrorism Database [Data File]," 2015.

3   Evidence for this may be found in an analysis of GTD data for ALF, ELF, anti-abortion terrorists and the activities of other related groups. Ibid.

4   Central Intelligence Agency, The World Factbook, "United States," https://www.cia.gov/library/publications/the-world-factbook/geos/us.html (last accessed 4 April 2016).

5   For an assessment of the effectiveness of counterterrorism in the United States, see Christopher Hewitt, "Law Enforcement Tactics and Their Effectiveness in Dealing with American Terrorism: Organizations, Autonomous Cells, and Lone Wolves," *Terrorism and Political Violence*, 26, no. 1 (2014); Central Intelligence Agency, The World Factbook, "United States."

6   See, for instance, Leonard Weinberg and William Eubank, "Terrorism and Democracy: What Recent Events Disclose," *Terrorism and Political Violence*, 10, no. 1 (1998); William Lee Eubank and Leonard Weinberg, "Does Democracy Encourage Terrorism?" *Terrorism and Political Violence*, 6, no. 4 (1994); William Eubank and Leonard Weinberg, "Terrorism and Democracy: Perpetrators and Victims," *Terrorism and Political Violence*, 13, no. 1 (2001).

7   See, for instance, David Pion-Berlin and George A. Lopez, "Of Victims and Executioners: Argentine State Terror, 1975–1979," *International Studies Quarterly*, 35, no. 1 (1991).

8   Jason Lyall, "Do Democracies Make Inferior Counterinsurgents? Reassessing Democracy's Impact on War Outcomes and Duration," *International Organization*, 64, no. 1 (2010).

9   See, for instance, Alex P. Schmid and Albert J. Jongman, *Political Terrorism: A New Guide to Actors, Authors, Concepts, Data Bases, Theories, and Literature* (New Brunswick, NJ: Transaction Publishers, 2005). "Terrorist Organization Profiles," National Consortium for the Study of Terrorism and Responses to Terrorism (START), www.start.umd.edu/tops/ (last accessed April 4, 2016).

10 "Global Terrorism Database [Data File]," 2015.

11 "Global Terrorism Database [Data File]," 2013. This data is from 1970, so it is most likely 2013, since we didn't need to update it. In two attacks, the GTD dataset records the number of fatalities as "unknown."

12 Ibid.

13 Boot, *Invisible Armies*, Appendix.

14 Sarkees and Wayman, *Resort to War: 1816–2007*; Connable and Libicki, *How Insurgencies End*; Fearon and Laitin, "Additional Tables For 'Ethnicity, Insurgency, and Civil War';" UCDP/PRIO, "Armed Conflict Dataset V.4–2014a, 1946–2013."

15 Leonard Weinberg and William Lee Eubank, *The Rise and Fall of Italian Terrorism* (Boulder CO: Westview Press, 1987) p. 56. For another discussion, see Claire Sterling, *The Terror Network* (New York: Holt, Rinehart and Winston, 1974), 25–41.

16 Weinberg and Eubank, *The Rise and Fall of Italian Terrorism*, 56–61.

17   For a widely admired analysis see Kalyvas, *The Logic of Violence in Civil War*, 249–328.

18   See George Kassimeris, *Inside Greek Terrorism* (London: Hurst & Company, 2013), 17–20.

19   For further discussion, see George Kassimeris, "Greece: The Persistence of Political Terrorism," *International Affairs*, 89, no. 1 (2013).

20   Rosenau, "'Our Backs Are against the Wall'."

21   Ibid.

22   See Christopher Hewitt, *Understanding Terrorism in America* (New York, NY: Routledge, 2003), 12–22.

23   See for example, Geoffrey Pridham, "Terrorism and the State in West Germany During the 1970s," in *Terrorism: A Challenge to the State*, ed. Juliet Lodge (New York, NY: St. Martin's, 1981), 11–56.

24   For a summary see John Parachini and Katushisa Furukawa, "Japan and Aum Shinrikyo," in *Democracy and Counterterrorism*, ed. Robert Art and Louise Richardson (Washington, DC: United States Institute of Peace Press, 2007), 531–62. See also Robert Jay Lifton, *Destroying the World to Save It: Aum Shinrikyo, Apocalyptic Violence, and the New Global Terrorism* (New York: Henry Holt and Company, LLC, 2000).

25   For a brief overview of the organization and its development, see Manabu Watanabe, "Religion and Violence in Japan Today: A Chronological and Doctrinal Analysis of Aum Shinrikyo," *Terrorism and Political Violence*, 10, no. 4 (1998).

26   Lifton, *Destroying the World to Save It*, see, for instance, Chapter 1.

27   See, for instance, Milton Leitenberg, "Aum Shinrikyo's Efforts to Produce Biological Weapons: A Case Study in the Serial Propagation of Misinformation," *Terrorism and Political Violence*, 11, no. 4 (1999). See also Lifton, *Destroying the World to Save It*, Introduction.

28   For further discussion, see Ian Reader, *Religious Violence in Contemporary Japan: The Case of Aum Shinrikyo*, Nordic Institute of Asian Studies Monograph Series, No. 82 (Richmond, UK: Curzon Press, 2000).

29   See, for instance, Robert Jay Lifton, "Reflections on Aum Shinrikyo," *Journal of Personal & Interpersonal Loss*, 3, no. 1 (1998).

30   See, for instance, Perliger, *Challengers from the Sidelines*.

31   Fearon and Laitin, "Additional Tables for 'Ethnicity, Insurgency, and Civil War'."

32   The literature on these subjects is vast. Readers might begin by reading the work of Rogelio Alonso. See, for instance, "Pathways Out of Terrorism in Northern Ireland and the Basque Country: The Misrepresentation of the Irish Model," *Terrorism and Political Violence*, 16, no. 4 (2004): 695–713.

33   See, for instance, Bureau of Counterterrorism, "Chapter 6. Foreign Terrorist Organizations," in *Country Reports on Terrorism 2014*.

34   Rohan Gunaratna, "Global Threat Forecast 2015," *RSIS Commentary*, 252 (2014).

35   States included in this list do not have insurgents operating during the time period under investigation, as designated by Boot. Boot, *Invisible Armies*.

36   "Global Terrorism Database [Data File]," 2015.

37   Ibid.

38   Refer to "GTD Codebook," 8.

39   Among the countries experiencing terrorism without insurgency or attempted insurgency, the average percentage of attacks perpetrated against non-state entities or private actors is 63.5 percent (the median is slightly higher at 65 percent). Terrorist attacks against government, military, and police targets are less common. The standard deviation of the mean is 17.4.

40 Ted Robert Gurr, *Why Men Rebel* (Princeton, NJ: Princeton University Press, 1970).

41 For additional information, see A. Perliger, "How Democracies Respond to Terrorism: Regime Characteristics, Symbolic Power and Counterterrorism," *Security Studies*, 21, no. 3 (2012); The Southern Poverty Law Center (SPLC), www.splcenter.org (last accessed April 4, 2016); Barkun, *Religion and the Racist Right.*

42 See for example, Peter Lehr, "Still Blind in the Right Eye?," in *Extreme Right-Wing Political Violence and Terrorism*, ed. Max Taylor, P. M. Currie, and Donald Holbrook (London: Bloomsbury, 2013), 187–211.

43 See, for instance, Jones and Libicki, *How Terrorist Groups End: Lessons for Countering Al Qa'ida*; Leonard Weinberg, *The End of Terrorism?* (New York, NY: Routledge, 2012); Cronin, *How Terrorism Ends.*

44 For a more detailed account, see Erica Baffelli, "Hikari No Wa: A New Religion Recovering from Disaster," *Japanese Journal of Religious Studies*, 39, no. 1 (2012)..

45 Kassimeris, "Greece." In this, Kassimeris draws on David Moss, "Politics, Violence, Writing: The Rituals of 'Armed Struggle' in Italy," in *The Legitimization of Violence*, ed. David Apter (London: Macmillan, 1997), 85.

46 For further discussion, see Connable and Libicki, *How Insurgencies End*, especially p. 165.

47 Fearon and Laitin, "Ethnicity, Insurgency, and Civil War;" Sambanis, "Do Ethnic and Nonethnic Civil Wars Have the Same Causes?"

48 Laqueur, *The Age of Terrorism*, 245–65.

49 For additional discussion of the tradeoffs between repression and concilia-tion as alternative means of addressing the threats posed by terrorists, see Laura Dugan and Erica Chenoweth, "Moving Beyond Deterrence: The Effectiveness of Raising the Expected Utility of Abstaining from Terrorism in Israel," *American Sociological Review*, 77, no. 4 (2012).

50 See for example, Peter Calvert, "Venezuela: The FALN-FLN," in *Democracy and Counterterrorism*, ed. Robert Art and Louise Richardson (Washington, DC: United States Institute of Peace Press, 2007), 167–93.

51 See, for instance, David Fielding and Anja Shortland, "The Dynamics of Terror During the Peruvian Civil War," *Journal of Peace Research*, 49, no. 6 (2012); Sergio Koc-Menard, "Switching from Indiscriminate to Selective Violence: The Case of the Peruvian Military (1980–95)," *Civil Wars*, 8, no. 3 (2006).

52 Jo-Marie Burt, "'Quien Habla Es Terrorista': The Political Use of Fear in Fujimori's Peru," *Latin American Research Review*, 41, no. 3 (2006).

53 Patricia Marchak, *God's Assassins: State Terrorism in Argentina in the 1970s* (Montreal, Canada: McGill-Queen's University Press, 1999), for instance p. 147.

54 Jennifer S. Holmes, Sheila Amin Gutierrez de Pineres, and Kevin M. Curtin, *Guns, Drugs, and Development in Colombia* (Austin, TX: University of Texas Press, 2008), 55.

55 United States Congress House Committee on Foreign Affairs,

Subcommittee on Western Hemisphere Affairs, "The Threat of the Shining Path to Democracy in Peru: Hearings before the Subcommittee on Western Hemisphere Affairs of the Committee on Foreign Affairs" (Washington, DC: U.S. Government Printing Office, 1992), 12–13.

56   See, for instance, Steven T. Zech, "Drug Trafficking, Terrorism, and Civilian Self-Defense in Peru," *CTC Sentinel*, 7, no. 4 (2014).

57   See for example, Michael Weiss and Hassan Hassan, *ISIS: Inside the Army of Terror* (New York, NY: Regan Arts, 2014); Jessica Stern and J. M. Berger, *ISIS: The State of Terror* (New York, NY: HarperCollins, 2015).

58   "Terrorist March in Iraq: The U.S. Response, Hearing before the Committee on Foreign Affairs, House of Representatives," ed. Committee on Foreign Affairs (Washington, DC: U.S. Government Printing Office, July 23, 2014). See also, Michael Knights, "ISIL's Political Military Power in Iraq," *CTC Sentinel*, 7, no. 8 (2014); Cronin, "ISIS Is Not a Terrorist Group."

59   Bureau of Counterterrorism, "Chapter 6. Foreign Terrorist Organizations," in *Country Reports on Terrorism 2014*.

60   Ibid.

61   For another summary of ISIL's changing names and designations, see Stern and Berger, *ISIS*.

62   This is nicely summarized with additional citations in the file on "Jabhat al-Nusra" available through "Mapping Militant Organizations," Stanford University, web.stanford.edu/group/mappingmilitants/cgi-bin/groups (last accessed April 4, 2016).

63   Knights, "ISIL's Political Military Power in Iraq."

64   "Global Terrorism Database [Data File]," 2015.

65   Khachig Tololyan, "Terrorism in Modern Armenian Culture," in *Political Parties and Terrorist Groups*, ed. Leonard Weinberg (London: Frank Cass and Company Limited, 1992), 8–22; Francis Hyland, *Armenian Terrorism* (Boulder, CO: Westview Press, 1991), 23–56.

66   See, for instance, Laura Dugan, Julie Huang, Gary LaFree, and Clark McCauley, "Sudden Desistance from Terrorism: The Armenian Secret Army for the Liberation of Armenia and the Justice Commandos of the Armenian Genocide," *Dynamics of Asymmetric Conflict*, 1, no. 3 (2008).

67   For a discussion of the relationship between this group of terrorists' use of violence and reactions among the diaspora communities on which the terrorists depend, see ibid.

68   This debate was set off by Claire Sterling's bestseller, *The Terror Network*, 228–46.

69   See, for instance, "Terrorist Organization Profiles."

70   Boot, *Invisible Armies*, Appendix.

71   Bureau of Counterterrorism, "Chapter 6. Foreign Terrorist Organizations," *Country Reports on Terrorism 2013* (Washington, DC: United States Department of State).

72   "Global Terrorism Database [Data File]," 2015.

73   Ibid.

74   Sterling, *The Terror Network*, 231.

75   Gunduz S. Aktan and Ali M. Koknar, "Turkey," in *Combating Terrorism: Strategies of Ten Countries*, ed. Yonah Alexander (Ann Arbor, MI: 2002), 261.

76   Henri Barkey, "Turkey and the PKK," in *Democracy and Counterterrorism*,

ed. Robert Art and Louise Richardson (Washington, DC: United States Institute of Peace Press, 2007), 348.

77 See, for instance, "Terrorist Organization Profiles: Kurdistan Workers' Party (PKK)," National Consortium for the Study of Terrorism and Responses to Terrorism (START), www.start.umd.edu/tops/terrorist_organization_profile. asp?id=63 (last accessed April 4, 2016).

78 See, for instance, ibid; "Terrorist Organization Profiles."

79 See, for instance, Ali Sarihan, "The Two Periods of the PKK Conflict: 1984–1999 and 2004–2010," in *Understanding Turkey's Kurdish Question*, ed. Fevzi Bilgin (Lanham, MD: Lexington Books, 2013).

80 See for example, Hamit Bozarslan, "The Kurdish Issue in Turkey Following the 2003 Iraq War," in *The Kurdish Question*, ed. Mohammad Ahmed and Michael Gunter (Costa Mesa, CA: Mazda Publishers, 2005), 123–35; Gulistan Gurbey, "Implications of Turkey's Constitutional Reforms for the Kurds," in *The Kurdish Question*, ed. Mohammad Ahmed and Michael Gunter (Costa Mesa, CA: Mazda Publishers, 2005), 136–62.

81 Gurbey, "Implications of Turkey's Constitutional Reforms for the Kurds," 152–62.

82 Sameer Lalwani, "India's Approach to Counterinsurgency and the Naxalite Problem," *CTC Sentinel*, 4, no. 10 (October 31, 2011).

83 "Global Terrorism Database [Data File]," 2015.

84 Ibid.

85 See, for instance, Mark Juergensmeyer, "The Logic of Religious Violence: The Case of the Punjab," *Contributions to Indian Sociology*, 22, no. 1 (1988).

86 See, for instance, Shale Horowitz, and Deepti Sharma, "Democracies Fighting Ethnic Insurgencies: Evidence from India," *Studies in Conflict & Terrorism*, 31, no. 8 (2008).

87 Boot, *Invisible Armies*, Appendix.

88 Paul Wallace, "Countering Terrorist Movements in India: Kashmir and Khalistan," in *Democracy and Counterterrorism: Lessons from the Past*, ed. Robert J. Art and Louise Richardson (Washington, DC: United States Institute of Peace Press, 2007), 428.

89 For example, "An Echo of Terrorism," *The Economist (Asia)* (June 12, 2003), www.economist.com/node/1852365 (last accessed April 4, 2016).

90 Horowitz and Sharma, "Democracies Fighting Ethnic Insurgencies: Evidence from India."

91 Ved Marwah, "India," in *Combating Terrorism: Strategies of Ten Countries*, ed. Yonah Alexander (Ann Arbor, MI: University of Michigan Press, 2002), 304–5.

92 Horowitz and Sharma, "Democracies Fighting Ethnic Insurgencies: Evidence from India."

93 "Global Terrorism Database [Data File]," 2013.

94 Ibid.

95 For a sense of the atmospherics, see Jessica Stern, *Terror in the Name of God* (New York, NY: Harper Collins, 2003), 107–37. For profiles of Islamist groups targeting India, see for instance "Mapping Militant Organizations."

96 See, for example, Mark J. Roberts, "Pakistan's Inter-Services Intelligence Directorate: A State within a State?," *Joint Force Quarterly*, 1, no. 48 (2008); Arjun Subramaniam, "Challenges of Protecting India from Terrorism,"

Terrorism and Political Violence, 24, no. 3 (2012). See also "Mapping Militant Organizations."

97 C. Christine Fair, "The 2008 Mumbai Attack," in *The Evolution of the Global Terrorist Threat*, ed. Bruce Hoffman and Fernando Reinares (New York, NY: Columbia University Press, 2014), 571–99; Husain Haqqani, "India's Islamist Groups," *Current Trends in Islamist Ideology*, 3 (2006).

98 See, for instance, Mohammad Sajjad Waqas and Ahmad Jawad, "Lashkar-e-Tayyiba and the Jamaat-Ud-Dawa: The Case for a Pakistani Narrative," *Strategic Studies*, 31, no. 3 (2011).

99 Subramaniam, "Challenges of Protecting India from Terrorism."

100 These figures are based on a count of cases made available via the "Global Terrorism Database [Data File]," 2014.

101 For a discussion of the Ottoman Empire's end, see Elie Kedourie, "The End of the Ottoman Empire," *Comtemporary History*, 3, no. 4 (1968).

102 See, for instance, Randall D. Law, *Terrorism: A History* (Malden, MA: Polity, 2009); Gerard Chaliand and Arnaud Blin, "The 'Golden Age' of Terrorism," in *The History of Terrorism: From Antiquity to Al Qaeda*, ed. Gerard Chaliand and Arnaud Blin (Berkeley, CA: University of California Press, 2007), 191–3.

103 Chaliand and Blin, "The 'Golden Age' of Terrorism," 191–2.

104 Alberto Ciria, "Peronism Yesterday and Today," *Latin American Perspectives*, 1, no. 3 (1974).

105 For further description, see Phyllis Auty, "9th Congress of League of Yugoslav Communists," *World Today*, 25, no. 6 (1969).

106 J. Bowyer Bell, *A Time of Terror* (New York, NY: Basic Books, 1978), 6–35.

107 Ibid., 16–17.

108 John Allcock, Marko Milivojevic, and John Horton, *Conflict in the Former Yugoslavia* (Santa Barbara, CA: ABC-CLIO, 1998), 291–3.

109 See, for instance, Aleksa Djilas, "Review: Tito's Last Secret: How Did He Keep the Yugoslavs Together?" *Foreign Affairs*, 74, no. 4 (1995).

110 See, for instance, James Gow, *The Serbian Project and Its Adversaries: A Strategy of War Crimes* (Montreal, Canada: McGill-Queen's University Press, 2003), 163–4.

111 We may distinguish between the ethnicity and the nationality or citizenship in the former Yugoslav republics. Serbs and Croats are ethnic groups identified largely on the basis of their religion. Serbs tend to be Orthodox; Croats tend to be Catholic. Serbian and Croatian are nationalities, or citizens of Serbia and Croatia, respectively. Bosnians are citizens of Bosnia. Bosnian Muslims are Bosnians who may also be referred to as "Bosniaks."

112 For a description of this, see for example, Samantha Power, *A Problem from Hell* (New York, NY: Harper, 2002), 247–327; Obrad Kesic, "Serbia – the Politics of Despair," *Current History*, 92, no. 577 (1993).

113 Power, *A Problem from Hell*; Kesic, "Serbia – the Politics of Despair."

114 United Nations, International Criminal Tribunal for the Former Yugoslavia, *20 Years of the ICTY: Anniversary Events and Legacy Conference Proceedings* (Sarajevo, Bosnia and Herzegovina: ICTY Outreach Programme, 2014); Ewa Tabeau, Jakub Bijak, and Neda Loncaric, "Death Toll in the Siege of Sarajevo, April 1992 to December 1995: A Study of Mortality Based on Eight Large Data Sources, Expert Report Prepared for the Case of Slobodan Milosevic – Bosnia and Herzegovina (It-02–54)" (International Criminal Tribunal for the Former Yugoslavia, 2003).

115 See, for instance, Damir Mirkovic, "Ethnic Conflict and Genocide: Reflections on Ethnic Cleansing in the Former Yugoslavia," *Annals of the American Academy of Political and Social Science*, 548 (1996); United Nations International Criminal Tribunal for the Former Yugoslavia, www.icty.org/. For additional information, see released CIA documents: "Bosnia, Intelligence, and the Clinton Presidency," Central Intelligence Agency, www.foia.cia.gov/collection/bosnia-intelligence-and-clinton-presidency (last accessed April 8, 2016).

116 Ariel Ahram, *Proxy Warriors* (Stanford, CA: Stanford University Press, 2011), 8.

117 See, for instance, Pedahzur and Perliger, "The Changing Nature of Suicide Attacks: A Social Network Perspective."

118 Ahram, *Proxy Warriors*, 8–9.

119 Martin Spegeli, "The First Phase, 1990–1992," in *The War in Croatia and Bosnia-Herzegovina*, ed. Branka Magas and Ivo Zanic (London: Frank Cass, 2001), 14–40.

4

Terrorism as a tactic of wider-scale warfare

In this chapter our focus is on insurgent groups that have used terrorism throughout their struggles to replace political regimes or in an effort to secede from a political community. First, though, we need to place this pattern of insurgency in context.

Some of the old generalizations about terrorism no longer match contemporary realities. The notion that "terrorism is a weapon of the weak" no longer applies to many twenty-first century insurgencies. In addition, the belief that terrorists are interested in the psychological effects of their violence while guerrillas seek to conquer territory no longer rings true. Terrorists as understood here may engage in guerrilla attacks to militarily weaken an adversary; many seek to control territory. Terrorists may concern themselves with the psychological effects of their attacks but they likely concern themselves with other potential effects of the various types of attacks they perpetrate. The same actors may be simultaneously terrorists and guerrillas. Moreover, while the expectation that "terrorists want a lot of people watching not a lot of people dead" may have had some resonance before 9/11, it has had far less since then.[1] Also outdated is the view that terrorism belongs in the initial "agitation propaganda" phase of an insurgency but then loses its *raison d'utilisation* as a violent conflict mounts and becomes more threatening to those holding power.

Consider the case of the jihadist group known as Boko Haram. The group emerged in 2009 in the heavily Muslim region of Northeastern Nigeria. Since that year, its militants have killed thousands of villagers and kidnapped hundreds of school-age girls, in many cases forcefully converting them to Islam or making them serve as sex slaves, or both. The group continues to send suicide bombers on missions to destroy various government targets. Over this same span of time, Boko Haram has also conquered territory, proclaimed a caliphate on the land under its control and proceeded to behead fellow Nigerians whom these jihadists believe have seriously violated Sharia law.

The situation in Afghanistan, though hardly identical, is similar. Although al-Qaeda Central is no longer able to use the country as a base of operations, the Taliban organization continues to be a serious contestant for power, thanks in part to its identification with the Pashtun ethnic group and its ability to operate from secure bases in Pakistan.[2]

Afghanistan's Taliban also draws its influence from Salafi jihadist ideology, though the movement is influenced by a distinct form of Sunni Islam, the "Hanafi Deobandi School."[3] The Afghan Taliban, with its more localized interests and activities, has not been labeled as a foreign terrorist organization, as designated by the U.S. Department of State.[4] There is also a Taliban in Pakistan, which goes by the name Tehrik-e Taliban Pakistan. This Taliban is an al-Qaeda affiliate and opponent of Pakistan's government. TTP is a designated FTO by the State Department operating on both sides of the Afghanistan–Pakistan border. Like the Taliban in Afghanistan before it, TTP provides a "safe haven" for al Qaeda, something al Qaeda lost with the 2001 invasion of Afghanistan.[5] Both Taliban organizations seek a form of religious control, and both seek to acquire and have acquired territory, especially in the heavily Pashtun areas of the countries involved. They have also carried out multiple suicide bombings and other terrorist attacks on civilian targets in contested areas.[6]

In Yemen the interplay between tribal politics and religious divisions has resulted in multiple armed insurgencies. Various claimants for power have been at war with one another in the country's capital at Sanaa since the forced departure of long-serving President Salah in 2005. Their tactics have included guerrilla operations in the countryside and terrorist attacks throughout Yemen. Al Qaeda in the Arabian Peninsula (AQAP) is also present. And, from bases in remote locales, AQAP seeks to topple the Saudi monarchy. Members of this al-Qaeda affiliate have also prepared difficult-to-detect bombs in order to blow up America-bound commercial airliners over the Atlantic. In addition, leaders of the Shiite Houthi population in the region launched an insurgency against the government and have captured significant territory, which the group presently seeks to rule.[7]

The case of ISIL also suggests we are dealing with a family of insurgencies that has become adept at combining tactics of guerrilla warfare and terrorism. ISIL emerged from AQI, which has been listed as a foreign terrorist organization by the United States Department of State since 2004 and which changed its name to Islamic State in Iraq (ISI) in 2006. ISIL has been described as an "umbrella organization."[8] Since its split from its own and al Qaeda's affiliate, the al-Nusra Front, in 2013 and from al Qaeda in 2014, ISIL has captured substantial territory in Syria and Iraq and proclaimed the formation of a new caliphate. In the course of its insurgencies against the Alawite and Shiite dominated regimes in Damascus and Baghdad, respectively, ISIL has carried out among the most brutal terrorist attacks known to humanity – beheadings, summary executions, and the enslavement of non-Muslim women. Shiites, as heretics, have been targeted for murder along with such non-Sunni religious minorities as Christians and the Yazidi.

What do these contemporary conflicts tell us about the evolving character of twenty-first century's "unconventional wars"?[9] To be more specific, why do we find terrorism so frequently used in conjunction with traditional guerrilla tactics to be so prevalent in the twenty-first century? Two answers come readily to mind.

First, there is the matter of location. In countries where the bulk of the population lives in the countryside, irregular warfare involving attacks on despised outposts of the central state makes good sense. Among other things, it provides the insurgents with an opportunity to win and maintain the support of the local population. The world's population has undergone considerable change since these tactics made sense. The irregular warfare analyst and U.S. Department of Defense advisor David Kilcullen calls attention to the fact that the world is going through a long-term population shift from rural areas to urban centers and from small towns to mega-cities, particularly to those located close to important waterways. As Kilcullen reasons, "the environment for future conflicts is clearly shifting. The four megatrends of population growth, urbanization, littoralization, and connectedness suggest that conflict is increasingly likely to occur in coastal cities, in underdeveloped regions of the Middle East, Africa, Latin America and Asia."[10] And, as examples of things likely to come, he cites Lashkar-e Tayyiba's 2008 attack on the Indian mega-city of Mumbai and the 1993 struggle for control of the Somali city of Mogadishu between a local warlord and American special forces.[11]

A second assessment about the changing nature of post-modern armed conflict emphasizes the importance of intelligence and cyber-security.[12] Such modern technologies as unmanned drones with their missile-firing capabilities are often mentioned along with the growing availability of miniaturized weapons, particularly valuable to insurgent groups. Most of all, though, this line of reasoning about the changing nature of war-making emphasizes new types of communication and the technologies that accompany them. Nowadays virtually all insurgent groups of any significance use websites to advertise their accomplishments and future aims. Some, such as ISIL, use blood-curdling graphics to get their messages across. Such writers as

Lorenzo Vidino echo alarms sounded by government officials about the ability of jihadist groups to radicalize and recruit new members via the Internet.[13]

Another answer to the question regarding why so many recent insurgencies seem to combine terrorist and guerrilla modes of action concerns the character of the states involved. The nature of the states where armed challengers seek to overturn established governments is likely an important consideration. In the early years of what the historian Walter Laqueur called the "Age of Terrorism," terrorism was largely the work of small clandestine bands typically operating within large cities. The groups, including, for example, the Red Brigades in Italy, the RAF in Germany, Popular Front for the Liberation of Palestine, and United Japanese Red Army, rarely consisted of more than a few hundred individuals operating on an underground basis.[14]

Despite threats to bring down the capitalist system on a worldwide basis and the claims these relatively small groups made about their inexorable momentum toward this objective, the reality was that they never seriously challenged the states and international institutions they sought to destroy. There are several reasons for this to have been the case. First, the groups involved were never able to win the support of any sizable constituency of potentially revolutionary supporters. Second, and clearly related, is the fact that these clandestine bands often targeted the world's most successful democracies. Not only did these democracies enjoy widespread legitimacy, they also had relatively strong institutions with which to enforce their rule throughout the national territory. The combination of political legitimacy and strong state institutions proved lethal for the terrorists.

Virtually the opposite situation prevails in countries where insurgents employ a mix of terrorism and tactics of guerrilla warfare. These are places where the state is usually corrupt and weak, whether nominally democratic or not. More to the point, their military and police establishments are unable or unwilling to enforce the law throughout the national territory. The tribal areas along the Pakistan–Afghanistan border, northern Mali, Somalia, and much of Yemen display these characteristics; they are weak states with ungoverned territory.[15] These are also places where local identities may overshadow a fragile or non-existent national identity. We could add much of Iraq, Syria, and Libya to this list.

Instead, in territories where these conditions prevail, there is little to inhibit insurgents from acting as guerrillas and terrorists simultaneously. Accordingly, in Iraq and Syria, ISIL directs its fighters to capture territory (e.g., Anbar Province) and carry out suicide bombings throughout Baghdad and its suburbs. The same tactics are used by the Taliban and its associates in Afghanistan and, to a lesser extent, in Pakistan as well.[16]

In Chapter 3, we discussed insurgencies in which those challenging the state used terrorism at the beginning or early phases of armed conflicts, which were initiated between 1970 and 2010. Now we turn our attention to situations in which insurgents employed terrorism throughout their challenges to the prevailing order.

Terrorism as a tactic of wider-scale armed conflict

There have been many instances in which militant groups have employed terrorist violence throughout their efforts in the context of wider-scale armed conflict. There are also a variety of patterns of terrorism used by groups engaging in armed conflict. In some cases, terrorism presents during an armed conflict, while being largely absent before or after the conflict. The terrorism credited to El Salvador's FMLN follows this pattern. The various Irish Republican Armies' use of terrorism also appears to follow this pattern. In other cases, terrorism is present outside of the period of wider-scale armed conflict but is present at a higher frequency during armed conflict. This was Algeria's experience with terrorism. The number of terrorist attacks peaked during the country's conflict with Algerian Islamist groups, including the GIA and the various armed Islamic movements associated with the Islamic Salvation Army. Many of the attacks between 1998 and 2008, including many occurring after the end of the period of wider-scale armed conflict, are credited to Algerian Islamic Extremists. In another set of cases, terrorism peaks at some point during an armed conflict. Guatemala's guerrilla fighters, including those affiliated with the Guatemalan National Revolutionary Unity (URNG), show this pattern in the context of Guatemala's thirty-six-year civil war. For still other groups, terrorism increases during armed conflict. Although their overall count of terrorist incidents is small, Sierra Leone's experience with terrorism also demonstrates this pattern during its two intra-state armed conflicts. The same can be said of Tajikistan's experience with terrorism during its war against the United Tajik Opposition (UTO), Liberia's insurgents, and El Salvador's FMLN. The presence of one or more peaks in the frequency of terrorist attacks is a relatively common feature of cases in which terrorism is used in the context of wars (see Figure 4.1).

In most of these cases, insurgent groups sought to replace a country's rulers or achieve some form of territorial separation. In the case of the loyalist groups of Northern Ireland, the goal was to avoid the separation sought by the competing Irish republicans. These cases are distinguished by their use of terrorism during a large part of their insurgent efforts, including the middle years of the period of wider-scale armed conflict. We should reiterate here that the period of "insurgency," as designated by Boot and used here, does not necessarily correspond with a period of wider-scale armed conflict (refer to Table 3.1, Table 3.2, and Table 3.3).[17]

The analysis here focuses on terrorism in the context of internal wars.[18] Patterns in the use of terrorism during and throughout internal wars vary. Some of the frequencies show one or more peaks; in some of these cases,

Guatemala's guerrillas, including the Guatemalan National Revolutionary Unity (1960–96)

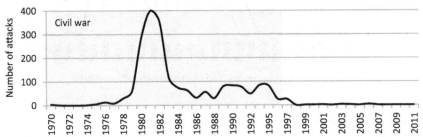

Provisional Irish Republican Army

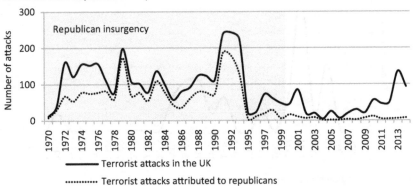

Eritrean Separatists (1961–83) and Anti-Derg Militias (1974–91)

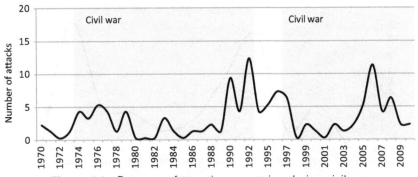

Figure 4.1   Patterns of terrorism occurring during civil war

El Salvador's Farabundo Marti National Liberation Front (1980–92)

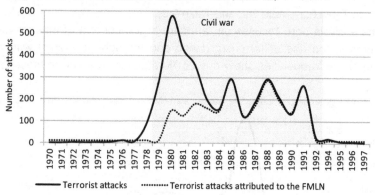

National Patriotic Front of Liberia (1989–92) and Liberians United for Reconciliation and Democracy, Movement for Democracy in Liberia (1999–2003)

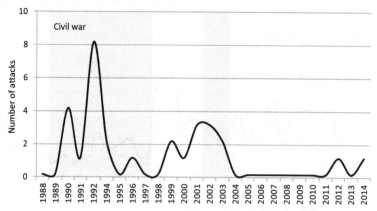

Terrorism during Sierra Leone's intra-state wars

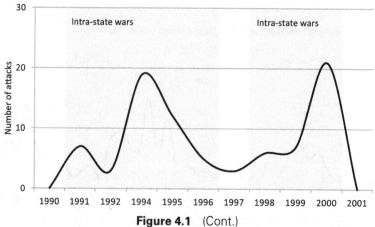

Figure 4.1   (Cont.)

Georgia's Abkhaz Secessionists (1992–93)

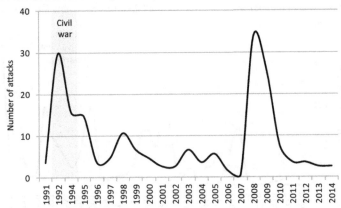

United Tajik Opposition (1992–97)

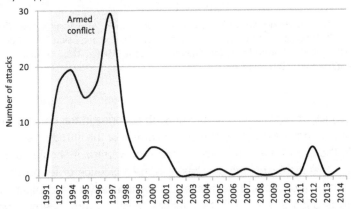

Armed Islamic Group of Algeria, Islamic Armed Movement/Islamic Salvation Front/Islamic Salvation Army (1992–2002)

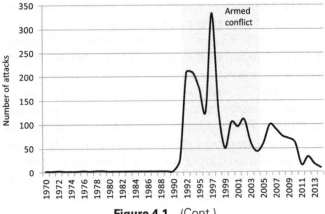

Figure 4.1   (Cont.)

Israel and various Palestinian groups: Hamas (1987–ongoing), Palestine Liberation
Organization (1965–ongoing), Popular Front for the Liberation of Palestine (1968–ongoing)

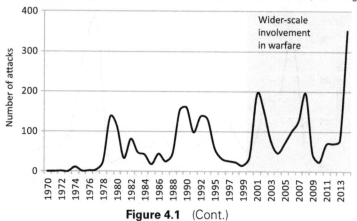

Figure 4.1   (Cont.)

Sources: Boot, *Invisible Armies*, 569–89; Connable and Libicki, *How Insurgencies End*,
157–62, 99–201; Sarkees and Wayman, *Resort to War*; Fearon and Laitin, "Additional
Tables;" UCDP/PRIO, "Armed Conflict Dataset V.4-2014a, 1946–2013," "Global Terrorism
Database [Data File]," 2012 and 2014.

the frequency of terrorism corresponds with changes in the conflict, such as
an increase or decrease in the intensity of conflict or the introduction of a new
actor. To the extent that terrorism is a tactic of warfare, it should not escape
our notice that increases and decreases in the incidence of terrorism should
equate with increases and decreases in the intensity of a conflict. Unless
terrorism is used in place of other tactics, such as rural guerrilla warfare,
increases in the numbers of attacks and casualties should follow increases in
the use of terrorist tactics, thereby leading to an increase in the overall level
of violence and the intensity of violence, to the extent that measures of these
are tied to numbers of attacks or numbers of casualties.

Of the patterns we observed, few show what might appear to be a
consistent use of terrorism for the duration of a conflict. Among these cases
were some with the lowest incidence of terrorism overall (e.g., Liberia and
Papua New Guinea). Moreover, in a small number of the cases examined
(including those of insurgents in Ethiopia, Nicaragua, and Sudan), the frequencies of terrorist attacks used throughout their efforts produce patterns
similar to those made by groups using terrorism at the later stages of insurgency or after wider-scale conflict has ended. The main differences are the
valleys that precede the peaks in frequencies of terrorism in some of the
cases and the sharpness of the spikes in the frequencies of terrorism in
others.

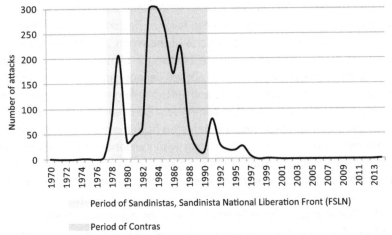

Period of Sandinistas, Sandinista National Liberation Front (FSLN)

Period of Contras

Figure 4.2   Terrorism in Nicaragua

Sources: Boot, *Invisible Armies*, 569–89; Connable and Libicki, *How Insurgencies End*, 157–62, 99–201; Sarkees and Wayman, *Resort to War*; Fearon and Laitin, "Additional Tables;" UCDP/PRIO, "Armed Conflict Dataset V.4-2014a, 1946–2013;" "Global Terrorism Database [Data File]," 2015.

For instance, in the case of the Sandinista-affiliated groups in Nicaragua, it is apparent that a later increase in terrorism was a response to a new insurgent threat, aimed directly at the Sandinistas by the Contras (see Figure 4.2). The Sandinistas gained power over the government in 1979 and were at this time, by definition, no longer insurgents. This was followed by the beginning of a new civil war involving the Contras. Terrorism was a tactic used in both episodes of civil war.

Not all or even most of the insurgencies were victorious in terms of toppling those in power or achieving a secessionist outcome. Despite employing a combination of terrorism and guerrilla warfare, some insurgent groups failed (e.g., the Tamil Tigers in Sri Lanka), others succeeded (e.g., in Nepal), while in other instances the question remains moot (e.g., Mali, Syria, and Iraq).

At this point in our discussion we intend to describe a number of cases in which insurgent groups employed both guerrilla tactics and terrorism for long periods in order to achieve their revolutionary aims. Latin America, the location of what Regis Debray labeled "the revolution in the revolution," provides us with a number of valuable cases for consideration.[19]

The emergence of these hybrid campaigns combining guerrilla warfare and terrorism should be linked to two significant developments: one political the other tactical. During the mid-to-late 1960s, the international communist movement experienced a serious schism. In China, Mao unleashed the

"Great Proletarian Cultural Revolution" while denouncing the Soviet Union for abandoning the revolutionary cause in favor of peaceful co-existence with the West. In Latin America and other parts of the world, communist parties mimicked this division. Factions developed within the parties, particularly prevalent among youth groups, which in many cases denounced the parties' officialdom for having become bureaucratized and far too willing to accommodate itself to the capitalist order. As a result, in some West European, South Asian, and Latin American countries these factions defected from the major communist parties in the names of Mao or Trotsky, along with indigenous revolutionary heroes from earlier times (e.g., Tupac Amaru, Farabundo Marti, Augusto Sandino). The result was a series of new revolutionary forces committed to political violence on behalf of the continent's vast number of impoverished masses.

The Cuban Revolution offered another example of what might be accomplished. If not exactly Robin Hood and his Merrie Men, Fidel Castro and Ernesto "Che" Guevara were treated as heroic revolutionary figures, who had defeated the reactionary government in Havana and forced the Americans out. It was hoped by many young revolutionaries throughout Latin America that the Cuban model could be successfully applied in their own countries. The problem with this formula was that Castro had called cities the "graveyards of revolution," and the Cuban model relied exclusively on guerrilla operations in the countryside.

Che Guevara attempted to replicate the Cuban revolution on a much wider scale. In 1967, Guevara and his small *foco* (i.e., guerrilla enclave) of fighters were defeated by the Bolivian military at their Andean base. Guevara himself was killed in these proceedings. For many disillusioned followers, the countryside by itself could not be the exclusive source of revolutionary activity. It needed augmentation.[20] Here we witness the arrival of the so-called "urban guerrilla" and serious campaigns of terrorism both in the cities and the countryside.

Colombia offers a vivid case of a protracted armed conflict, one whose insurgents have employed a mix of guerrilla warfare and urban terrorism for some decades in the hope of bringing an end to the democratically elected government in Bogota. It is also a country in which both Castroite and Maoist ideas were at work at various times. This is one of the four cases we discuss in greater detail.

Terrorism in the context of wider-scale warfare

We now turn to a discussion of instances in which insurgent groups use terrorism in the context of wider-scale warfare. These are cases in which a state's challengers employed terrorism throughout the course of their struggles in order to change the prevailing political order.

Colombia's leftist guerrillas

Colombia has a number of features that made it exceptionally vulnerable to an armed insurgency. The first is its geography: "Colombia is a mountainous, diverse region with a strong African heritage along the Atlantic coast, an overwhelmingly indigenous population in the southwestern mountains, and a mixed population in the interior. Before air travel in the 1920s, the country was a union in name only because intra-national communication and travel was difficult. Indeed, some have argued that the nation's violence and entire political structure stems from a lack of geographic cohesion."[21]

These physical and human characteristics would lead an observer to predict that Colombia would be governed by a military junta or some other authoritarian arrangement, but this has not been the case at all. Unlike many of its counterparts in much of Latin America, Colombia has not suffered a military coup or populist dictatorship since 1953. Moreover, between 1958 and 1974, Colombia resembled a "consociational democracy" with a power-sharing coalition that included the two leading political forces in the country.

Despite, or perhaps because of, this democratic tradition Colombia is also distinguished by its long history of both public and private violence. Over time, the country's murder rate has been among the highest in the world, rivaling that of South Africa, though it is lower than Venezuela's and some of its Central American neighbors.[22] In addition, Colombia attracted international attention beginning in the 1970s based on the role played by some of its residents in the cocaine business. The Cali and Medellin drug cartels became notorious for their key roles in the refining and shipment of drugs to North America and elsewhere.[23] The drug traffickers offered bribes to public officials and were willing to kill those judges, local mayors, and others who refused to accept their offers.

There is also the matter of Colombia's "La Violencia." During the first two thirds (approximately) of the twentieth century, Colombian politics was dominated by two hegemonic political parties: the Conservatives and Liberals. Both parties reflected the interests of the country's upper-middle classes. The Liberals, though, tended to be anti-clerical, opposed to the highly conservative views of the Church hierarchy. The Conservatives, on the other hand, were more likely to express the views of the country's wealthy landowners as well as those of the Church.[24] This duopoly came to an end in the years immediately following World War II. The Liberals divided into competing factions in 1946, following the government's suppression of the communist-led farm workers' union. Meanwhile, the Conservatives attempted to control all or most of the levers of power both in Bogota and in the countryside. Following the assassination of a Liberal leader in 1948, crowds in downtown Bogota attacked the presidential palace and burned much of the city's business district. What followed was a virtual civil war, as Liberals took up arms against the Conservative-dominated state. According to Waldmann, "Between 1949 and 1958, about 250,000 people were killed in a conflict that initially bore resemblance to a party conflict in the traditional sense, then developed its own dynamics. Banditry and criminal violence expanded into the countryside and superseded the political motives of violence."[25]

The National Front agreement between contending Liberal and Conservative forces was one outcome of "La Violencia." This was the era between 1958 and 1974 when the contending Liberal and Conservative forces reached an agreement that would re-establish order based on what amounted to a power-sharing arrangement. The resulting coalition between Liberals and Conservatives was in place at all levels of government, while the two parties alternated in holding the presidency.[26]

It was against this background that the revolutionary ideas of Castro, Mao, and Latin America's own advocates of the urban guerrilla took hold. According to Eduardo Pizarro, an immediate trigger to the ignition of an armed revolutionary struggle was the Colombian Communist Party's decision to endorse the National Front, the power-sharing coalition of Conservatives and Liberals. Instead of insurrection, the Party called for "peaceful revolutionary struggle through the progressive democratization of the country."[27] In other words, the Party was endorsing "revisionism," heresy in classical Marxism.

It is no doubt a simplification, but what followed was the appearance of some half-dozen groups committed to the overthrow of the National Front by violent means. The most long-lasting of these formations were the ELN (National Liberation Army), M-19 (Movement of April 19) and FARC. FARC especially was rooted in the Colombian Communist experience. The ELN emerged in the early 1960s after some dozens of university students returned from Cuba where they had been inspired by Castroite ideas about revolution and Guevara's thoughts on the ability of *foci* to establish a revolutionary atmosphere through revolutionary action. M-19, a late-comer, was organized in protest against the rigging of the country's April 19, 1970, presidential election.

The ELN has proven to be the most reluctant of these armed struggle groups to compromise in reaction to the government's various peace initiatives. During the 1980s and after, ELN militants specialized in sabotaging Colombia's oil fields and kidnapping business executives, both foreign and domestic. The ELN has also been able to establish a handful of territorial enclaves within Colombia.

Throughout its own, by-now long career, FARC has proven to be the most serious challenger to a succession of Colombian governments. It has conquered substantial territory and has specialized in murdering police officers and civilian opponents in the big cities and kidnapping prominent figures in Colombian life, including politicians, high-ranking military officers, and celebrities. According to various accounts, FARC has also gone into the drug business. During the 1980s and 1990s, FARC offered protection to cocaine traffickers as they shipped the raw coca from Bolivia and Peru to refiners and shippers in the Colombian hinterland. Neither the ELN nor FARC has made much of an effort to win the hearts and minds of the people falling under their control. If anything, the two groups' leaders have behaved more arbitrarily than the government in Bogota when given the chance to rule. And, from time-to-time, both the ELN and FARC have employed terrorism to maintain their control. As Waldmann reports: "When a guerrilla group feels weakened or is not being taken seriously by the authorities, it often commits spectacular acts of terrorism to win back the attention and respect of the government and general public."[28] As an illustration, in 1985, M-19 militants invaded the Palace of Justice in Bogota and took hostage members of the Colombian Supreme Court. Somewhat later, FARC launched a bombing campaign in downtown Bogota in response to the election of a presidential candidate of whom it disapproved.

Over the decades the government has sought to end the insurgency through the use of "carrots and sticks." For example, at various times the government has offered the insurgents opportunities to rejoin the democratic political process by running candidates for the presidency and other public offices. FARC entered the political process through its association with the Patriotic Union party, though many thousands of party members were assassinated, reportedly by FARC's competitors in the drug-trafficking business and along the ideological spectrum, including right-wing militant groups, who may have operated "with the complicity of the government."[29] A democratically elected constituent assembly produced a new constitution in 1991 in the hope that this document would end the insurgency.

The effect of these and other measures was to end M-19 and the other minor groups' involvement in the revolutionary armed struggle. The ELN and FARC, on the other hand, have persisted in their campaigns well into the twenty-first century. At the same time, their capacity to do more than cause highly publicized annoyances seems to have become increasingly remote.[30]

In Colombia's case, terrorism has been used throughout the period under discussion (see Figure 4.3). Recorded incidences of terrorism have increased over the duration of the conflict, which began in 1963. Terrorism

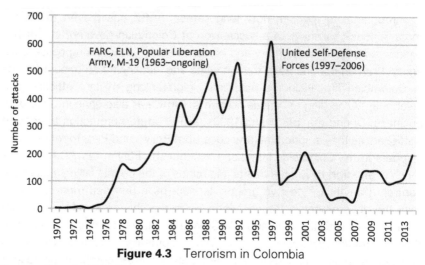

Figure 4.3 Terrorism in Colombia

Sources: Boot, *Invisible Armies,* 569–89; Connable and Libicki, *How Insurgencies End,* 157–62, 99–201; Sarkees and Wayman, *Resort to War;* Fearon and Laitin, "Additional Tables;" UCDP/PRIO, "Armed Conflict Dataset V.4-2014a, 1946–2013;" "Global Terrorism Database [Data File]," 2014.

data for this earlier period is not available. The number of terrorist attacks in Colombia peaked with the initiation of operations by the United Self-Defense Forces (AUC). The AUC formed as a right-wing paramilitary group in 1997 in response to the threats posed by Colombia's leftist rebels. The group carried out various atrocities during its tenure. The group was also a competitor in the drug trafficking business. Terrorism decreased considerably in the years after the introduction of the AUC and its apparent dissolution in 2006.[31]

FARC has survived more than fifty years and the loss of several of its leaders to natural causes as well as an effective and internationally sponsored effort to weaken the group. Moreover, despite the wealth the group has accumulated from its criminal activities, it has lost support as a result of effective counterterrorism. Seeking the most favorable exit from their current predicament – and perhaps as part of an effort to realize some of the group's original political objectives – FARC began working with Colombia toward a negotiated peace.

Peru and the Shining Path

At the beginning of the 1980s, Peru had experienced more than a decade of military dictatorship. After years of largely failed efforts to promote economic and social development, the ruling junta decided to return power to the civilian politicians. The outcome of the 1980 balloting was the election of a socialist to the presidency, one committed to reform within the context of the newly restored constitutional order. However, as David Scott Palmer and others have observed, Peru had an exceptionally vibrant Marxist-Leninist and Maoist subculture centered in the universities and labor unions.[32] One outcome of this mix of revolutionary leftist groups was the formation of the Communist Party of Peru – Shining Path (Sendero Luminoso).

The Shining Path emerged from a series of factional fights and splits among Peru's newly liberated Marxist revolutionary organizations. Its origins derive from political life not in the capital city, Lima, but in the remote area of Ayacucho, in a city by the same name. It is a community in the southwest of the state, high in the Andes at more than 9,000 feet above sea level and separated around 350 miles from Lima by road. This is also the home of the San Cristobal de Huamanga University.

At the time the Shining Path began, the region had only one dirt road leading to Lima, no telephones, a single radio station and one weekly newspaper. Still, or perhaps because of, Ayacucho's remoteness, the university attracted a young revolutionary professor of philosophy, Abimael Guzman. A charismatic figure, Guzman had visited China on several occasions during the 1960s at the time when the Great Proletarian Revolution was in full swing. Of course following Mao's death in 1976 China's new leadership abandoned the Cultural Revolution in favor of economic reforms that led, eventually, to the country's transformation into an economic giant. But it was the Maoist experience that impressed Guzman and a small group of other Peruvian intellectuals who joined him on his pilgrimage.[33]

As David Scott Palmer points out, Guzman's small Peruvian Maoist party was cast adrift when the Cultural Revolution was abandoned in China at the end of the 1970s. At this time Guzman underwent a transformation into "Commandante Gonzolo." He then devised his own revolutionary doctrine. His was not a modest exercise. After Marx, Lenin, and Mao, Guzman regarded himself as adding a new star to the communist firmament. Despite Peru's poverty and vast economic inequalities, both rural and urban, most Peruvian Marxists concluded that a revolutionary condition did not exist. Guzman disagreed. He believed in the revolutionary potential of the country's impoverished indigenous population of peasants and the profoundly alienated dwellers of Lima's slums. His objective, which was largely Maoist, also drew on local experiences and pre-Colombian traditions. According to Gordon McCormick, Guzman supplemented Mao's thinking with that of Jose Carlos Mariategui, who advocated indigenous organization and a "rejuvenated Andean socialism."[34]

Initially, Shining Path acquired the weapons and ammunitions it needed to begin its revolutionary campaign by stealing them from isolated police stations. Similarly, the group stole dynamite sticks from mining operations located on the slopes of the Andes. By the mid-1980s and as the organization gathered momentum, Shining Path was able to impose a tax on coca producers and Colombian-based drug traffickers.

Shining Path announced its presence and revolutionary goals at the beginning of the decade (1980) by bombing a number of banks and police stations in some of Peru's provincial capitals. The group was also known for strange acts, including a ghoulish display in Lima on December 26, 1980. One description of the scene paints a terrible, and somewhat confusing, picture of early Shining Path terrorism: "Several dogs met the morning hung from street lights in central Lima. Tied at the neck, almost without struggling in the still air of the Lima dawn, their sad bodies were wrapped in cloth painted with strident colors."[35] Not all that easy to understand, the message was intended for China's new post-Mao leadership: the "lap dogs of capitalism" would meet a similar end to that met by the canines.

Although Guzman regarded himself as a Maoist, he believed he had made an independent contribution to Mao's revolutionary theories. In 1981, he received the approval of the organization's central committee for "The Beginning Plan." For Mao, the path to revolution involved various stages of peasant insurrection in the countryside. These would culminate with the revolutionaries' seizure of the national capital and their triumphant march through Peking, Saigon, Havana, and elsewhere. Instead of this revolutionary choreography, Guzman stressed the importance of urban violence (i.e., terrorism) in Lima and Peru's other major cities.

As with the Shining Path's hanging of dogs, some of the group's urban terrorism had a symbolic quality. Another example was when the group's cadres were able to shut down Lima's lighting system to coincide with the Pope's visit to the city and to commemorate Guzman's birthday. More frequently, however, the Shining Path's urban operations involved more than hijinks. The group's terrorism was among the most macabre. Cynthia McClintock describes this type of terrorism.

> For perhaps the first time in the history of Latin America, nuns, priests, journalists, agronomists, food aid workers, even human rights activists were directly targeted and killed ... Sendero killed not only routinely, but savagely ... One of the most common tactics was the beheading of victims. Also, eyes were gouged out; men were castrated; children were disemboweled; and human bonfires set.[36]

We should stress that the Shining Path was different from a classic rural insurgency following Mao's teachings. Measured in terms of targets, the group tended to attack civilians more often than the police or security forces. Its militants created widespread terror by attacking and executing peasants in the Andes from whom they seized land. Another consideration involves not only against whom but also where the Shining Path carried out its attacks. According to data reported by David Scott Palmer, between 1980 and 1987, the organization carried out 11,796 attacks.[37] Of this number more than 3,000 attacks occurred in Lima. And, if we add the province of Ayacucho's total (2,756) we account for more than half of the Shining Path's attacks at the height of its operations.[38] Rather than a rural strategy of encircling the cities, we see an organization pursuing the tactics of urban terrorism in conjunction with more conventional guerrilla operations and terrorism in the countryside.[39]

By the late 1980s it appeared as if the Shining Path had become a serious contender for power. However, within a few years its challenge to the state had greatly diminished. How did this defeat occur?

At least to some extent Sendero's defeat was self-inflicted. Instead of following Mao's dictum about winning the support of the peasantry, Guzman's followers seemed to go out of their way to antagonize and in many instances terrorize their potential supporters. In Cambodia, the Khmer Rouge was able to rule by terror until they were overthrown by Vietnamese forces. But Pol Pot's terror was imposed not before, but after the Khmer conquered the capital city and the previous government had fled. In the case of the Shining Path, Peru's peasants had options. By cooperating with the government, the people could receive some protection from the organization's torments. As Palmer puts it, "While Shining Path's radical Maoist ideology had been a potent unifying force for its supporters and helps explain how the group could justify even the most barbaric acts, the ideology simultaneously served to alienate most of the presumed beneficiaries of the revolution."[40]

Second, the organization suffered a leadership "decapitation." On September 8, 1992, Peruvian security forces broke into a dance studio in a high-income suburb of Lima and arrested Guzman.[41] After questioning, he was put on display in a cage in the middle of Lima wearing a striped black and white prisoner's uniform so as to make clear his humiliation.

For an organization whose members had come to venerate Guzman much in the way Mao, "the Great Helmsman," had come to be worshipped in China, Commandante Gonzolo's arrest and humiliation had a profoundly demoralizing effect on thousands of his worshippers. The Shining Path has not regained its momentum since this time.

A final consideration includes the changes in the Peruvian state apparatus that were triggered by the threat posed by Sendero and another revolutionary group, the Tupac Amaru. During the term of Peruvian President Alan Garcia

(1985–90), the government pursued a by-now classic counterinsurgency strategy of winning the peasantry's hearts and minds. Garcia's government instituted a policy of respect for human rights and limiting the discretionary powers of the military. In addition, Garcia undertook serious efforts at land reform and rural development. These progressive steps, perhaps worthwhile by themselves, did little to weaken the Shining Path.

By the time Alberto Fujimori was elected to the presidency in 1990, Peru's military leaders were thoroughly alienated from the civilian politicians – often a formula for a *coup d'état* in much of Latin America. Fujimori, a less than admirable figure in many ways, quickly reconciled with the generals and strengthened the roles of Peru's military counterterrorism intelligence agency and the special civilian tribunals, begun under Garcia, to hear cases involving terrorism, a measure intended to prevent the intimidation of judges in the regular court system.[42] It was this combination of events, including Sendero's self-defeating behavior, the arrest of Guzman, and smarter and harsher government measures, that seem to have brought about the end of Peru's revolutionary episode.

In summary, the use of terrorism by Peru's Shining Path is one of the clearest examples of terrorism being used in the context of wider-scale warfare. The group escalated its use of terrorism shortly after it formed and the group's defeat, achieved for the most part in 1992, corresponded with the rapid decline in the group's use of terrorism. The group also escalated its attacks on harder targets, including the government, military, and police, during the years of wider-scale warfare. This pattern is also evident during the years in which the group perpetrated comparatively fewer attacks (1985, 1988, and 1990). Attacks on private, non-state entities made up a larger proportion of the Shining Path's attacks both earlier and later in the group's insurgent campaign, at times when the group was presumably weaker. Although terrorism continued to be used by remaining members of the group through the end of Peru's civil war in 1995 and shortly thereafter, the numbers of attacks were far smaller in comparison to the years of active insurgency and war (see Figure 4.4).

In fact, there is almost no Shining Path terrorism after 1997. A survey of data on terrorism in Peru shows that the same is true of terrorism, in general, in Peru after 1997.[43]

Sri Lanka

Citizens of Sri Lanka, a teardrop-shaped island off India's southeast coast, experienced an insurgency which brought about substantially more fatalities than Peru's over the last decades of the twentieth century and first decade of the twenty-first. The cause for which so many died had very little to do with

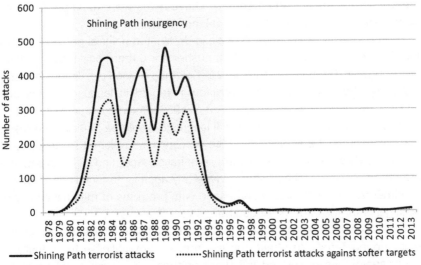

Figure 4.4 Shining Path terrorism and insurgency (1978–2013)

Sources: Boot, *Invisible Armies*, 569–89; Connable and Libicki, *How Insurgencies End*, 157–62, 99–201; Sarkees and Wayman, *Resort to War*; Fearon and Laitin, "Additional Tables;" UCDP/PRIO, "Armed Conflict Dataset V.4-2014a, 1946–2013;" "Global Terrorism Database [Data File]," 2014.

the ideas of Marx or Mao and far more to do with an ethnic struggle involving the status of the country's minority Tamil population. Sri Lanka was and is divided between a majority Buddhist Sinhalese population and the Hindu Tamils (estimated at between 8 and roughly 17 percent of the population) whose members are concentrated in Sri Lanka's northeast region and, in particular, on the Jaffna Peninsula.[44]

The British had brought much of the Tamil population from India during the nineteenth century to work on the colony's (then called Ceylon's) tea plantations. Over time the British administrators chose the Tamils to be the instruments for its colonial domination. Accordingly, Tamils populated the country's bureaucracy, courts, and school system. In short, the Tamils became what scholars of colonialism often describe as "state people," enjoying a preferred position vis-à-vis the British as compared to other populations, including indigenous ones.

Sri Lanka became independent of British control in 1948. The latter bequeathed to the new nation a democratic constitution, one designed along Westminster lines. Democratic elections were to be conducted in accordance with a "one-man, one-vote" principle. Winning parliamentary candidates would be decided on the basis of a first-past-the-post rule. Also in keeping with British tradition, no written provision was included protecting the freedom of speech and assembly. These rights were to be protected by normal statutory law. Trouble was not long in coming.

Shortly after independence, Sinhalese-dominated political parties, notably the Sri Lanka Freedom Party (SLFP), pushed for a more egalitarian distribution of power. The unitary parliament in Colombo passed legislation seriously impacting the Tamils' preferred position in regard to language, schooling, and employment. The Sinhala Only Act of 1956 was a key source of conflict. By this law, the country's sole official language would be Sinhala. The result was widespread Tamil protests: "These responses resulted in violence, of which Tamils were frequently victims. A spiral of escalating violence saw the growth of Sinhalese chauvinism ... whereby appeals to Sinhalese Buddhist sentiments were inextricably enmeshed with promises of material and symbolic gains for the underprivileged masses ..."[45]

If the Sinhala-only requirement excited the Sinhalese masses, it infuriated many young Tamils. In effect, the law made them ineligible for virtually all public sector jobs and placed limitations on their schooling. To make matters worse, from the Tamil perspective, was the imposition of a quota system limiting Tamil access to higher education. Sri Lanka's constitution was revised in 1972 and 1978 to strengthen Sinhalese domination. Among other additions to the legal code, an amendment was added prohibiting the formation of political parties advocating independence for any ethnic group.[46]

In 1972, the initial Tamil reaction to what many regarded as their "oppression" was the formation of a political party, Tamil United Liberation Front (TULF). Its leaders sought to achieve regional autonomy for the Tamils. At a more radical level a number of small "coffee house" revolutionary groups appeared who used the language of Marx and Lenin and theories of national liberation to demand a completely independent country of Tamil Eelam. By 1975, these groups had coalesced into the Eelam Revolutionary Group of Students (EROS). EROS militants, some of whom had trained at PLO bases in Lebanon, began a series of terrorist attacks on Sinhalese targets. These included assassination attempts against government officials and the bombing of various public facilities.[47]

A new violent revolutionary organization appeared in 1976 under these heightening tensions. This was the Liberation Tigers of Tamil Eelam. By contrast to its "coffee house" revolutionary predecessors the LTTE was able to win a level of popular support from among the masses. In large measure this was achieved through the presence of a new charismatic and ruthless leader, Vellupillai Prabhakaran. Within a few years Prabhakaran had managed to eliminate his revolutionary Tamil rivals and then launch a violent campaign against the Sri Lankan government.

Although the Tamil Tigers were responsible for most of the terrorism in

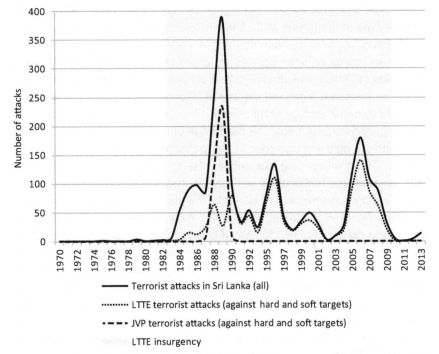

Figure 4.5 Comparison of JVP and LTTE terrorism (1970–2013)

Sources: Boot, *Invisible Armies*, 569–89; Connable and Libicki, *How Insurgencies End*, 157–62, 99–201; Sarkees and Wayman, *Resort to War*; Fearon and Laitin, "Additional Tables;" UCDP/PRIO, "Armed Conflict Dataset V.4-2014a, 1946–2013;" "Global Terrorism Database [Data File]," 2014.

Sri Lanka and operated for the longest period of time, they were not responsible for the spike in terrorism in 1989. This spike is a result of attacks perpetrated by another group, the People's Liberation Front (JVP), which carried out attacks between 1987 and 1990 (see Figure 4.5). Unlike the LTTE's other challengers, the JVP was not competing for the support of the Tamil population, rather it was a nationalist group appealing to the Sinhalese majority. The JVP's threat dissipated before the height of LTTE terrorism.[48]

A crucial year in the history of the conflict was 1983. The LTTE executed eighteen Sri Lankan soldiers after a shootout in Tamil territory. At the funerals for the soldiers in Colombo (the government had put their mutilated bodies on display), Tamil residents of the capital were attacked by mobs of infuriated Sinhalese. These indiscriminate assaults left over 300 Tamils dead. Tamil-owned shops and homes were set on fire by the thousands.[49] Some 100,000 fled Sri Lanka for the safety of the southeastern Indian state of Tamil Nadu.

The LTTE's large scale insurgency, which was waged from 1983 to 2009, cost the lives of thousands of Sri Lankans on both sides of the ethnic divide. The fighting involved guerrilla operations and direct military engagements as well as waves of terrorism. As an organization, the LTTE consisted of thousands of Tamils, including men and women fighters. And, as is the case with other insurgent organizations, the LTTE consisted of political and military wings, both dominated by Prabhakaran: "The cult of personality at the apex of the organization is reflected in the pledge of allegiance made by cadres to the Eelam struggle and also specifically to Prabhakaran."[50]

The LTTE's military wing included an elite special operations unit used for raids penetrating into Sinhalese territory. There were also an amphibious Sea Tigers; a branch resembling an air force, the Air Tigers; and a suicide squad, the Black Tigers. Put another way, at the height of its operations the LTTE was able to deploy a fighting force that bore some resemblance to the military organization of a nation-state or at least a state in the making. Furthermore, the LTTE developed links to and support from external groups. It received weapons and other war materiel from Indian Tamils in the state of Tamil Nadu, located a few miles across the narrow waterway that separates the island state from mainland India. Support also came from the Tamil diaspora. Tamil communities in Britain, Canada, France, and elsewhere in the Western world sent the LTTE money to sustain the struggle. On occasion, they sent recruits.

The Black Tigers, in particular, require some attention. The Black Tigers were a suicide group, which consisted of men and women (known as Birds of Paradise). Black Tigers were expected to wear amulets containing cyanide capsules around their necks. They were instructed to kill themselves if their capture was imminent. We normally associate suicide terrorism with Middle Eastern jihadist groups. Yet, before the surge in suicide attacks after the turn of the twenty-first century, the LTTE was responsible for more such operations than any other terrorist organization worldwide.[51] In fact, the number of suicide attacks attributed to the Tamil Tigers exceeded the number of suicide attacks perpetrated by all other actors during this time, combined.[52]

The Black Tigers carried out suicide attacks against three types of targets: the military, prominent political figures, and members of the Sinhalese public.[53] The Black Tigers assassinated one Sri Lankan President, Renasinghe Premadasa, and almost succeeded in killing another. Perhaps the most spectacular killing often attributed to the Tamil Tigers was the murder of Indian Prime Minister Rajiv Gandhi during his campaigning for India's 1991 national elections. The Black Tigers suicide attacks also involved igniting themselves in such public places as Colombo's central bus station, which left 113 Sinhalese dead in 1987 and which, in turn, led to reprisals by the military against Tamil civilians on the Jaffna Peninsula.

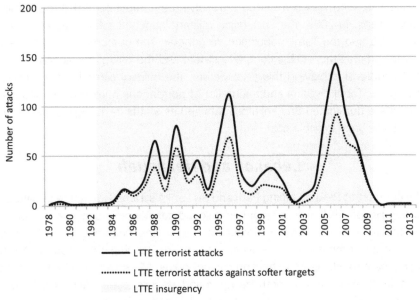

Figure 4.6 LTTE terrorism

Sources: Boot, *Invisible Armies*, 569–89;Connable and Libicki, *How Insurgencies End*, 157–62, 99–201; Sarkees and Wayman, *Resort to War*, Fearon and Laitin, "Additional Tables;" UCDP/PRIO, "Armed Conflict Dataset V.4-2014a, 1946–2013;" "Global Terrorism Database [Data File]," 2014.

LTTE terrorism included attacks on harder and softer targets, replicating a combination of tactics characteristic among the serious insurgent groups discussed thus far. The pattern of LTTE terrorism suggests that the group's terrorist activities occurred in waves, with each successive wave involving more attacks than the previous one (see Figure 4.6).

The fighting was so brutal that it led foreign powers to attempt to mediate the conflict in order to bring about a negotiated settlement. India's New Delhi government made a serious attempt to do so in 1987. India went as far as sending peace-keeping forces to Sri Lanka in 1987. Initially the effort was to provide some protection for the Tamil population while negotiations between the sides were pursued under Indian auspices. The goal was to provide the Tamils with enough local autonomy to satisfy Prabhakaran while retaining a single Sri Lanka. These efforts did not succeed. In fact, the LTTE leader eventually accused India of siding with the government in Colombo and his Tigers became involved in fighting with the Indian military and targeting the government (hence the Gandhi assassination).[54] The Norwegian government also made an attempt to achieve a negotiated settlement, but to no avail.

Finally, in 2005 Sri Lankan voters elected a new president, Mahinda

Rajapaksa, who was committed to resolving the Tamil conflict through military means. In 2006, the Sri Lankan military launched a full-scale attack on the LTTE and the Tamil population, in general. The outcome of this military campaign was the LTTE's complete defeat and the killing of Prabhakaran. In the course of achieving this total victory, the military carried out the mass killings of Tamil civilians and a long list of horrendous human rights abuses. Sinhalese-dominated Sri Lanka has retained its status as a single state but at a virtually unimaginable cost.[55]

Lebanon and Hezbollah

By contrast to Peru's Shining Path and Sri Lanka's Tamil Tigers, the Lebanese group Hezbollah (Party of God) has enjoyed considerable success to a point where it currently plays a significant role in the country's more or less democratic process, with political participation ranging from competing in parliamentary elections to holding cabinet posts. Moreover, this Party of God is able to exert control, both *de facto* and *de jure*, over much of southern Lebanon. It has its own media outlets, social service agencies and, in conjunction with its Iranian patron, a foreign military and diplomatic presence. There is also what seems to be greater international involvement in Lebanon's conflicts in the forms of state support and intervention.

Not only is Lebanon a state with a history of terrorism, it is also a state with a relatively recent record of wider-scale warfare and insurgency. Terrorism has taken place in the context of both. Moreover, it appears that the frequency of terrorism has followed the patterns we have come to expect in the context of wider-scale warfare. The frequencies of terrorist incidents have increased with the onset of insurgency, increased when more than one insurgent group is operating, and decreased with the ends of insurgencies. Terrorism rose over the course of Lebanon's civil war, remained high during the overlap between this war and the initiation of conflicts between Israel and militants in southern Lebanon, and decreased as these conflicts came to an end (see Figure 4.7).

The historical context from which Hezbollah appeared is entwined with the experience of Lebanon's Shiite population.[56] After the country's achievement of independence from France in 1943, Lebanon's large Shi'a community was politically and economically subordinated to its Maronite Christian and Sunni Muslim populations. These groups held the levers of power in Beirut and, along with Druze and Greek minorities, controlled most of Lebanon's economic enterprises. Shiites were largely confined to the rural south and the eastern Bekaa Valley, bordering Syria. The decrepit zones of south Beirut also had a large Shiite population.

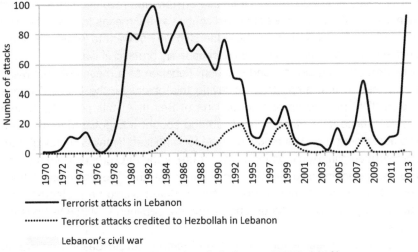

Terrorist attacks in Lebanon

Terrorist attacks credited to Hezbollah in Lebanon

Lebanon's civil war

Figure 4.7 Terrorism in Lebanon (1970–2013)

Sources: Boot, *Invisible Armies*, 569–89; Connable and Libicki, *How Insurgencies End*, 157–62, 99–201; Sarkees and Wayman, *Resort to War*; Fearon and Laitin, "Additional Tables;" UCDP/PRIO, "Armed Conflict Dataset V.4-2014a, 1946–2013;" "Global Terrorism Database [Data File]," 2014.

There was a Shiite awakening in the 1970s. A number of factors contributed to this awakening. First was the appearance of a charismatic imam from Iran, Musa al-Sadr. During the first half of the decade, al-Sadr led representatives of the Shi'a, particularly in the south, to overturn the community's traditional land-owning elites and demand substantial improvements in its economic, social, and political status. He also organized a Shi'a militia, Amal, to defend the population when the Lebanese civil war broke out in 1975.[57] Another important reason for the Shiite mobilization during Lebanon's fifteen-year civil war (1975–90) was the presence of Palestinian militant groups on the border with Israel. These groups, operating in what came to be known as "Fatahland," clashed with the indigenous Shiite farmers. Amal was at first a response to the threat posed by the presence of the armed PLO groups, which were representing the national aspirations of Palestinian Sunnis, on historic Shiite territory.

Abu Sadr "disappeared" while on a visit to Colonel Qaddafi's Libya in 1978. (The suspicion is that he was killed by the Colonel's agents.)[58] The presumed death of the charismatic leader hardly put an end to Lebanon's Shiite mobilization. The Iranian revolution of 1979 excited the religious enthusiasm of Shiites in Lebanon and throughout the Middle East. Hagiographic pictures of the Ayatollah Khomeini were quickly put on display in south Beirut and elsewhere in Lebanon. Furthermore, shortly after the revolution's success, the new clerical regime in Tehran sent members of its Islamic Revolutionary Guards to the

Bekaa Valley to imbue young Lebanese Shiites with revolutionary ideas and train them in the techniques of armed conflict as the means for implementing these ideas. Sensibly enough, the leadership did not want to leave Lebanon's Shiites helpless in the midst of an exceptionally brutal civil war.

In 1982, the Israelis invaded southern Lebanon as a means of destroying PLO bases in that area. After achieving this objective, the Israeli Defense Forces (IDF) pushed on to the outskirts of Beirut. At this point the United States, France, and others intervened and sought a negotiated settlement. The agreement that was reached called for a phased Israeli withdrawal from the Beirut area in exchange for the departure of the PLO groups from the city. The understanding also included a guarantee that the Palestinian populations housed in refugee camps in the vicinity of Beirut would be protected from attacks by opposing militia groups, especially Lebanon's Maronite Christian forces.

The following year voters elected the Maronite leader Bashir Gemayel to the Lebanese presidency. Shortly afterward Gemayel and his associates were killed when the house where they were conferring was blown up. Although evidence discovered later attributed responsibility to the Syrian government,[59] the initial Maronite reaction was to blame the Palestinians for the killings.

In revenge for the killing, Gemayel elements of the Lebanese Forces invaded the Palestinian camps of Sabra and Shatilla and proceeded to carry out a massacre of all the women and children they could locate. The IDF was criticized severely and justifiably for turning its back while the murders were under way. The condemnation of Israeli inaction was sufficiently intense so as to convince the government of Menachem Begin to accelerate its withdrawal from greater Beirut, although the IDF did retain control over much of southern Lebanon, home to a substantial percentage of the country's Shiite population.

In response to the Palestinian murders, an international force acting under UN auspices returned to Beirut in an attempt to restore some semblance of order and to strengthen the Lebanese government and its armed forces. The United States and France took the lead in this effort; a small Italian contingent also participated.

All three Western countries sent military contingents to promote an end to the civil war. This goal was to be achieved largely by strengthening the national government in Beirut, and in particular its armed forces. What Washington and Paris did not understand was that this effort was widely perceived by the Druze, Sunni, and Shiite militias as the Americans and French (the former mandate power, after all) taking the side of Lebanon's Christians. During 1983, the American Marine contingent, a peacekeeping force, became embroiled in the fighting. Even the aging Battleship New Jersey became involved. From off-shore it began lobbing sixteen-inch projectiles at Druze targets in the Shouf Mountains, southeast of Beirut.

It was during this period that Hezbollah was formed, "born as an umbrella organization encompassing a group of clerics and their followers, individual militants, and smaller factions ..."[60] The new Party of God received the spiritual blessing of Iran's Ayatollah Khomeini and logistical help from Hafez al-Asad's regime in Damascus. Hezbollah would be a nationalist group representing the interests of the Shiite community, as well as an Islamist group with political objectives that were also religious.[61]

Hezbollah began to make its presence felt in the spring of 1983. The American and French peacekeepers were targets of suicide bombing attacks. Some credit for these attacks was taken by individuals whose handlers claimed they belonged to a shadowy Shiite group Islamic Jihad Organization (IJO),[62] which many attribute to being Hezbollah in its formative stage. Then in October, a truck bomb was detonated at the U.S. Marine Corps' barracks near Beirut's international airport, killing 241 Americans. Almost simultaneously, another attacker drove his explosive-laden truck into the French barracks, leaving fifty-eight French soldiers dead. This pair of attacks is widely attributed to Hezbollah, the group that soon became known as the "founding father" of suicide terrorism.[63]

Discretion overcame belligerency and within a few months, in 1984, American, French, and Italian forces withdrew from Lebanon. The suicide attacks had forced this departure. Despite a failed attempt to assassinate Hezbollah's spiritual guide, Sheik Fadlallah, and efforts by the Reagan administration to cover the defeat with a diplomatic fig leaf, the attackers had inflicted what was seen as an embarrassing defeat on the Americans. Hezbollah soon became a powerful force in Lebanese politics.

By the mid-1980s, Hezbollah turned its attention to aircraft hijacking and the kidnapping or killing of Western hostages. As Robin Wright puts it, "The Marine withdrawal did not, however, end the crusade against the American presence in Lebanon. The Shi'a commandos instead began a second phase of attacks, as American individuals rather than institutions became the targets."[64] Among the most spectacular of these attacks were the assassination of Malcolm Kerr, the president of the American University in Beirut; the torture and killing of William Buckley, the CIA station chief in the city; and the skyjacking of TWA Flight 847 in which an American sailor was murdered.

In addition to these acts of terrorism, Hezbollah also kidnapped a list of American reporters and reporters from other Western countries. Most of these were held until 1986, when members of the Reagan Administration made a secret deal with Iran (Hezbollah's patron) to free the hostages in exchange for weapons the country could use in its long war with Saddam Hussein's Iraq.

To this point Hezbollah appears as almost exclusively a militant organization willing to use terrorism to achieve its goals, or perhaps the goals of its patrons. The group's main targets were not the softer civilian targets, however. Hezbollah's earliest attacks in Lebanon, both credited and "suspected,"[65] were directed against harder targets, such as foreign diplomats, the military, and police. This seems to be a trend that continued, with more than 70 percent of the group's attacks being aimed at states or armed actors (including military, police, and armed non-state groups) within them.[66] This is not unexpected given the group's emergence in the context of wider-scale warfare and its subsequent participation in intra-state and inter-state wars against state and non-state actors. Even in the midst of Lebanon's civil war Hezbollah's targets were not limited to its immediate neighborhood. Among the incidents credited to the group include several attacks in Kuwait as well as attacks in Saudi Arabia, Egypt, and Europe, to name a few.

By the end of the 1980s, this Party of God underwent a significant transformation. It acquired a mass following by developing schools and various social service programs for the Shiite community.[67] With the return of democratic elections and under the leadership of Sheik Hassan Nasrallah, Hezbollah entered the political party realm. It is through these activities that the group elected deputies to Lebanon's parliament and found positions within the cabinet. Hezbollah also developed a strong network for mass communications, including its own television station, Al-Manar, which it has used for the purposes of spreading propaganda.[68]

These social and political transformations may be less about organizational change than about competition for support, resources, and, ultimately, power.[69] Hezbollah's rivals included another local group, Amal, which was a secular competitor for the support of Lebanon's Shiite community and presumably, to some extent, for state support from both groups' external benefactors. Though they have been known to cooperate more recently, these two groups went to war with each other in 1988.[70]

Hezbollah emerged from these wars as a strong competitor to Lebanon's state and its military. In addition to providing services typically provided by a state, Hezbollah would become a military force that could pose a challenge to the Lebanese state.[71]

It was Hezbollah's armed conflict with Israel that led it to become an insurgent organization whose repertoire of tactics included but was no longer limited to suicide attacks and terrorism. Hezbollah's militant wing had become a force that could carry out attacks on military targets in the context of wider-scale warfare. In addition to a handful of suicide bombings aimed at IDF outposts in occupied southern Lebanon, Hezbollah engaged in a significant wave of guerrilla operations against regular IDF patrols in Israel's zones of occupation. The government in Jerusalem even created a South Lebanese Army to join in the struggle against Hezbollah's increasingly sophisticated fighters.

In 2000 and in the face of mounting Israeli casualties the Israeli government of Ehud Barak withdrew its forces from southern Lebanon including those located in a buffer zone the IDF had sought to maintain.

This move brought ramifications within and outside Lebanon. Hezbollah's presumed success in fighting and eventually expelling the Israelis served as an inspiration to Hamas, Islamic Jihad, and other Palestinian groups who came to believe that they would be able to end Israel's occupation of their own land by similar means.[72]

For Hezbollah, engaging in international warfare would likely be viewed as complementary to, rather than in competition with, the party's role in domestic politics. Presumably, these roles would serve the same population, albeit in different ways. At the same time, from the perspectives of others within Lebanon, the group's "independent military agenda"[73] would not necessarily be consistent with the interests of the Lebanese state or its residents. Moreover, Hezbollah's actions showed that the Lebanese state lacked a monopoly on the use of force.[74] Some have accused Hezbollah of using violence against the Lebanese state and its members, including former Lebanese Prime Minister Rafik Hariri, who was assassinated in 2005. The timing and circumstances surrounding Hariri's exit from political office suggest a motive: Hariri's opposition to Syrian intervention in Lebanese politics. The International Criminal Court at The Hague may decide on the question of Hezbollah members' responsibility (with or without Syrian sponsorship) for Hariri's murder. Regardless of responsibility, Hezbollah has not substituted the olive branch for the gun.

More recent events suggest that this has not changed. In 2006 Hezbollah waged a month-long war with the Israelis in which they succeeded in bombarding northern Israel with some thousands of Iranian-supplied missiles. Hezbollah emerged bloody but unbowed. Under Sheik Nasrallah's leadership Hezbollah fighters have begun playing an active role in the defense of Bashar al-Assad's Syrian dictatorship against the Sunni groups fighting to topple it.[75] More interestingly, perhaps, the "founding father" of suicide attacks is now among its most recent targets.[76]

In this same context, the Lebanese state and the Lebanese Armed Forces (LAF) have faced an additional conundrum. Hezbollah, with its own agenda and substantial support from the Shiite population within Lebanon, is again able to act independently of the Lebanese state while pursuing its interests in Syria. With the threat of war near its borders, the LAF has called on Hezbollah for assistance in protecting Lebanon. From a position of relative weakness, the Lebanese state and its military have faced repercussions from not preventing Hezbollah-affiliated Shiite fighters from participating in the conflict in neighboring Syria, while simultaneously stopping Sunnis from doing much the same. These developments combine with perceptions that the LAF is more Shiite than Sunni and biased in favor of Shiite interests. Such perceptions reinforce sectarian divisions, which could destroy the Lebanon's fragile national unity. This is a situation that could produce a conflict within Lebanon's borders to complement the threat coming from outside, potentially drawing Lebanon's Shiite and Sunni populations onto opposite sides of a broader conflict like those taking place in Syria and Iraq.[77]

A look at the frequencies of terrorism by Hezbollah and other groups reveals some interesting patterns. First, peaks in Hezbollah's use of terrorism do not coincide with peaks in others' uses of terrorism. This suggests that Hezbollah's use of terrorism may be motivated by different events than those motivating other terrorists. For instance, Hezbollah perpetrated its highest numbers of terrorist attacks in 1985, 1994, and 1999 (coincidentally, this was also the last year Hezbollah carried out a suicide attack).[78] In 1998–99, Hezbollah's number of terrorist attacks surpassed that of all other actors perpetrating attacks in Lebanon. With the exceptions of 1999 and 2008, Hezbollah's use of terrorism peaks at times when the numbers of attacks perpetrated by other groups were decreasing (see Figure 4.8).

Since forming, Hezbollah has used terrorism along with guerrilla tactics

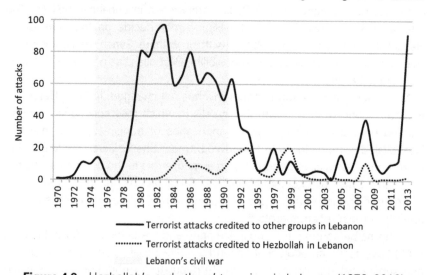

Figure 4.8 Hezbollah's and others' terrorism in Lebanon (1970–2013)

Sources: Boot, *Invisible Armies*, 569–89; Connable and Libicki, *How Insurgencies End*, 157–62, 99–201; Sarkees and Wayman, *Resort to War*; Fearon and Laitin, "Additional Tables;" UCDP/PRIO, "Armed Conflict Dataset V.4-2014a, 1946–2013;" "Global Terrorism Database [Data File]," 2014.

in the context of insurgencies and wider-scale warfare. Hezbollah's origins midway through Lebanon's civil war coincided with "the peak of a crisis in the Lebanese system."[79] Between its formation and 2001, the group has carried out attacks against combatant and noncombatant targets. The lull in Hezbollah attacks around 1988 corresponds approximately with the end of Lebanon's sectarian civil war in 1990; terrorist attacks against noncombatant targets were nearly non-existent in 1990. This was not the end of war, however. The Southern Lebanon War between Hezbollah and Israel coincided with this timeline between 1982 and 1990. Hezbollah's attacks on noncombatant and non-state targets did not return to their civil-war-era levels; however, attacks on combatant targets and non-terrorist attacks rose. Hezbollah continued using terrorism after the end of Lebanon's civil war.

Although the group has carried out fewer terrorist attacks since 2001, this change may be better explained by a transition from a clandestine militant group operating in the shadows into an armed force operating in public. The escalation to war between Hezbollah and Israel in 2006 is not recorded as terrorism but rather as war. Fewer than ten terrorist attacks were attributed to Hezbollah in 2006; these were mostly against private entities and all but one took place in Israel; only one of these attacks exclusively targeted the military, and this one attack occurred in Lebanon.[80] Hezbollah's conduct during its 2006 war with Israel was that of a non-state or quasi-state military, rather than a clandestine organization engaging in terrorism or even guerrilla warfare. Nevertheless, Hezbollah was relatively weak in this confrontation, and the group relied primarily on rockets, which were fired over the border into Israel. In response, Israel engaged in ground and air offensives targeting Hezbollah's stronghold within Lebanon. There were more than 1,100 deaths in Lebanon, slightly more than twenty times the number of Israeli deaths; most of the fatalities were civilians.[81] While neither side could claim a victory, the weaker side – Hezbollah – was not defeated (see Figure 4.9). As was the case in 2006, Hezbollah's participation in Syria's ongoing civil war is that of a military, not that of a terrorist group.

India and the Naxalites

India's Naxalites (its name is taken from the community where the group was born) harbor no such separatist or religious ambition. Instead, this Indian Maoist organization seeks to follow along the Chinese leader's revolutionary path by overthrowing the regime in New Delhi and replacing it with something approaching a people's republic.[82]

In fact, the Naxalites (rather like Peru's Shining Path) were the result of the Sino-Soviet split dating from 1964 and involving a division within India's

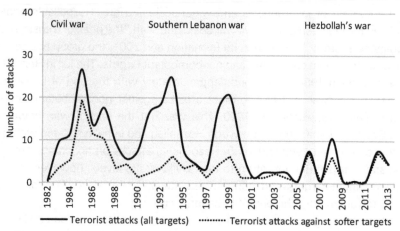

Figure 4.9 Hezbollah's terrorist attacks within and outside Lebanon (1982–2013)

Sources: Boot, *Invisible Armies*, 569–89; Connable and Libicki, *How Insurgencies End*, 157–62, 99–201; Sarkees and Wayman, *Resort to War*; Fearon and Laitin, "Additional Tables;" UCDP/PRIO, "Armed Conflict Dataset V.4-2014a, 1946–2013;" "Global Terrorism Database [Data File]," 2014.

Communist Party. Followers of Maoism rejected revisionism, split off, and established their own organization. Two leaders of the new party's Politburo, Kanu Sanyal and Charu Majumdar, called for the adoption of what became known as "the annihilation line." According to this line, which obviously includes elements of anarchism, revolution could be achieved by dramatic campaigns of violence involving peasants led by radical party leaders killing their class enemies.

The first manifestation of this tactic was an uprising of tea plantation workers in the fall of 1967. Led by Sanyal and Majumdar, the tea workers in Naxalbari ransacked government offices, chased off the police, and killed those they regarded as their "class enemies." After some weeks the Indian military re-occupied the area and brought this rural rebellion to an end.[83]

The defeat did not bring an end to the Naxalites. In 1969 its operations spread to Calcutta, capital of West Bengal, where cadres seized control of the Presidency College and converted its chemistry lab into a bomb-making factory. Over the next few years the Naxalites fought for control of the entire city. Gun battles between the police and the Maoists became daily occurrences. By 1971, the authorities managed to regain control of the situation via widespread arrests and extra-judicial killings.

From this point the Naxalites, following Mao, pursued a rural strategy. Their insurgency has involved operating from the forests and fields of central and eastern India, impoverished areas far removed from the country's moderniz-ing cities. In these zones the Maoists have won the support of large numbers of tribal peoples. As one recent analyst puts it:

> From their isolated origins, the insurgents had become a unified and highly disciplined fighting force whose writ replaced that of the government across large parts of the country ... The insurgency has intensified in both scope and scale. Across much of the country, the war has led to the total collapse of the state and the emergence of a kind of anarchical warlordism more often associated with countries such as Somalia.[84]

By the beginning of the twenty-first century the Naxalites had grown to include a force of between 15,000 and 20,000 well-equipped combatants. This is a force with very few recorded terrorist attacks, at least under the "Naxalite" name (see Figure 4.10). Despite this, the threat they posed was so substan-tial that, in 2006, Prime Minister Singh referred to this Maoist insurgency as "the single greatest security challenge" confronting India.[85] In 2009, the government launched Operation Green Hunt, a large-scale counterinsurgency effort involving the deployment of thousands of troops. Thus far, however, Operation Green Hunt and succeeding efforts have proven unsuccessful.

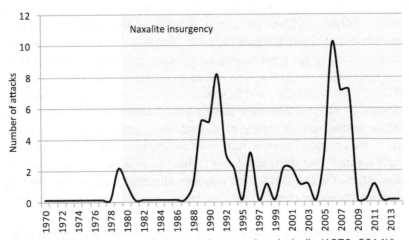

Figure 4.10 Naxalite and communist terrorism in India (1970–2014)*

* The terrorist attacks counted here include those credited to the Naxalites, as well as those credited to various communist parties and organizations in India.

Sources: Boot, *Invisible Armies*, 569–89; Connable and Libicki, *How Insurgencies End*, 157–62, 99–201; Sarkees and Wayman, *Resort to War*; Fearon and Laitin, "Additional Tables;" UCDP/PRIO, "Armed Conflict Dataset V.4-2014a, 1946–2013;" "Global Terrorism Database [Data File]," 2015.

While the terrorist campaigns launched by the Sikh secessionists in the Punjab and the persistent terrorist attacks staged by Lashkar-e Tayyiba and the other Pakistani-based jihadist groups on behalf of Jammu Kashmir have not as yet transformed into a full-scale insurgency, the Naxalite struggle against the Indian state, by contrast, certainly has. From a band of Maoists carrying out terrorist attacks in Calcutta, the Naxalites have gone on to take control of territory through a combination of terrorist and guerrilla tactics. They also have developed a significant mass following among the impoverished classes of West Bengal and elsewhere.

Final observations

How do we distinguish the winners from the losers in the five cases we have just reviewed? In Colombia, Peru, Sri Lanka, Lebanon, and India the groups involved were all able to escalate their operations by using some combination of guerrilla warfare, highly theatrical propaganda, and terrorism. Yet, Hezbollah and the Naxalites endure while the Shining Path and the Liberation Tigers have largely passed from the scene, likely to be followed shortly by Colombia's FARC. Why would this be the case?

In the case of Hezbollah we are dealing with an organization that is much more than a terrorist group. Hezbollah was able to command the respect and loyalty of Lebanon's Shiite population. It achieved this initially receiving the endorsement of highly admired clerics in both Iran and Lebanon. Hezbollah appealed to its target constituency on religious grounds. In addition to religious symbolism, Hezbollah also added to its appeal by providing tangible benefits, such as schools and hospitals, to the Shiite population and other residents of the predominantly Shiite parts of Lebanon. Hezbollah became institutionalized with a variety of organizations active in Shiite-dominated parts of the country. These, in turn, provided many of the social services that people wanted. Hezbollah acted as a "state" by making services available in places where the Lebanese state was less effective. Beyond this, Hezbollah controls a significant military branch, which it has employed in defense of its community.

On the other hand, Shining Path and the LTTE seemed to go out of their way to antagonize the very populations in whose names they claimed to act. This brutality toward Peruvian peasants (including enslaving them) and Tamil opponents of Prabhakaran was self-defeating in that it undercut, rather than built support for, the insurgencies. These were, among other things, a major violation of Maoist ideas.

Then, there is the matter of "charismatic" leadership. After the Shining

Path and the Tamil Tiger organizations were decapitated by the arrest of Guzman and the killing of Prabhakaran, the insurgencies themselves collapsed. This was not the case with Hezbollah. After the Israelis assassinated Abbas al-Musawi, an early leader of the group, the organization continued to develop and thrive under Sheik Hassan Nasrallah.

Lebanon was and is a weak state with a military often divided along sectarian lines, which has been unable to exert control over Hezbollah or much else. Peru and Sri Lanka had somewhat stronger states, also with relatively fragile democratic institutions. Initially leaders in both Peru and Sri Lanka seemed befuddled by the insurgencies with which they were confronted. They seemed to oscillate between repression and conciliation.[86] It was only after the elections of Fujimori in Peru and Rajapaksa in Sri Lanka that both governments succeeded in repressing their respective insurgencies. Repression coincided with authoritarian regressions and violations of basic human rights. In these ways, we may presume that the costs of countering the insurgent groups were spread wider than was responsibility for carrying out the insurgencies. With some outside assistance, Colombia's counterinsurgency efforts have become more effective in recent years.

Finally, we need to stress the vast differences in external support for these groups. Hezbollah has been the beneficiary of enormous support from Iran and the now-embattled Syrian dictatorship. The Naxalites seem to have the support of local populations, despite being labeled a significant threat within India. FARC's journey to the negotiating table likely has something to do with the group's label as a threat to U.S. national security and the cooperative counterinsurgency effort that followed this label. By contrast, the Tamil Tigers managed to alienate a potentially powerful patron – the government in New Delhi. Otherwise, it had to depend on the philanthropy of the Tamil diaspora. The Shining Path had virtually to light its own way.

Notes

1   Jenkins, "Will Terrorists Go Nuclear?"; J. Craig Jenkins, Thomas V. Maher, and Chuck Fahrer, "Seedbeds of Insurgency: Structure and Dynamics in the Egyptian Islamist Insurgency, 1986–99," *Journal of Peace Research*, 51, no. 4 (2014).

2   See for example, Thomas Barfield, *Afghanistan: A Political and Cultural History* (Princeton, NJ: Princeton University Press, 2010), 272–336; Bergen, *The Longest War*, 177–83; Carlota Gall, *The Wrong Enemy* (Boston, MA: Houghton-Mifflin, 2014), 119–46.

3   See, for instance, Assaf Moghadam, *The Globalization of Martyrdom: Al Qaeda, Salafi Jihad, and the Diffusion of Suicide Attacks* (Baltimore, Maryland: Johns Hopkins University Press, 2008), 157.

4   See, for instance, "Chapter 6. Foreign Terrorist Organizations," in *Country Reports on Terrorism 2013*.
5   Ibid.
6   See, for instance, "Mapping Militant Organizations;" Chicago Project on Security and Terrorism (CPOST), "Suicide Attack Database (December 19, 2014 Release)."
7   Gregory Johnson, *The Last Refuge: Yemen, Al Qaeda and America's War in Arabia* (New York, NY: W.W. Norton, 2013), 150–4.
8   See, for instance, BBC News Middle East, "What Is Islamic State?" December 2, 2015, www.bbc.com/news/world-middle-east-29052144 (last accessed April 8, 2016).
9   See also Martin and Weinberg, "Terrorism in an Era of Unconventional Warfare."
10   David Kilcullen, *Out of the Mountains* (New York, NY: Oxford University Press, 2013), 107.
11   Ibid.
12   See for example, Berkowitz, *The New Face of War*; Richard Clarke, *Cyber War* (New York, NY: Harper Collins, 2010), 70–101.
13   Lorenzo Vidino, *Al Qaeda in Europe* (New York, NY: Prometheus Books, 2006).
14   Donatella Della Porta, *Clandestine Political Violence* (New York, NY: Cambridge University Press, 2014). See especially Laqueur, *The Age of Terrorism*, 1.
15   See for example, Angel Rabasa, Steven Boraz, Peter Chalk, Kim Cragin, Theodore W. Karasik, Jennifer D. P. Moroney, Kevin A. O'Brien, and John E. Peters, *Ungoverned Territories: Understanding and Reducing Terrorism Risks* (Santa Monica, CA: RAND Corporation, 2007), 49–74.
16   According to the Chicago Project on Suicide Terrorism (CPOST), the number of suicide attacks in Afghanistan since 2003 exceeds that of Pakistan by more than four times. Chicago Project on Security and Terrorism, "Suicide Attack Database (December 19, 2014 Release)."
17   Boot, *Invisible Armies*.
18   Sarkees and Wayman, *Resort to War: 1816–2007*; UCDP/PRIO, *UCDP/PRIO Armed Conflict Dataset Codebook, Version 4–2014a*; "Global Terrorism Database [Data File]," 2012, 2013, 2014, 2015; Fearon and Laitin, "Additional Tables For 'Ethnicity, Insurgency, and Civil War';" Connable and Libicki, *How Insurgencies End*.
19   Debray, *Revolution in the Revolution*, 67.
20   Walter Laqueur, *Terrorism* (Boston, MA: Little, Brown, 1977), 178–9.
21   Cynthia Watson, "Guerrilla Groups in Colombia," in *Political Parties and Terrorist Groups*, ed. Leonard Weinberg (London: Frank Cass, 1992), 85.
22   World Bank, "Intentional Homicides (Per 100,000 People)."
23   For a summary see Tina Rosenberg, *Children of Cain* (New York, NY: William Morrow & Co., 1991), 23–76.
24   See for example, Peter Waldmann, "Colombia and the FARC," in *Democracy and Counterterrorism*, ed. Robert Art and Louise Richardson (Washington, DC: United States Institute of Peace Press, 2007), 222–7.
25   Ibid., 223.
26   Gonzalo Sanchez, "The Violence: An Interpretive Synthesis," in *Violence in Colombia*, ed. Charles Berquist, Ricardo Penarada, and Gonzalo Sanchez (Wilmington, DE: SR Books, 1992), 75–124.

27   Quoted in Eduardo Pizarro, "Revolutionary Guerrilla Groups in Colombia," in *Violence in Colombia*, ed. Charles Berquist, Ricardo Penarada, and Gonzalo Sanchez (Wilmington, DE: SR Books, 1992), 173.
28   Waldmann, "Colombia and the FARC," 230.
29   BBC News Latin American & Caribbean, "Farc's Political Party Regains Legal Status," www.bbc.com/news/world-latin-america-23251500 (last accessed April 8, 2016).
30   Ana Maria Bejarano, "The Constitution of 1991," in *Violence in Colombia, 1990–2000*, ed. Charles Berquist, Ricardo Penarada, and Gonzalo Sanchez (Wilmington, DE: SR Books, 2001), 53–74.
31   See "Mapping Militant Organizations."
32   See especially David Scott Palmer, "Terror in the Name of Mao," in *Democracy and Counterterrorism*, ed. Robert Art and Louise Richardson (Washington, DC: United States Institute of Peace Press, 2007), 195–220; Palmer, "The Revolutionary Terrorism of Peru's Shining Path," 249–308.
33   Gustavo Gorriti, *The Shining Path* (Chapel Hill, NC: University of North Carolina Press, 1999), 55–76.
34   Gordon H. McCormick, "The Shining Path and Peruvian Terrorism," in *Inside Terrorist Organizations*, ed. David C. Rapoport (Portland, OR: Frank Cass, 2001), 113.
35   Gorriti, *The Shining Path*, 76.
36   Cynthia McClintock, *Revolutionary Movements in Latin America* (Washington, DC: United States Institute of Peace Press, 2005), 68.
37   This is nearly four times the number of attacks coded in the Global Terrorism Database for all of Peru between 1980 and 1987 ($n = 3{,}238$ attacks). Refer to "Global Terrorism Database [Data File]," 2015.
38   Again, this count differs from the number of attacks recorded in the Global Terrorism Database. The GTD records just over 440 Shining Path attacks in the Ayacucho area and just over 1,360 Shining Path attacks in the Lima area. Almost all of these attacks occurred between 1980 and 1987. Moreover, the sum of these attacks still adds up to more than half of all Shining Path attacks during this time period. Ibid.
39   Palmer, "The Revolutionary Terrorism of Peru's Shining Path," 272–3.
40   Palmer, "Terror in the Name of Mao," 203.
41   The owner of the dance studio had been a Sendero sympathizer.
42   McClintock, *Revolutionary Movements in Latin America*, 142–9.
43   "Global Terrorism Database [Data File]," 2014.
44   Brendan O'Duffy, "LTTE: Majoritarianism, Self-Determination, and Military to Political Transition in Sri Lanka," in *Terror, Insurgency, and the State: Ending Protracted Conflicts*, ed. Marianne Heiberg, Brendan O'Leary, and John Tirman (Philadelphia, PA: University of Pennsylvania Press, 2007), 257–87. This estimate is based on various reports regarding the size of the Tamil population and data on ethnic identification and primary language spoken. See, for instance, Central Intelligence Agency, The World Factbook, "Sri Lanka," https://www.cia.gov/library/publications/the-world-factbook/geos/ce.html (last accessed April 4, 2016).
45   Thomas Marks, "Sri Lanka and the Liberation Tigers of Tamil Eelam," in *Democracy and Counterterrorism*, ed. Robert Art and Louise Richardson (Washington, DC: United States Institute of Peace Press, 2007), 486.
46   For further description, see Jason G. Stone, "Sri Lanka's Postwar Descent,"

Journal of Democracy, 25, no. 2 (2014); Neil DeVotta, "Illiberalism and Ethnic Conflict in Sri Lanka," *Journal of Democracy*, 13, no. 1 (2002).

47 Marks, "Sri Lanka and the Liberation Tigers of Tamil Eelam," 487–8.

48 "Global Terrorism Database [Data File]," 2014.

49 For a description see Stephen Hopgood, "Tamil Tigers, 1987–2002," in *Making Sense of Suicide Missions*, ed. Diego Gambetta (New York, NY: Oxford University Press, 2005), 43–76.

50 O'Duffy, "LTTE: Majoritarianism, Self-Determination, and Military to Political Transition in Sri Lanka," 264.

51 Bloom, *Dying to Kill*, 50–1.

52 Rapoport, "The Four Waves of Modern Terrorism."

53 Chicago Project on Security and Terrorism, "Suicide Attack Database (December 19, 2014 Release)."

54 Martha Crenshaw, "Democracy, Commitment Problems, and Managing Ethnic Violence: The Case of India and Sri Lanka," in *The Democratic Experience and Political Violence*, ed. David C. Rapoport and Leonard B. Weinberg (London: Frank Cass, 2001), 135–59.

55 Robert Kaplan, "Buddha's Savage Peace," *The Atlantic*, September 2009, 56–61; Human Rights Watch, "Recurring Nightmare: State Responsibility for 'Disappearances' and Abductions in Sri Lanka" (2008), www.hrw.org/reports/2008/srilanka0308/srilanka0308web.pdf (last accessed April 16, 2016).

56 For a general discussion see Augustus Richard Norton, *Hezbollah* (Princeton, NJ: Princeton University Press, 2007), 29–68.

57 Daniel Byman, "Israel and the Lebanese Hizbollah," in *Democracy and Counterterrorism*, ed. Robert Art and Louise Richardson (Washington, DC: United States Institute of Peace Press, 2007), 305–41.

58 Fuad Ajami, *The Vanished Imam* (Ithaca, NY: Cornell University Press, 1986), ad passim.

59 Marius Deeb, *Syria's War on Lebanon* (New York, NY: Palgrave Macmillan, 2003), 79–81.

60 Benedetta Berti, *Armed Political Organizations: From Conflict to Integration* (Baltimore, MD: Johns Hopkins University Press, 2013), 33.

61 Norton, *Hezbollah*, 35–40.

62 Robin Wright, *Sacred Rage: The Wrath of Militant Islam* (New York, NY: Touchstone, 2001 (updated edition)), 107.

63 Pedahzur, *Suicide Terrorism*, 52.

64 Robin Wright, *Sacred Rage: The Wrath of Militant Islam* (New York, NY: Simon and Schuster, 1985), 100.

65 See, for instance, "Global Terrorism Database [Data File]," 2015.

66 Hezbollah's history of attacking harder state and armed targets is well known. The calculation offered here is based on data on Hezbollah's attacks available via the Global Terrorism Database, in which Hezbollah is credited with 384 attacks, 274 of which were against government, military, police, or violent or armed non-state groups. If only terrorist attacks are taken into account, assaults on softer targets make up closer to 50 percent (as opposed to 30 percent) of the group's attacks. Ibid.

67 Eitan Azani, *Hezbollah: The Story of the Party of God, from Revolution to Institutionalization* (New York, NY: Palgrave MacMillan, 2009), 71–5.

68 For further discussion, see, for instance, ibid., 73; Maura Conway, "Terror TV? An Exploration of Hizbollah's Al-Manar Television," in *Countering*

Terrorism in the 21st Century: Internatinoal Perspectives, ed. James J. F. Forest (Westport, CT: Greenwood Publishing Group, 2007), 405–19.

69   For further discussion, see Martin, "Dilemmas of 'Going Legit': Why Should Violent Groups Engage in or Avoid Electoral Politics?"

70   See, for instance, Norton, *Hezbollah*; Azani, *Hezbollah*.

71   For instance, Berti, *Armed Political Organizations*, 72; Jeffrey White, "Hizb Allah at War in Syria: Forces, Operations, Effects and Implications," *CTC Sentinel*, 7, no. 1 (2014).

72   For further discussion, see Bruce Hoffman, "The 'Cult of the Insurgent': Its Tactical and Strategic Implications," *Australian Journal of International Affairs*, 61, no. 3 (2007).

73   Berti, *Armed Political Organizations*, 58.

74   Ibid.

75   White, "Hizb Allah at War in Syria: Forces, Operations, Effects and Implications."

76   "Recent Highlights in Political Violence," *CTC Sentinel*, 7, no. 1 (2014): 22; Chris Zambelis, "Hizballah's Lebanese Resistance Brigades," *CTC Sentinel*, 7, no. 11 (2014). See also Chicago Project on Security and Terrorism, "Suicide Attack Database (December 19, 2014 Release)."

77   Mona Alami, "The Lebanese Army and the Confessional Trap," *Sada*, June 25, 2014.

78   See, for instance, Chicago Project on Security and Terrorism, "Suicide Attack Database (December 19, 2014 Release)."

79   Azani, *Hezbollah*, ix.

80   "Global Terrorism Database [Data File]," 2015.

81   See, for instance, Human Rights Watch, "Why They Died: Civilian Casualties in Lebanon During the 2006 War" (2007), www.hrw.org/report/2007/09/05/why-they-died/civilian-casualties-lebanon-during-2006-war (last accessed April 16, 2016).

82   Rabindra Ray, *The Naxalites and Their Ideology* (Calcutta: Oxford University Press, 1988), 28–51.

83   Prakash Singh, *The Naxalite Movement in India*, rev. edn. (New Delhi: Rupa Publications (Kindle Edition), 2006).

84   Michael Spacek, "India's Enduring Naxalite Insurgency," *World Politics Review* (February 22, 2011): 5.

85   This is a widely cited statement. See, for instance, Jonathan Kennedy and Sunil Purushotham, "Beyond Naxalbari: A Comparative Analysis of Maoist Insurgency and Counterinsurgency in Independent India," *Comparative Studies in Society and History* 54, no. 4 (2012): 832.

86   For more on the various pay-offs associated with state policies of repression and conciliation, see Dugan and Chenoweth, "Moving Beyond Deterrence: The Effectiveness of Raising the Expected Utility of Abstaining from Terrorism in Israel."

5

Terrorism after wars: the weapon of the weakest?

We have come across a number of instances in which serious terrorist violence followed rather than preceded insurgencies. Much of the writing on the subject has suggested that terrorism is used during an early attention-getting stage of an insurgency (see Chapter 3). In this chapter we investi-gate circumstances in which terrorist violence appears to follow or increase toward the end of an internal war.

Unlike wars between states, internal wars are usually depicted as fights to the finish: either the challengers win or the incumbents retain power. The winners occupy or retain control over the levers of power in govern-ment while the losers face prison, exile, or worse. The Russian, Chinese, Vietnamese, and Iranian revolutions followed this pattern, with the challeng-ers taking power. The Latin American insurgencies of the 1960s and 1970s in Argentina and Brazil produced outcomes favorable to the incumbents. In a few recent cases compromise settlements were achieved as in El Salvador and in Northern Ireland following the 1998 Good Friday agreement.[1] But, do these outcomes necessarily mean an end to terrorism?

The answer is pretty clearly "no." In the case of Northern Ireland, dissident elements within the IRA regarded the compromise agreement involving the region's continued status as part of the United Kingdom as a betrayal of the cause seeking a united Ireland. Accordingly, the Real IRA and like-minded bands launched a series of terrorist attacks intended to "sabotage the peace."[2] Likewise, the 1979 Iranian Revolution produced a decisive outcome. Iran's monarchy was toppled. The Shah, his family, and key supporters fled into exile. Revolutionaries quickly established ad hoc courts for the trial and execution of the Shah's military and police officers. This decisive victory, though, did not bring an end to terrorism; in fact, the success of the revolutionaries fostered it.

The dominant faction among the revolutionaries was the followers of the Muslim cleric, the Ayatollah Khomeini. To gain complete control of the new regime, though, they had to defeat other revolutionary groups who wanted to move Iran in a secular direction. One of these groups, an offshoot of the Iranian communist party, sought unsuccessfully to prevent the country from becoming a Muslim theocracy. Despite carrying out a wave of assassinations and bombings lasting over a year (1982–83), the Ayatollah's forces prevailed and the dissident terrorists were either killed or forced into exile.

As these examples suggest, the end of wider-scale armed confrontations do not necessarily produce peace, nor do peace agreements necessarily lead to peace. On occasion, these outcomes set the stage for new warfare. This is true of "great wars" and the peace agreements formulated at their ends. The 1919 Peace Treaty at Versailles ending World War I created conditions for World War II twenty years later. It is also true of smaller wars. An agreement reached in Geneva in 1954 ended French involvement in the war over Vietnam. After this, Vietnam was divided into two independent states, South Vietnam and a communist North Vietnam. These same Geneva Accords were followed by a long-fought war aimed at achieving the merger of the two states under communist auspices by one side and the prevention of this outcome by the other. It also led to the ill-fated American military involvement on behalf of the losing South Vietnamese side. Our own data indicates the existence of some fourteen instances in which outbreaks of terrorism occurred after what seemed to be the conclusion of an armed insurgency. Table 5.1 lists instances in which terrorism seems to occur toward the end of armed conflict.

Assigning meaning to these cases is not without its difficulties. The situations appear to be divisible, roughly, into those where the terrorism represents the last gasp of what the French would call *irredusibles*, groups or factions that refuse to accept the apparent outcome and choose to fight on until they are induced to stop or decide to stop themselves (e.g., Northern Ireland, Cambodia). Second, we come across cases where the terrorism or violence, in general, is chronic (e.g., Tajikistan, Ethiopia, Burundi). The apparent end of many of the insurgencies we examine here is an illusion caused by the limited timeframe captured by our data. What seems to be an end to insurgency is really simply a pause before the outbreak of another one. Multi-ethnic countries where hostility between groups along ethnic, geographic, and religious lines is a fact of life are particularly susceptible to this chronic pattern. Third, we find episodes where an insurgency, successful or not, has so weakened the state that it no longer possesses the ability to maintain public order. In this situation new or newly revived terrorist groups take advantage of the chaos to achieve their objectives. Later in the chapter we consider a number of

Table 5.1   Terrorism at the end of wider-scale armed conflict

Insurgents	Internal war	Peaks and patterns	Place
Terrorism increasing or peaking after internal war			
Communist Party of the Philippines/ New People's Army (1969–ongoing)	1972–92, 2005–6	Terrorism increased during the latter half of the war. First peaks toward the end of the earlier war (1988 and 1990). Subsequent peaks following latter war (2008). Terrorism increasing 2012–13.	Philippines
Sandinistas (1961–79)	1978–79	The war came at the end of the Sandinista's insurgency. There were several peaks: first peak in 1978, followed by terrorism used again during and after the 1981–90 civil war and another peak after that war in 1991–92.	Nicaragua
Contras (1981–90)	1981–90	Terrorism was used during and after the war, the peak in 1991–92 is credited to the Recontras.	Nicaragua
Sudan People's Liberation Movement (1983–2005)	1983–2004	Terrorism used throughout war (small numbers) and continuing after, peaked in 2012.	Sudan
Panama (1989)	1989*	The 20 December Movement (M-20) carried out terrorism after Operation Just Cause. Attacks between 1990 and 1992 (small number of attacks).	Panama
Serbian Republic (1992–94)	1992–95	Terrorism in the state peaked after the civil war. Peak in 1997, most attackers "unknown."	Bosnia and Herzegovina
Kosovo Liberation Army (1996–99)	1996–99	Terrorism peaked in 2000.	Kosovo
Communist Party of Nepal (1996–2006)	1997–2006	Terrorism was used during the conflict in small numbers, but peaked afterward. Sharp increase in terrorism in 2013.	Nepal

Insurgents	Internal war	Peaks and patterns	Place
Terrorism increasing in the later stages of internal war			
African National Congress, Pan Africanist Congress, Azanian People's Organization (1961–90)	1983–94**	There is some disagreement on this case. • The period of insurgency may have ended in 1990 for the ANC; however, this period of time coincided with an intra-state war that lasted until 1994. As such, the peak in terrorism in 1988 may be an end-of-insurgency event or a beginning-of-insurgency event. • Another spike in the incidence of terrorism after the insurgency may be attributed to white supremacists, many attackers are "unknown."	South Africa
Eritrean separatists (1961–93) and Anti-Derg militias (1974–91)	1974–92	Terrorism increased at the end of the insurgencies, peaking in 1992. The overall number of attacks is small and the perpetrators are largely "unknown."	Ethiopia
Free Aceh Movement (1976–2005)	1975–2005	Terrorism peaked in 2001, toward the latter part of the civil war.	Indonesia
Mozambican National Resistance (1976–92)	1976–95	Terrorism peaked in 1989 and dropped afterward. Very little terrorism recorded after 1992 until a new spike in terrorism began in 2012.	Mozambique
Shanti Bahini (1973–97)	1976–97	Terrorism perpetrated during the latter half of the insurgency.	Bangladesh
Khmer Rouge and Khmer nationalists (1979–93)	1978–97	Terrorism peaked toward the end of the war (1992–96).	Cambodia

(Continued)

Table 5.1   *(Continued)*

Insurgents	Internal war	Peaks and patterns	Place
Terrorism increasing in the later stages of internal war			
Allied Democratic Forces National Army for the Liberation of Uganda (ADF-NALU) (1986–2000)	1986–2000	Most attacks credited to NALU and ADF occurred between 1997 and 2001.	Uganda
National Patriotic Front of Liberia (NPFL) (1989–92)	1989–97	Terrorism peaked toward the end of the civil war and after the insurgency, the numbers of overall attacks (*n* = 32) and NPFL-credited attacks are small (*n* = 6).	Liberia
Nagorno-Karabakh (1988–94)	1992–94	Terrorism peaked during the civil war, though this was late in terms of the insurgents' activities.	Azerbaijan

* This incident is not described as an intra-state war or civil war according to some sources; however, it is described as a "minor" armed conflict in the UCDP/PRIO dataset. UCDP/PRIO codes other events as a combination of "minor," "intermediate," and "war" that are described as insurgencies, civil wars, or intra-state, extra-state, and non-state wars by the other sources we consulted.

** These are the years coded as "civil war." The time period of insurgency is given as 1960–94; the time period of intra-state war is given as 1987–94.

Sources: Boot, *Invisible Armies*, 569–89; Connable and Libicki, *How Insurgencies End*, 157–62, 99–201; Sarkees and Wayman, *Resort to War*; Fearon and Laitin, "Additional Tables;" UCDP/PRIO, "Armed Conflict Dataset V.4-2014a, 1946–2013;" "Global Terrorism Database [Data File]," 2013.

these failed state cases, along with the implications these cases have for the warfare that likely remains to be seen in the twenty-first century.

Terrorism as a trailing indicator

The last gasp of terrorism may be the result of very different developments. On the one hand, an increase or continuation of terrorism may follow the formation of divisions within a militant organization between those ready to abandon armed struggle and those who are unwilling to end their wars. This may lead to the creation of splinter groups. The many factions of the

Irish Republican Army exemplify this trend. Two examples include the appearances of the militant Real IRA and Continuity IRA factions during the period in which the political wing of the Provisional IRA seemed to be gaining influence. Another example occurred a generation earlier with the formation of the Provisional IRA in 1969 and its split from the Official IRA. Within a few years, the Official IRA declared an end to its use of violence. The factions are not necessarily weaker or stronger than their counterparts (the PIRA was the stronger faction; the Continuity and Real IRAs are weaker). They simply are not finished with their fight.

Terrorism may also increase following the military defeat of an insurgent group. This may have been the case in parts of Asia during the eighteenth and nineteenth centuries. Stephen Frederic Dale tells the story of Muslim communities fighting European colonization along the coast of India in Malabar, as well as in Atjeh, Sumatra and Mindanao and Sulu in the Philippines. According to his account, the established Muslim communities – themselves former colonizers – used military means against the new colonizers until they could no longer fight the superior European militaries; they then turned to jihad and terrorism, in particular suicide terrorism.[3] A similar story could be told of the military defeat of the original Irish Republican Army, which sought a free Ireland during the early twentieth century. The Irish War of Independence was partially successful in producing a free Republic of Ireland in the southern counties and western counties. The reality of a divided Ireland with the six northern counties remaining part of the United Kingdom, however, fell short of the republican movement's objectives. The war continued, though the Troubles and the associated terrorism took decades to materialize.

Drawing on these examples, we may presume that the remnants of other armed groups which are presumed to have been militarily defeated may also turn back to terrorism. We face at least two dilemmas in our search for more recent examples. First, data on terrorism is confined to a relatively short period of time in recent history. We simply do not have much data with which to work. Moreover, many of the groups that have turned to insurgency during the time period for which we have data on terrorist attacks are still active; others have been defeated only recently. As such, it may be too soon for evidence of a return to terrorism to materialize. Attention tends to turn away from wars or other conflicts after military victory. Perhaps evidence of groups' operations remains scarce for these reasons, as well. One recent example helps to highlight the problem to which we refer. It appeared that the Shining Path was defeated in 1992 or shortly thereafter with the arrest of the group's leader, Abimael Guzman. Shining Path was influenced by Marxist thought and Maoist revolutionary action.[4] Similarly, another group, the Marxist Tupac Amaru Revolutionary Movement (MRTA), also continued its activities for a period of time after that group's leadership was arrested the same year. Peru's civil war also lasted for several more years, eventually ending in 2000. While we know now that both groups were severely weakened, the Shining Path was apparently not dead. The Shining Path continues as a militant and political group with limited influence.[5] There has been a small increase in terrorism attributed to the group in recent years, though the numbers of events come nowhere close to those found during the groups active years prior to and just after the capture of Abimael Guzman, the group's leader.[6]

Patterns of trailing terrorism

We identify three patterns of terrorism as a trailing indicator. In one set of cases, terrorism increases or peaks after an internal war has ended. In some of these cases, the peak is sharp and the use of terrorism ends quickly. In others, terrorism peaks but continues for a time. Several of the examples that seem to fit this pattern are of groups engaging in terrorism in the context of an ongoing competition between militarized groups. In a second set of cases, a different pattern emerges. Rather than an abrupt end, terrorism increases over the course of an insurgency. A pattern such as this may indicate a gradual weakening of an insurgent group relative to the state. As groups weaken, they may be left relying more and more on terrorist attacks, or attacks on softer civilian targets. A third set of cases are of considerable interest to us. These are the cases in which years pass between campaigns of terrorism. Perhaps the organization has renewed itself or found a new base of support. Alternatively, something within the environment within which these groups operate may have changed, leading to a new set of grievances and new opportunities to challenge the status quo. Rather than an end to militant activities, increases in terrorism may represent the beginnings of new armed conflicts, which may or may not materialize.

Nicaragua's warring Contras and Sandinistas demonstrate the first pattern. Terrorist attacks credited to the left-leaning Sandinistas peaked in frequency during the latter part of their insurgency in 1979 (see Figure 5.1). Coincidentally, this is also the period described as war (1978–79) following a longer period of insurgency, which began in 1961. For the Sandinistas, 1979 was the year they successfully pressured long-time dictator Anastasio Somoza to resign his presidency. A few years later, the Sandinistas gained another victory, this one electoral. In 1984, Sandinista leader José Daniel Ortega was elected president.

The Sandinistas have acted as an insurgent group and as a political party. They have faced violent forms of competition from local rebels in the form of the counterrevolutionary Contras. These rebels – not a single group, but a collection of groups – carried on an externally sponsored campaign to unseat the Sandinistas. This Contra campaign was not successful, though neither was the Sandinistas' effort to counter them. There was no decisive winner or loser.

In electoral terms, however, there was a new winner. The 1990 presidential election gave voters the chance to choose between the Sandinistas and the Contras. The opposition candidate, Violeta Chamorro defeated incumbent Daniel Ortega, bringing a centrist National Opposition Union party. Chamorro was also a symbolic candidate, the widow of a journalist whose assassination in 1978 "served as a catalyst for civil war."[7] In an electoral sense, the victory was short (neither party won the subsequent presidential election), but the peace was shorter. Despite an end to war in 1990, representatives of both groups returned to violent tactics in 1991.

The pattern of terrorism credited to the Sandinistas toward the ends of Nicaragua's civil wars is more dramatic than that of the Contras and their successors, the Recontras. The numbers of terrorist attacks perpetrated in Nicaragua peaked briefly in 1991 following the end of the Nicaragua's Contra-led insurgency and civil war in 1990. This peak was evident in the numbers of attacks carried out by Sandinistas and Contras. The number increased from very few attacks in 1990, with none credited to the Sandinistas that year, to dozens of attacks the following year. Of eighty recorded attacks, seventy-seven met GTD's three terrorism criteria. Just under half of these attacks in 1991 ($n = 36$) were perpetrated against unarmed, non-state targets.[8]

Another pattern emerges from taking a closer look at the targets of each of the groups. The increase in terrorist violence is more noticeable for the Sandinistas, for which very few terrorist attacks were recorded during the duration of the 1980 and 1990 conflict. In fact, the Sandinistas were in power much of this time, with Daniel Ortega serving in the presidency from 1984 through 1990. As such, attacks perpetrated as part of a state response to the rebels would be unlikely to meet the definitional criteria of terrorism. Most of the terrorist attacks credited to the Sandinista groups after 1990 were aimed at government targets (thirteen out of eighteen in 1991). The remaining Sandinista-credited attacks in this year were aimed at civilian targets, including journalists. The Contras (or Recontras) targeted different entities. Almost half of the Recontra-credited terrorist attacks in 1991 were aimed at government, military, police, and other armed groups (fifteen of thirty-three).[9] Terrorist attacks credited to the Sandinistas peaked much more dramatically toward the end of the earlier conflict, in 1979 (see Figure 5.1).

These patterns tell us something interesting about the groups and their insurgent activities. The Sandinista and Contra groups' use of terrorism

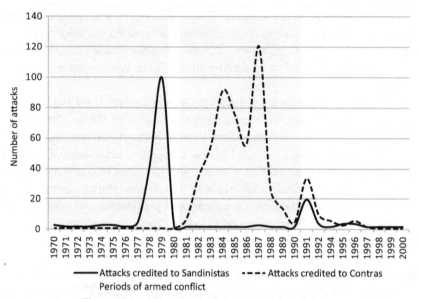

Figure 5.1   Nicaragua's Contras and Sandinistas

Sources: Boot, *Invisible Armies*, 569–89; Connable and Libicki, *How Insurgencies End*, 157–62, 99–201; Sarkees and Wayman, *Resort to War*; Fearon and Laitin, "Additional Tables;" UCDP/PRIO, "Armed Conflict Dataset V.4-2014a, 1946–2013;" "Global Terrorism Database [Data File]," 2015.

(including attacks on government and other armed and unarmed actors) peaked following Nicaragua's 1981–90 civil war. Neither side emerged as a victor from this war. While a peace was reached, elections were held, and a centrist candidate was chosen as the country's new president, some within these groups seem to have retained an interest in continuing their violent struggle. In fact, according to the timeline of attacks, the Sandinistas and Contras appear to trade violence, with clusters of attacks credited to one or the other group. In addition, several clusters of attacks are recorded as having "unknown" attackers (*n* = 23).[10]

Perhaps 1991 was the decisive year for both parties. After twenty years of terrorism and civil war, Nicaragua's rebels no longer fight each other. For their part, the Sandinistas have returned to the presidency. José Daniel Ortega was elected as Nicaragua's president by a majority of Nicaragua's voters. Ortega re-entered office in 2007, was re-elected in November 2011, and will likely have the opportunity to run for a third successive term in 2016.[11] The Sandinistas are the leading party in much of the country.

In Nicaragua's case, the end of the civil war turned into the beginning of another (albeit shorter and less violent) episode of terrorism. In another example, that of South Africa, a spike in terrorism coincides with the end of one period of insurgency and the early years of an intra-state war, both of which involved the same party, the African National Congress (ANC).

According to some accounts, the end of a thirty-year insurgency on the part of the ANC, Pan Africanist Congress (PAC), and Azanian People's Organization (AZAPO) came around 1988 and 1990.[12] An intra-state war began around the same time in 1987 and lasted until 1994, the year ANC leader Nelson Mandela was elected to South Africa's presidency. The insurgency and intra-state wars overlap for a period of years. A depiction of the timing of terrorist attacks credited to the ANC, PAC, and AZAPO reveals a related ambiguity: it is difficult to discern whether terrorism was increasing toward the end of the insurgency or at the beginning of the intra-state war. Was terrorism being used by increasingly weak actors or increasingly strong actors in the years leading up to the insurgents' victory around 1990?

The answer to this question may be found in part by consideration of the longer-term trend. The frequency of terrorist attacks by these three groups, the overwhelming majority of which were credited to the ANC (the PAC and AZAPO are credited with carrying out a total of nine terrorist attacks between 1990 and 1994, four and five attacks respectively), increased gradually over the two and a half decades leading up to the insurgents' victory. The attacks peak in 1988 and decline rapidly to almost zero before peaking again for a brief period, and at a much lower count, around 1992. Terrorism was a tool used in the period leading up to the end of the insurgency, abandoned with

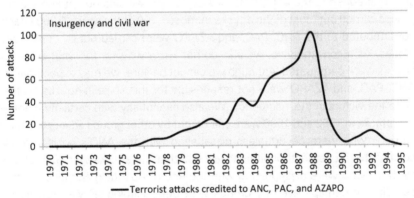

Figure 5.2   South Africa's ANC, PAC, and AZAPO*

* The incidents included in the counts above meet GTD's three criteria for terrorism. This count excludes "ambiguous" cases, but includes terrorist attacks on state, military, and police targets.

Sources: Boot, *Invisible Armies*, 569–89; Connable and Libicki, *How Insurgencies End*, 157–62, 99–201; Sarkees and Wayman, *Resort to War*; Fearon and Laitin, "Additional Tables;" UCDP/PRIO, "Armed Conflict Dataset V.4-2014a, 1946–2013;" "Global Terrorism Database [Data File]," 2015.

the pending victory of the equality movement, and used again, though briefly, afterward, though also in the context of internal war.

The ANC, PAC, and AZAPO were not alone in their participation in wider-scale warfare in South Africa. Other groups seeking racial equality and those opposing it engaged in militant activities throughout these time periods under consideration. What can we learn about the use of terrorism by other partici-pants in South Africa's internal war?

One way to answer this question is to look at the overall pattern of ter-rorist attacks taking place in South Africa. Shifting our focus away from the ANC, PAC, and AZAPO, we can see what other groups were active during this time and, to some extent, what objectives they sought. In the case of South Africa, there have been almost 1,200 terrorist attacks, meeting the three definitional criteria while including attacks on the state, its military, police, and violent political parties. Plotting the frequencies of terrorist attacks by years, we find a tremendous spike in terrorism in 1992 followed by a smaller spike in 1996.[13] These spikes correspond to the period following the ANC, PAC, and AZAPO insurgency and the period following the end of internal war in South Africa. They are also part of an trend showing an increasing frequency in the use of terrorism over time. As such, the patterns suggest support for terror-ism as a trailing indicator used toward the end or after armed confrontation (see Figure 5.3).

We must reserve judgment for the moment, however. We know the attacks are not credited to the ANC, PAC, or AZAPO, yet we also do not know which groups carried out most of the attacks. Almost 1,100 of the nearly 1,200 attacks not attributed to the ANC, PAC, and AZAPO were carried out by "unknown" groups. As a consequence, we also do not know why –or for what end – the attacks were perpetrated. Although we cannot be sure, we may expect that the ANC, PAC, and AZAPO were not responsible for this spike in attacks, as they were the victors in the insurgency. We also cannot say with certainty whether the attacks in 1992 and 1996 were carried out by other groups advocating racial equality, who were nevertheless dissatisfied with the ANC's position at the head of this movement, or alternatively whether the attacks were perpetrated by those who were disappointed with the end of Apartheid and its system of benefits, or perhaps even by groups with other ideologies. We also do not know the extent to which these attacks may have been retribution carried out by either side against their presumed adversaries as part of a continuation of a culture of violence following decades of violence in the country.

The data available via the GTD is not sufficiently informative for us to use it to make such determinations. We have information on the targets of attacks, but not sufficient information on whether these targets were sym-pathizers or opponents of South Africa's new status quo or the specifics of

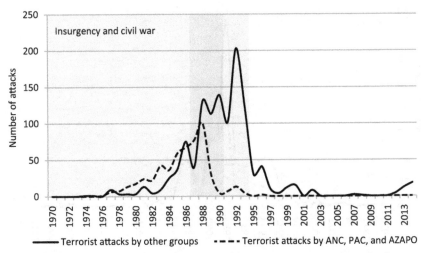

Terrorist attacks by other groups ▪-▪-▪ Terrorist attacks by ANC, PAC, and AZAPO

Figure 5.3 South Africa's terrorism in comparative perspective*

* Terrorism here includes cases meeting GTD's three criteria. This count excludes "ambiguous" cases, but includes terrorist attacks on state, military, and police targets.

Sources: Boot, *Invisible Armies*, 569–89; Connable and Libicki, *How Insurgencies End*, 157–62, 99–201; Sarkees and Wayman, *Resort to War*, Fearon and Laitin, "Additional Tables;" UCDP/PRIO, "Armed Conflict Dataset V.4-2014a, 1946–2013;" "Global Terrorism Database [Data File]," 2015.

the contexts within which each attack took place. What we can do is disaggregate these attacks by the targets. Attacks on the government shortly before and after 1994, when the ANC's leader Nelson Mandela was elected to office, are more likely to be attacks perpetrated against the new regime.

This appears to be the case. A look at the total number of terrorist attacks against government targets seems to support the assumption that groups other than the ANC, PAC, and AZAPO were responsible for most of the attacks on South Africa's government after 1988, or after the beginning of the end of the insurgency. The ANC is responsible for proportionately more attacks on government targets (as compared to others) for the period between 1982 and 1986 and in the year 1988 (the PAC and AZAPO are not credited with attacks on government targets). This last year was also the peak of ANC attacks on government targets. Figure 5.4 shows the number of attacks credited to other groups or "unknown" groups as well as the total number of attacks on government entities, including those credited to the ANC. Attacks by the ANC are represented by the gap between the two lines (the line representing the total number of attacks and the line for attacks presumably carried out by others). The three groups are credited with comparatively few attacks on government targets between 1989 and 1996, as

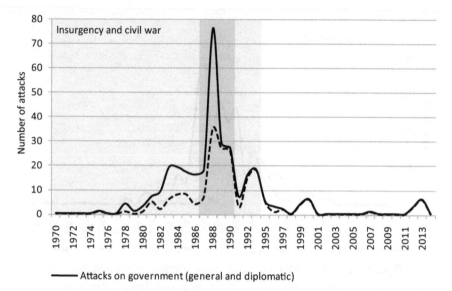

—— Attacks on government (general and diplomatic)

▬ ▬ ▬ Attacks on government (general and diplomatic), excluding attacks
credited to the ANC, PAC, or AZAPO

Figure 5.4   Terrorism* against government targets

* Terrorism here includes cases meeting the GTD's three criteria. This count excludes
"ambiguous" cases.

Sources: Boot, *Invisible Armies*, 569–89; Connable and Libicki, *How Insurgencies End*,
157–62, 99–201; Sarkees and Wayman, *Resort to War*; Fearon and Laitin, "Additional
Tables;" UCDP/PRIO, "Armed Conflict Dataset V.4-2014a, 1946–2013;" "Global Terrorism
Database [Data File]," 2015.

illustrated by the closing of the gap between total attacks and attacks by
others and unknowns (see Figure 5.4).

A similar pattern is observable for terrorism against police targets. Attacks
by the ANC peaked in 1987 before dropping to zero in 1990. A handful of
PAC- and AZAPO-credited attacks on police targets were confined to the
latter 1990–92 period. In the absence of data on terrorist attacks in 1993, it
is hard to ascertain whether this pattern continued or changed during the following year. Based on data for 1994 and the end of terrorism for these groups
in 1996, however, it seems probable that the ANC, PAC, and AZAPO were
not the main perpetrators of terrorist attacks on the police after 1989 (see
Figure 5.5).

When it comes to a discussion of South Africa's recent experience with
terrorism and internal warfare, one coincidence stands out. The frequency of
terrorist attacks declined noticeably following the end of the country's internal
war in 1994.

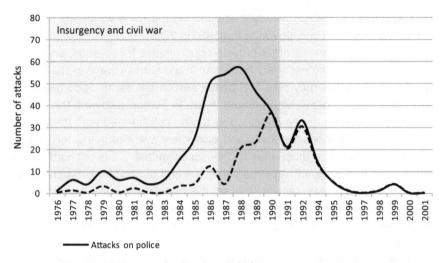

Figure 5.5 Terrorism* against police targets

* Terrorism here includes cases meeting the GTD's three criteria. This count excludes "ambiguous" cases.

Sources: Boot, *Invisible Armies*, 569–89; Connable and Libicki, *How Insurgencies End*, 157–62, 99–201; Sarkees and Wayman, *Resort to War*; Fearon and Laitin, "Additional Tables;" UCDP/PRIO, "Armed Conflict Dataset V.4-2014a, 1946–2013;" "Global Terrorism Database [Data File]," 2015.

The end or the beginning of war?

In *Violence after War*, Michael Boyle treats the problem of postwar war systematically.[14] Here it seems helpful to quote Boyle in defining our terms.

> A post-conflict state is defined here by four conditions: 1) the state experienced an armed conflict between at least two parties; 2) the fighting for the war has been conducted on its own territory; 3) there was an explicit and formal termination of the war; and 4) the peace settlement must last for at least one year.[15]

Given these criteria, what are the circumstances that stimulate violence after the termination of an internal war? Boyle answers by pointing out that often governments are weakened as a result of the fighting, leaving a gap in terms of the state's ability to provide public security. With law enforcement agencies diminished, criminals may seize new opportunities available to them.

One example to which Boyle calls attention is the massive looting that followed the American occupation of Baghdad in 2003.

Postwar environments often provide opportunities for revenge, and internal wars are often exceptionally brutal. As in the Greek Civil War (1945–49), the brutalized often may take the peace settlement as an opportunity for revenge against those who brutalized them. In Europe following the end of the Nazi occupation, those identified as having collaborated with the enemy in France, the Netherlands, Italy, and elsewhere were targeted for various forms of retaliation by those they had earlier assaulted.[16] It is not hard to see similar circumstances arising in Iraq after the end of Saddam Hussein's rule. Hussein's regime was secular, though the benefits accrued disproportionately to members of the minority Sunni sect within the majority Shi'a state. Moreover, the regime's treatment of minorities, and especially the Kurds, was brutal.

Based on these and other conditions, Boyle distinguishes between types of post-conflict states, between those he identifies as operating in hard or soft environments. Soft environments are ones in which the violence is primarily criminal and predatory. Some of the violence, though, may serve a political purpose – acts of individual or small-group terrorism, for example – but this low level activity lacks an overall strategic design. Hard environments, on the other hand, are ones in which groups, either new or old, pose serious challenges to the incumbents. Oftentimes new or renewed insurgencies are launched against severely weakened post-conflict states.[17]

Boyle then employs the Uppsala Conflict Termination Dataset to measure the prevalence of renewed violence following the peace agreements that occurred between 1989 and 2007. Of the fifty-two cases the dataset identifies as wars that ended in these years, Boyle reports that there were nineteen instances in which insurgencies followed the termination of war. If we add to this figure soft environments in which terrorist bombings and politically motivated assassinations were carried out, we are dealing with a rather common occurrence: the end of a war leads to renewed warfare within a relatively short period of time. We now draw attention to three current episodes that should at least illustrate the issue.

In all three of the cases we are considering – Libya, Yemen, and Afghanistan – serious bouts of terrorism followed the overthrow of central governments and the prevailing political order. Inter-tribal violence followed the death of Qaddafi in Libya, the departure of former President Saleh of Yemen, and the chaos in Kabul in the aftermath of the 2001 defeat of the Taliban regime (and the forced departure of al Qaeda's central command). In addition to the tribal element, religion has certainly been a crucial ingredient in the conflicts. Terrorist violence was based on Salafi-jihadists' and other ultra-conservative fundamentalist groups' aim to impose Sharia law on often unwilling populations, including Shiite minorities.

The intervention of outside powers intent on restoring order typically made things worse. The involvement of the United States, the European powers, and the United Nations became an independent source of conflict. Those external forces that became embroiled or sought to play a mediating role in the conflicts often found themselves targets of terrorist attacks.

In short, what we have witnessed is the violence that, with few exceptions, occurs in the wake of the collapse of state authority. Unfortunately the database at our disposal does not capture developments such as this when the result is something less than war. In addition, we are constrained by the recentness of some developments and the limitations of data on terrorism in terms of the timeframe of interest, including the most recent two years (2014–15). While we include our usual array of graphs below, we caution the reader to understand these examples as cases in which terrorism follows state collapse. In these cases, wider-scale warfare is a symptom of terrorism, rather than the other way around.

Libya

Libya is a multi-tribal country which was conquered by the Ottomans (1835). The geographic space that is considered to be part of Libya is relatively large (seventeenth in terms of land mass) and the population relatively small (108th in the world) by comparison to other states.[18] As was true before the Ottoman victory, the country remained divided into three separate entities: Tripolitania, Cyrenaica, and Fazzan. Despite stiff resistance from the Ottoman Turks and indigenous groups, Libya was conquered by Italy in 1912. Over the succeeding years the Italians tried to promote political and economic development. Particularly after Mussolini came to power, the Italians (who integrated the three regions into one colony) sought to incorporate Libya into what the Fascists believed would become a significant part of a new Roman Empire.[19] This was, of course, not a goal that would be realized. During World War II, British and American armed forces drove the Italians and their German allies out of Libya. What followed the war were several years of negotiations among the victorious powers, involving the United Nations. Finally, Libya gained its independence in 1951 under the leadership of a monarch, the Western-oriented King Idris al-Sanussi. With British and American assistance, the monarch ruled until 1969. During that year and while on a tour of Eastern Europe, King Idris was overthrown by a group of young military officers led by a young (twenty-eight-year-old) colonel, Muammar al-Qaddafi.

Lasting until the uprisings of the Arab Spring, the Qaddafi regime's exploits have produced voluminous commentary. Suffice it to say here that the young colonel came to power as an advocate of pan-Arabism, intending to walk in the footsteps of the Egyptian leader Gammal Nasser. Unlike his hero to the east, Qaddafi had resources to invest in his pan-Arab cause and related interests. Libya's small population and vast oil wealth, which had been discovered by British engineers, provided its leader immense wealth.

Over the next four decades Qaddafi devoted large amounts of money to promoting the Palestinian cause by supporting Fatah and the various groups falling under the PLO umbrella. His anti-imperialism led him to sponsor various terrorist operations on his own. The Qaddafi regime's most notorious association with terrorism was the December 1988 bombing of Pam Am Flight 103 over Lockerbie, Scotland. Qaddafi is also associated with offering sanctuary to "Carlos the Jackal" (Vladamir Ilyich Sanchez) after the latter's band seized those attending a meeting of the OPEC oil ministers in Vienna and held them hostage.[20] Further, Qaddafi was known to have equipped and funded terrorist groups on a virtually worldwide basis ranging from the IRA to Philippine separatists.[21]

It was not long before the Libyan dictatorship came into open conflict with the United States. In 1986, American intelligence sources reported that Libyan agents were responsible for a bombing at a Berlin disco frequented by American service personnel. This terrorist act led the Reagan administration to retaliate. Taking-off from bases in Great Britain, American bombers staged raids on training camps used by terrorist in and near Tripoli. Qaddafi's compound in the city also came under attack, killing one of his children in the process.

During the last decade of the twentieth century, Qaddafi, an erratic figure if there ever was one, launched a campaign to acquire WMDs. Poison gas facilities were under construction in Libya's desert, and surreptitious negotiations were under way, via Pakistan, for nuclear weapons technology.

Qaddafi began to make an about-face, or a political u-turn, shortly before the turn of the twenty-first century. Faced with continuing international isolation and repeated condemnations by the United Nations, the Libyan dictator sought to re-integrate his country into the international community. In 2003, he signed an agreement to abandon his quest for WMDs. He agreed to a settlement with the families of the Lockerbie victims. He also agreed that Libya would no longer promote or sponsor terrorism. In view of these changes, Western businesspeople flocked to Tripoli. Libya was open for business.

The Libyan revolution, which followed in 2011–12, should be seen in the context of the Arab Spring.[22] The spring of 2011 saw the outbreak of popular protest movements in Tunisia, Egypt, Libya, Yemen, and Syria, all aimed at compelling authoritarian and corrupt rulers to relinquish power. Western observers hoped these uprisings would lead the countries involved in a democratic direction. Although the situation remains fluid, with the exception of Tunisia, these hopes have not been realized.

Libya is a state with divided loyalties.[23] Tribal affiliations survived under the dictatorial regime. Benghazi, and the eastern part of the country as a whole, had not been favored by the regime in Tripoli. The various tribes loyal to Qaddafi – including his own – were located in the western part of Libya. Qaddafi's interest in promoting a pan-Arab identity is interesting when considered in the context of the country's relative lack of a Libyan national identity.

In the Libyan case, protests broke out in February 2011 in Benghazi over the detention of an anti-Qaddafi lawyer. In any case the regime reacted to the Benghazi protests with the indiscriminate use of force, with bullets rather than tear gas. This over-reaction was the spark that ignited the civil war. The fighting lasted until October 2011 when Qaddafi was cornered and killed by insurgents in his home base at Sirte. The fighting on the ground had involved a constellation of militia groups drawn largely from the eastern part of Libya (one estimate puts the number at 500).[24] In addition to these ground operations, largely fighting along the country's Mediterranean coast, NATO carried out air attacks on the regime's key outposts. A UN Security Council resolution and support from the Arab League justified the air operations in the name of protecting Libyan civilians.[25] Qaddafi had threatened to execute all who opposed him.

Libya after Qaddafi was and is a very weak state; many would argue it is in a process of complete disintegration.[26] The late Colonel's legacy was a set of poorly developed "people's committees" based on his *Green Book*, a volume in which he described plans for a new type of democracy, one with direct rule by the people. In effect, this meant rule by Qaddafi and the retinue of people around him.[27]

Despite optimism that might have existed at the outset of Libya's Arab Spring, Libya's transition to some weak version of democratic rule proceeded slowly. No longer working toward democracy, some of the largely eastern-based militias transformed themselves into terrorist groups whose aims were Islamist rather than secular democratic. With UN observers in place, general elections were held in July 2012 to select a governing body and issue a constitutional declaration. Constituent assembly elections in 2014 were organized in order to write a more permanent document. The net result of these institution-making efforts has been the formation of a weak government in Tripoli, one with a limited ability to control, much less monopolize, the use of force on its own territory. If parts of the state are not under warlord rule, something approaching this appears to prevail. For example, in 2014 one of the militia groups seized control of the new National Congress in Tripoli and refused to leave the premises until its demands were met.

The weakness of the Libyan state, competition among the local armed groups, and the lack of a broader community from which to draw national unity have also left openings for outsiders who can influence domestic politics. Moreover, the country's oil wealth provides additional incentives for those interested in taking advantage of the ungoverned spaces. Voids such as these are large enough and appealing enough for transnational actors like al Qaeda and ISIL to seek a space for themselves, their ideas, and operations.[28] Salafi-jihadist ideologies have followed the influence of these groups, giving religious divisions a more central role in what was otherwise a tribal conflict.

Against this background a number of violent Islamist groups have emerged, ones located largely in the eastern part of the country, Benghazi especially. The most powerful of these Islamist organizations appear to be Dawn of Libya, Ansar al-Sharia (with branches in Benghazi and the nearby port city of Dern), the Raf al-Sahati Brigade, and the February 17 Martyrs Brigade.

The U.S. State Department now designates both branches of Ansar al-Sharia as FTOs. The reason for this designation was its role in the September 11, 2012, attack on the U.S. Mission in Benghazi. This attack involved the murder of the United States' Ambassador Christopher Stevens and three members of his staff. The killings also had political ramifications in the United States. Members of Congress accused the State Department of having failed to provide adequate security and, initially, having misled the American public about the terroristic nature of the attack. The group has also carried out a series of assassinations and bombings on behalf of the jihadist cause. Described as being "more ... a label than an organized group," Ansar al-Sharia, along with like-minded groups in Tunisia and elsewhere in North Africa, may have some ideological affinity, if not direct ties, to al Qaeda.[29] For its part, al Qaeda seemed unable to offer advice for the development of a post-Qaddafi Libyan state.[30]

What appears to be the relatively recent arrival of ISIL to Libya may challenge the positions of these groups, including Ansar al-Sharia.[31] Volunteers from Libya have recently made their way to the Islamic State (ISIL) and now participate in its struggles to establish a new caliphate.[32] ISIL has sought land, formed alliances, made enemies, and carried out attacks, including executions, on soil that would be Libyan were there a Libyan state to exert control over it.[33] ISIL's movement into Libya seems more like an invasion and co-optation from outside, not unlike a foreign occupation. Tales of ISIL's brutal approach to gaining the allegiance of its new Libyan subjects supports this view.[34]

The number of terrorist incidents in Libya has increased dramatically in recent years. Despite being a tactic that was hardly recorded in Libya's past, terrorism has come to play an increasing role in competition among Libya's

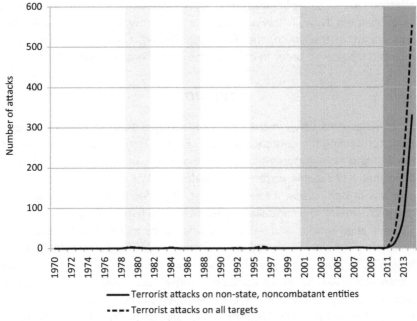

Terrorist attacks on non-state, noncombatant entities

- - - - Terrorist attacks on all targets

Figure 5.6 Terrorism in Libya*

*Shaded areas denote periods of armed conflict and war. Darker shaded areas represent periods of more than one war and/or armed conflict.

Sources: Boot, *Invisible Armies*, 569–89; Connable and Libicki, *How Insurgencies End*, 157–62, 99–201; Sarkees and Wayman, *Resort to War*, Fearon and Laitin, "Additional Tables;" UCDP/PRIO, "Armed Conflict Dataset V.4-2014a, 1946–2013;" "Global Terrorism Database [Data File]," 2015.

insurgents. Terrorist attacks on all types of targets increased more than twofold between 2013 and 2014. Terrorist attacks on non-state and unarmed targets increased almost four-fold during the same time (see Figure 5.6). In the Libyan case, terrorism was not present before or during wider-scale armed confrontations until quite recently, following the Arab Spring and the collapse of the Libyan state. While there is little reason to expect an end of war in Libya in the near future, there is good reason to view the use of terrorism in Libya as a weapon of weak actors increasingly resorting to terrorism as a tactic in ongoing warfare. These are the same weak groups, unable to rule by other means, which must compete with each other for primacy within the largely ungoverned state.

We should add before concluding our discussion of Libya that violence carried out by terrorist groups has largely been confined to the northern part of the country. While southern Libya has not been a peaceful and tranquil region, the dynamics of conflict in this area have been different. The various

Arab tribes in this Sahel/Sahara region enjoyed the colonel's patronage during the Qaddafi era. Now, following Qaddafi's overthrow, the two major African communities in the south, the Tubu and Tuareg, have from time-to-time employed violence in order to enhance their situations vis-à-vis the Arabs.[35]

Yemen

Yemen resembles Libya in the sense of lacking a state capable of governing and protecting the country's territory. Francis Fukuyama reminds us that "the first and most important institution that fragile or failing states lack is an administratively capable government. Before a state can be constrained by either law or democracy, it needs to exist. This means, in the first instance, the establishment of a centralized executive and a bureaucracy."[36]

Yemen is an ancient land – there are references to it in both the Bible and the Koran – but one which has experienced great difficulty in establishing a modern state. Yemen's history has been violent and bloody, even by Middle Eastern standards. In recent centuries, Yemen was ruled by the Ottoman Turks. Following World War I, the British ruled the territory, or at least the major port of Aden.[37] The hinterland was dominated by tribes; most were Sunni though at least one was Shiite.

In recent decades, Yemen has been both an importer and exporter of terrorism. So far as the latter is concerned, members of AQAP have used their bases in Yemen to launch attacks on Western targets. These attention-getting events include an effort in 2000 to sink an American destroyer, the *USS Cole,* while at anchor in the port of Aden; an unsuccessful attempt by a Yemeni-trained Nigerian student to detonate a bomb on Northwest Airlines Flight 253 over Detroit at Christmastime in 2009 (the underwear bomber); and an attempt the following year to send computer-based time bombs to various targets in the United States. Another effort was the unsuccessful attempt by a suicide bomber to kill a Saudi prince, who was also a deputy minister and involved in counterterrorism, at his office in Riyadh.[38] The most spectacular was the successful attempt by two AQAP-trained French Muslims to murder the staff of the satirical French magazine, *Charlie Hebdo*, in January 2015.

AQAP's outpost in Yemen is the locale from which its expert bomb-maker Ibrahim al-Asiri develops his weapons. This was also the place where the late American-born preacher of jihad Anwar al-Awalki delivered his appeals to the believers. Al-Awalki was killed in 2012, the result of a Hellfire missile strike fired from an American drone.

The al-Awalki episode calls our attention to the role of the United States (and Saudi Arabia) in Yemen's domestic politics.[39] What type of rule did these foreign powers have to confront in meeting the threats posed by AQAP?

Until the British withdrawal from Aden in 1967, most of northern Yemen was ruled as an imamate based on a branch of Shi'a Islam known as Zaydism. "Politics in the time of the imams was the preserve of ... factions; and was conducted on a personal face-to-face basis."[40] Political assassinations were a common practice in this tribal setting.

During the era of the People's Republic, South Yemen became a haven for various revolutionary terrorist organizations. Not unlike Libya, the regime in Aden provided training camps for the United Japanese Red Army and the German RAF. It was the Palestinian groups, most notably the Marxist-Leninist PFLP, that were the principal beneficiaries. Raids on Israeli targets, such as the 1972 massacre at Lod Airport, were planned and launched from the People's Republic.

Fighting between the North and South took on the look of a Cold War confrontation between the Soviet Union (South Yemen) and the U.S.- and the Saudi-funded North. Finally in 1990, as the USSR was in the process of disintegration, leaders in Sana and Aden reached an agreement to merge the two states under the auspices of President Ali Abdullah Saleh, an exceptionally shrewd politician from northern Yemen. His opposite number from the erstwhile People's Republic became the prime minister.

The newly united Yemen under Saleh made an effort to contain AQAP. These efforts were heavily subsidized by the Saudis and the Americans. In the latter case Predator drones have been used to maintain surveillance and occasionally carry out missile strikes against AQAP bases and human targets of significance. Saudi Arabia's interest is not difficult to understand. The monarchist regime in Riyadh shares a border with Yemen. In this case, however, the term "border" really belongs in quotation marks. The territory involved is largely ungoverned, without effective security on either side. Moreover, the territory is suitable for the type of clandestine activities often associated with insurgents: "On the Arabian Peninsula, it is possible for terrorist groups to maintain a low profile and hide. Large spaces are hidden as a result of the hostile environments for non-indigenous visitors ... Terrorists can take advantage of this situation by staying where outsiders and law enforcement cannot see them."[41]

Accordingly, from 2004 forward Saleh's army fought at least six rounds of rebellion in Yemen's northwest, an area sharing that porous border with Saudi Arabia. A Zaydi group known as the "Believing Youth" (or Houthi) led the main challenge.

In the aftermath of 9/11, Saleh was reluctant to side with the Americans and Saudis, despite the substantial subsidy that had been provided to him and despite the fact that large numbers of Yemenis were employed at jobs in the Kingdom. On pain of losing his subsidy and having his workers sent home, Saleh was coerced into cooperating with his benefactors. Saleh continued to rule Yemen until 2011, the year of the Arab Spring (he had been in power in the North from 1978). Saleh managed this through multiple re-elections to the presidency and his ability to manipulate and maneuver among the various tribes as religious groups that collectively constituted Yemen's population.

As dictators were being toppled in Tunisia and Egypt in 2011, a similar effort was undertaken in Yemen. In this case, the Arab Spring consisted of thousands of young Yemenis gathering in Sana, Aden, and other cities. Their demand was for Saleh's resignation. After a brief interlude the protests became violent. Saleh's presidential palace was attacked and he was himself injured by shell fire.

The Americans and Saudis could read the handwriting on the wall and persuaded Saleh to resign. After this was accomplished, a new democratic constitution was approved so that large numbers of Yemenis believed that they could look forward to something approaching democratic rule. This was not to be, however. In January 2015, the popularly elected government was the victim of a coup staged by the Shi'a Zaydi fighters, the Houthi.

With Yemen's state falling into disarray, AQAP continues to be a powerful force, one that is now able to control significant swaths of territory. In 2014, AQAP announced its plan to establish a state – an Islamic emirate – in an eastern part of Yemen's Hadrawmat Province, a province that divides the country into eastern and western parts.[42] Houthi influence seems to be concentrated in the southwestern areas of Yemen and especially along the border with Saudi Arabia.[43] Their areas of influence, or at least presence, overlap in places with each other and with that of Yemen's government.[44] Civil war followed the escalation of violence in 2014. The main parties in the conflict are Shi'a Houthis, Salafi-jihadist al-Qaeda affiliates, and the Yemeni government. In a state with a majority Sunni population, the civil war appears to be a competition among denominational groups.

The use and frequency of terrorism in Yemen follows a trend roughly similar to that in Lebanon. The rough similarity is represented by the large increase in the use of terrorism since 2010 and a more dramatic increase in the number of terrorist incidents as the conflict escalated to civil war. The number of terrorist incidents recorded in Yemen jumped by more than 70 percent between 2013 and 2014. This increase in terrorism may not coincide with the end of the current armed conflict, but it is also not the beginning. Terrorism in Yemen prior to 2015 does not follow the logic of a leading indicator; armed conflicts have been ongoing in Yemen for more than twenty years. Terrorism is also not evident during the earlier periods in which armed conflicts overlapped (2004–5 and 2007) or throughout the periods of armed conflicts (see Figure 5.7). Terrorism has not been used consistently in the context of Yemen's wider-scale warfare. Instead, it appears that terrorism is a tactic used increasingly by the

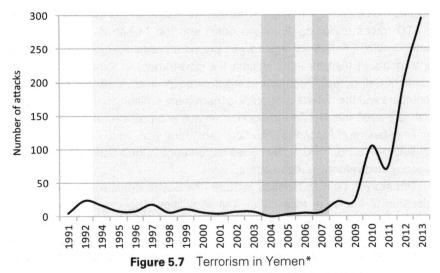

Figure 5.7   Terrorism in Yemen*

*Shaded areas denote periods of war and insurgency. Darker shaded areas represent periods of more than one war and/or armed conflict.

Sources: Boot, *Invisible Armies*, 569–89; Connable and Libicki, *How Insurgencies End*, 157–62, 99–201; Sarkees and Wayman, *Resort to War*; Fearon and Laitin, "Additional Tables;" UCDP/PRIO, "Armed Conflict Dataset V.4-2014a, 1946–2013;" "Global Terrorism Database [Data File]," 2014.

various terrorist-insurgent groups competing for control and operational space within Yemeni territory. It may also be that terrorism is a tactic of future warfare.

Afghanistan

As is true for Yemen, so too with recent conflicts in Afghanistan, it requires some understanding of the international milieu in which these conflicts have occurred to capture their internal developments. First, we should pay attention to Pakistan's role in Afghanistan. Over the post-independence decades, rulers in Islamabad have worried about their power vis-à-vis India. On occasion this relationship has led to full-scale war between the two countries. More often, however, the friction has encouraged state-sponsored terrorism. Islamist groups have carried out attacks on the Indian Parliament in New Delhi. The most spectacular attack was the 2011 raid on the city of Mumbai.[45] Much of this violence has been based on the struggle over Jammu and Kashmir, the only Indian state with a Muslim majority.

Pakistani leaders, both civilian and military, have come to see Afghanistan as a buffer between the two now-nuclear-armed antagonists. Pakistan, though, is not always a unitary actor. On occasion, the state's Inter-Service Intelligence agency has pursued its own goals irrespective of those expressed by decision-makers in Islamabad. Insofar as the struggle between NATO forces (including American ones) and the Taliban is concerned, the Inter-Service Intelligence agency has played a crucial role in supporting the insurgents in their struggle against the government in Kabul, Afghanistan. Carlotta Gall notes, "Afghan investigators soon discovered that the suicide bombers and the networks supplying them were emanating from Pakistan. In January 2006 the Afghan intelligence service and police rounded up a group of Pakistanis and Afghans in Kandahar who, they said, were behind the string of suicide attacks."[46] Gall then goes on to suggest Inter-Service Intelligence agency involvement in these operations.

The story is by now familiar. In 1979, the Soviet Union made the ill-fated decision to intervene militarily in Afghan politics. This decision was based on the fact that its pro-communist client government in Kabul was in danger of being defeated on the battlefield by a coalition of religiously inspired tribal groups, notably the Pashtuns, a group whose members resided in Afghanistan as well as Pakistan.

As the fighting persisted, both the United States and Pakistan became engaged in the effort to resist Soviet domination.[47] This was a war within the Cold War, the outcome of which could presumably alter the balance of power between the United States and the Soviet Union. It was in America's interests, as they were understood at the time, to support the Afghan fighters and whoever else was willing to help the Afghans defeat the Soviet occupiers. The Inter-Service Intelligence agency served to funnel weapons and other material support to opponents of the Afghanistan's communist government. And, with the help of the Saudis, a network was created to send Muslim fighters, mujahideen warriors, to wage a defensive jihad against the Soviet forces, which were viewed as atheists seeking to control part of the House of Islam. Imams throughout the Arab world made appeals for young men to take up arms and fight the Soviets.

The Pakistani city of Peshawar, close to the Afghan border, was used as a jumping off place for people and supplies crossing the Afghan border into the war zone. By the mid-1980s, the flow of people was also going in the other direction, into Pakistan. The Soviets were particularly brutal in dealing with the Afghans. Refugees fleeing the fighting crossed into Pakistan, where they were then housed in refugee camps.

This combination of actors scattered along the Afghanistan–Pakistan border brought serious consequences for subsequent developments in South Asia, the Middle East, and beyond. Arab volunteers flocked to Peshawar. From 1984, they were met by representatives of the Services Office whose key figures were the Sheik Abdullah Azzam and Osama bin Laden. Bin Laden was a son (one of fifty-seven) of a wealthy Saudi-Yemeni businessman, as well as a wealthy businessman in his own right.[48]

The origins of al Qaeda ("the Base") are to be found in this organized effort to funnel support to the Afghans and their largely Arab allies (the Afghan-Arabs) in their mission to remove the Soviet presence from Afghanistan. This goal was achieved in 1989, when the last Soviet soldier crossed the border back into the USSR.

This event marked a victory of the comparatively weak Afghan forces against the superior Soviet military. How could the weaker party win in such a brutal conflict? We know, of course, that insurgents enjoy significant benefits when fighting on their home soil, where they speak the languages, know the terrain and can blend with the local population. We also know that the insurgents benefited from outside support, including support from some of the states against which the same insurgents would later turn. From the perspective of the Afghan-Arab fighters and their leaders, however, the interpretation of this victory was one of good triumphing over evil. It was a powerful victory that was used to send an influential message.

Discussions followed among members of "the Base" about what additional steps should be taken to protect the House of Islam on a worldwide basis. The decision was made (following the mysterious death of Azzam) to engage "the far enemy." The United States, especially, became a target because it posed what was viewed as a greater threat to Islam than the "near enemy," the Arab World's collection of corrupt dictators.

The return of Afghan-Arabs to their countries of origin had a blowback effect. Holy warriors from Algeria, Saudi Arabia, Yemen, and elsewhere launched terrorist campaigns aimed at the local authoritarian regimes. Many of these inspired young men coalesced around Osama bin Laden.

Bin Laden became angered when the Saudi royal family chose the United States and its allies to protect the Kingdom from the threat of an Iraqi invasion after the latter's seizure of neighboring Kuwait in the summer of 1990.[49] The result of operations Desert Shield and Desert Storm was the liberation of Kuwait from Saddam Hussein's grasp and the elimination of the Iraqi threat to the Saudis.

The following year, under pressure from the Kingdom, bin Laden and his followers departed for the Sudan. Over the next several years, al Qaeda began its attacks on the "far enemy" in a number of locations. One of these attacks was the 1993 bombing of New York's World Trade Center.[50]

At the time that the Sudanese government came under pressure from Washington and Riyadh either to expel bin Laden or accept sanctions, a new force was emerging in Afghanistan. The departure of the Soviets led to the formation of a provisional government, which was composed of the country's major ethnic groups: the Pashtun, Tajiks, Uzbeks, and various Pakistan-supported personalities. What followed was a short-lived civil war among the competing tribal warlords.[51]

Rather than continue to observe the chaos across its border the Pakistanis promoted a new force. Thanks to Saudi funding, thousands of religious schools were established to serve the Afghan refugee population. These schools, or madrasas, became the training grounds for a new and largely Pakistani-controlled fighting force: the Taliban.

The Taliban, under leadership of the late one-eyed cleric, Mullah Omar, fought their way to Kabul. They were highly motivated and, by the second half of the1996, had taken control of a large swath of the country. At this point, the Taliban seemed triumphant. Over the next few years the Taliban imposed a form of terror on the country. Girls, for example, were prohibited from attending school and corporal punishment was administered on those who violated minor provisions of the religious code.

In 1998, the Taliban regime in Kabul offered sanctuary to bin Laden and his al-Qaeda organization. They were joined by the Egyptian radical Ayman al-Zawahiri, his followers, and Salafists from other parts of the Muslim world. From here, al Qaeda then proceeded to launch a series of highly visible terrorist attacks on American targets. These terrorist spectaculars culminated with the 9/11 attacks on the Pentagon and the World Trade Center. The response was an attack on bin Laden's safe haven in Afghanistan.

With the less-than-enthusiastic support of the Pakistani military, the American administration and a handful of its allies committed their special forces to the fight. Within a few months, they had chased al Qaeda into the tribal areas of northern Pakistan. The Taliban also took flight, many of whose leading personalities took sanctuary in the Baluchistan province of Pakistan.

The concerned parties then held a UN-sponsored conference in Berlin (2001), which selected a Pashtun notable named Hamad Karzai as interim president. Karzai was subsequently elected to the office on a continuing basis (he left office in 2014).

For its part, the Bush Administration turned its attention elsewhere. Having routed al Qaeda and chased the Taliban into Pakistani exile, the time had come to end Saddam Hussein's rule in Iraq.

The Taliban were hardly a spent force. Mullah Omar and his followers resumed their struggle shortly after Karzai's assumption of power in Kabul. The United States and its NATO allies sought to defeat a new generation of Pakistan-based jihadis. The effort to fight back against the renewed insurgency was hampered by the new government's own corruption and incompetence.

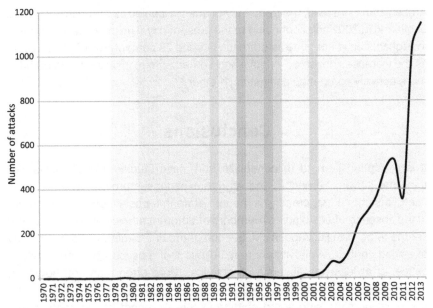

Figure 5.8 Terrorism in Afghanistan*

* The count here includes attacks meeting the GTD's three terrorism criteria. The count includes attacks on state, military, police, and other armed groups. "Ambiguous" cases are not included. Shaded areas denote periods of insurgency and war. Darker shaded areas represent periods of more than one war and/or armed conflict.

Sources: Boot, *Invisible Armies*, 569–89; Connable and Libicki, *How Insurgencies End*, 157–62, 99–201; Sarkees and Wayman, *Resort to War*; Fearon and Laitin, "Additional Tables;" UCDP/PRIO, "Armed Conflict Dataset V.4-2014a, 1946–2013;" "Global Terrorism Database [Data File]," 2014.

Little was done, for example, to vet military and police recruits. As a result individual soldiers and police officers occasionally turned on their fellow officers or sold weapons and other supplies on the black market. American air strikes often did not help matters, especially when the arsenals of drones and manned jets hit innocent civilians.

Given these conditions, we might expect the Taliban revival to succeed without all that much difficulty. This has proved not to be true, however. Many Afghans who experienced brutal Taliban rule during the last decade of the twentieth century have little interest in witnessing a repeat performance in the twenty-first century.

The increasing frequency of terrorism recorded in Afghanistan resembles those found in Libya and Yemen. As with the former cases, terrorism is neither present prior to or throughout earlier armed confrontations. There is very little terrorism recorded for the two decades of earlier insurgency and warfare in

Afghanistan.[52] Instead, the frequency of attacks labeled as terrorism increases beginning in 2002 and continuing to the present day. The increase in terrorism in Afghanistan is not quite as dramatic (around 25 percent from 2013 to 2014) as the increases observed in Libya and Yemen, where insurgents are perhaps more actively competing against each other.[53]

Conclusions

It is exceptionally hard to generalize from case studies. Nevertheless, we think the Libyan, Yemenite, and Afghan experiences provide us with some useful insights. First, creating a modern state in a post-colonial environment in the absence of ties binding members of different ethnicities to one another seems to be virtually impossible. Second, there is the matter of the durability of armed conflict. Well-wishers may believe that a peace agreement means peace, or at least the absence of violence. More often than not, however, a peace agreement means a rest period between rounds before the fight resumes, perhaps with some shifting in the alignment of the contestants. Some of the old contestants drop out while new ones enter the fray. In each of the above cases, long histories of armed conflict and instability combine to create conditions for a continuation of war involving new or old insurgent groups in new insurgencies. Afghanistan's current insurgency and sharp increase in the use of terrorism should be seen not simply as terrorism occurring in the context of wider-scale insurgency, but rather as terrorism following two decades of insurgencies, occurring back-to-back and involving some of the same cast of insurgent groups. Similarly, in the cases of Libya and Yemen, we have reason to believe that the next round of wars – or the continuations of ongoing conflict in these locations – will involve the extensive use of terrorism.

We view the patterns of increasing terrorism in today's "terrorism hot spots"[54] as distinct from the leading indicators discussed in Chapter 3 and distinct from the concurrent indicators discussed in Chapter 4. It may be that sharp increases in terrorism's use will coincide with the latter stages of armed conflict, though it is too soon to know for sure whether this will be the outcome. We concede that the pattern of increasing terrorism observed in the cases of Libya, Yemen, and Afghanistan may be something other than a trailing indicator, as seen in the cases of Nicaragua and South Africa. The difference between the former and latter cases is partly the fact that the war ended in the latter cases while they are continuing in the former. Two other – likely relevant – difference involve location and timing. The wars in Nicaragua and South Africa ended. The wars in North Africa, the Middle East, and

Central Asia are ongoing. Furthermore, the wars in the Libya, Yemen, and Afghanistan involve Islamist groups. It is possible that these groups, with their more global objectives and operations, their transnational affiliations and appeal, and their religious rhetoric and justifications will engage in warfare differently than their predecessors of the earlier generations of terrorism. The increasing frequency of terrorism as a tactic of armed groups engaging in insurgency in the twenty-first century may be indicative of a new pattern in the use of terrorism by groups engaging in wider-scale warfare, a pattern that involves attacks perpetrated by weak actors operating outside of what is commonly considered to be legitimate warfare, pursuing political objectives through tactics intended to spread fear to larger audiences. We cannot be sure what the future holds.

Notes

1   Enrique Baloyra, "El Salvador: From Reactionary Despotism to Partidocracia," in *Postconflict Elections*, ed. Krishna Kumar (Boulder, CO: Lynne Rienner, 1998), 15–37; Roger MacGinty and John Darby, *Guns and Government* (New York, NY: Palgrave, 2002), 86–106.
2   See, for instance, Andrew H. Kydd, and Barbara F. Walter, "Sabotaging the Peace: The Politics of Extremist Violence," *International Organization*, 56, no. 2 (2002); Kydd and Walter, "The Strategies of Terrorism."
3   S. F. Dale, "Religious Suicide in Islamic Asia – Anticolonial Terrorism in India, Indonesia, and the Philippines," *Journal of Conflict Resolution*, 32, no. 1 (1988); Stephen F. Dale, "The Islamic Frontier in Southwest India: The Shahid as a Cultural Ideal among the Mappillas of Malabar," *Modern Asian Studies*, 11, no. 1 (1977).
4   See, for instance, "Terrorist Organization Profiles: Shining Path," National Consortium for the Study of Terrorism and Responses to Terrorism (START), 2015.
5   See, for instance, numerous reports in recent years of Shining Path members seeking to form a political party while also engaging in militant and criminal activities in Peru's countryside. BBC News, Latin America & Caribbean, "Peru Admits Shining Path Rebels Have Not Been 'Exterminated'," August 6, 2015, www.bbc.com/news/world-latin-america-33813695 (last accessed May 3, 2016).
6   "Global Terrorism Database [Data File]," 2013; see also William Neuman, "Peru Forced to Confront Deep Scars of Civil War," *New York Times*, May 26, 2012.
7   U.S. Department of State, Office of the Historian, "Central America, 1977–1980," https://history.state.gov/milestones/1977-1980/central-america-carter (last accessed March 15, 2016).
8   "Global Terrorism Database [Data File]," 2013.
9   These numbers are derived from an analysis of GTD data. Ibid.
10 Ibid.

11 See, for instance, Forrest D. Colburn and Arturo S. Cruz, "Personalism and Populism in Nicaragua," *Journal of Democracy*, 23, no. 2 (2012).

12 Boot, *Invisible Armies*; UCDP/PRIO, "Armed Conflict Dataset V.4–2014a, 1946–2013."

13 Being able to compare frequencies for 1993 would likely add to this discussion; however, data for this year is not available through the GTD dataset.

14 Michael Boyle, *Violence after War* (Baltimore, MD: Johns Hopkins University Press, 2014).

15 Ibid., 48.

16 Ibid., 52–5. See, for example, Istvan Deak, Jan Gross, and Tony Judt, eds, *The Politics of Retribution in Europe* (Princeton, NJ: Princeton University Press, 2000).

17 For Boyle's description, see Boyle, *Violence after War*.

18 Central Intelligence Agency, The World Factbook, "Libya," https://www.cia.gov/library/publications/the-world-factbook/geos/ly.html (last accessed April 4, 2016).

19 See, Dirk Vanderwalle, *A History of Modern Libya*, 2nd edn (New York, NY: Cambridge University Press, 2012), 11–32.

20 Colin Smith, *Carlos: Portrait of a Terrorist* (New York, NY: Holt, Rinehart and Winston, 1976), 221–44.

21 For further discussion, see Byman, *Deadly Connections: States that Sponsor Terrorism*; Eben Kaplan, "How Libya Got Off the List," www.cfr.org/libya/libya-got-off-list/p10855 (last accessed April 12, 2016).

22 James Gelvin, *The Arab Uprisings: What Everyone Needs to Know* (New York, NY: Oxford University Press, 2012); Lin Noueihed and Alex Warren, *The Battle for the Arab Spring* (New Haven, CT: Yale University Press, 2012).

23 For further discussion, see, for instance, Edward Randall, "After Qadhafi: Development and Democratization in Libya," *The Middle East Journal*, 69, no. 2 (2015). See also Geoffrey Howard, "Libya's South: The Forgotten Frontier," *CTC Sentinel*, 7, no. 11 (2014).

24 Mirco Keilberth and Christoph Reuter, "A Threat to Europe: The Islamic State's Dangerous Gains in Libya," *Spiegel Online International*, February 23, 2015.

25 Christopher S. Chivvis, Keith Crane, Peter Mandaville, and Jeffrey Martini, *Libya's Post-Qaddafi Transition: The Nation-Building Challenge*, National Security Research Division (Santa Monica, CA: RAND Corporation, 2012), www.rand.org/content/dam/rand/pubs/research_reports/RR100/RR129/RAND_RR129.pdf (last accessed May 2, 2016).

26 For an excellent summary of Libya's myriad woes see "Libya's Civil War: The Four-year Descent from Arab Spring to Factional Chaos," *The Economist*, January 10, 2015, 21–3.

27 Muammar Al-Qadhafi, *The Green Book*, London: Martin Brian & O'Keeffe, 1976. *The Green Book* was first published in Arabic in 1975, and widely circulated throughout Libya. It was to be Qaddafi's answer to Mao's Little Red Book. For a description, see BBC News Africa, "What Now for Colonel Gaddafi's Green Book?," April 29, 2011, www.bbc.com/news/world-africa-13235981 (last accessed April 8, 2016).

28 Keilberth and Reuter, "A Threat to Europe."

29 Tim Lister and Paul Cruickshank, "What Is Ansar Al Sharia, and Was It Behind the Consulate Attack in Benghazi?" *CNN Politics*, November 16, 2012.

30   Barak Barfi, "Al-Qa'ida's Confused Messaging on Libya," *CTC Sentinel*, 4, no. 8 (2011).

31   See, for instance, Ganor, "Four Questions on ISIS." See also Aaron Y. Zelin, "The Rise and Decline of Ansar Al-Sharia in Libya," *Current Trends in Islamist Ideology*, 18 (2015).

32   Alison Pargeter, "Islamist Militant Groups in Post-Qadhafi Libya," *CTC Sentinel*, 6, no. 2 (2013).

33   Zelin, "The Rise and Decline of Ansar Al-Sharia in Libya."

34   Government of the United Kingdom, "Foreign Travel Advice: Libya," www.gov.uk/foreign-travel-advice/libya/terrorism (last accessed April 12, 2016).

35   Howard, "Libya's South."

36   Francis Fukuyama, *Political Order and Political Decay* (New York, NY: Farrar, Straus, Giroux, 2014), 51.

37   Paul Dresch, *A History of Modern Yemen* (New York, NY: Cambridge University Press, 2000), 28–57.

38   For further discussion, see Caryle Murphy, "AQAP's Growing Security Threat to Saudi Arabia," *CTC Sentinel* 3, no. 10 (2010).

39   Gregory Johnson, *The Last Refuge: Yemen, Al-Qaeda and America's War in Arabia* (New York, NY: W.W. Norton, 2014).

40   Robert Burrowes, *The Yemen Arab Republic* (Boulder, CO: Westview Press, 1987), 19.

41   Theodore Karasik and Kim Cragin, "Case Study: The Arabian Peninsula," in *Ungoverned Territories: Understanding and Reducing Terrorism Risks*, ed. Angel Rabasa, et al. (Santa Monica, CA: RAND Corporation, 2007), 103.

42   "Recent Highlights in Political Violence."

43   See, for instance, BBC News Middle East, "Yemen Crisis: Who Is Fighting Whom," March 26, 2015, www.bbc.com/news/world-middle-east-29319423 (last accessed April 12, 2016). See also Stratfor Global Intelligence, "In Yemen, Anti-Houthi Operations Confront Forceful Opposition," www.stratfor.com/analysis/yemen-anti-houthi-operations-confront-forceful-opposition (last accessed April 12, 2016).

44   "In Yemen, Anti-Houthi Operations Confront Forceful Opposition."

45   Fair, "The 2008 Mumbai Attack," 571–99.

46   Gall, *The Wrong Enemy*, 147.

47   For an introductory discussion see Seth G. Jones, *In the Graveyard of Empires* (New York, NY: Norton, 2010), 3–51.

48   Bergen, *The Longest War*, 11–35.

49   Ibid., 19.

50   Peter Bergen, *Holy War, Inc.* (New York, NY: The Free Press, 2001), 167–94.

51   Barfield, *Afghanistan*, 250–2.

52   "Global Terrorism Database [Data File]," 2015

53   This calculation is based on a review of the updated GTD data for 2014. "Global Terrorism Database [Data File]," 2015.

54   This phrase is borrowed from Braithwaite and Li, "Transnational Terrorism Hot Spots: Identification and Impact Evaluation."

6

Conclusions and forecasts

This effort to understand the place of terrorism in twenty-first century warfare began with a review of the explanations for why terrorism may have been used during discrete phases of insurgencies, as proposed by revolutionary theorists such as Mao, General Giap, and others. Current circumstances suggest a more complicated picture, however, than these theorists supposed. It may be that the strategies of insurgent groups have changed over time. The causes may lie in the enormous population shift from rural to urban and the increasing permeability of national borders.[1] The latter point, at least, may seem counterintuitive in an era in which border security commands so much attention. The reality, however, is that a number of weak states are unable to monitor or control their borders. Even strong states find this challenging. The border between Mexico and the United States demonstrates this. Those wanting to cross borders tend to find ways of doing so.

The former point also raises questions. Urbanization is not a new phenomenon. Yet, it seems that insurgents today have found haven in the ungoverned spaces of weak or failing states, where they can operate without much interference. At the same time, the maps showing the territories presumed to be occupied by groups such as ISIL suggest that the territories under insurgent groups' control include towns and the roadways connecting them.[2] Even if ISIL's control does not extend beyond these roadways and outside of the urban centers, it is worth asking whether alternatives to ISIL exist in these empty spaces.[3]

For insurgent groups, terrorism may serve as a tool for capturing the allegiance, or at least acquiescence, of the stranded masses residing within the territories these groups claim. Urbanization and border insecurity may create incentives for the groups seeking to radically change the existing order to launch insurgencies that combine guerrilla operations and terrorism. These groups may organize along military lines, claim territories, and create terror in urban and rural settings. In addition, insurgent groups now have means at their disposal to challenge the incumbents' dominance over the dissemination of information. They can produce their own media. With the aid of Internet communications, they can send their messages directly to their desired audiences.

In Greece, Turkey, and elsewhere small, clandestine terrorist groups continue to carry out assassinations and other terrorist operations.[4] But these attacks clearly represent a dead end for those who hoped for bigger and better things. Despite the fragility of governments in Athens and Ankara, these revolutionary groups have failed to capture much, if any, popular support.

The most significant terrorist campaigns in recent years have been ones waged in the name of jihad. The most prominent groups waging insurgencies and using terrorism have fundamentalist religious ideologies and associations (current or former) with al Qaeda. These include the Islamic State (ISIL), the Pakistani Taliban and their allies, Afghanistan's Taliban, Nigeria's Boko Haram, Somalia's al Shabaab, and al Qaeda, along with its other franchises and affiliates. Several of these groups have managed to seize significant territory, including major cities, such as ISIL's capture of Mosul in northern Iraq, not far from the Syrian and Turkish borders, and to stage attacks on the incumbents, their regular armed forces, and civilian populations. Al-Qaeda Central appears to play an inspirational role with its calls for jihad against the West and corrupt Arab regimes. It is through its AQAP franchise in Yemen that al Qaeda most resembles other twenty-first century insurgents.

To what extent does the behavior of these relatively new and religiously motivated organizations constitute an evolution of terrorist violence? It is difficult to say for sure, but some signs point in the direction of change. We refer to the use of beheadings on both an individual and mass basis accompanied by a narration by what is, in effect, a public announcer. These performances seem to represent exemplary deeds similar to the airline skyjackings characteristic of earlier waves of terrorism and the suicide bombings found in more recent examples. The difference today is that insurgents control the media and the message. They need not carry out large-scale attacks to gain attention for their group or their cause.

The combination of guerrilla tactics, terrorist campaigns, and territorial conquest appears at least to be an unusual phenomenon in the modern history of insurgencies. Rather than advancing from terrorism to guerrilla warfare to conventional military tactics, today's insurgents are finding their strength in a combination of these, though one that relies more heavily on terrorism and guerrilla tactics than military confrontations. Insurgents must take advantage of the weak, finding their safety in the absence of a state capable of respond-ing to the insurgents' threats. Regardless of their strength, support, and sophistication, insurgent groups cannot hope to succeed by confronting stronger militaries on a battlefield, and it is unlikely that an insurgent group's best strategy would include such an attempt.

Perhaps more importantly, the battlefield has changed in recent years. There are few scenarios in which militaries would challenge other militaries on a field of battle. Wars are fought differently today than they were fifty years ago. To the extent that warfare can be managed remotely, the battlefield may come to the insurgents rather than the other way around. Insurgents may seek, even gain, the sophisticated technologies to carry out remote warfare; however, this should not give them hope that they can or should face a greater adversary directly. Instead, insurgent groups may confront competing insur-gent groups. ISIL turned on the al-Nusra Front, its former progeny and ally, in response to that group's opposition to being absorbed into the Islamic State. ISIL and al Qaeda have turned on each other following quarrels over operations and which person would assume the network's highest leadership position.

The new practitioners are also different than their predecessors. The "new" terrorists are more than terrorists. Former American Secretary of Defense Chuck Hagel went so far as to say that ISIL is "beyond just a terrorist group;" it is a new phenomenon not encountered before by the American military.[5] The highly respected analyst Audrey Kurth Cronin has argued that the Islamic State is not a terrorist group as she has come to understand such groups.[6]

Insurgents today are spreading their operations and setting up training camps in weakened states, such as Syria and Iraq, Libya and Sudan. They are claiming to establish their own states, something their predecessors, includ-ing the Tamil Tigers, Basques, and Irish republicans, did not try. Even the Colombian guerrillas, after fifty years of fighting from their safe havens in rural Colombia, did not do this. The territory they controlled or sought to control may have had a name (e.g., "Farc-land") and they may have demanded taxes, yet even the most ambitious of these groups did not claim or attempt to create a state. ISIL's declaration of an Islamic State stands out in opposition to al Qaeda's failure to do so. Libya's rebel groups are competing for their portion of the Libyan state; AQAP and the Houthi rebels are on the same track in Yemen.

Today's terrorist networks operate outside of domestic spheres. Their oper-ations are not international in the sense of earlier terrorist networks; instead, many are transnational. They may not have a homeland for which to fight. They may operate in a virtual reality in terms of their communications, propaganda, and terrorism. And, although they may be more loosely connected to their comrades – local and foreign – than were their predecessors, it is possible that their weak ties may give strength to their organizational structure.[7] Networks may be more difficult to counter than hierarchical organizations, and they seem to facilitate greater flexibility in terms of operations and decision-making.

Despite their differences, however, there are also similarities between today's insurgents and their predecessors. The dominant ideology of the terrorists today is religious, in most cases fundamentalist and Islamist. Religion serves the same unifying function that nationalism or class-based identities did for previous generations of terrorists, though religion may be a stronger unifying ideology in terms of being shared among peoples of different nationalities and residing in different states and because of its relationship to individuals' identity, prosperity in this world, and personal salvation for the next.[8] On the other hand, Salafi jihadists and others with fundamentalist religious doctrines make up only a small minority within the larger Muslim community. Salafi jihadists, in particular, are a minority within the small community of Salafists. Most Salafists are nonviolent; Salafi jihadists use violence. Salafists, in turn, are a small community that fits within the larger, and quite diverse, community of Sunni Muslims. The Salafi-jihadist doctrine, at least as it is practiced by terrorists, excludes moderates within their larger community, not to mention those outside of it.

Although their ideologies differ from those that came before them, modern Islamist groups are similar to their predecessors in having ideas and goals that are unlikely to find a broader base of support. They have big aims but limited appeal. Their natural allies are a minority. Without the support – or submission – of masses, they cannot win the wars they have started. Eventually, they will moderate or they will lose; perhaps both.

The largest and most influential Salafi-jihadist groups have another weakness. Not only do they have limited appeal among the masses, they have almost no appeal as an ally of groups with other religious or nationalist objectives. The world in which a Salafi-jihadist group achieves its stated objectives would look very different from the world today. The borders between states would likely disappear. The national interests and identities that so many have fought to achieve would disappear. Whether or not the Palestinian people should have a state would not matter; there would be no Palestinian state. There would not be an Egyptian or Saudi or other national state within an Islamic caliphate. There would also be no room for religious diversity. Muslims of different backgrounds and beliefs would be expected to unite within a single, larger community. The varying interpretations of Islam would be inconsistent with those espoused by the Salafi-jihadist interpretation. This very different world seems unattainable for the Salafi jihadists and unpalatable for a majority of their presumed constituents.

In addition, if insurgent groups must find support at the local level in order to survive, they will have to appeal to the local populations and their local interests. These are unlikely to include erasing local identities, abandoning local practices, or converting to a more literal interpretation of Islam. If insurgent groups do not require local support – for instance, if they have external support or are sufficiently self-funded – they will likely need local submission, which they may achieve through a strategy that includes terrorism.

Finally, as has happened with their predecessors, cracks have appeared within larger terrorist networks and organizations. The competition over who would lead the movement after Osama bin Laden's death seems to have taken a toll. The network has split. A competing center of power was born in ISIL and the group (previously al Qaeda in Iraq) has been expelled from the al-Qaeda ranks. Now, the two former allies seem to be engaged in their own form of war, this one against each other. With this has come the news of defections among other al-Qaeda affiliates to the side of the Islamic State. This is a process that may lead to an even more obvious competition between the groups for allegiance, support, and prestige.

Two potential outcomes of this competition come to mind. We may expect the groups to compete in order to enhance their appeal to their target audiences. Rivalry between ISIL and al Qaeda could contribute to moderation, in the case that their global vision is subsumed to the more localized objectives and interests of their affiliates and potential affiliates. This seems like an unlikely scenario at this time. Alternatively, competition could push the groups to carry out more spectacular attacks – the types of attacks that gain attention and create terror, along with the guarantee of greater death and destruction – as means of demonstrating which of the groups has the most strength and highest likelihood of success. What will happen – perhaps some other outcome – remains to be seen.

What is clear, however, is that today's insurgent-terrorists, like their predecessors, will likely pursue the same intermediate outcome their predecessors sought – the production of fear. Fear remains the most important tool of today's terrorists. Beyond this, there are suggestions that today's insurgents are participants in a new era of warfare. They claim territory, proclaim new states within the shells of weak or failed states, and use terrorism and guerrilla tactics to achieve these goals. Today's insurgents seem to be changing how wars are fought in the twenty-first century.

Warfare in the twenty-first century

At the beginning of this book we suggested a number of expectations and raised questions regarding relationships between the time at which insurgents launch terrorist attacks and the ultimate fates of their armed struggles. Was the terrorism a leading indicator, forecasting future and wider conflicts? Alternatively, did the terrorism occur throughout the conflict from beginning to end? And finally, what was the significance, if any, for groups, new or old, that employed terrorism toward the end of the fighting? We began this study with expectations drawn from the largely distinct literatures on terrorism and insurgency. Let us briefly restate these expectations.

> Expectation #1 – Terrorism will be used during the early stages of armed struggles and subsequently abandoned as a group gathers strength and becomes more capable of engaging in guerrilla warfare or other forms of armed confrontation.

Our first expectation was based on an understanding – and common expectation, as explained in the literature – that insurgents will prefer to abandon the irregular or illegitimate forms of armed confrontation associated with terrorism and guerrilla warfare. After all, these are seen as the tactics of weak actors, who can presumably do no better. This will occur as (and if) the armed groups progress through the phases of insurgency, which will lead them eventually into more direct confrontations with their adversaries. Once sufficient capacity is achieved – in the forms of support, territory, and ammunitions – the insurgents should establish regular armed forces and graduate to more conventional military tactics. If using terrorism and guerrilla tactics is a sign of weakness; confronting adversaries on battlefields would be the opposite.

We may expect today's insurgents to be equally – or even more – aware of their relative weakness and their relative strength. Insurgents cannot hope to win an armed confrontation against a conventionally equipped military. Avoiding direct confrontations, they can hope to survive the duration of wider-scale warfare. Little has changed in this sense from past to present.

Additionally, leaders of conventional armed forces have learned lessons from past experiences in places like Malaya, Vietnam, and Afghanistan. It is difficult for conventional forces to defeat insurgents on insurgents' home soil. This is likely a lesson that has also been learned by insurgents. Insurgents need not attempt conventional warfare when they have the benefits of hiding among locals and staging guerrilla-style attacks and acts of terrorism. The involvement of multiple competing rebel groups in some of today's conflicts – Syria, Iraq, Yemen – may go part of the way toward explaining why insurgents seem to be relying so heavily on terrorism. In some cases, it is clear that the insurgent groups are in direct competition with each other and are attacking each other as a result. It has become clear in other cases that the groups are competing to show the level of brutality they are willing to use. Support for some of these groups seems to come from outsiders seeking to affiliate with the "winning team" or looking for an outlet for their own aggressive tendencies.[9] Yet, these groups remain relatively weak, and they are left fighting other weak actors. The recognition of terrorism as a tactic of warfare leads us to the second expectation discussed and examined in this study.

> Expectation #2 –Terrorism will be used throughout armed conflicts under specific circumstances. One circumstance is a group's inability to change tactics. Another is a group's need to subdue a population while simultaneously engaging in a guerrilla confrontation.

We suspect – again drawing on what seems to be the conventional wisdom – that groups use terrorist tactics because they have no viable alternatives. Those that can confront a state or its armed forces, even as guerrillas operating in the shadows, will do so. Those that cannot will continue to aim attacks at the oftest" targets, hoping in the meantime to use their target audience as an intermediary to influence the state. If the goal were only to draw attention, using terrorism would be sufficient. For insurgents, however, the goal is to change the political system, acquire territory, or something of the sort. Gaining attention – even sympathy – is unlikely to be enough to produce these outcomes. In this sense, terrorism looks like a dead end.

On the other hand, some insurgent forces often use terrorism alongside other tactics associated with guerrilla warfare. Insurgent groups may terrorize a civilian population in order to deter civilians from defecting to an opponent's side. In doing so, insurgent groups exercise authority over their presumed constituency. They police and punish, demonstrating their strengths and others' weaknesses. They may collect rents to fund their operations, similar to collecting taxes. Although using terrorism during warfare is not new for non-state actors – as demonstrated by the example of the Viet Cong using terrorism against civilians while engaging in guerrilla warfare against regular armed forces – it seems to have become a more common tactic of warfare.

Many of today's insurgents have rebel groups as adversaries, not just states. They also have external adversaries in the forms of foreign states and international governmental organizations. One byproduct of the global war on terrorism is the emphasis that has been placed on terrorist entities and the international scope of the threat posed by these groups. Even though this may be an overstatement of insurgents' or terrorists' capabilities, carrying out spectacular attacks is one way these groups may fulfill these expectations. It is also a way in which insurgent groups send messages to their "far enemies." And, as ISIL has shown, using terrorism is one way for the insurgents to communicate with their "near enemies," potential recruits, supporters, and other target audiences.

While noting each of these possibilities, it is important to point out that many of the twenty-first century's insurgent groups – ISIL included – are still active. They are continuing to use terrorism and to do so in some cases in the context of wider-scale warfare. These are our examples of twenty-first century insurgents engaging in twenty-first century warfare.

Expectation #3 – Armed groups operating in the twenty-first century are more likely to use terrorism throughout wider-scale armed confrontations than they were during previous eras.

The expectation that terrorism has become a regular aspect of irregular warfare is based in part on the documented increase in the incidence of terrorism since 2001 (or at least the documented increase in the counting of terrorist attacks since this time). This is further substantiated by the increased incidence of terrorism in places where insurgents are actively operating. Even though this may not seem like a surprising association, given recent events in the post-2001 era, it should give cause for concern. Terrorism is a tactic used against softer targets by non-state actors who presumably desire to be more than that. While it has not been all that uncommon in the past for civilians to be targeted during wartime, the difference is that insurgents tend also to operate at times and in places where there is not wider-scale war. In some cases, there is minor armed conflict. Moreover, the presumption has been that insurgents may gain power and reach the point where they will prefer to abandon terrorism for other, more respectable targets and tactics.

As with our first expectation, the likelihood of this type of transition will depend on an insurgent group's strength. It may also depend on how insurgents view their opponents and how they perceive their likelihood of success. Another assumption associated with this evolution in tactics is that insurgents will eventually fight conventional forces. Today's insurgents operating in lawless lands may not face states or conventional armies. They may not have states as adversaries. Instead, they may fight other insurgents. They may find otherwise unprotected populations to control. Insurgent groups may use terrorism rather than expending the effort to establish a more legitimate basis of control. Perhaps these expectations belong in more democratic settings, such as in Nicaragua, where the people have had expectations regarding those claiming to fight on their behalf. Without competition for legitimacy, and perhaps without an expectation that legitimacy may be achieved, insurgent groups may not make a transition away from terrorism.

Today's insurgents face other hurdles, tremendous ones compared to those faced by their predecessors. Counterterrorism and counterinsurgency policies and practices have improved since the turn of the twenty-first century. While these policies have been consistently adapted in response to changes in the threats posed by terrorists, the response to the 9/11 attacks has perhaps been the most concerted, organized, and comprehensive effort to interfere with terrorists' activities, identify potential terrorist threats, and prevent terrorist attacks, especially mass-casualty events. In the process, some states and their militaries have become harder targets than they once were. When facing these stronger states, insurgent groups may have no alternative other than remaining weak and operating in the shadows, for fear of being targeted and eliminated. Their survival depends on their ability to maintain clandestine activities and avoid detection when operating in such locations. On the other hand, these issues are less relevant for militants operating in ungoverned spaces. That is, unless there is a concerted effort by an external force to find and eliminate a group, regardless of its location. Al Qaeda is one example of a targeted group lacking a true safe haven. It is also a group that is weakening.

While some states have become stronger, other states and their militaries are weaker now than they were in the past. In places with weak or failing states, insurgent groups seem to have more success. Lebanon's civil war left room for Hezbollah to operate as a quasi-state offering various types of social assistance and protection, services the group still provides. Iraq's transition to democracy created conditions conducive to sectarian conflict among the groups competing for power. Syria's civil war left a void, which ISIL and others have attempted to fill. There are many similar accounts among the insurgents operating in the twenty-first century.

In failed or failing states, insurgent groups operate in the absence of a competing state authority. They may not have combatants or a state to target. Failed and failing states provide a type of safe haven for the strongest of the weak non-state actors. One problem, of course, is that the actors may not know in advance which of them is the strongest. Gathering this information requires armed confrontation, likely in the forms of terrorist attacks and guerrilla tactics.

   Expectation #4 – Armed groups will use terrorism toward the end of wider-scale conflicts as they become weaker.

The idea that weak actors will adopt the tactics of conventional militaries as they gain strength seems to defy much of what we have learned about insurgents since 9/11. Insurgent groups remain relatively weak, though so do the states in which they operate. They may gain the capacity to launch more sophisticated attacks, but they are nowhere close to having the military capacity states have. Even those operating in ungoverned spaces face stronger adversaries dedicated to carrying out the global war on terrorism. With effective counterterrorism and counterinsurgency, harder targets should become more difficult for insurgents to attack. There will be little consolation for those groups that manage to obtain more sophisticated military capabilities. State sponsors of insurgent groups are unlikely to share their most valuable technologies today for the same reasons they were reluctant to share them in the past. For instance, states are unlikely to share weapons of mass destruction. Technologies are traceable and weapons can be used against the states supplying them.[10] Terrorism remains the tactic of the weakest actors, and today's insurgents are these weakest actors. Terrorism may be their only option.

On the whole, today's insurgents seem to be more brutal in their tactics than they were in the past. For ISIL, at least, the group's spectacular attacks include executions via beheadings and burning captives alive. This is not to say that bombs and bullets are no longer part of their arsenal; rather, they may not be as useful for the purposes of propaganda as the brutal, personal attacks against very specific enemies of the new state. When it comes to carrying out larger-scale attacks, today's insurgents may rely on relatively unsophisticated weaponry, such as suicide bombs and other types of assaults on vulnerable populations. These are the types of attacks that gain news coverage reaching a larger audience than the insurgent groups' own propaganda mill.

Insurgent groups' attacks on civilians seem to receive more attention than attacks on other targets. In recent years insurgents have targeted children in elementary schools, kidnapped girls and young women by the hundreds, and massacred college students on their campus. Part of the explanation for the reliance on these types of targets may be that insurgents see civilians as legitimate targets. Osama bin Laden declared this much when he was al Qaeda's leader.

Another issue, and one that compounds the former, is the possibility that insurgents rationalize their kidnappings as beneficial to the victims. At least from the perspective of the insurgents, self-serving as it may be, the kidnapped can be indoctrinated. This, in particular, applies in the cases of kidnapped girls and women, who may be forced to convert to the insurgents' way of thinking or mistreated for refusing the offer. Such activities may be supported by interpretations (or misinterpretations) of religious texts. Interpretations that encourage death sentences for nonbelievers, resisters, moderates, and others may lend legitimacy to savage acts. Female prisoners may also be commissioned to provide services for male militants.[11] Providing wives – as has been the case with some female prisoners – may be a form of payment for fighters' service.

Many of today's insurgents have or are seeking control over territory. Holding territory does not necessarily add to insurgents' security today the way it may have done in the past. The challenge to insurgent groups is greater when counterinsurgency and counterterrorism are carried out by stronger states – as is the case in the context of the global war on terrorism – and not only by the weak states in which the groups seem to thrive. Improvements in surveillance technologies and the availability of unmanned attack crafts facilitate targeted attacks against far-off insurgents. In short, insurgents remain weak, even when they hold territory and control populations, and the tactics they use reflect this weakness.

Is insurgency changing?

To determine the extent our expectations were supported by the evidence we examined the distributions of terrorist events in the context of wider-scale warfare. How commonly do we find terrorism occurring at the beginning, throughout, and toward the end of insurgencies?

A number of observations stand out and merit consideration. Cases where terrorist attacks appear at the beginning of insurgencies are relatively rare in recent decades. The type of progression from an "agitation-propaganda" phase to full-scale war as described by revolutionary writers earlier in the twentieth century rarely coincides with current realities. Among other things, this finding calls into question the status of terrorism as a leading indicator of wider conflict.

Far and away, the pattern we find most frequently is the use of terrorism throughout the course of an insurgency. Our evidence suggests that insurgent groups active during the late twentieth and early twenty-first centuries have incorporated terrorism into their standard repertoire of operations. The advantages to the insurgents include maintaining a condition of chronic fear and uncertainty among both the authorities and the civilian population. The insurgents may be engaged in what the philosopher of jihad, Abu Bakr Naji, describes as the "management of savagery."[12]

Terrorism was more commonly a trailing indicator than a leading one. It is more frequent for terrorism to appear or peak toward the latter stages of an armed conflict than during its initial phases. The cases, or at least their central tendencies, suggest explanations. First, terrorism appears to be a tactic employed by those whose challenges are losing ground. Second, endgame terrorism also may be carried out in retaliation against segments of a population who are perceived to have betrayed the cause for which the insurgents have been fighting. And, third, there may be a certain amount of desperation involved. The late surge in terrorism may reflect the fact that authorities (or rival groups) are closer to victory. The use of terrorism may reflect desperation and frustration.

In the process of conducting this analysis, another, somewhat unexpected, pattern emerged. The study of insurgent groups operating in the twenty-first century is limited by the fifteen year timeframe. This seems quite short by insurgent standards, at least in terms of those insurgencies that manage to get off the ground. We focused much of our attention on the tactics of insurgent groups operating in a handful of the states where insurgencies are ongoing. Of these, several share a similar pattern, which does not match any of our initial expectations. We observe in some places very sharp increases in the use of terrorism in places where there was very little or no recorded history of terrorism. States with this pattern include Afghanistan, Yemen, and Libya, as discussed in Chapter 5. Insurgencies in these countries are not likely to be nearing their ends, though some of the armed groups participating in them may be. These are interesting patterns for further observation and analysis, in large part because we do not know how they may change in the years to come. We may wonder what insurgent groups' choices of tactics suggest about their trajectories as political actors and perhaps as future state-builders. One conclusion we can suggest is that the insurgents relying on terrorism are unlikely to be the ones who will win the hearts and minds of the masses.

We also detect contradictory tendencies with contemporary terrorist activity. We have observed, on the one hand, many instances in which terrorism has been incorporated into the repertoire of tactics employed on a continuing basis by insurgents seeking to destroy incumbent regimes. These are tactics used on the ground where insurgents operate, typically against weak or failing states. On the other hand, we are aware that insurgent groups such as al Qaeda, ISIL, and other holy warriors have used the Internet to stimulate "lone wolves," especially in places that are out of these groups' reach. This is one way these groups may target the Western democracies they oppose, yet do so from a distance. Their secret weapon is the disenfranchised, perhaps naïve, maybe even "notoriety-seeking"[13] individuals who reside in every society. In democratic societies, these individuals tend to enjoy the types of freedoms that allow them to associate, organize, and act, and maybe even to arm themselves.

We may wonder how this works. Small groups and individuals may develop a vicarious attachment to a terrorist group via social media. Radicalization over the Internet works by first inviting an individual to feel as though he or she is part of a larger community of people who share similar beliefs. Perhaps an individual's beliefs are already radical or extreme, or perhaps they become more so through a process that involves education and indoctrination. A virtual community may seem larger than it is. As part of a virtual community, an individual may mistakenly come to think of a set of shared beliefs as more mainstream and acceptable than they are. This would be an illusion (or delusion). The job of the far-away terrorists is to encourage local actors to engage in acts of violence against their neighbors, the citizens of democracies. These are populations within reach of "lone wolf" terrorists operating in an open and free environment. This is also where the terrorists are likely to do the most harm and achieve the most publicity with the least effort.

At least for the near future it seems safe to say that twenty-first century warfare will continue to take on these characteristics. "Lone wolves" will continue operating in the Western democracies and elsewhere insurgent groups will continue to combine terrorism, guerrilla warfare, and the media, both mass and social. This is largely a response to successful counterterrorism and counterinsurgency policies that make it increasingly difficult for insurgent groups to operate outside of the weak or failed states over which they are competing. It is also an innovation on the part of today's terrorists, who are learning how to use technology to their benefit and, not unlike greater military powers, to engage in warfare from a distance.

Even so, today's insurgent-terrorists should be desperate and frustrated. More than many of their predecessors, they have ideas and goals that lack mass appeal, even among those within their presumed constituency. This is apparent despite their unprecedented access to media and faraway audiences. Today's insurgent-terrorists must rely on terror to take territory and control populations. They are faced with international cooperation in what has turned into an effective effort at interrupting their operations. Traditionally soft targets have become harder. Even their ability to employ guerrilla tactics has been compromised. Despite all of their new tools, in comparison to their predecessors, it appears that today's insurgents are by far the weakest actors.

Notes

1   Kilcullen, *Out of the Mountains*.
2   BBC, "Islamic State Group: Crisis in Seven Maps," 27 April 2016, www.bbc.com/news/world-middle-east-27838034 (last accessed April 27, 2016).
3   Kathy Gilsinan, "The Many Ways to Map the Islamic 'State'," *The Atlantic*, August 27, 2014.
4   See for example Ayala Albayrak and Joe Pakinson, "Attacks Roil Turkey Ahead of Elections," *Wall Street Journal*, April 2, 2015, 8; National Counterterrorism Center, "Counterterrorism Guide, Historical Timeline, 2014," www.nctc.gov/site/timeline.html (last accessed April 12, 2016).

5 This statement was widely reported. See, for instance, "Chuck Hagel: ISIS 'Beyond Anything We've Seen'," *CBS News*, August 22, 2014.

6 Cronin, "ISIS Is Not a Terrorist Group."

7 For the foundational work on the subject, see Mark S. Granovetter, "The Strength of Weak Ties," *American Journal of Sociology*, 78, no. 6 (1973).

8 Iannaccone and Berman, "Religious Extremism: The Good, the Bad, and the Deadly."

9 For instance, Cronin, "ISIS Is Not a Terrorist Group."

10 For a discussion, see J. J. Castillo, "Nuclear Terrorism: Why Deterrence Still Matters," *Current History*, 102, no. 668 (2003).

11 Cohen, "Explaining Rape During Civil War: Cross-National Evidence (1980–2009)."

12 Abu Bakr Naji, *The Management of Savagery: The Most Critical Stage through which the Umma Will Pass*, trans. William McCants (Cambridge, MA: John M. Olin Institute for Strategic Studies, 2006).

13 W. Kassel, "Terrorism and the International Anarchist Movement of the Late Nineteenth and Early Twentieth Centuries," *Studies in Conflict & Terrorism*, 32, no. 3 (2009).

Appendices

Appendix 1: Insurgents organized by territory (1970–2012)

Territory	Timeline	Insurgents (n = 169 group-territory pairs)	Status*
Afghanistan	1980–89	Afghan and Arab insurgents (vs. Soviets)	insurgents won
	1989–92	Afghan Mujahideen	insurgents won
	1992–96	Taliban	insurgents won
	1996–2001	Northern Alliance	insurgents won
	2001–ongoing	Taliban, Haqqani Network, Hizb-i Islami Gulbuddin	ongoing
Algeria	1992–2002	Armed Islamic Group of Algeria (GIA), Islamic Armed Movement/ Islamic Salvation Front/ Islamic Salvation Army (MIA/FIS/AIS)	Algeria won
Angola	1961–75	Angolan insurgents (independence)	insurgents won
	1975–2002	National Union for the Total Independence of Angola (UNITA)	Angola won
	1975–ongoing	Cabinda rebels	ongoing
Argentina	1976–82	Revolutionary Armed Forces (FAR), People's Revolutionary Army/All for the Fatherland Movement (ERP/MTP)	no victor
Azerbaijan	1988–94	Nagorno-Karabakh	no victor
Bangladesh	1971	Bangladeshi insurgents (versus Pakistan)	insurgents won
	1973–97	Shanti-Bahini	no victor

Territory	Timeline	Insurgents (n = 169 group-territory pairs)	Status*
	1992–ongoing	Harakat ul-Jihad-i-Islami (HUJI)	ongoing
Bosnia-Herzegovina	1992–94	Serbian Republic militants	no victor
Brazil	1968–71	National Liberation Action (ALN), Popular Revolutionary Vanguard (VPR)	Brazil won
Burundi	1972	Hutu rebels	Burundi won
	1988	Hutu rebels	Burundi won
	1993–2005	Civil war	insurgents won
Cambodia	1968–75	Khmer Rouge	insurgents won
	1979–93	Khmer Rouge and Khmer nationalists	no victor
Canada	1963–71	Quebec Liberation Front (FLQ)	Canada won
Central African Republic	1994–97	Movement for the Liberation of the Central African People (MLPC)	Central African Republic won
Chad	1965–79	Front for National Liberation of Chad (FROLINAT)	insurgents won
	1991–98	Movement for Democratic Development (MDD), Chadian National Front (FNT), Committee for Action for Peace and Democracy (CSNDP), Armed Forces for a Federal Republic (FARF)	no victor
	2003–ongoing	Darfuri rebels	ongoing
Chile	1965–ongoing	Movement of the Revolutionary Left (MIR)	ongoing
China	1996–ongoing	Uighur insurgents	ongoing
Colombia	1963–ongoing	Revolutionary Armed Forces of Colombia (FARC), National	ongoing

Territory	Timeline	Insurgents (*n* = 169 group-territory pairs)	Status*
		Liberation Army (ELN), Popular Liberation Army (EPL), 19th April Movement (M-19)	
	1997–2006	United Self-Defense Forces of Columbia (AUC)	Colombia won
Congo (Brazzaville)	1997–99	Cobra and Ninja Rebels	Congo won
Congo (DRC)	1977	Front for the National Liberation of the Congo (FLNC)	DRC won
(Zaire) (Kinshasa)	1986–ongoing	Lord's Resistance Army (LRA)	ongoing
	1996–97	Alliance of Democratic Forces for the Liberation of Congo (AFDL)	insurgents won
	1998–ongoing	Eastern Congolese militias	ongoing
Croatia	1990–95	Republic of Serbian Krajina	Croatia won
Djibouti	1991–2001	Afar insurgents	no victor
Egypt	1973–ongoing	Gama'a al-Islamiyya	ongoing
El Salvador	1980–92	Farabundo Marti National Liberation Front (FMLN)/ leftists	El Salvador won
Ethiopia	1961–93	Eritrean separatists	insurgents won
	1974–91	Anti-Derg militias	insurgents won
France	1979–87	Action Directe	France won
Georgia	1992–93	Abkhaz secessionists	insurgents won
Germany	1970–98	Red Army Faction (RAF)	Germany won
Greece	1975–2002	Revolutionary Organization 17 November (17N)	Greece won
	2003–ongoing	Revolutionary Struggle (EA)	ongoing
Guatemala	1960–96	Guatemalan National Revolutionary Unity (URNG)/leftists	Guatemala won

Territory	Timeline	Insurgents (*n* = 169 group-territory pairs)	Status*
Guinea-Bissau	1962–74	Independence-seeking insurgents	insurgents won
	1998–99	Military junta	insurgents won
India	1966–ongoing	Mizo National Front (MNF)	ongoing
	1967–ongoing	Naxalites	ongoing
	1984–ongoing	Sikh separatists	ongoing
	1989–ongoing	Kashmiri separatists	ongoing
	1989–ongoing	Lashkar-e-Taiba (LET)	ongoing
	1989–ongoing	Harakat-ul-Mujahideen (HUM)	ongoing
Indonesia	1976–2005	Free Aceh Movement (GAM)	Indonesia won
	1993–ongoing	Jemaah al-Islamiyah (JI)	ongoing
Iran	1965–ongoing	Mujaheedin-e-Khalq (MEK)	ongoing
	1979–ongoing	Kurdish Democratic Party Iran (KDPI)	ongoing
	2003–ongoing	People's Resistance Movement of Iran (PRMI/Jundallah)	ongoing
Iraq	1980–88	Kurdish Peshmerga	Iraq won
	1991	Shiite and Kurdish insurgents	Iraq won
	2001–ongoing	Ansar al-Islam	ongoing
	2003–ongoing	Al Qaeda Iraq (AQI), Jaish al-Mahdi (JAM), Kata'ib Hizballah, Baathist Nationalists	ongoing
Israel	1965–ongoing	Palestine Liberation Organization (PLO)	ongoing
	1968–ongoing	Popular Front for the Liberation of Palestine-General Command (PFLP-GC)	ongoing
	1974–ongoing	Abu Nidal Organization	ongoing
	1982–2000	Hezbollah	insurgents won
	1987–ongoing	Hamas	ongoing
	1987–93	First Palestinian Intifada	no victor
	1990–ongoing	Kahane Chai	ongoing

Territory	Timeline	Insurgents (*n* = 169 group-territory pairs)	Status*
	2000–05	Second Palestinian Intifada	Israel won
	2006	Hezbollah	no victor
Italy	1970–88	Red Brigades	Italy won
Ivory Coast	2002–ongoing	Forces Nouvelles (FN)	ongoing
Japan	1969–2000	Japanese Red Army (JRA)	Japan won
	1984–ongoing	Aum Shinrikyo	ongoing
Jordan	1970	Palestine Liberation Organization (PLO)	Jordan won
	1974–ongoing	Abu Nidal Organization (ANO)	ongoing
Kenya	1998–ongoing	Al Qaeda in East Africa	ongoing
Laos	1953–75	Pathet Lao	insurgents won
Lebanon	1975–90	Sunni, Shia, and Christian militias	no victor
	1982–2000	Hezbollah	insurgents won
	1991–ongoing	Asbat al-Ansar	ongoing
Liberia	1989–92	National Patriotic Front of Liberia (NPFL)	no victor
	1999–2003	Liberians United for Reconciliation and Democracy (LURD), Movement for Democracy in Liberia (MODEL)	insurgents won
Libya	1995–ongoing	Libyan Islamic Fighting Group (LIFG)	ongoing
	2011	Transitional National Council	insurgents win
Mali	1990–95	Tuareg insurgents	no victor
	2007–09	Tuareg insurgents	ongoing
	2012–ongoing	Tuareg insurgents, Ansar-al-Dine	no victor
Mexico	1994–ongoing	Zapatista Army of National Liberation (EZLN)	ongoing
Moldova	1990–92	Dniestr separatists	insurgents won
Morocco	1976–91	Polisario Front	Morocco won
	1990–ongoing	Moroccan Islamic Combatant Group (GICM)	ongoing

Territory	Timeline	Insurgents ($n = 169$ group-territory pairs)	Status*
Mozambique	1962–75	Mozambican guerrillas (independence)	insurgents won
	1976–92	Mozambican National Resistance (RENAMO)	Mozambique won
Myanmar (Burma)	1948–ongoing	Kachin and Karen (KNU)	ongoing
Namibia	1960–90	South West Africa People's Organization (SWAPO)	insurgents won
Nepal	1996–2006	Communist Party of Nepal (CPN)	no victor
Nicaragua	1961–79	Sandinistas	insurgents won
	1981–1990	Contras	no victor
Nigeria	1967–70	Biafran insurgents	Nigeria won
	1980–85	Maitatsine Sect	Nigeria won
	1991–ongoing	Niger Delta rebels	ongoing
Northern Ireland/ Great Britain	1966–2007	Ulster Volunteer Force, Loyalist Volunteer Force (UVF, LVF)	no victor
	1969–97	Provisional Irish Republican Army (IRA)	British won
	1995–ongoing	Continuity Irish Republican Army (CIRA)	ongoing
Oman	1962–83	Dhofari rebels	Oman won
Pakistan	1973–ongoing	Baluchi separatists	ongoing
	1989–ongoing	Harakat-ul-Mujahideen (HuM)	ongoing
	1996–ongoing	Lashkar-e-Jhangvi (LeJ)	ongoing
	2000–ongoing	Jaish-e-Mohammed (JeM)	ongoing
	2002–ongoing	Taliban supporters/Tehrik-e-Taliban Pakistan (TTP)	ongoing
Panama	1989	Panama (versus United States)	United States won

Territory	Timeline	Insurgents (n = 169 group-territory pairs)	Status*
Papua New Guinea	1988	Bougainville Revolutionary Army (BRA)	insurgents won
Peru	1980–ongoing	Shining Path	ongoing
Philippines	1968–96	Moro National Liberation Front (MNLF)	Philippines won
	1969–ongoing	Communist Party of the Philippines/New People's Army (NPA)	ongoing
	1977–ongoing	Moro Islamic Liberation Front (MILF)	ongoing
	1991–ongoing	Abu Sayyaf Group (ASG)	ongoing
Portugal	1983–84	Popular Forces 25 April (FP-25)	Portugal won
Russia	1994–96	Chechen insurgents	insurgents won
	1999–ongoing	Chechen insurgents	ongoing
Rwanda	1990–94	Rwandan Patriotic Front (RPF)	insurgents won
	1994–ongoing	Interahamwe	ongoing
Saudi Arabia	2000–ongoing	Al Qaeda of the Arabian Peninsula (AQAP)	ongoing
Senegal	1982–2004	Movement of Democratic Forces of Casamance (MFDC)	Senegal won
Kosovo/ Serbia-Montenegro	1996–99	Kosovo Liberation Army (KLA)	insurgents won
Sierra Leone	1991–2002	Revolutionary United Front (RUF), Armed Forces Revolutionary Council (AFRC)	Sierra Leone won
Slovenia/ Yugoslavia	1991	Slovenian nationalist-separatist	insurgents won
Somalia	1980–91	Anti-Barre groups (Somali National Movement, Somali Salvation	insurgents won

Territory	Timeline	Insurgents (*n* = 169 group-territory pairs)	Status*
		Democratic Front, Isaaq clans)	ongoing
	1991–ongoing	Competing clans and Islamists	
South Africa	1961–90	African National Congress (ANC), Pan Africanist Congress (PAC), Azanian People's Organization (AZAPO)	insurgents won
South Yemen	1986	Civil war	S. Yemen won
	1994	South Yemeni separatists	no victor
Spain	1959–2011	Basque Fatherland and Liberty (ETA)	Spain won
Sri Lanka	1971	People's Liberation Front (JVP)	Sri Lanka won
	1983–2009	Tamil Tigers	Sri Lanka won
Sudan	1963–72	Anya Nya	no victor
	1983–2005	Sudan People's Liberation Movement (SPLM)	insurgents won
	1986–ongoing	Lord's Resistance Army (LRA)	ongoing
	2003–ongoing	Darfuri Rebels	ongoing
Syria	1976–82	Muslim Brotherhood	Syria won
	2011–ongoing	Free Syrian Army	ongoing
Tajikistan	1992–1997	United Tajik Opposition (UTO)	Tajikistan won
Tanzania	1998–ongoing	Al Qaeda in East Africa	ongoing
Thailand	1965–83	Communist Party	Thailand won
	2004–ongoing	South Thailand rebels	ongoing
Timor-Leste	1974–99	Revolutionary Front for an Independent East Timor (FRETILIN)	no victor
	1975–99	East Timorese insurgents	insurgents won

Territory	Timeline	Insurgents (*n* = 169 group-territory pairs)	Status*
Turkey	1978–ongoing	Revolutionary People's Liberation Party	ongoing
	1983–ongoing	Kurdish Workers' Party (PKK)	ongoing
Uganda	1981–86	National Resistance Army (NRA)	insurgents won
	1986–93	Uganda People's Army (UPA), Uganda Freedom Movement (UFM)	Uganda won
	1986–2000	Allied Democratic Forces National Army for the Liberation of Uganda (ADF-NALU)	Uganda won
	1986–ongoing	Lord's Resistance Army (LRA)	ongoing
United States	1969–77	Weather Underground (Weathermen)	United States won
	1973–75	Symbionese Liberation Army (SLA)	United States won
	1992–2001	Patriot Movement	United States won
Uruguay	1963–73	Tupamaros	Uruguay won
Uzbekistan	1991–ongoing	Islamist Movement of Uzbekistan (IMU)	ongoing
	2004–ongoing	Islamic Jihad Union (IJU)	ongoing
Vietnam	1955–75	Viet Cong, People's Army of Vietnam (PAVN)	insurgents won
Yemen	1994	South Yemeni separatists	no victor
	2004–ongoing	Houthi rebels	ongoing
Zimbabwe (Rhodesia)	1964–79	Zimbabwe African National Movement – Patriotic Front (ZANU-PF)	insurgents won
International	1988–ongoing	Al Qaeda	ongoing

* The outcomes given here are based on Boot's assessments of the status of the insurgents in 2012.

Source: Max Boot, *Invisible Armies*, Appendix, 569–89.

Appendix 2: States with two or more overlapping insurgencies (1970–2012)

Location	Years of overlapping insurgencies	Approximate number of years of overlapping insurgency (to 2012)
India	1967–ongoing	46
Israel	1968–ongoing	45
Philippines	1969–ongoing	44
Angola	1975–ongoing	38
Sudan	1972–83 1986–ongoing	38
Iran	1979–ongoing	34
Turkey	1983–ongoing	30
Northern Ireland/Great Britain	1969–97	29
Congo (DRC, Zaire)	1986–ongoing	27
Timor-Leste/Indonesia	1975–99	25
Pakistan	1989–ongoing	24
Lebanon	1982–2000	19
Ethiopia	1974–91	18
Japan	1984–2000	17
Uganda	1986–2000	15
Indonesia	1993–2005	13
Iraq	2001–ongoing	12
Colombia	1997–2006	10
Uzbekistan	2004–ongoing	9
Bangladesh	1973–97	5
United States	1973–75	3
Morocco	1990–91	2
Libya	2011	1

* The outcomes given here are based on Boot's assessments of the status of the insurgents in 2012.

** We list the Lord's Resistance Army (LRA) in each of the three states in which it was active.

Source: Max Boot, *Invisible Armies*, Appendix, 569–89.

Appendix 3:   Internal wars (1970–2010)

Territory	Time period	Internal war
Afghanistan	1978-2001	Insurgency, civil war (anti-Soviet, Afghan Mujahideen, Taliban, Northern Alliance)
	2001–ongoing	Insurgency (Anti-Coalition/Afghan Resistance)
Algeria	1992–2004	Insurgency, civil war (Islamic groups)
Angola	1961–75	Insurgency, civil war (Angolan independence)
	1975–2002	Insurgency, civil war (UNITA)
	1975–ongoing	Insurgency, civil war (Cabinda rebels)
Argentina	1968–79	Insurgency, civil war (Leftists)
Azerbaijan	1992–94	Insurgency, civil war (Nagorno-Karabakh)
Bangladesh	1971–72	Insurgency, civil war (Bangladesh)
	1974–97	Insurgency, civil war (Shanti-Bahini)
Bosnia-Herzegovina	1992–95	Insurgency, civil war (Serbian Republic)
Brazil	1965–72	Insurgency (Leftists)
Burundi	1972, 1988	Insurgency
Burundi	1993–2004	Insurgency and civil war
Cambodia	1968–75	Insurgency, civil war (Khmer Rouge)
	1978–98	Insurgency, civil war (Khmer Rouge and Khmer nationalists)
Central African Republic	1996–97	Civil war (MLPC)
Chad	1965–88	Insurgency, civil war (FROLINAT)
	1991–2002	Insurgency, civil war (MDD, FNT, CSNDP, FARF)
	2005–06	Intra-state war (Darfuri rebels)
Chile	1973	Intra-state war, armed conflict
China	1991–ongoing	Uighur insurgency, civil war
Colombia	1963–ongoing	FARC (and others) insurgency and civil war

Territory	Time period	Internal war
Congo	1997–2003	Cobra and Ninja Rebel insurgency, civil war
D.R. Congo	1977–78	FLNC insurgency, civil war
	1996	AFDL insurgency, civil war
	1998–2003	Eastern Congolese insurgency, civil war
Croatia	1991–95	Republic of Serbian Krajina insurgency, civil war
Djibouti	1991–94	Afar insurgency, civil war
El Salvador	1979–92	FMLN insurgency, civil war
Ethiopia	1960–93	Eritrean separatist insurgency and civil war
	1974–92	Anti-Derg militia, civil war
Georgia	1992–94	Abkhaz secessionist insurgency, civil war
Guatemala	1960–96	URNG insurgency, civil war
Guinea-Bissau	1962–74	Independence-seeking insurgency and civil war
	1998–99	Military junta, insurgency, civil war
India	1952–ongoing	Insurgency and civil war in the Northeast (various groups)
	1970–71, 1980–ongoing	Naxalite insurgency, civil war
	1982–93	Insurgency, civil war (Sikh separatists)
	1989–ongoing	Insurgency, civil war (Kashmiri separatists)
	1989–ongoing	Insurgency (Pakistan-India border)
Indonesia	1975–2005	Insurgency and civil war (GAM)
Iran	1979–93, 1996–2001	Insurgency, civil war (various groups)
Iraq	1961–75, 1985–88	Insurgency, civil war
	1991	Insurgency (Shiite and Kurds)
	2003–ongoing	Insurgency (various groups)
Israel	1965–2004	Insurgency (various groups)
	2000–ongoing	Insurgency (various groups)
Ivory Coast	2002–04	Insurgency, intra-state war

Territory	Time period	Internal war
Jordan	1970	Civil war (Fedayeen)
Laos	1960–79	Insurgency, civil war, intra-state war (Pathet Lao)
Lebanon	1975–90	Civil war (Sectarian)
	1982–2000	Intra-state war (Hezbollah)
Liberia	1989–97	Insurgency, civil war (NPFL)
Mali	1989–94	Insurgency, civil war (Tuareg)
Moldova	1990–92	Insurgency, civil war (Dniestr separatists)
Morocco	1975–91	Insurgency, civil war (Polisario Front)
Mozambique	1962–75	Insurgency, civil war (FRELIMO)
	1976–95	Insurgency, civil war (RENAMO)
Myanmar	1946–2006	Insurgency, civil war (KNU)
Namibia	1960–89	Insurgency, civil war (SWAPO)
Nepal	1997–2006	Insurgency, civil war (CPN)
Nicaragua	1978–79	Insurgency, civil war (Sandinistas)
	1981–90	Insurgency, civil war (Contras)
Nigeria	1967–70	Insurgency, civil war (Biafran)
	1980–81	Intra-state war
	1991–ongoing	Insurgency (Niger Delta rebels)
Northern Ireland	1969–99	Insurgency (IRA)
Oman	1968–71, 1973–75	Non-state war
Pakistan	1973–77	Insurgency, civil war (Baluchi separatists)
	1989–92, 1996–2004	Armed conflict and war (various groups)
	2004–06	Intra-state war (Waziristan)
Papua New Guinea	1988–98	Insurgency, civil war
Peru	1981–88	Insurgency, civil war, armed conflict (Shining Path)
Philippines	1968–2006	Insurgency, civil war (various)

Territory	Time period	Internal war
Russia	1994–96	Insurgency, intra-state war (Chechen)
	1999–ongoing	Insurgency, intra-state war (Chechen)
Rwanda	1990–94	Insurgency, civil war (RPF)
	1998–2002	Civil war, intra-state war (Interahamwe)
Senegal	1980–2003	Insurgency, civil war (MFDC)
Kosovo	1996–99	Insurgency, war (KLA)
Sierra Leone	1991–2002	Insurgency, intra-state war (RUF, AFRC)
Slovenia	1991	Insurgency (separatist)
Somalia	1980–91	Insurgency, intra-state war (Anti-Barre groups)
	1991–ongoing	Insurgency, intra-state war (various)
South Africa	1960–94	Insurgency, civil war (various)
South Yemen	1986	Insurgency, civil war
	1994	Insurgency, civil war (separatists)
Sri Lanka	1971, 1989	Insurgency, civil war (JVP)
	1983–2009	Insurgency, civil war (LTTE)
Sudan	1963–72	Insurgency, intra-state war (Anya Nya)
	1983–2004	Insurgency, civil war (SPLM)
	2003–06	Insurgency, intra-state war (Darfuri rebels)
Syria	1978, 1981, 1982	Intra-state war (Muslim Brotherhood)
	2001–ongoing	Civil war (various)
Tajikistan	1992–97	Insurgency, intra-state war (UTO)
Thailand	1972–73, 1974–82	Intra-state war, armed conflict (communists)
	2004–ongoing	Insurgency (South Thailand rebels)
Timor-Leste	1975–2005	Insurgency, civil war (FRETILIN)
	1975–78	War (East Timor)
Turkey	1977–80	Insurgency, civil war (DHKP-C)
	1984–99	Insurgency, civil war (PKK)
Uganda	1981–87	Insurgency, civil war (NRA)
	1986–87, 1989, 1991	Intra-state war (UPA, UFM)
	1986–2000	Insurgency (ADF-NALU)

Territory	Time period	Internal war
	1986–2004	Insurgency, civil war, intra-state war, armed conflict (LRA)
Uruguay	1963–73	Tupamaros
Uzbekistan	2000	"minor" armed conflict (IMU)
	2004	"minor" armed conflict
Vietnam	1960–75	Insurgency, civil war (Viet Cong, PAVN)
Yemen	2004–05, 2007	Intra-state war (Houthi rebels)
Zimbabwe	1965–80	Insurgency, civil war, intra-state war (ZANU-PF)

Sources: Max Boot, *Invisible Armies*, 569–89, Ben Connable and Martin Libicki, *How Insurgencies End*, 157–62, 99–201; Meredith Reid Sarkees and Frank Wayman, *Resort to War*, James D. Fearon and David D. Laitin, "Additional Tables;" UCDP/PRIO, "Armed Conflict Dataset V.4–2014a, 1946–2013."

Bibliography

Abrahms, Max. "Why Terrorism Does Not Work." *International Security*, 31, no. 2 (2006): 42–78.

Abrahms, Max. "What Terrorists Really Want." *International Security*, 32, no. 4 (2008): 78–105.

Abrahms, Max. "The Political Effectiveness of Terrorism Revisited." *Comparative Political Studies*, 45, no. 3 (2012): 366–93.

Abrahms, Max, and Philip B. K. Potter. "Explaining Terrorism: Leadership Deficits and Militant Group Tactics." *International Organization*, 69, no. 2 (2015): 311–42.

Ahram, Ariel. *Proxy Warriors*. Stanford, CA: Stanford University Press, 2011.

Ajami, Fuad. *The Vanished Imam*. Ithaca, NY: Cornell University Press, 1986.

Aktan, Gunduz S., and Ali M. Koknar. "Turkey." In *Combating Terrorism: Strategies of Ten Countries*, edited by Yonah Alexander. Ann Arbor, MI: University of Michigan Press, 2002, 260–300.

Alami, Mona. "The Lebanese Army and the Confessional Trap." *Sada*, June 25, 2014.

Albayrak, Ayala, and Joe Pakinson. "Attacks Roil Turkey Ahead of Elections." *Wall Street Journal*, April 2, 2015.

Alkhouri, Laith, and Alex Kassirer. "Governing the Caliphate: The Islamic State Picture." *CTC Sentinel*, 8, no. 8 (2015): 17–20.

Allcock, John, Marko Milivojevic, and John Horton. *Conflict in the Former Yugoslavia*. Santa Barbara, CA: ABC-CLIO, 1998.

Alonso, Rogelio. "Pathways Out of Terrorism in Northern Ireland and the Basque Country. The Misrepresentation of the Irish Model." *Terrorism and Political Violence*, 16, no. 4 (2004): 695–713.

Andrews, Edmund L., and John Kifner. "George Habash, 82, Founder of Popular Front for the Liberation of Palestine." *New York Times*, January 27, 2008.

Arreguín-Toft, Ivan. *How the Weak Win Wars: A Theory of Asymmetric Conflict*. New York, NY: Cambridge University Press, 2005.

Arreguín-Toft, Ivan. "Contemporary Asymmetric Conflict Theory in Historical Perspective." *Terrorism and Political Violence*, 24, no. 4 (2012): 635–57.

August, Oliver. "Al-Qaeda's Land Grab." *The Economist: The World in 2013* (2013).

Auty, Phyllis. "9th Congress of League of Yugoslav Communists." *World Today*, 25, no. 6 (1969): 264–76.

Ayers, Nick. "Ghost Martyrs in Iraq: An Assessment of the Applicability of Rationalist Models to Explain Suicide Attacks in Iraq." *Studies in Conflict & Terrorism*, 31, no. 9 (2008): 856–82.

Azani, Eitan. *Hezbollah: The Story of the Party of God, from Revolution to Institutionalization*. New York, NY: Palgrave MacMillan, 2009.

Baffelli, Erica. "Hikari No Wa: A New Religion Recovering from Disaster." *Japanese Journal of Religious Studies*, 39, no. 1 (2012): 29–49.

Baloyra, Enrique. "El Salvador: From Reactionary Despotism to Partidocracia." In

Postconflict Elections, edited by Krishna Kumar. Boulder, CO: Lynne Rienner, 1998, 15–37.

Bandura, Albert. "Mechanisms of Moral Disengagement." In *Origins of Terrorism: Psychologies, Ideologies, Theologies, States of Mind*, edited by Walter Reich. New York, NY: Cambridge University Press, 1990, 161–91.

Barfi, Barak. "Al-Qa'ida's Confused Messaging on Libya." *CTC Sentinel*, 4, no. 8 (2011): 8–12.

Barfield, Thomas. *Afghanistan: A Political and Cultural History*. Princeton, NJ: Princeton University Press, 2010.

Barkey, Henri. "Turkey and the PKK." In *Democracy and Counterterrorism*, edited by Robert Art and Louise Richardson. Washington, DC: United States Institute of Peace Press, 2007, 343–81.

Barkun, Michael. *Religion and the Racist Right: The Origins of the Christian Identity Movement*. Chapel Hill, NC: The University of North Carolina Press, 1997.

BBC, "Islamic State Group: Crisis in Seven Maps," April 27, 2016. www.bbc.com/news/world-middle-east-27838034 (last accessed April 27, 2016)

BBC News Africa. "What Now for Colonel Gaddafi's Green Book?" April 29, 2011. www.bbc.com/news/world-africa-13235981 (last accessed April 8, 2016).

BBC News Africa. "Who Are Somalia's Al-Shabab?" April 3, 2015. www.bbc.com/news/world-africa-15336689 (last accessed April 4, 2016).

BBC News Latin American & Caribbean. "Farc's Political Party Regains Legal Status," July 10, 2013. www.bbc.com/news/world-latin-america-23251500 (last accessed April 8, 2016).

BBC News Latin America & Caribbean. "Peru Admits Shining Path Rebels Have Not Been 'Exterminated'," August 6, 2015. www.bbc.com/news/world-latin-america-33813695 (last accessed April 8, 2016).

BBC News Middle East. "Yemen Crisis: Who Is Fighting Whom," March 26, 2015. www.bbc.com/news/world-middle-east-29319423 (last accessed April 12, 2016).

BBC News Middle East. "What Is Islamic State?" December 2, 2015. www.bbc.com/news/world-middle-east-29052144 (last accessed April 8, 2016).

Bejarano, Ana Maria. "The Constitution of 1991." In *Violence in Colombia, 1990–2000*, edited by Charles Berquist, Ricardo Penarada and Gonzalo Sanchez. Wilmington, DE: SR Books, 2001, 53–74.

Bell, J. Bowyer. *A Time of Terror*. New York, NY: Basic Books, 1978.

Bergen, Peter. *Holy War, Inc.* New York, NY: The Free Press, 2001.

Bergen, Peter. *The Longest War*. New York, NY: The Free Press, 2011.

Berkowitz, Bruce. *The New Face of War: How Wars Will Be Fought in the 21st Century*. New York, NY: The Free Press, 2003.

Berti, Benedetta. *Armed Political Organizations: From Conflict to Integration*. Baltimore, MD: Johns Hopkins University Press, 2013.

Betts, Richard K. "The Soft Underbelly of American Primacy: Tactical Advantages of Terror." *Political Science Quarterly*, 117, no. 1 (2002): 19–36.

Betz, David. "Cyberspace and Insurgency." In *The Routledge Handbook of Insurgency and Counterinsurgency*, edited by Paul Rich and Isabelle Duyvesteyn. New York, NY: Routledge, 2014, 54–66.

Bloom, Mia M. "Palestinian Suicide Bombing: Public Support, Market Share, and Outbidding." *Political Science Quarterly*, 119, no. 1 (2004): 61–88.

Bloom, Mia M. *Dying to Kill: The Allure of Suicide Terror*. New York: Columbia University Press, 2005.

Boot, Max. *Invisible Armies: An Epic History of Guerrilla Warfare from Ancient Times to the Present*. New York, NY: Liveright Publishing Corporation, 2013.

Boot, Max. "The Evolution of Irregular War: Insurgents and Guerrillas from Akkadia to Afghanistan." *Foreign Affairs*, 92, no. 2 (2013): 100–14.

Boyle, Michael. "Do Counterterrorism and Counterinsurgency Go Together?" *International Affairs*, 86, no. 2 (2010): 333–53.

Boyle, Michael. "Progress and Pitfalls in the Study of Political Violence." *Terrorism and Political Violence*, 24, no. 4 (2012): 527–43.

Boyle, Michael. *Violence after War.* Baltimore, MD: Johns Hopkins University Press, 2014.

Bozarslan, Hamit. "The Kurdish Issue in Turkey Following the 2003 Iraq War." In *The Kurdish Question*, edited by Mohammad Ahmed and Michael Gunter. Costa Mesa, CA: Mazda Publishers, 2005, 123–35.

Braithwaite, Alex. "Transnational Terrorism as an Unintended Consequence of a Military Footprint." *Security Studies*, 24, no. 2 (2015): 349–75.

Braithwaite, Alex, and Quan Li. "Transnational Terrorism Hot Spots: Identification and Impact Evaluation." *Conflict Management and Peace Science*, 24, no. 4 (2007): 281–96.

Brym, R. J., and Bader Araj. "Palestinian Suicide Bombing Revisited: A Critique of the Outbidding Thesis." *Political Science Quarterly*, 123, no. 3 (2008): 485–500.

Bunce, Valerie, and Sharon Wolchik. "A Regional Transition: The Diffusion of Democratic Change under Communism and Postcommunism." In *Democracy and Authoritarianism in the Poscommunist World*, edited by Valerie Bunce, Michael McFaul and Kathryn Stoner-Weiss. New York, NY: Cambridge University Press, 2010, 30–56.

Burdette, Jeff. "Why the ISIS-Al-Qaeda Conflict Isn't All Good News." *Georgetown Security Studies Review*, March 26, 2014.

Bureau of Counterterrorism. "Chapter 6. Foreign Terrorist Organizations." In *Country Reports on Terrorism 2013*. Washinton, DC: United States Department of State, 2013.

Bureau of Counterterrorism. "Chapter 6. Foreign Terrorist Organizations." In *Country Reports on Terrorism 2014*. Washinton, DC: United States Department of State, 2014.

Burrowes, Robert. *The Yemen Arab Republic.* Boulder, CO: Westview Press, 1987.

Burt, Jo-Marie. "'Quien Habla Es Terrorista': The Political Use of Fear in Fujimori's Peru." *Latin American Research Review*, 41, no. 3 (2006): 32–62.

Byman, Daniel. *Deadly Connections: States that Sponsor Terrorism.* New York, NY: Cambridge University Press, 2005.

Byman, Daniel. "Israel and the Lebanese Hizbollah." In *Democracy and Counterterrorism*, edited by Robert Art and Louise Richardson. Washington, DC: United States Institute of Peace Press, 2007, 305–41.

Calvert, Peter. "Venezuela: The FALN-FLN." In *Democracy and Counterterrorism*, edited by Robert Art and Louise Richardson. Washington, DC: United States Institute of Peace Press, 2007, 167–93.

Castillo, J. J. "Nuclear Terrorism: Why Deterrence Still Matters." *Current History*, 102, no. 668 (2003): 426–31.

Chaliand, Gerard, and Arnaud Blin. "The 'Golden Age' of Terrorism." In *The History of Terrorism: From Antiquity to Al Qaeda*, edited by Gerard Chaliand and Arnaud Blin. Berkeley, CA: University of California Press, 2007, 175–96.

Chaliand, Gerard, and Arnaud Blin, eds. *The History of Terrorism.* Berkeley, CA: University of California Press, 2007.

Chenoweth, Erica. "Terrorism and Democracy." *Annual Review of Political Science*, 16 (2013): 355–78.

Chenoweth, E., N. Miller, E. McClellan, H. Frisch, P. Staniland, and M. Abrahms. "Correspondence: What Makes Terrorists Tick." *International Security*, 33, no. 4 (2009): 180–6.

Chicago Project on Security and Terrorism (CPOST). "Suicide Attack Database (December 19, 2014 Release)."

Chivvis, Christopher S., Keith Crane, Peter Mandaville, and Jeffrey Martini. *Libya's Post-Qaddafi Transition: The Nation-Building Challenge.* National Security Research Division. Santa Monica, CA: RAND Corporation, 2012. www.rand.org/content/dam/rand/pubs/research_reports/RR100/RR129/RAND_RR129.pdf (last accessed May 2, 2016).

"Chuck Hagel: ISIS 'Beyond Anything We've Seen'." *CBS News*, August 22, 2014.

Central Intelligence Agency (CIA). "Bosnia, Intelligence, and the Clinton Presidency." www.foia.cia.gov/collection/bosnia-intelligence-and-clinton-presidency (last accessed April 8, 2016).

Central Intelligence Agency (CIA). The World Factbook. "Libya." https://www.cia.gov/library/publications/the-world-factbook/geos/ly.html (last accessed April 4, 2016).

Central Intelligence Agency (CIA). The World Factbook. "Sri Lanka." https://www.cia.gov/library/publications/the-world-factbook/geos/ce.html (last accessed April 4, 2016).

Central Intelligence Agency (CIA) The World Factbook. "United States." https://www.cia.gov/library/publications/the-world-factbook/geos/us.html   (last accessed April 4, 2016).

Ciria, Alberto. "Peronism Yesterday and Today." *Latin American Perspectives*, 1, no. 3 (1974): 21–41.

Clarke, Richard. *Cyber War*. New York, NY: Harper Collins, 2010.

Clausewitz, Carl von. *On War*. Princeton, NJ: Princeton University Press, 1976.

Cohen, D. K. "Explaining Rape During Civil War: Cross-National Evidence (1980–2009)." *American Political Science Review*, 107, no. 3 (2013): 461–77.

Colburn, Forrest D., and Arturo S. Cruz. "Personalism and Populism in Nicaragua." *Journal of Democracy*, 23, no. 2 (2012): 104–18.

Collier, David, and James E. Mahon. "Conceptual Stretching Revisited – Adapting Categories in Comparative-Analysis." *American Political Science Review*, 87, no. 4 (1993): 845–55.

Connable, Ben, and Martin Libicki. *How Insurgencies End*. Santa Monica, CA: RAND, 2010.

Conrad, Justin, and Kevin Greene. "Competition, Differentiation, and the Severity of Terrorist Attacks." *Journal of Politics*, 77, no. 2 (2015): 546–61.

Conway, Maura. "Terror TV? An Exploration of Hizbollah's Al-Manar Television." In *Countering Terrorism in the 21st Century: International Perspectives*, edited by James J. F. Forest. Westport, CT: Greenwood Publishing Group, 2007, 401–19.

Coulter, John. "Guerrilla Tactics." *China Business Review*, May 1, 2007, 52–5.

Crawford, Neta C. "Assessing the Human Toll of the Post-9/11 Wars: The Dead and Wounded in Afghanistan, Iraq, and Pakistan, 2001–2011." 2011. http://watson.brown.edu/costsofwar/files/cow/imce/papers/2011/Assessing%20the%20Human%20Toll%20of%20the%20Post911%20Wars.pdf (last accessed April 20, 2016).

Crawford, Neta C. "Costs of War: War-Related Death, Injury, and Displacement in Afghanistan and Pakistan 2001–2014." Watson Institute for International Studies, Brown University, 2015, 1–31. http://watson.brown.edu/costsofwar/files/cow/imce/papers/2015/War%20Related%20Casualties%20Afghanistan%20and%20Pakistan%202001-2014%20FIN%20%288%29.pdf (last accessed April 20, 2016).

Crenshaw, Martha. "The Causes of Terrorism." *Comparative Politics*, 13, no. 4 (1981): 379–99.

Crenshaw, Martha. "Theories of Terrorism – Instrumental and Organizational Approaches." *Journal of Strategic Studies*, 10, no. 4 (1987): 13–31.

Crenshaw, Martha. "Democracy, Commitment Problems, and Managing Ethnic Violence: The Case of India and Sri Lanka." In *The Democratic Experience and Political Violence*, edited by David C. Rapoport and Leonard B. Weinberg. London: Frank Cass, 2001, 135–59.

Crenshaw Hutchinson, Martha. "The Concept of Revolutionary Terrorism." In *Terrorism: The Second or Anti-Colonial Wave*, edited by David C. Rapoport. New York, NY: Routledge, 2006. 70–87.

Criado, Henar. "Bullets and Votes: Public Opinion and Terrorist Strategies." *Journal of Peace Research*, 48, no. 4 (2011): 497–508.

Cronin, Audrey Kurth. *How Terrorism Ends: Understanding the Decline and Demise of Terrorist Campaigns*. Princeton, NJ: Princeton University Press, 2009.

Cronin, Audrey Kurth. "ISIS Is Not a Terrorist Group: Why Counterterrorism Won't Stop the Latest Jihadist Threat." *Foreign Affairs*, 94, no. 2 (2015): 87–98.

Crozier, Brian. *The Rebels*. Boston, MA: Beacon Press, 1960.

Dale, S. F. "Religious Suicide in Islamic Asia – Anticolonial Terrorism in India, Indonesia, and the Philippines." *Journal of Conflict Resolution*, 32, no. 1 (1988): 37–59.

Dale, Stephen F. "The Islamic Frontier in Southwest India: The Shahid as a Cultural Ideal among the Mappillas of Malabar." *Modern Asian Studies*, 11, no. 1 (1977): 41–55.

Deak, Istvan, Jan Gross, and Tony Judt, eds. *The Politics of Retribution in Europe*. Princeton, NJ: Princeton University Press, 2000.

Debray, Regis. Revolution in the Revolution? New York, NY: Grove Press, Inc., 1967.

Deeb, Marius. *Syria's War on Lebanon*. New York, NY: Palgrave Macmillan, 2003.

Della Porta, Donatella. *Clandestine Political Violence*. New York, NY: Cambridge University Press, 2014.

Dershowitz, Alan. *Why Terrorism Works: Understanding the Threat, Responding to the Challenge*. New Haven, CT: Yale University Press, 2002.

DeVotta, Neil. "Illiberalism and Ethnic Conflict in Sri Lanka." *Journal of Democracy*, 13, no. 1 (2002): 84–98.

Dew, Andrea J. "The Erosion of Constraints in Armed-Group Warfare: Bloody Tactics and Vulnerable Targets." In *Armed Groups: Studies in National Security, Counterterrorism, and Counterinsurgency*, edited by Jeffrey H. Norwitz. Newport, RI: U.S. Naval War College, 2008, 255–68.

Djilas, Aleksa. "Review: Tito's Last Secret: How Did He Keep the Yugoslavs Together?" *Foreign Affairs*, 74, no. 4 (1995): 116–22.

Dresch, Paul. *A History of Modern Yemen*. New York, NY: Cambridge University Press, 2000.

Dugan, Laura, and Erica Chenoweth. "Moving Beyond Deterrence: The Effectiveness of Raising the Expected Utility of Abstaining from Terrorism in Israel." *American Sociological Review*, 77, no. 4 (2012): 597–624.

Dugan, Laura, Julie Huang, Gary LaFree, and Clark McCauley. "Sudden Desistance from Terrorism: The Armenian Secret Army for the Liberation of Armenia and the Justice Commandos of the Armenian Genocide." *Dynamics of Asymmetric Conflict*, 1, no. 3 (2008): 231–49.

Duyvesteyn, Isabelle. "How New Is the New Terrorism?" *Studies in Conflict & Terrorism*, 27, no. 5 (2004): 439–54.

Easterbrook, G. "The End of War?" *New Republic*, 232, no. 20 (2005): 18–21.

"An Echo of Terrorism." *The Economist (Asia)* (June 12, 2003). www.economist.com/node/1852365 (last accessed April 4, 2016).

Edwards, Aaron. "Abandoning Armed Resistance? The Ulster Volunteer Force as a Case Study of Strategic Terrorism in Northern Ireland." *Studies in Conflict & Terrorism*, 32, no. 2 (2009): 146–66.

Ensalaco, Mark. *Middle Eastern Terrorism: From Black September to September 11*. Philadelphia, PA: University of Pennsylvania Press, 2008.

Eubank, William Lee, and Leonard Weinberg. "Does Democracy Encourage Terrorism?" *Terrorism and Political Violence*, 6, no. 4 (1994): 417–35.

Eubank, William, and Leonard Weinberg. "Terrorism and Democracy: Perpetrators and Victims." *Terrorism and Political Violence*, 13, no. 1 (2001): 155–64.

Fair, C. Christine. "The 2008 Mumbai Attack." In *The Evolution of the Global Terrorist Threat*, edited by Bruce Hoffman and Fernando Reinares. New York, NY: Columbia University Press, 2014, 571–99.

Fall, Bernard B. "The Theory and Practice of Insurgency and Counterinsurgency." *Military Review*, 95, no. 5 (2015): 40–8.

Fanon, Frantz. *The Wretched of the Earth*. New York, NY: Grove Press, 1963.

Fearon, James D., and David D. Laitin. "Review: Violence and the Construction of Ethnic Identity." *International Organization*, 54, no. 4 (2000): 845–77.

Fearon, James D., and David D. Laitin. "Additional Tables For 'Ethnicity, Insurgency, and Civil War'." Stanford University, Department of Political Science, February 6, 2003.

Fearon, James D., and David D. Laitin. "Ethnicity, Insurgency, and Civil War." *American Political Science Review*, 97, no. 1 (2003): 75–90.

Fielding, David, and Anja Shortland. "The Dynamics of Terror During the Peruvian Civil War." *Journal of Peace Research*, 49, no. 6 (2012): 847–62.

Flood, Derek Henry. "An Overview of Syria's Armed Revolution." *CTC Sentinel*, 5, no. 4 (2012): 1–5.

Fujii, Lee Ann. "The Puzzle of Extra-Lethal Violence." *Perspectives on Politics*, 11, no. 2 (2013): 410–26.

Fukuyama, Francis. "The End of History?" *The National Interest*, 16 (1989): 3–18.

Fukuyama, Francis. *Political Order and Political Decay*. New York, NY: Farrar, Straus, Giroux, 2014.

Gall, Carlota. *The Wrong Enemy*. Boston, MA: Houghton-Mifflin, 2014.

Galula, David. *Counterinsurgency Warfare: Theory and Practice*. Westport, CT: Praeger Security International, 2006.

Ganor, Boaz. *The Counter-Terrorism Puzzle*. New Brunswick, NJ: Transaction, 2005.

Ganor, Boaz. "Four Questions on ISIS: A 'Trend' Analysis of the Islamic State." *Perspectives on Terrorism*, 9, no. 3 (2015): 56–64.

Garthoff, Raymond L. "Unconventional Warfare in Communist Strategy." *Foreign Affairs*, 40, no. 4 (1962): 566–75.

Gelvin, James. *The Arab Uprisings: What Everyone Needs to Know*. New York, NY: Oxford University Press, 2012.

Gerges, Fawaz A. "The Transformation of Arab Politics: Disentangling Myth from Reality." In *The 1967 Arab-Israeli War: Origins and Consequences*, edited by Avi Shlaim and William Roger Louis. New York, NY: Cambridge University Press, 2012, 285–314.

Gillespie, Richard. *Soldiers of Peron*. Oxford: Clarendon Press, 1982.

Gilsinan, Kathy. "The Many Ways to Map the Islamic 'State'." *The Atlantic*, August 27, 2014.

Gleditsch, Nils Petter, Steven Pinker, Bradley A. Thayer, Jack S. Levy, and William R. Thompson. "The Forum: The Decline of War." *International Studies Review*, 15, no. 3 (2013): 396–419.

"Global Terrorism Database (GTD) Codebook: Inclusion Criteria and Variables." START, October 2012.

"Global Terrorism Database [Data File]." National Consortium for the Study of

Terrorism and Responses to Terrorism (START), 2013, 2014 and 2015. www. start.umd.edu/gtd (last accessed 4 April 2016).

Goldstein, Joshua S. *Winning the War on War: The Decline of Armed Conflict Worldwide.* New York, NY: Dutton, 2011.

Gorriti, Gustavo. *The Shining Path.* Chapel Hill, NC: University of North Carolina Press, 1999.

Gourevitch, Philip. *We Wish to Inform You That Tomorrow We Will Be Killed with Our Families: Stories from Rwanda.* New York, NY: Farrar, Straus and Giroux, 1998.

Government of the United Kingdom. "Foreign Travel Advice: Libya." www.gov. uk/foreign-travel-advice/libya/terrorism (last accessed April 12, 2016).

Gow, James. *The Serbian Project and Its Adversaries: A Strategy of War Crimes.* Montreal, Canada: McGill-Queen's University Press, 2003.

Granovetter, Mark S. "The Strength of Weak Ties." *American Journal of Sociology,* 78, no. 6 (1973): 1360–80.

Guevara, Che. *Guerrilla Warfare.* New York, NY: Monthly Review Press, 1961.

Guillen, Abraham. "Urban Guerrilla Strategy." In *Guerrilla Strategies: An Historical Anthology from the Long March to Afghanistan,* edited by Gerard Chaliand. Berkeley, CA: University of California Press, Ltd., 1982, 317–23.

Gunaratna, Rohan. "Global Threat Forecast 2015." *RSIS Commentary,* 252 (2014).

Gurbey, Gulistan. "Implications of Turkey's Constitutional Reforms for the Kurds." In *The Kurdish Question,* edited by Mohammad Ahmed and Michael Gunter. Costa Mesa, CA: Mazda Publishers, 2005, 136–62.

Gurr, Ted Robert. *Why Men Rebel.* Princeton, NJ: Princeton University Press, 1970.

Habash, George, and Mahmoud Soueid. "Taking Stock: An Interview with George Habash." *Journal of Palestine Studies,* 28, no. 1 (1998): 86–101.

Hafez, Mohammed M. "Suicide Terrorism in Iraq: A Preliminary Assessment of the Quantitative Data and Documentary Evidence." *Studies in Conflict & Terrorism,* 29, no. 6 (2006): 591–619.

Hamilton, Lawrence C., and James D. Hamilton. "Dynamics of Terrorism." *International Studies Quarterly,* 27, no. 1 (1983): 39–54.

Hammes, Colonel Thomas X. "Fourth Generation Warfare Evolves, Fifth Emerges." *Military Review,* 87, no. 3 (2007): 14–23.

Haqqani, Husain. "India's Islamist Groups." *Current Trends in Islamist Ideology,* 3 (2006): 10–23.

Hewitt, Christopher. *Understanding Terrorism in America.* New York, NY: Routledge, 2003.

Hewitt, Christopher. "Law Enforcement Tactics and Their Effectiveness in Dealing with American Terrorism: Organizations, Autonomous Cells, and Lone Wolves." *Terrorism and Political Violence* 26, no. 1 (2014): 58–68.

Hoffman, Bruce. "The Changing Face of Al Qaeda and the Global War on Terrorism." *Studies in Conflict & Terrorism* 27, no. 6 (2004): 549–60.

Hoffman, Bruce. *Inside Terrorism.* New York, NY: Columbia University Press, 2006.

Hoffman, Bruce. "The 'Cult of the Insurgent': Its Tactical and Strategic Implications." *Australian Journal of International Affairs,* 61, no. 3 (2007): 312–29.

Hoffman, Bruce. "Leaderless Jihad: Terror Networks in the Twenty-First Century." *Foreign Affairs* 87, no. 3 (2008): 133–8.

Holmes, Jennifer S., Sheila Amin Gutierrez de Pineres, and Kevin M. Curtin. *Guns, Drugs, and Development in Colombia.* Austin, TX: University of Texas Press, 2008.

Hopgood, Stephen. "Tamil Tigers, 1987–2002." In *Making Sense of Suicide Missions,* edited by Diego Gambetta. New York, NY: Oxford University Press, 2005, 43–76.

Horne, Alistair. *A Savage War of Peace: Algeria, 1954–1962*. New York, NY: New York Review of Books, 2006.

Horowitz, Michael C. "Nonstate Actors and the Diffusion of Innovations: The Case of Suicide Terrorism." *International Organization*, 64, no. 1 (2010): 33–64.

Horowitz, Shale, and Deepti Sharma. "Democracies Fighting Ethnic Insurgencies: Evidence from India." *Studies in Conflict & Terrorism*, 31, no. 8 (2008): 749–73.

Hosmer, Stephen. *Viet Cong Repression and Its Implications for the Future*. Lexington, MA: Heath Lexington Books, 1970.

Howard, Geoffrey. "Libya's South: The Forgotten Frontier." *CTC Sentinel*, 7, no. 11 (2014): 12–16.

Human Rights Watch. "Why They Died: Civilian Casualties in Lebanon During the 2006 War." 2007.

Human Rights Watch. "Recurring Nightmare: State Responsibility for 'Disappearances' and Abductions in Sri Lanka." 2008.

Human Security Report Project. *Human Security Report 2013: The Decline in Global Violence: Evidence, Explanation, and Contestation*. Vancouver, Canada: Human Security Press, 2014.

Huntington, Samuel P. *The Clash of Civilizations and the Remaking of World Order*. New York, NY: Simon and Schuster, 1996.

Hyland, Francis. *Armenian Terrorism*. Boulder, CO: Westview Press, 1991.

Iannaccone, Laurence R., and Eli Berman. "Religious Extremism: The Good, the Bad, and the Deadly." *Public Choice*, 128, no. 1–2 (2006): 109–29.

Janos, Andrew C. "Unconventional Warfare: Framework and Analysis." *World Politics* 15, no. 4 (1963): 636–46.

Jenkins, Brian Michael. "Will Terrorists Go Nuclear?" (November 1975). www.rand.org/content/dam/rand/pubs/papers/2006/P5541.pdf.

Jenkins, Brian Michael. "The New Age of Terrorism (Chapter 8)." In *Mcgraw-Hill Homeland Security Handbook*. McGraw-Hill Companies, Inc., 2006.

Jenkins, Brian Michael. "Brothers Killing Brothers: The Current Infighting Will Test Al Qaeda's Brand." Santa Monica, CA: RAND Corporation, 2014. www.rand.org/pubs/perspectives/PE123.html (last accessed April 20, 2016)

Jenkins, J. Craig, Thomas V. Maher, and Chuck Fahrer. "Seedbeds of Insurgency: Structure and Dynamics in the Egyptian Islamist Insurgency, 1986–99." *Journal of Peace Research*, 51, no. 4 (2014): 470–86.

Jensen, Richard. "The United States, International Policing and the War against Anarchist Terrorism, 1900–1914." *Terrorism and Political Violence*, 13, no. 1 (2001): 15–46.

Jensen, Richard. "The International Campaign against Anarchist Terrorism, 1880–1930s." *Terrorism and Political Violence*, 21, no. 1 (2009): 89–109.

Jensen, Richard. *The Battle against Anarchist Terrorism*. New York, NY: Cambridge University Press, 2014.

Jensen, Richard. "The Pre-1914 Anarchist 'Lone Wolf' Terrorist and Governmental Responses." *Terrorism and Political Violence*, 26, no. 1 (2014): 86–94.

Jervis, Robert. "Theories of War in an Era of Leading-Power Peace, Presidential Address, American Political Science Association, 2001." *American Political Science Review*, 96, no. 1 (2002): 1–14.

Joes, Anthony. *Urban Guerrilla Warfare*. Lexington, KY: The University of Kentucky Press, 2007.

Johnson, Gregory. *The Last Refuge: Yemen, Al Qaeda and America's War in Arabia*. New York, NY: W.W. Norton, 2013.

Johnson, Gregory. *The Last Refuge: Yemen, Al-Qaeda and America's War in Arabia*. New York, NY: W.W. Norton, 2014.

Johnson, Thomas, and M. Chris Mason. "Terrorism, Insurgency and Afghanistan."

In *Countering Terrorism and Insurgency in the 21st Century*, edited by James Forrest. Westport, CT: Praeger International, 2007, 453–78.

Jones, B. D. "Bounded Rationality." *Annual Review of Political Science*, 2 (1999): 297–321.

Jones, Seth G. *In the Graveyard of Empires*. New York, NY: Norton, 2010.

Jones, Seth G., and Martin C. Libicki. *How Terrorist Groups End: Lessons for Countering Al Qa'ida*. Santa Monica, CA: RAND Corporation, 2008.

Juergensmeyer, Mark. "The Logic of Religious Violence: The Case of the Punjab." *Contributions to Indian Sociology*, 22, no. 1 (1988): 65–88.

Juergensmeyer, Mark. "Understanding the New Terrorism." *Current History*, 99, no. 636 (2000): 158–63.

Kaldor, Mary. *New and Old Wars: Organized Violence in a Global Arena*. Stanford, CA: Stanford University Press, 2001.

Kaldor, Mary. *New and Old Wars*, 2nd edn. Stanford, CA: Stanford University Press, 2006.

Kalinovsky, Artemy M. *A Long Goodbye: The Soviet Withdrawal from Afghanistan*. Cambridge, MA: Harvard University Press, 2011.

Kalyvas, Stathis N. "The Paradox of Terrorism in Civil War." *Journal of Ethics*, 8 (2004): 97–138.

Kalyvas, Stathis N. *The Logic of Violence in Civil War*. New York, NY: Cambridge University Press, 2006.

Kalyvas, Stathis N. "Review Symposium: Counterinsurgency Manual." *Perspectives on Politics*, 6, no. 2 (2008): 351–3.

Kalyvas, Stathis N., and Matthew Adam Kocher. "The Dynamics of Violence in Vietnam: An Analysis of the Hamlet Evaluation System (HES)." *Journal of Peace Research*, 46, no. 3 (2009): 335–55.

Kaplan, Eben. "How Libya Got Off the List." www.cfr.org/libya/libya-got-off-list/p10855 (last accessed April 12, 2016).

Kaplan, Fred. *The Insurgents*. New York, NY: Simon and Schuster, 2013.

Kaplan, Jeffrey. "The Fifth Wave: The New Tribalism?" *Terrorism and Political Violence*, 19, no. 4 (2007): 545–70.

Kaplan, Robert. "Buddha's Savage Peace." *The Atlantic*, September 2009.

Karasik, Theodore, and Kim Cragin. "Case Study: The Arabian Peninsula." In *Ungoverned Territories: Understanding and Reducing Terrorism Risks*, edited by Angel Rabasa, Steven Boraz, Peter Chalk, Kim Cragin, Theodore W. Karasik, Jennifer D. P. Moroney, Kevin A. O'Brien, and John E. Peters. Santa Monica, CA: RAND Corporation, 2007, 77–110.

Kassel, W. "Terrorism and the International Anarchist Movement of the Late Nineteenth and Early Twentieth Centuries." *Studies in Conflict & Terrorism*, 32, no. 3 (2009): 237–52.

Kassimeris, George. "Greece: The Persistence of Political Terrorism." *International Affairs*, 89, no. 1 (2013): 131–42.

Kassimeris, George. *Inside Greek Terrorism*. London: Hurst & Company, 2013.

Kaufman, S. J. "Symbolic Politics or Rational Choice? Testing Theories of Extreme Ethnic Violence." *International Security*, 30, no. 4 (2006): 45–86.

Kearns, Erin M., Brendan Conlon, and Joseph K. Young. "Lying About Terrorism." *Studies in Conflict & Terrorism*, 37, no. 5 (2014): 422–39.

Kedourie, Elie. "The End of the Ottoman Empire." *Comtemporary History*, 3, no. 4 (1968): 19–28.

Keefer, Philip, and Norman Loayza, eds. *Terrorism, Economic Development, and Political Openness*. New York, NY: Cambridge University Press, 2008.

Keilberth, Mirco, and Christoph Reuter. "A Threat to Europe: The Islamic State's Dangerous Gains in Libya." *Spiegel Online International*, February 23, 2015.

Kennedy, Jonathan, and Sunil Purushotham. "Beyond Naxalbari: A Comparative Analysis of Maoist Insurgency and Counterinsurgency in Independent India." *Comparative Studies in Society and History*, 54, no. 4 (2012): 832–62.

Kesic, Obrad. "Serbia – the Politics of Despair." *Current History*, 92, no. 577 (1993): 376–80.

Khalil, James. "Know Your Enemy: On the Futility of Distinguishing between Terrorists and Insurgents." *Studies in Conflict & Terrorism*, 36, no. 5 (2013): 419–30.

Kilcullen, David. *The Accidental Guerrilla*. New York, NY: Oxford University Press, 2009.

Kilcullen, David. *Counterinsurgency*. New York, NY: Oxford University Press, 2010.

Kilcullen, David. *Out of the Mountains*. New York, NY: Oxford University Press, 2013.

Knights, Michael. "ISIL's Political Military Power in Iraq." *CTC Sentinel*, 7, no. 8 (2014): 1–7.

Koc-Menard, Sergio. "Switching from Indiscriminate to Selective Violence: The Case of the Peruvian Military (1980–95)." *Civil Wars*, 8, no. 3 (2006): 332–54.

Kurtulus, Ersun N. "The 'New Terrorism' and Its Critics." *Studies in Conflict & Terrorism*, 34, no. 6 (2011): 476–500.

Kydd, Andrew H., and Barbara F. Walter. "Sabotaging the Peace: The Politics of Extremist Violence." *International Organization*, 56, no. 2 (2002): 263–96.

Kydd, Andrew H., and Barbara F. Walter. "The Strategies of Terrorism." *International Security*, 31, no. 1 (2006): 49–80.

LaFree, Gary. "Editorial Introduction: Loner Attacks and Domestic Extremism, Lone-Offender Terrorists." *Criminology and Public Policy*, 12, no. 1 (2009): 59–62.

LaFree, Gary, and Bianca E. Bersani. "County-Level Correlates of Terrorist Attacks in the United States." *Criminology and Public Policy*, 13, no. 3 (2014): 455–81.

LaFree, Gary, and Gary Ackerman. "The Empirical Study of Terrorism: Social and Legal Research." *Annual Review of Law and Social Science*, 5 (2009): 347–74.

LaFree, Gary, Sue-Ming Yang, and Martha Crenshaw. "Trajectories of Terrorism: Attack Patterns of Foreign Groups that Have Targeted the United States, 1970–2004." *Criminology and Public, Policy*, 8, no. 3 (2009): 445–73.

Lalwani, Sameer. "India's Approach to Counterinsurgency and the Naxalite Problem." *CTC Sentinel*, 4, no. 10 (October 31, 2011): 5–8.

Laqueur, Walter. *Guerrilla*. Boston, MA: Little, Brown and Company, 1976.

Laqueur, Walter. *Terrorism*. Boston, MA: Little, Brown, 1977.

Laqueur, Walter. *The Age of Terrorism*. Boston, MA: Little, Brown and Company, 1987.

Laqueur, Walter. "Postmodern Terrorism." *Foreign Affairs*, 75, no. 5 (1996): 24–36.

Laqueur, Walter. "The New Face of Terrorism." *Washington Quarterly*, 21, no. 4 (1998): 169–78

Laqueur, Walter. *The New Terrorism: Fanaticism and the Arms of Mass Destruction*. New York, NY: Oxford University Press, 1999.

Laqueur, Walter. *A History of Terrorism*. New Brunswick, NJ: Transaction Publishers, 2012.

Law, Randall D. *Terrorism: A History*. Malden, MA: Polity, 2009.

Lehr, Peter. "Still Blind in the Right Eye?" In *Extreme Right-Wing Political Violence and Terrorism*, edited by Max Taylor, P. M. Currie, and Donald Holbrook. London: Bloomsbury, 2013, 187–211.

Leitenberg, Milton. "Aum Shinrikyo's Efforts to Produce Biological Weapons: A Case Study in the Serial Propagation of Misinformation." *Terrorism and Political Violence*, 11, no. 4 (1999): 149–58.

Levitt, Matthew. "Al-Qa'ida's Finances: Evidence of Organizational Decline?" *CTC Sentinel*, 1, no. 5 (2008): 7–9.

"Libya's Civil War: The Four-year Descent from Arab Spring to Factional Chaos." *The Economist*, January 10, 2015, 21–3.

Lieber, K. A., and D. G. Press. "Why States Won't Give Nuclear Weapons to Terrorists." *International Security*, 38, no. 1 (2013): 80–104.

Lifton, Robert Jay "Reflections on Aum Shinrikyo." *Journal of Personal & Interpersonal Loss*, 3, no. 1 (1998): 85–97.

Lifton, Robert Jay. *Destroying the World to Save It: Aum Shinrikyo, Apocalyptic Violence, and the New Global Terrorism*. New York, NY: Henry Holt and Company, LLC, 2000.

Lister, Tim, and Paul Cruickshank. "What Is Ansar Al Sharia, and Was It Behind the Consulate Attack in Benghazi?" *CNN Politics*, November 16, 2012.

Lyall, Jason. "Do Democracies Make Inferior Counterinsurgents? Reassessing Democracy's Impact on War Outcomes and Duration." *International Organization*, 64, no. 1 (2010): 167–92.

MacGinty, Roger, and John Darby. *Guns and Government*. New York, NY: Palgrave, 2002.

Marchak, Patricia. *God's Assassins: State Terrorism in Argentina in the 1970s*. Montreal, Canada: McGill-Queen's University Press, 1999.

Marighella, Carlos. *Manual of the Urban Guerrilla*, The Terrorist Classic. Chapel Hill, NC: Documentary Publications, 1985.

Marks, Thomas. "Sri Lanka and the Liberation Tigers of Tamil Eelam." In *Democracy and Counterterrorism*, edited by Robert Art and Louise Richardson. Washington, DC: United States Institute of Peace Press, 2007, 483–530.

Marshall, Monty G., and Ted Robert Gurr. *Peace and Conflict 2005: A Global Survey of Armed Conflicts, Self-Determination Movements, and Democracy*. College Park, MD: Center for International Development and Conflict Management, 2005.

Martin, Susanne. "From Parliamentarianism to Terrorism and Back Again." Austin, TX: University of Texas at Austin, 2011.

Martin, Susanne. "Dilemmas of 'Going Legit': Why Should Violent Groups Engage in or Avoid Electoral Politics?" *Behavioral Sciences of Terrorism and Political Aggression*, 6, no. 2 (2014): 81–101.

Martin, Susanne, and Arie Perliger. "Turning to and from Terror: Deciphering the Conditions under Which Political Groups Choose Violent and Nonviolent Tactics." *Perspectives on Terrorism*, 6, no. 4–5 (2012): 21–45.

Martin, Susanne, and Leonard B. Weinberg. "Terrorism in an Era of Unconventional Warfare." *Terrorism and Political Violence* (forthcoming).

Marwah, Ved. "India." In *Combating Terrorism: Strategies of Ten Countries*, edited by Yonah Alexander. Ann Arbor, MI: University of Michigan Press, 2002, 301–36.

McBeth, John. "Technology May Hold Key to Answers About Malaysia Airlines Flight Mh370." *China Post (The Straits Times/Asia News Network)*, March 12, 2014.

McClintock, Cynthia. *Revolutionary Movements in Latin America*. Washington, DC: United States Institute of Peace Press, 2005.

McCormick, Gordon H. "The Shining Path and Peruvian Terrorism." In *Inside Terrorist Organizations*, edited by David C. Rapoport. Portland, OR: Frank Cass, 2001, 109–26.

Merari, Ariel. "Terrorism as a Strategy of Insurgency." *Terrorism and Political Violence*, 5, no. 4 (1993): 213–51.

Metz, Steven. "Rethinking Insurgency." In *The Routledge Handbook of Insurgency and Counterinsurgency*, edited by Paul Rich and Isabelle Duyvesteyn. New York, NY: Routledge, 2014.

Midlarsky, M. I., Martha Crenshaw, and F. Yoshida. "Why Violence Spreads – the Contagion of International Terrorism." *International Studies Quarterly*, 24, no. 2 (1980): 262–98.

Mili, Hayder, and Jacob Townsend. "Tribal Dynamics of the Afghanistan and Pakistan Insurgencies." *CTC Sentinel*, 2, no. 8 (2009): 1–4. www.ctc.usma.edu/v2/wp-content/uploads/2010/06/Vol2Iss8-Art3.pdf (last accessed April 29, 2016).

Mirkovic, Damir. "Ethnic Conflict and Genocide: Reflections on Ethnic Cleansing in the Former Yugoslavia." *Annals of the American Academy of Political and Social Science*, 548 (1996): 191–9.

Moghadam, Assaf. *The Globalization of Martyrdom: Al Qaeda, Salafi Jihad, and the Diffusion of Suicide Attacks*. Baltimore, Maryland: Johns Hopkins University Press, 2008.

Moghadam, Assaf. "Motives for Martyrdom: Al-Qaida, Salafi Jihad, and the Spread of Suicide Attacks." *International Security*, 33, no. 3 (2009): 46–78.

Moss, David. "Politics, Violence, Writing: The Rituals of 'Armed Struggle' in Italy." In *The Legitimization of Violence*, edited by David Apter. London: Macmillan, 1997, 83–127.

Mueller, John. *The Remnants of War*. Ithaca, NY: Cornell University Press, 2004.

Mueller, John. "War Has Almost Ceased to Exist: An Assessment." *Political Science Quarterly*, 124, no. 2 (2009): 297–321.

Murphy, Caryle. "AQAP's Growing Security Threat to Saudi Arabia." *CTC Sentinel*, 3, no. 10 (2010): 1–4.

Nagl, John. *Learning to Eat Soup with a Knife*. Westport CT: Praeger, 2002.

Nagl, John A. *Learning to Eat Soup with a Knife: Counterinsurgency Lessons from Malaya and Vietnam*. Chicago, IL: University of Chicago Press, 2005.

Naji, Abu Bakr. *The Management of Savagery: The Most Critical Stage through which the Umma Will Pass*. Translated by William McCants. Cambridge, MA: John M. Olin Institute for Strategic Studies, 2006.

National Counterterrorism Center. "Counterterrorism Guide, Historical Timeline, 2014." www.nctc.gov/site/timeline.html (last accessed April 12, 2016).

"National Strategy for Combating Terrorism." The White House, President George W. Bush, September 2006.

Neuman, William. "Peru Forced to Confront Deep Scars of Civil War." *New York Times*, May 26, 2012.

Norton, Augustus Richard. *Hezbollah*. Princeton, NJ: Princeton University Press, 2007.

Noueihed, Lin, and Alex Warren. *The Battle for the Arab Spring*. New Haven, CT: Yale University Press, 2012.

"Obama's Claim He Called Benghazi an 'Act of Terrorism'." *Washington Post*, May 14, 2014.

O'Duffy, Brendan. "LTTE: Majoritarianism, Self-Determination, and Military to Political Transition in Sri Lanka." In *Terror, Insurgency, and the State: Ending Protracted Conflicts*, edited by Marianne Heiberg, Brendan O'Leary and John Tirman. Philadelphia, PA: University of Pennsylvania Press, 2007, 257–87.

Office of the Coordinator for Counterterrorism. *Country Reports on Terrorism 2009*. Washington, DC: United States Department of State, 2010.

O'Neil, A. "Terrorist Use of Weapons of Mass Destruction: How Serious Is the Threat?" *Australian Journal of International Affairs*, 57, no. 1 (2003): 99–112.

O'Neill, Bard E. "Forward." In *War of the Flea: The Classic Study of Guerrilla Warfare*. Washington, DC: Potomac Books, Inc., 2002, vii–xi.

O'Neill, Bard E. *Insurgency and Terrorism: From Revolution to Apocalypse*, 2nd edn. Washington, DC: Potomac Books, Inc., 2005.

Palmer, David Scott. "The Revolutionary Terrorism of Peru's Shining Path." In *Terrorism in Context*, edited by Martha Crenshaw. University Park, PA: Pennsylvania University Press, 1995, 249–308.

Palmer, David Scott. "Terror in the Name of Mao." In *Democracy and Counterterrorism*, edited by Robert Art and Louise Richardson. Washington, DC: United States Institute of Peace Press, 2007, 195–220.

Pape, R. A. "The Strategic Logic of Suicide Terrorism." *American Political Science Review*, 97, no. 3 (2003): 343–61.

Parachini, John, and Katushisa Furukawa. "Japan and Aum Shinrikyo." In *Democracy and Counterterrorism*, edited by Robert Art and Louise Richardson. Washington, DC: United States Institute of Peace Press, 2007.

Pargeter, Alison. "Islamist Militant Groups in Post-Qadhafi Libya." *CTC Sentinel*, 6, no. 2 (2013): 1–4.

Pedahzur, Ami. *Suicide Terrorism*. Malden, MA: Polity Press, 2005.

Pedahzur, Ami, and Arie Perliger. "The Changing Nature of Suicide Attacks: A Social Network Perspective." *Social Forces*, 84, no. 4 (2006): 1987–2008.

Peresin, Anita. "Fatal Attraction: Western Muslimas and ISIS." *Perspectives on Terrorism*, 9, no. 3 (2015): 21–38.

Perliger, A. "How Democracies Respond to Terrorism: Regime Characteristics, Symbolic Power and Counterterrorism." *Security Studies*, 21, no. 3 (2012): 490–528.

Perliger, Arie. *Challengers from the Sidelines: Understanding America's Violent Far-Right*. West Point, NY: The Combating Terrorism Center at West Point, 2012.

Perliger, Arie, and Ami Pedahzur. "Social Network Analysis in the Study of Terrorism and Political Violence." *Ps-Political Science & Politics*, 44, no. 1 (2011): 45–50.

Pinker, Steven. *The Better Angels of Our Nature: Why Violence Has Declined*. New York, NY: Viking Penguin, 2011.

Pion-Berlin, David, and George A. Lopez. "Of Victims and Executioners: Argentine State Terror, 1975–1979." *International Studies Quarterly*, 35, no. 1 (1991): 63–86.

Pizarro, Eduardo. "Revolutionary Guerrilla Groups in Colombia." In *Violence in Colombia*, edited by Charles Berquist, Ricardo Penarada and Gonzalo Sanchez. Wilmington, DE: SR Books, 1992, 169–94.

Post, Jerrold. "Terrorist Psycho-Logic: Terrorist Behavior as a Product of Psychological Forces." In *Origins of Terrorism: Psychologies, Ideologies, Theologies, States of Mind*, edited by Walter Reich. New York, NY: Cambridge University Press, 1990, 25–40.

Power, Samantha. *A Problem from Hell*. New York, NY: Harper, 2002.

Pridham, Geoffrey. "Terrorism and the State in West Germany During the 1970s." In *Terrorism: A Challenge to the State*, edited by Juliet Lodge. New York, NY: St. Martin's, 1981, 11–56.

Rabasa, Angel, Steven Boraz, Peter Chalk, Kim Cragin, Theodore W. Karasik, Jennifer D. P. Moroney, Kevin A. O'Brien, and John E. Peters. *Ungoverned Territories: Understanding and Reducing Terrorism Risks*. Santa Monica, CA: RAND Corporation, 2007.

Randall, Edward. "After Qadhafi: Development and Democratization in Libya." *The Middle East Journal*, 69, no. 2 (2015): 199–221.

Rapoport, David C. "Fear and Trembling – Terrorism in 3 Religious Traditions." *American Political Science Review*, 78, no. 3 (1984): 658–77.

Rapoport, David C. "The Fourth Wave: September 11 in the History of Terrorism." *Current History*, 100, no. 650 (2001): 419–24.

Rapoport, David C. "The Four Modern Waves of Terrorism." In *Attacking Terrorism*, edited by Audrey Kurth Cronin and James Ludes. Washington, DC: Georgetown University Press, 2004, 87–98.

Rapoport, David C. "The Four Waves of Modern Terrorism." In *Terrorism Studies: A Reader*, edited by John Horgan, and Kurt Braddock. New York, NY: Routledge, 2012, 41–60.

Ray, Rabindra. *The Naxalites and Their Ideology*. Calcutta: Oxford University Press, 1988.

Reader, Ian. *Religious Violence in Contemporary Japan: The Case of Aum Shinrikyo*, Nordic Institute of Asian Studies Monograph Series, No. 82. Richmond, UK: Curzon Press, 2000.

"Recent Highlights in Political Violence." *CTC Sentinel*, 7, no. 1 (2014): 21–4.

Reed, Donald J. "Beyond the War on Terror: Into the Fifth Generation of War and Conflict." *Studies in Conflict & Terrorism*, 31, no. 8 (2008): 684–722.

Roberts, Mark J. "Pakistan's Inter-Services Intelligence Directorate: A State within a State?" *Joint Force Quarterly*, 1, no. 48 (2008): 104–10.

Rosenau, W. "'Our Backs Are against the Wall': The Black Liberation Army and Domestic Terrorism in 1970s America." *Studies in Conflict & Terrorism*, 36, no. 2 (2013): 176–92.

Rosenau, William. "Counterinsurgency: Lessons from Iraq and Afghanistan." *Harvard International Review*, 31, no. 1 (2009): 52–6.

Rosenberg, Tina. *Children of Cain*. New York, NY: William Morrow & Co., 1991.

Ryan, Henry Butterfield. *The Fall of Che Guevara: A Story of Soldiers, Spies, and Diplomats*. New York, NY: Oxford University Press, 1998.

Sageman, M. "Does Osama Still Call the Shots? Debating the Containment of Al Qaeda's Leadership." *Foreign Affairs*, 87, no. 4 (2008): 163–5.

Sageman, Marc. *Leaderless Jihad: Terror Networks in the Twenty-First Century*. Philadelphia, PA: University of Pennsylvania Press, 2008.

Sageman, Marc, and Bruce Hoffman. "The Reality of Grass Roots Terrorism [with Reply]." *Foreign Affairs*, 87, no. 4 (2008): 163–6.

Sambanis, N. "Do Ethnic and Nonethnic Civil Wars Have the Same Causes? A Theoretical and Empirical Inquiry (Part 1)." *Journal of Conflict Resolution*, 45, no. 3 (2001): 259–82.

Sambanis, N. "What Is Civil War? Conceptual and Empirical Complexities of an Operational Definition." *Journal of Conflict Resolution*, 48, no. 6 (2004): 814–58.

Sanchez, Gonzalo. "The Violence: An Interpretive Synthesis." In *Violence in Colombia*, edited by Charles Berquist, Ricardo Penarada, and Gonzalo Sanchez. Wilmington, DE: SR Books, 1992, 75–124.

Sanchez-Cuenca, Ignacio. "The Dynamics of Nationalist Terrorism: ETA and the IRA." *Terrorism and Political Violence*, 19, no. 3 (2007): 289–306.

Sarihan, Ali. "The Two Periods of the PKK Conflict: 1984–1999 and 2004–2010." In *Understanding Turkey's Kurdish Question*, edited by Fevzi Bilgin. Lanham, MD: Lexington Books, 2013, 89–102.

Sarkees, Meredith Reid, "Codebook for the Intra-State Wars v.4.0. Definitions and Variables," COW Project. www.correlatesofwar.org/data-sets/COW-war (last accessed April 28, 2016).

Sarkees, Meredith Reid, and Frank Wayman. *Resort to War: 1816–2007*. Washington, DC: CQ Press, 2010.

Schmid, Alex P., and Albert J. Jongman. *Political Terrorism: A New Guide to Actors, Authors, Concepts, Data Bases, Theories, and Literature*. New Brunswick, NJ: Transaction Publishers, 2005.

Schulze, Kirsten E. *The Arab-Israeli Conflict*. 2nd edn. New York, NY: Routledge, 2013.

Scott, James M. *Deciding to Intervene: The Reagan Doctrine and American Foreign Policy*. Durham, NC: Duke University Press, 1996.

Shapiro, Jacob N. *The Terrorist's Dilemma: Managing Violent Covert Organizations*. Princeton, NJ: Princeton University Press, 2013.

Shelley, Louise. "Blood Money: How ISIS Makes Bank." *Foreign Affairs*, November 30, 2014.

Shelley, Louise I. *Dirty Entanglements: Corruption, Crime, and Terrorism*. New York, NY: Cambridge University Press, 2014.

Sherman, Lawrence W., Patrick Gartin, and Michael Buerger. "Hot Spots of Predatory Crime: Routine Activities and the Criminology of Place." *Criminology and Public Policy*, 27, no. 1 (1989): 27–55.

Shimko, Keith. *The Iraq Wars and America's Military Revolution*. New York, NY: Cambridge University Press, 2010.

Silitski, Vitali. "Contagion Deferred: Preemptive Authoritarianism in the Soviet Union (the Case of Belarus)." In *Democracy and Authoritarianism in the Postcommunist World*, edited by Valerie Bunce, Michael McFaul and Kathryn Stoner-Weiss. New York, NY: Cambridge University Press, 2010.

Singh, Prakash. "The Naxalite Movement in India." New Delhi: Rupa Publications (Kindle Edition), 2006 (rev. edn).

Slaughter, Anne-Marie. "The Real New World Order." *Foreign Affairs*, 76, no. 5 (1997): 183–7.

Slaughter, Anne-Marie. *A New World Order*. Princeton, NJ: Princeton University Press, 2004.

Smith, Colin. *Carlos: Portrait of a Terrorist*. New York, NY: Holt, Rinehart and Winston, 1976.

Sobieck, Stephen M. "Democratic Responses to International Terrorism in Germany." In *The Deadly Sin of Terrorism: Its Effect on Democracy and Civil Liberty in Six Countries*, edited by David A. Charters. Westport, CT: Greenwood Press, 1994, 43–72.

The Southern Poverty Law Center (SPLC). www.splcenter.org (last accessed April 4, 2016).

Spacek, Michael. "India's Enduring Naxalite Insurgency." *World Politics Review* (February 22, 2011).

Spector, Regine A. "The Anti-Revolutionary Toolkit." *CACI Analyst* (2006).

Spegeli, Martin. "The First Phase, 1990–1992." In *The War in Croatia and Bosnia-Herzegovina*, edited by Branka Magas and Ivo Zanic. London: Frank Cass, 2001, 14–40.

Stanford University. "Mapping Militant Organizations." web.stanford.edu/group/mappingmilitants/cgi-bin/groups (last accessed April 4, 2016).

Sterling, Claire. *The Terror Network*. New York, NY: Holt, Rinehart and Winston, 1981.

Stern, Jessica. *Terror in the Name of God*. New York, NY: Harper Collins, 2003.

Stern, Jessica, and J. M. Berger. *ISIS: The State of Terror*. New York, NY: HarperCollins, 2015.

Stone, Jason G. "Sri Lanka's Postwar Descent." *Journal of Democracy*, 25, no. 2 (2014): 146–57.

Stratfor Global Intelligence. "In Yemen, Anti-Houthi Operations Confront Forceful Opposition." www.stratfor.com/analysis/yemen-anti-houthi-operations-confront-forceful-opposition (last accessed April 12, 2016).

Subramaniam, Arjun. "Challenges of Protecting India from Terrorism." *Terrorism and Political Violence*, 24, no. 3 (2012): 396–414.

Tabeau, Ewa, Jakub Bijak, and Neda Loncaric. "Death Toll in the Siege of Sarajevo, April 1992 to December 1995: A Study of Mortality Based on Eight Large Data Sources, Expert Report Prepared for the Case of Slobodan Milosevic – Bosnia and Herzegovina (It-02–54)." 0329–6653 – 0329–6663: International Criminal Tribunal for the Former Yugoslavia, 2003.

Tarrow, Sidney. *The New Transnational Activism*. New York, NY: Cambridge University Press, 2005.

"Terrorist March in Iraq: The U.S. Response, Hearing before the Committee on Foreign Affairs, House of Representatives," edited by Committee on Foreign Affairs. Washington, DC: U.S. Government Printing Office, July 23, 2014.

"Terrorist Organization Profiles." National Consortium for the Study of Terrorism and Responses to Terrorism (START). www.start.umd.edu/tops/ (last accessed April 4, 2016).

"Terrorist Organization Profiles: Kurdistan Workers' Party (PKK)." National Consortium for the Study of Terrorism and Responses to Terrorism (START). www.start.umd.edu/tops/terrorist_organization_profile.asp?id=63 (last accessed April 4, 2016).

"Terrorist Organization Profiles: Shining Path." National Consortium for the Study of Terrorism and Responses to Terrorism (START), 2015.

Thornton, Thomas. "Terror as a Weapon of Political Agitation." In *Internal War*, edited by Harry Eckstein. New York, NY: The Free Press, 1964, 71–99.

Thucydides. *Thucydides: History of the Peloponnesian War*. Translated by C. Forster Smith. Cambridge, MA: Harvard University Press, 1951.

Tilly, Charles. *The Politics of Collective Violence*. New York, NY: Cambridge University Press, 2003.

Tololyan, Khachig. "Terrorism in Modern Armenian Culture." In *Political Parties and Terrorist Groups*, edited by Leonard Weinberg. London: Frank Cass and Company Limited, 1992, 8–22.

Tse-Tung, Mao. *Selected Works of Mao Tse-Tung*. Vol. 1. Elmsford, NY: Pergamon Press, Inc., 1965.

Tse-Tung, Mao. *On Guerrilla Warfare*. Translated by Samuel B. Griffith: BN Publishing, 2007.

Tucker, David. "What Is New About the New Terrorism and How Dangerous Is It?" *Terrorism and Political Violence*, 13, no. 3 (2001): 1–14.

UCDP/PRIO. "Armed Conflict Dataset V.4–2014a, 1946–2013." (2014).

UCDP/PRIO. *UCDP/PRIO Armed Conflict Dataset Codebook, Version 4–2014a*: Uppsala Conflict Data Program (UCDP). Centre for the Study of Civil Wars, International Peace Research Institute, Oslo (PRIO), 2015.

United Nations International Criminal Tribunal for the Former Yugoslavia. www. icty.org/.

United Nations, International Criminal Tribunal for the Former Yugoslavia. *20 Years of the ICTY: Anniversary Events and Legacy Conference Proceedings*. Sarajevo, Bosnia and Herzegovina: ICTY Outreach Programme, 2014.

United States Congress House Committee on Foreign Affairs, Subcommittee on Western Hemisphere Affairs. "The Threat of the Shining Path to Democracy in Peru: Hearings before the Subcommittee on Western Hemisphere Affairs of the Committee on Foreign Affairs." Washington, DC: U.S. Government Printing Office, 1992.

United States Department of the Army. *Counterinsurgency*, Field Manual No. 3-24/ Marine Corps Warfighting Publication No. 3-33.5. Washington, DC: Department of the Army, December 15, 2006. http://usacac.army.mil/cac2/Repository/Materials/COIN-FM3-24.pdf (last accessed 20 April 2016).

United States Department of the Army. *Military Police Operations*, Field Manual No. 3-39, August 26, 2013.

U.S. Department of State, Office of the Historian. "Central America, 1977–1980." https://history.state.gov/milestones/1977-1980/central-america-carter (last accessed March 15, 2016).

Valentino, Benjamin A. *Final Solutions: Mass Killing and Genocide in the 20th Century*. Edited by Robert J. Art, Robert Jervis and Stephen M. Walt, Cornell Studies in Security Affairs. New York, NY: Cornell University Press, 2004.

van Creveld, Martin. *The Transformation of War: The Most Radical Reinterpretation of Armed Conflict since Clausewitz*. New York, NY: The Free Press, 1991.

Vanderwalle, Dirk. *A History of Modern Libya*, 2nd edn. New York, NY: Cambridge University Press, 2012.

Vidino, Lorenzo. *Al Qaeda in Europe*. New York, NY: Prometheus Books, 2006.

Waldmann, Peter. "Colombia and the FARC." In *Democracy and Counterterrorism*, edited by Robert Art and Louise Richardson. Washington, DC: United States Institute of Peace Press, 2007, 221–60.

Wallace, Paul. "Countering Terrorist Movements in India: Kashmir and Khalistan." In *Democracy and Counterterrorism: Lessons from the Past*, edited by Robert J. Art and Louise Richardson. Washington, DC: United States Institute of Peace Press, 2007, 425–82.

Waqas, Mohammad Sajjad, and Ahmad Jawad. "Lashkar-e-Tayyiba and the Jamaat-Ud-Dawa: The Case for a Pakistani Narrative." *Strategic Studies*, 31, no. 3 (2011): 59–90.

Watanabe, Manabu. "Religion and Violence in Japan Today: A Chronological and Doctrinal Analysis of Aum Shinrikyo." *Terrorism and Political Violence*, 10, no. 4 (1998): 80–100.

Watson, Bruce. *When Soldiers Quit*. Westport, CT: Praeger, 1997.

Watson, Cynthia. "Guerrilla Groups in Colombia." In *Political Parties and Terrorist Groups*, edited by Leonard Weinberg. London: Frank Cass, 1992, 84–102.

Weinberg, Leonard. "Turning to Terror: The Conditions under Which Political Parties Turn to Terrorist Activities." *Comparative Politics*, 23, no. 4 (1991): 423–38.

Weinberg, Leonard. *Global Terrorism*. New York, NY: The Rosen Publishing Group, Inc., 2009.

Weinberg, Leonard. *The End of Terrorism?* New York, NY: Routledge, 2012.

Weinberg, Leonard, and William Eubank. *The Rise and Fall of Italian Terrorism*, New Directions in Comparative and International Politics. Boulder, CO: Westview Press, 1987.

Weinberg, Leonard, and William Eubank. "Terrorism and Democracy: What Recent Events Disclose." *Terrorism and Political Violence*, 10, no. 1 (1998): 108–18.

Weinberg, Leonard, and William Eubank. "An End to the Fourth Wave of Terrorism?" *Studies in Conflict & Terrorism*, 33, no. 7 (2010): 594–602.

Weinberg, Leonard, Ami Pedahzur, and Arie Perliger. *Political Parties and Terrorist Groups*. New York, NY: Routledge, 2008.

Weinstein, Jeremy. *Inside Rebellion: The Politics of Insurgent Violence*. New York, NY: Cambridge University Press, 2007.

Weiss, Michael, and Hassan Hassan. *ISIS: Inside the Army of Terror*. New York, NY: Regan Arts, 2014.

White, Jeffrey. "Hizb Allah at War in Syria: Forces, Operations, Effects and Implications." *CTC Sentinel*, 7, no. 1 (2014): 14–18.

The White House, Office of the Press Secretary. "Remarks by the President on the Deaths of U.S. Embassy Staff in Libya." September 12, 2012.

Wiktorowicz, Quintan, and John Kaltner. "Killing in the Name of Islam: Al-Qaeda's Justification for September 11." *Middle East Policy*, 10, no. 2 (2003): 76–92.

Wilkinson, Paul. *Terrorism Versus Democracy: The Liberal State Response*, 2nd edn. New York, NY: Routledge, 2006.

Winkler, Carol K. *In the Name of Terrorism: Presidents on Political Violence in the Post-World War II Era*. Albany, NY: State University of New York Press, 2006.

Wolchik, Sharon L. "Can There Be a Color Revolution?" *Journal of Democracy*, 23, no. 3 (2012): 63–70.

World Bank. "Intentional Homicides (Per 100,000 People)."

Wright, Robin. *Sacred Rage: The Wrath of Militant Islam*. New York, NY: Simon and Schuster, 1985.

Wright, Robin. *Sacred Rage: The Wrath of Militant Islam*. New York, NY: Touchstone, 2001 (updated edition).

Wright, Thomas C. *Latin America in the Era of the Cuban Revolution*. Westport, CT: Praeger Publishers, 2001.

Yacoubian, Mona. "Hezbollah's Gamble in Syria: The Dangerous Calculation Behind the Group's Decision to Back Assad." *Foreign Affairs*, June 2, 2013.

Zambelis, Chris. "Hizballah's Lebanese Resistance Brigades." *CTC Sentinel*, 7, no. 11 (2014): 9–12.

Zech, Steven T. "Drug Trafficking, Terrorism, and Civilian Self-Defense in Peru." *CTC Sentinel*, 7, no. 4 (2014): 18–22.

Zelin, Aaron Y. "The Rise and Decline of Ansar Al-Sharia in Libya." *Current Trends in Islamist Ideology*, 18 (2015): 104–18, 20.

Zenn, Jacob. "A Biography of Boko Haram and the Bay'a to Al-Baghdadi." *CTC Sentinel*, 8, no. 3 (2015): 17–21.

Index